# MAYA SACRED GEOGRAPHY
# AND THE CREATOR DEITIES

# Maya Sacred Geography and the Creator Deities

KAREN BASSIE-SWEET

University of Oklahoma Press : Norman

Also by Karen Bassie-Sweet

*From the Mouth of the Dark Cave: Commemorative Sculpture of the Late Classic Maya* (Norman, 1991)
*At the Edge of the World: Caves and Late Classic Maya World View* (Norman, 1996)

Library of Congress Cataloging-in-Publication Data

Bassie-Sweet, Karen, 1952–
Maya sacred geography and the creator deities / Karen Bassie-Sweet.
p.    cm.
Includes bibliographical references and index.
ISBN 978-0-8061-3957-9 (hardcover : alk. paper)
1. Popol vuh. 2. Maya mythology. 3. Maya cosmology.
4. Creation—Mythology—Guatemala. I. Title.
P1465.P8B37 2008
299.7'8423—dc22
2008012966

Copyright © 2008 by the University of Oklahoma Press, Norman, Publishing Division of the University. Manufactured in the U.S.A.

1 2 3 4 5 6 7 8 9 10

For Mary

# CONTENTS

# ILLUSTRATIONS

## FIGURES

## Maps

## CHART

# ACKNOWLEDGMENTS

I began the research for this book more than twelve years ago. My work was interrupted in January of 2000 when I made a visit to Jolja' Cave, Chiapas, to see its Early Classic murals. The imminent danger of vandalism led me to initiate the Jolja' Cave Project to properly document these paintings, and for several years my deity study often took a backseat to this field work. My collaboration with Robert Laughlin, who became one of my Jolja' co-directors, and Allen Christenson, whom I first met at the 1999 Mesa Redonda de Palenque, dramatically altered the course of my deity investigation in many positive ways. Allen's work at Santiago Atitlán and his remarkable new translation and analysis of the *Popol Vuh* changed my understanding of the core creation story, and his work was a major catalyst for my new interpretations. Bob's lifetime of research with the Tzotzil Maya was an endless source of inspiration and vital information. Whenever I was in doubt or required clarification, Bob and Allen provided the answers and input that moved me forward. It is not an exaggeration to say that this book would not exist without the productive partnership I have had with my two dear friends, and I am deeply indebted to them for their insights and support. Without them, I would still be sitting in a dark cave.

In 1978, I met Alfonso Morales at the Mesa Redonda de Palenque, and we have been great friends ever since. Alfonso taught me to pay close attention to the everyday practices of the Maya—in particular, their agricultural techniques. Although Alfonso has regrettably not published his important insights about Maya corn production and its economic implications, his conversations with many Mayanists have inspired them to write about the imbalance of corn production and its effect on society, the trade advantages of smoking corn to preserve it, and the significance of raiding cornfields during periods of scarcity as a source of conflict and war. My dialogues with Alfonso re-centered my attention on corn production and the vital role this staple has in Maya life. I thank him for generously sharing his exceptional knowledge.

I am truly fortunate to be a research associate in an archeology department that includes Geoffrey and Sharisse McCafferty. Over the years, they have forcibly opened my eyes to the aesthetics of other Mesoamerican cultures—not an easy task, given my lifelong obsession with the Maya. They patiently answered my questions and willingly shared much of their outstanding research with me. I am grateful to them for this, and for their steady friendship. I have also enormously benefited from exchanges with John Pohl, whose extraordinary work inspired me to move in directions I would never have otherwise considered. John's responses to my ideas have always been full of encouragement and important suggestions that take my research to higher levels. I thank him for his enthusiastic collaboration.

I also thank John Fought, who always points me in the right direction and then gently shoves me down the path. It was John's Ch'orti' tale about the laughing falcon that convinced me that the bird manifestation of Itzamnaaj found in many of the blowgun scenes on Maya pottery represented Wak, the laughing falcon of the *Popol Vuh* that was shot by the hero twins.

For many years, Elin Danien invited me to participate in the Maya Weekend at the University of Pennsylvania, where I was able to meet and interact with a wide range of Maya researchers. I treasure our close friendship that developed during these meetings, and I greatly appreciate her unfailing support and encouragement. Joel Skidmore has been a steady source of information, advice, and encouragement. I greatly value his kindness and generosity, and thank him for allowing me to express many of my concepts on his marvelous website, www.mesoweb.com.

My personal experiences in highland Guatemala have been limited, and I have relied on the exemplary publications of dozens of scholars to understand the landscape and culture of this region. In particular, the research and publications of Edwin Braakhuis, Margaret Bruchez, Robert Burkitt, Garrett Cook, Lawrence Feldman, Maud Oakes, Jon Schackt, Richard Wilson, Charles Wisdom, and Ruud van Akkeren have been vital sources of information and ideas. I have also been extremely fortunate to have the advice and support of many other fine scholars who have significantly contributed to the interpretations in this book. Michael Carrasco, Michael Coe, Enrique Florescano, Falken Forshaw, Jill Furst, Hal Green, Christina Halperin, Nick Hopkins, Kerry Hull, Alonso Méndez, Julie Miller, John Sosa, Jon Spenard, and Marc Zender have my sincere gratitude. I also want to thank Iris Morgan of the University of Calgary Map Library, who assisted me in obtaining various maps of Guatemala, and Leon Reinhart for providing the Lake Atitlán photograph. I am also indebted to Merle Greene Robertson for allowing me to publish her Palenque drawings, and to Justin and Barbara Kerr for providing access to their database of Maya pottery. I also warmly thank John Drayton, director of the University of Oklahoma Press, who has consistently been receptive to my ideas, and Alessandra Jacobi Tamulevich, Julie Shilling, and Katrin Flechsig for their excellent editorial work.

As always, I am grateful for the support of my husband, Rick, and my daughter, Elizabeth, who endure my absences from family activities with patience and understanding, and who forgive my sharpness when I am tired and cranky. They are my shining lights in the dark night.

My final acknowledgment and thanks are for Mary Ciaramella, who has been my friend and travel companion since I first met her in Guatemala in 1977. Mary's publications on the everyday activities found in the codices, such as weaving, pottery production, idol making, and beekeeping, are exceptional, detailed studies that inspired me to continue researching the ordinary in order to discover the extraordinary. Without her encouragement, input, and support, I would have given up long ago. I dedicate this book to her.

# INTRODUCTION

The ancient Maya were, first and foremost, cultivators of corn, their single most important commodity. Although the contemporary Maya eat a variety of foods, they still consider corn to be their one true sustenance, and they believe that without this most sacred food their souls would surely perish. The great reverence the Maya have for corn is indicated by the widespread practice of treating each kernel with care and respect and by the elaborate ceremonies that they undertake to ensure the protection of the corn's soul.

Given the important role corn plays in Maya society, it is not surprising that their stories concerning the creation of the earth and its preparation for human habitation revolve around establishing the corn cycle. The sacred geography of the ancient Maya was based on the way they modified and changed the natural landscape to produce corn. The deities who the Maya believed created the corn cycle and controlled the forces of nature were the focus of rituals they practiced over centuries to ensure an abundant harvest. One of the purposes of this study is to identify and describe the agricultural nature of these deities who were thought to be responsible for the initial creation and ordering of the world and its cyclical renewal.

The *Popol Vuh* is a sixteenth-century manuscript written by literate members of the Postclassic K'iche' elite of highland Guatemala. It explains the creation of the world, the role of the major deities in this creation, and the history of the K'iche' (Brasseur de Bourbourg 1861; Recinos 1950; Edmonson 1971; Tedlock 1985, 1996; Christenson 2003a). As the seminal work of Michael Coe has demonstrated, the creation mythology narrated in the *Popol Vuh* reveals many core beliefs also found in Preclassic and Classic Period art. By analyzing the *Popol Vuh* as well as Maya art and hieroglyphic texts, and making analogies with contemporary sources, the major themes concerning Maya cosmology can be explored.

More than thirty Mayan languages are spoken in southern Mexico, Guatemala, Belize, and parts of Honduras. All of these languages descended from an ancient form called Proto-Mayan that existed in the distant past sometime before 2000 B.C.. Proto-Mayan diversified into four branches (Wastekan, Yukatekan, Western Mayan, and Eastern Mayan), and as time progressed, Eastern Mayan separated into Mamean-Ixilik and K'iche'an-Poqom-Q'eqchi', while Western Mayan separated into Chujean-Q'anjob'alan and Ch'olan-Tzotzilan. The Classic Period hieroglyphic texts of the lowlands represent a Ch'olan language. Map 1 represents the distribution of Mayan languages at the time of the Spanish conquest. The Maya area can be divided into three geographic zones: the Pacific coastal plain and piedmont in the south, the highlands and northern piedmont in the middle, and the lowlands in the north. Areas of maximum linguistic diversity are customarily assumed to be places of origin. The concentration of Eastern and Western Mayan languages in the highlands and northern piedmont of Guatemala indicates that the Maya originally dispersed from this area into the lowlands (Kaufman 1976; Josserand 2006; John Robertson, personal communication). The landscape of central highland Guatemala was the environment where the basic template of Maya world view was created.

The *Popol Vuh* relates the deeds of three generations of deities: the creator grandparents, Xpiyacoc and Xmucane; their sons, One Hunahpu and Seven Hunahpu; and One Hunahpu's sons, named One Chouen, One Batz, Hunahpu, and Xbalanque (Christenson 2003a). Lowland Classic Period parallels for all of these gods have been identified (Coe 1973, 1977, 1989; Taube 1985, 1992a; Bassie-Sweet 1996; Zender 2004a) (Chart 1). Some researchers question the validity of comparing these deities because of the significant transformations and changes that occurred in the Maya region from the Classic to Postclassic Period. In addition, it has been pointed out that the highland and lowland Maya inhabited vastly different ecosystems, which in itself suggests that they would have had significantly different world views. Yet the parallels in their creation myths are strikingly similar. One of the obvious reasons for these consistencies is that they were agricultural societies based on corn production, and their world views evolved out of ancient beliefs concerning the role of the corn cycle in the creation of the world. This set of core beliefs is the subject of this book, and it is my contention that the basic creation myth was established at a very early date.

The *Popol Vuh* explicitly states that only a small part of the story about One Hunahpu is told (Christenson 2003a:112). The Classic Period parallel of One Hunahpu was named One Ixim. Many Classic Period scenes are directly related to the story of One Hunahpu as told in the *Popol Vuh*, but numerous additional scenes record the other part of his tale. In this book, I reconstruct as much of One Ixim/One Hunahpu's story as possible and analyze his role in Maya world view.

The first chapter of this book is an overview of concepts essential for understanding the Maya world, including the male/female principle of complementary opposition and the nature of deities and humans. Beliefs related to corn and its

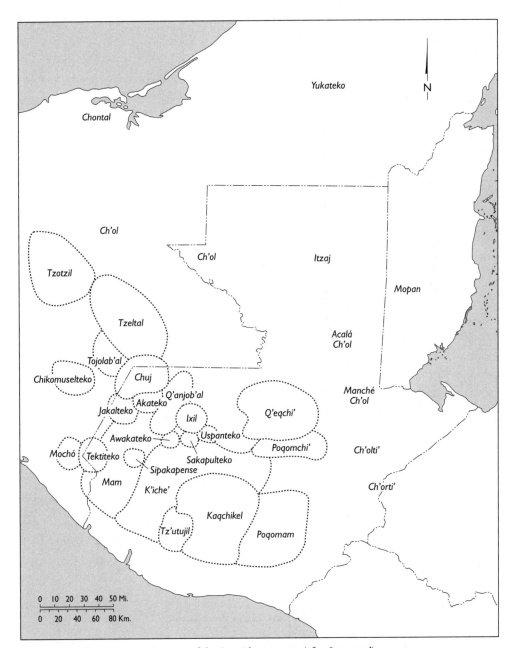

Map 1. Mayan languages at the time of the Spanish conquest (after Josserand)

annual cycle, the methods that the Maya used to time agricultural events, and the fundamental ceremonies that they conducted to ensure a bountiful harvest are discussed in chapters 2 and 3.

The Maya believed that the surface of the earth was flat and that it floated on a body of water. On the surface of this flat world was a quadrilateral space. The rising and setting points of the sun at solstice established the corners of the quadrilateral

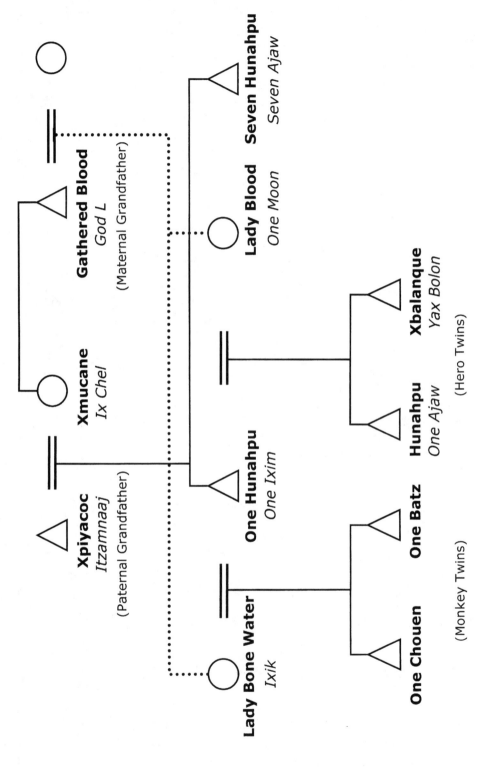

Chart 1. Genealogy chart of major creator deities

world, while the zenith passage of the sun marked its center. From the center of the world, four roads radiated out to the four directions. Quadrilateral platforms with radial staircases, such as the one found at the center of the Palenque Cross Group, represented these four world roads. The Maya used many other metaphors—such as a human body, a house, or a cornfield—to describe the quadrilateral world. The center of the world was defined as a heart or navel when referring to the body metaphor. In house metaphors, the center was defined by a fire surrounded by three stones like the three stones that surround a typical Maya cooking fire. When a farmer first sows his field, he plants his first seeds in a ritual mound at the center of the field. The Maya do not remove large trees from their new *milpas*, or cornfields. In particular, ceiba trees are left standing. In milpa metaphors, the center could be defined either by the ritual mound or the adjacent tree. Chapter 4 reviews the concepts associated with these metaphors, while chapter 5 deals with the nature of water, wind, and divination.

Chapters 6 through 12 describe the essential characteristics of the primary deities and present a model for their genealogy. I argue that the original house and milpa at the center of the world were those of the creator grandparents and their offspring. Chapter 13 explores how the Maya world view was based on the landscape of highland Guatemala, and how specific volcanoes and mountains in this region were thought to be manifestations of the primary deities. I present evidence that the mythological actions recorded in the *Popol Vuh* and in the Classic Period texts were thought to have happened at specific locations in the highland region. I argue that the three dominant volcanoes of Lake Atitlán marked the center of the quadrilateral world and represent the three hearthstones of the center fire. The headwaters of the four major river systems of the Maya region are located just northwest of Lake Atitlán, and I further propose that the four world roads radiating out from the center of the world represent these four rivers.

Chapter 14 reviews the evidence that the Milky Way, the ecliptic, and the constellations were also identified with specific highland locations, and that the progression of the Milky Way, planets, and constellations across the sky reenacted Maya mythology on a nightly basis. In chapter 15, I reconstruct the primary elements of the Maya creation and world-ordering story and attempt to flesh out the details of this core myth. The concluding chapter explores some of the implications of this model.

Schellhas (1904) categorized the various supernatural beings found in the Postclassic codices and gave them alphabetic designations such as God A, God B, and so on. With some modifications, these are still valid categories, and I employ them when applicable. I have used the Thompson catalog numbers to identify certain hieroglyphs (Thompson 1964). Pottery identified by the designation BOD refers to Francis Robicsek's (1981) publication *The Maya Book of the Dead*. I also make reference to pottery vessels identified by the letter K and a number. These designations are from the Kerr database of pottery, which can be accessed on the Internet at http://research.famsi.org/kerrmaya.html. Color illustrations of the Maya codices can also be found on the website of the Foundation for the Advancement of Mesoamerican Studies (FAMSI), www.famsi.org. The illustrations of Maya art in this book have been simplified to highlight the pertinent elements in the discussion. The reader is encouraged to see the original work in detail on the FAMSI website. In cited material, I have chosen to retain the orthography used by the author.

The term "Yucatan" in this book refers to the area of the Yucatan peninsula that incorporates the Mexican states of Yucatán, Quintana Roo, and Campeche. Although the indigenous people of this area refer to their language as simply "Maya," linguists use the term "Yucatec" or "Yucatec Maya" because the term "Maya" has been used to refer to all people who speak a Mayan language. When referring to activities or beliefs of the contemporary Maya, I identify the language of the community in question when necessary.

In discussing the Maya calendar, I have retained the terms *b'aktun*, *k'atun*, and *tun* for units of the Long Count, even though epigraphers now believe that these units of time were called *pik*, *winikha'b'*, and *ha'b'* (Stuart 1996, 2006). I have also employed the names for the *tzolk'in* days and *haab* periods that were used in northern Yucatan at the time of the conquest, but I have spelled these names using the orthography now accepted by most researchers. During the Classic Period, these calendar names were somewhat different, but I have chosen to retain the colonial Yucatec names for consistency. When referring to highland Maya calendar names, I have put the Yucatec colonial equivalent in brackets afterward for clarity. I have used the Thompson correlation number of 584,285 to convert Maya dates to the Gregorian calendar.

# MAYA SACRED GEOGRAPHY
# AND THE CREATOR DEITIES

# 1

# OVERVIEW

The Maya world view embraces several fundamental concepts that provide a framework for understanding their beliefs. These key concepts include the male/female principle of complementary opposition, the nature of deities and humans, the manner in which mountains are depicted, directional terms, and the calendar system.

## THE MALE/FEMALE PRINCIPLE OF COMPLEMENTARY OPPOSITION

The Maya frequently categorize according to pairs of complementary opposites such as male/female, right/left, hot/cold, senior/junior, and dry/wet. In many modern Maya communities, a human being is considered to be both male and female. The right side of the body is male and the left side is female (Cook 1981:155; B. Tedlock 1982; Christenson 2003b:98). The right/male orientation is also found in the *Popol Vuh,* where One Hunahpu impregnates Lady Blood with the male twins Hunahpu and Xbalanque by spitting in her right hand (Christenson 2003a:129).

Despite the male/female nature of each individual, it is thought that an adult has to be married in order to become a complete person (Wagley 1949; Maynard 1963; Vogt 1969, 1976; Devereaux 1987; Morris 1987; Carlsen and Prechtel 1991; Joyce 1992, 1993; Bassie-Sweet 2002). Immediately after creating the first four men, the deities make a wife for each one. Husbands and wives work in unison in their tasks just as the right side of the body works with the left. Perhaps the best expression of this complementary nature is that a man may plant and harvest corn, but he must have a wife to transform it into food. Furthermore, it is common practice for a farmer and his wife to conduct the agricultural rituals together (Wagley 1941:35). The notion that a husband and wife are intrinsically bonded is found in modern Atiteco beliefs:

Atiteco thought conceives of male and female as aspects of one original unit and that no unit can be other than both male and female. Certainly, nothing complete, nothing fully fulfilling its function in the world, can be other than this. Thus, a man cannot take office before marriage and all offices have complementary tasks for the husband/wife pair, whether they function together on any given occasion or not. (Tarn and Prechtel 1986:173)

The *Popol Vuh* refers to the first males as "our first grandfather, our first father" as well as "our first mother-father" (Edmonson 1971:153). The Ch'ol term for an ancestor is "our father-mother." The term "mother-father" or "father-mother" is also given to certain leaders of the community. Nicholas Hopkins (1996; personal communication) identifies this term as a metonym in which two typical members of a class are juxtaposed to stand for the whole domain. He notes that in such metonyms the two members are usually the best examples of the domain. Such terms are also called *merismus*, defined as an abbreviated reference to a whole by naming representative or complementary parts. In the Poqomam town of Palin, the position of mother-father "is considered to be held by a man and his wife although the man may act alone and be called *tutat* [mother-father]. The wife, however, shares the position and its prestige, and the couple often function as a unit" (Maynard 1963:62). In the modern Tzotzil area, the wife of an office holder holds the same status as her husband (Guiteras Holmes 1961:98, 223, 241; Morris 1987:64, 209). At Santa Eulalia, the prayer maker's wife shares in the responsibility for the success of his administration, and in the event of his death she finishes his term of office (La Farge 1947:133). At Chamula, the wife of a cargo holder holds the title of her husband prefixed by *me?*, "mother." Single men can not hold office in Q'eqchi' *cofrades* (Wilson 1990:51, 1995:164). The *mayordomo* of the *cofradía* must have the support of his wife (called the *mayordoma*) to function. These male leaders can not attain their positions or function in the community without their wives. The sharing of status is seen in Classic inscriptions where the wife of the ruler has many of the same titles as her husband. An example of this is found in the parentage statement for the Yaxchilan ruler Bird Jaguar. On Stela 11, his mother (Lady Ik Skull) is named as an Ixik Bakab, "lady Bakab," while his father is called a five *k'atun* Bakab.

## DEITIES

In a previous publication, I defined a deity as an entity who owns, protects, or controls some force, element, or object that humans think they must have to survive, and who thus must be respected, worshipped, or appeased (Bassie-Sweet 1996:13). For the purposes of this book, I will retain this general definition. The Maya word for god or sacred object is *k'uh*, while the word for holiness is *k'uhul*. Hieroglyphic signs representing these words have been identified in Classic Period texts (Ringle

1988; Houston and Stuart 1996:291–94). The logographic sign used to express the word *k'uh* is composed of a supernatural head (God C) with a "water group" sign attached to the front (see chapter 5 for a review of the components of this sign). It is used in contexts where it clearly refers to gods, such as on K2796 and K7750. The God C head is also employed as the adjective *k'uhul*, and one of the most common occurrences is in the emblem-glyph title that occurs in the name phrases of certain elite members. The title is composed of the God C *k'uhul* sign, a place name and the title *Ajaw*, "lord." The Palenque emblem glyph title would be glossed in English as "the holy Palenque lord."

The Classic Maya had a standardized set of creator gods, and the evidence for this is embedded in their calendar system. The Maya believed that each interval such as the day, the night, the month, the solar year, the *k'atun* (twenty-*tun* period), the lunar cycle, and the greater Venus cycle was ruled by a different deity or set of deities. Their calendar was not just a method for tracking the various celestial cycles, but a complex system used to ascertain which of the many deities ruled a particular moment. As Thompson (1950) and Kelley (1976) have demonstrated, the regents of the time periods were standardized and venerated across the Classic Maya realm. These calendar-related deities were worshipped for more than just their roles in divination; they also played a key part in creating, ordering, and renewing the world and all the beings in it.

In addition to this core set of deities, the Maya also had patron deities specific to their group. For example, each community in Postclassic Chiapas had a unique patron deity, but there was one set of deities who were recognized and worshipped over the whole region (Calnek 1988:45–47). These latter deities were thought to have brought the earth, sky, and humans into existence. The *Popol Vuh* provides a model for patron deities. In this story, each of the four K'iche' lineages receives a god whose role is to protect the community. The narrative focuses on the qualities of the god Tohil, who became the patron deity for the leading lineage as well as several other groups. The text specifically states that Tohil is the substitute and remembrance of the Framer and the Shaper (the creator deities; Christenson 2003a:215), and as the story unfolds, it is apparent that Tohil manifests several key qualities of the creator deities, such as fire and thunder. Patron gods associated with specific sites have been identified in Classic Maya art, and these deities frequently have attributes of the primary creator deities as well (Houston and Stuart 1996). The same can be said for the name phrases of humans in which various god names are combined. For example, the name of the Dos Pilas ruler Itzamnaaj K'awiil contains the name of the creator grandfather and one of the primary lightning bolt gods.

Deities appeared in a variety of forms that reflected their spheres of control and responsibilities. These manifestations could take the appearance of plants, animals, natural formations, and phenomena such as wind, lightning, thunder, and fire. Many of the manifestations of the major deities also had four different aspects, one for each direction. Evidence from colonial documents suggests that these four directional aspects were viewed as siblings who were ranked in a hierarchy just as siblings were in Maya society (Tozzer 1941:135). In mythological times, the creator deities underwent birth, stages of growth, rites of passage, transformations, death, and rebirth. They created cornfields, planted and harvested corn, performed divinations, conducted business, fought, formed alliances, and intermarried. From all of these actions and interactions a hierarchy was formed in which members had overlapping duties and responsibilities.

The behavior of the deities was a model for appropriate human conduct and provided justification and rationalization for elite activities, social hierarchy, political structure, and economic strategies. Maya elites were frequently illustrated wearing the costumes of certain deities, including face masks in the likeness of the god. When humans donned the costume of a deity, they assumed the traits of the deity or were temporarily transformed into the deity (Houston and Stuart 1996).

The *Popol Vuh* begins with a list of paired male and female names for the creator grandparents:

> Framer and Shaper
> She Who Has Borne Children and He Who Has Begotten Sons
> Hunahpu Possum and Hunahpu Coyote
> Great White Peccary and Coati
> Sovereign and Quetzal Serpent
> Heart of Lake and Heart of Sea
> Creator of the Green Earth and Creator of the Blue Sky
> Midwife and Patriarch
> Xpiyacoc and Xmucane
> Protector and Shelterer
> Twice Midwife and Twice Patriarch (Christenson 2003a)

Later in the text, Hunahpu Possum/Hunahpu Coyote, Great White Peccary/Coati and Creator of the Green Earth/Creator of the Blue Sky are specifically said to be names for the creator grandparents called Xpiyacoc and Xmucane. Dennis Tedlock (1996) views Framer/Shaper, She Who Has Borne Children/He Who Has Begotten Sons, and Sovereign/Quetzal Serpent as a set of deities who are distinct from Xpiyacoc and Xmucane. Christenson (2003a) views Framer/Shaper and Sovereign/Quetzal Serpent as distinct gods, but sees She Who Has Borne Children/He Who Has Begotten Sons as manifestations of Xpiyacoc and Xmucane. The principal reason for dividing these deities into separate groups is that Framer/Shaper and Sovereign/Quetzal Serpent speak with the creator grandparents. Given the evidence for interaction between various manifestations of a deity, the simplest explanation of the *Popol Vuh* list seems to be that it names the different manifestations of the creator grandparents.

The role of thunderbolts in Maya mythology is widespread. It is thought that leaders are capable of using thunderbolts to defend their communities and that lightning strikes germinate the corn seed. Lightning also plays a role in transferring knowledge from the deities to human diviners (see chapter 5). Many contemporary stories describe how the deities send thunderbolts as punishment for inappropriate behavior. In the Maya area, rain and storms are invariably announced by the sound of distant thunder and are accompanied by dramatic displays of thunderbolts. The frequent flashes of intense light and loud booms are an awesome display of power as they strike the ground, splitting trees and setting the landscape on fire. Colonial Period sources indicate that the gods identified with lightning were called *chahks*, which literally means lightning. Although their appearance changes slightly over time, deities identified as chahks (God B of the codices) are illustrated in Maya art from the Preclassic to the Postclassic. In Classic Period art, chahks are shown with a zoomorphic face with serpents emanating from the mouth, and they wear a *Spondylus* (thorny or spiny oyster) shell earring. In hieroglyphic writing, the name "Chahk" is most often represented by a portrait of this deity. One of the hieroglyphic writing conventions is to reduce a logographic sign to a single element. This element is then used to represent the entire sign. In the case of the name "Chahk," the *Spondylus* shell earring is often used to represent his entire portrait.

Ethnographic sources indicate that lightning bolts were thought to be flint axes thrown by the chahks, and numerous illustrations show chahks wielding their lightning axes. These axes often take the form of a lightning serpent. Many chahks are named with appellatives such as the "First Mist in the Sky Chahk" and the "Fire That Burns in the Sky Chahk." In the *Popol Vuh*, three of the primary creator deities are named as thunderbolt gods, and they have Classic Period parallels (see chapter 6).

## Humans

The *Popol Vuh* indicates that the creator deities attempted to create humans from a variety of materials before they finally succeeded. In the final creation, the creator grandmother ground corn seeds into a fine paste and mixed this dough with water; from this mixture the first human bodies were modeled (Christenson 2003a:193–95). The text specifically states that the corn dough became flesh and the water became blood. The corn seeds were obtained from a sacred mountain known as Paxil, "split," and Cayala, "lime water, bitter or stagnant water." Paxil Mountain is located in north-western Guatemala and is discussed more fully in chapter 13. Although the source of the water used to create the blood of humans is not discussed in the *Popol Vuh*, I present evidence in chapter 15 that this water came from Meauan Mountain on the Chixoy River. I will also demonstrate that the cave illustrated in the Preclassic San Bartolo murals represents a cave on this mountain.

There are numerous contemporary stories about the discovery of corn seed within a mountain. These tales do not mention that humans were made from this corn; rather, they focus on how the corn was freed from the mountain so that humans could have access to it. In these tales, the corn was found hidden behind a cliff or inside a cave. To access the seed, a god had to strike open the stone with a thunderbolt (Burkitt 1920; Oakes 1951:244; Thompson 1954:273; 1970:354; Mayers 1958; Miles 1960; Vogt 1969; Edmonson 1971:146; Laughlin and Karasik 1988:203; Montejo and Campbell 1993; Preuss 1993; Christenson 2001). The *Popol Vuh* does not directly say that lightning was used to get at the corn seed used to create humans, but the name Paxil, "split," implies this (Edmonson 1971:146; D. Tedlock 1985:328, 1996:288, 357). Furthermore, Fray Thomás de Coto writes in his seventeenth-century dictionary that the word *paxil* specifically refers to breaking an ear of corn in two (Christenson 2003a:193).

Human beings were thought to be much more than just flesh and blood, but to have spirits or souls. The concepts associated with human spirituality in Mesoamerica are complex. In central and southern Mexico, a person was thought to have several types of soul-like essences centered in or identified with different parts of the body such as the head, heart, liver, blood, and breath, and each of these souls was related to different, but overlapping or interconnected, functions (López Austin 1988; Furst 1995). They could be manifested as breath, wind, or winged beings that either left the body after death or died with it. It was believed that the creator gods breathed and drilled the soul into a fetus or child. Children also received a spiritual force from the day of the 260-day calendar on which they were born, and this day name dictated the fate of the child.

Maya concepts concerning the spiritual nature of an individual are not well understood, but some information has been gleaned from the inscriptions and from comparisons with ancient Mesoamerican and contemporary beliefs (Stuart 1988, cited in Freidel, Schele, and Parker 1993:440; Houston and Stuart 1989, 1998; Grube and Nahm 1994; Houston and Taube 2000). The belief that people's destinies or characteristics were received on the day of their birth is well documented. The many heart metaphors found in Mayan languages indicate that one of the soul essences was located in the heart. This heart essence gave animation to humans and was thought to be the centering force of the body (Hill and Fischer 1999; Laughlin 2004).

The importance of what some have termed the "breath soul" is stated in the *Popol Vuh* episode that describes the creation of the first four men: "They had their breath, therefore they became" (Christenson 2003a:197). A widespread death expression found in hieroglyphic texts refers to the departure of the breath soul from the body at death, and this phrase has been translated as "diminished, his white T533 breath/wind" (Stuart, cited in Houston and Taube 2000:267). The T533 sign itself has not been deciphered, but epigraphers believe it may refer to some kind of flower, seed, or egg (see chapters 8 and 15). Anyone who has been present when a person dies is aware of a common after-death occurrence when the muscles of the body release and a final gasp of air seems to be taken in and then forcefully exhaled. This dramatic and somewhat frightening occurrence is surely related to the belief in a breath soul departing the body (Furst 1995). Las Casas records that a jade bead was placed in the mouths of Poqom Maya lords just after they expired in order to capture the breath soul: "When it appears then that some lord is dying, they had ready a precious stone which they placed at his mouth when he appeared to expire, in which they believe that they took the spirit, and on expiring they very lightly rubbed his face with it. It takes the breath, soul, or spirit" (Miles 1957:749). Furst (1995:54–55) notes that a similar procedure was carried out by the Aztecs, who placed a green stone representing the soul of the deceased in the mouth. How the breath of the lord was captured when he died in circumstances that did not allow for this practice is not known, but Taube (2005:31) suggests that the jade masks placed on the deceased ruler were probably "a means of holding and sustaining the living soul of the dead king." There is considerable evidence that the death and funeral rites of Maya lords were modeled after those of One Hunahpu and his Classic Period parallel, the corn god One Ixim (see chapter 15). In the *Popol Vuh*, the skull of the deity One Hunahpu is brought back into existence when his sons adorn him. Classic Period scenes indicate that this adornment involved dressing him in his jade costume. The placing of a jade mask and jade jewelry on a ruler may have mimicked this act and ensured that the ruler would continue to function in the afterlife in the role of One Ixim.

In the world view of some contemporary Maya communities, the human soul may have thirteen parts, or may simultaneously exist in the body of an individual and in the body of several supernatural co-essences who live in a sacred mountain cave. In some cases, a person can have as many as thirteen different co-essences, or companion spirits, and they may take the form of animals or natural phenomena such as lightning, meteors, and whirlwinds. While ordinary people have little control over them, the spiritually strong can direct their co-essences to perform certain benevolent or malevolent functions such as protecting the community from supernatural forces and causing or curing illness. In contemporary healing ceremonies, the first act is often to determine who the source of such an illness is. Co-essences called *way*, "companion spirit," have been identified in Classic Maya inscriptions and art (Houston and Stuart 1989; Grube and Nahm 1994). These *way* co-essences are often portrayed in Maya art as hybrid animals with menacing characteristics. Stuart comments on the nature of these *way* beings and suggests that the elite used them to mete out punishment and cause illness:

> My contention, based on specific evidence presented at the Forum, is that the *way* beings are representations of the animated dark forces wielded by Classic Maya sorcerers in their attempts to influence other people, and perhaps other rulers. One could think of them as spells, curses, or other sorts of enchantments wielded by *brujos*. These could be manifested as diseases and afflictions of the body, or perhaps as some other misfortune, but the point always seems to be their harmful effects on others. (Stuart 2005a:160)

Contemporary accounts of sorcerers who send their co-essences to inflict disease indicate that these spirits can also take the form of wind or the breath of the sorcerer.

Another well-documented concept in Maya beliefs is the notion that powerful humans can transform into animals and natural phenomena. Many stories relate how the transformed sorcerer is prevented by a clever person from transforming back into his human form.

The modern Tz'utujil use to the terms *jal* and *k'ex* to refer to the cycles of life and regeneration (Carlsen and Prechtel 1991:26). The changes experienced through an individual life cycle are called *jal*, while the change from one generation to the next is *k'ex*. Children are thought to be the embodiment and replacement of the parent or grandparent. The same concept is found among the Ixil, where a child is named after a relative from the grandparents' generation. The child is thought to be the present and future replacement of this person. After the death of the older person, the namesake is expected to remember the departed in prayers and rituals (Colby and Colby 1981:303). In the K'iche' town of Momostenango, dance festivals play an important role in ceremonial life, and the concept of replacement (*c'axel*) is also evident: "there is a tendency for sons to follow their fathers in particular dances, 'like an unbroken chain,' although they do not necessarily dance in the same part, and in fact father and son will often dance together for nine or even eighteen years until the father becomes too infirm to continue. By this time a grandson may be ready to take his place as the *c'axel* for the retiring elder" (Cook 1981:85). The Tzotzil also express the replacement concept in their beliefs concerning the community leaders: "The authorities do not act in their own name: each one represents or is the personification of all those who preceded him back to the 'beginning of the world'" (Guiteras Holmes 1961:78).

The notion that the Classic ruler was the replacement of the founding ancestor and subsequent leaders is highlighted on several monuments. For example, Copan Altar Q refers to the accession of the ruler Yax Pasaj. The fifteen previous rulers, beginning with the founding ancestor Yax K'uk' M'o', are shown validating Yax Pasaj's accession. At Yaxchilan, the narrative of Structure 12 gives the names of the preceding Yaxchilan rulers beginning with the founding ancestor Yoaat B'alam and ending with the protagonist of the story. This continuity with the preceding rulers is also seen in the Palenque inscriptions of Pakal and Kan B'ahlam.

During pre-Columbian times, a young lord rose through the civil-religious hierarchy of his community by progressing through a succession of offices. The acquisition of offices previously held by his father or grandfather validated him as their replacement. The *Popol Vuh* makes it clear that the essential skill of the first leaders was their ability to communicate with the creator deities. As the living replacement of the ancestral leaders, the current leader also had this skill. He was the crucial link between the community and these supernatural beings.

## MOUNTAINS

The Maya viewed mountains as manifestations of their deities, and they identified many of their primary gods with specific mountains in the Guatemalan highlands.

A zoomorphic mountain with a cave mouth is frequently illustrated in Classic Period art (Stuart 1987). The body of this creature is often decorated with elements that are found on the T528 sign used to represent the day name *Kawak*, "lightning." Stuart identified the syllabic rendering of the word *witz*, "mountain," in the hieroglyphic texts, as well as the logographic sign that represents this word. The latter sign is a variant of the T528 sign, and these witz glyphs function in the hieroglyphic texts as place names (Stuart and Houston 1994). Some of these witz monsters and logograms have split-open heads and corn foliage growing from them. Phonetic complements on some of the logograms suggest that these split signs actually represent the word *pax*, "split," in these contexts (Martin 2004). Other signs can be added to these various witz glyphs to specify particular mountains. For example, locations called Five Flower Mountain and Macaw Mountain are mentioned in the hieroglyphic texts (Stuart and Houston 1994). It is apparent from this usage that the image of Paxil Mountain was used as the generic word for *witz*, "mountain," and that the additional signs on these witz monsters indicate whether the motif represents Paxil Mountain or some other mountain. Some of the most common elements found on witz monsters include various flowers, birds, and snakes.

In addition to its use in the day name *Kawak* and in the glyph for mountain, the T528 sign appears with phonetic complements that indicate it is read *tuun*, "stone," in certain contexts. For the Maya, one of the most important stones was the limestone used to create lime for processing corn and for constructing buildings. Although it does not represent the word for cave, the T528 sign is a stylized drawing of a cave in a cutaway profile view (Bassie-Sweet 1987, 1991:102–26). The mouth is pictured as an overhanging shelf with a cluster of stalactites hanging from it. In many examples of witz monsters, the teeth of the monster have the form of T528 *tuun* "stone" signs, which further reinforces T528's association with limestone and cave formations. On the north wall of the San Bartolo murals, the tooth of the witz monster has the form of a stalactite marked with striations of black stripes and beads (Saturno, Taube, and Stuart 2005).

The Maya collected water from drip-water formations for their rituals (Thompson 1959, 1975; Bonar 1989; Bassie-Sweet 1991, 1996). At the caves of Jolja' in Chiapas, Mexico, cave water is still used in rain ceremonies by the adjacent Ch'ol Maya community of Joloniel. Community members have broken off numerous stalactites from the cave for use in rain rituals because it is believed that they have the power to create rain. The rain-making aspect of the San Bartolo cave will be discussed in chapter 15.

## DIRECTIONAL TERMS

There has been considerable debate about the use of Maya directional terms and precisely what they mean. Several hieroglyphic texts indicate that the Maya had four directional terms that referred to north, south, east, and west. It has been proposed that the north and south glyphs were not identified with these directions, but rather with the zenith (heaven) and nadir (the underworld). The layout of the Tikal twin pyramid complexes has been used as evidence for this interpretation. These twin pyramid complexes are composed of a square plaza with twin radial pyramids demarcating the east and west sides. The south side is bounded by a long, narrow building with nine doorways, while the north is marked by a roofless house that contains a stela and altar. The stela illustrates the ruler performing a Period Ending event. Coggins (1980) proposed that the east and west pyramids represented the locations of the rising and setting sun, while the north building represented the zenith position of heaven and the south building represented the underworld. To orient such a cosmogram to the natural world requires rotating the plaza on its side so that north is up and south is down. In Coggins's interpretation, the ruler was conceptually performing the Period Ending rituals at the zenith, and the nine doorways of the southern building represented the underworld. In a previous publication, I questioned the validity of this proposal, and I continue to assert that this identification is seriously flawed (Bassie-Sweet 1996:196–99). As noted by León Portilla (1988:204), a clear example of the use of the north and south directional glyphs oriented to north and south is found on the walls of Río Azul Tomb 12. Each wall of the tomb is painted with its appropriate directional glyph. In Maya categories of up and down, east is associated with "up" and the rising sun, while west is identified with "down" and the setting sun. This is reflected in indigenous maps, where east is invariably placed at the top and west at the bottom.

## CATHOLIC MYTHOLOGY AND MAYA WORLD VIEW

In this book, I use a wide variety of contemporary stories to shed light on the themes found in the *Popol Vuh* and in Maya art. The strategies that the Spanish priests utilized to convert the Maya to Catholicism and the methods the Maya utilized to try to retain their pre-Columbian customs and beliefs were varied, but an important aspect of this conversion process was that many of the Maya deities shared significant traits with Catholic deities. For example, the corn god One Ixim/One Hunahpu was a primary deity in Maya world view, and the cross-shaped ceiba tree (*yaxche*) at the center of the world was one of his manifestations. One Ixim/One Hunahpu lived on the surface of the earth; he was the son of the creator grandfather Itzamnaaj/Xpiyacoc; he was the role model for appropriate human behavior; and he was killed by his enemies but was later resurrected. These characteristics are found in Jesus Christ, who was thought to be the son of the Christian creator god. He, too, lived on the surface of the earth; his actions provided the role model for humans to emulate; he died and was later resurrected; and he was identified with a cross. In some Ch'orti' areas, Catholic beliefs play a strong role in the tales related to the origin of corn, and the people associate corn with Christ: "It is said that when Christ was crucified, Saint Magdalene was at the foot of the cross, holding a basin in her hand. After the lance-thrust she caught the blood in the basin. Though his enemies ran to drink the blood, it turned at once into small corn plants. . . . Because of this, Magdalene has all the corn in her grasp, and men must pray to her in order that the harvest may abound" (Mayers 1966:240). Some Tzotzil also believe that the first corn came from the body of Christ (Gossen 1974:40). There were also significant parallels between pre-Columbian patron deities and Christian saints (Christenson 2001). These various parallels made the Maya more receptive to Catholic mythology but also permitted them to merge Catholic beliefs into their own system.

The relationship between the yaxche tree of One Ixim/One Hunahpu and the cross of Christ illustrates this point. The Grijalva expedition of 1518 noted a large number of stone crosses when it circumnavigated the coast of Yucatan. The next year when the Cortez expedition landed on Cozumel Island, the Spaniards found many temples that were several stories high, and in the courtyard of one of these temples they saw a stone cross that was said to be the emblem of the rain god (Prescott 1979:148, 159). The priest Francisco Hernández also noted that this cross was a symbol of the Maya rain god (Saville 1921:209), and as will be discussed in later chapters, this rain god was a manifestation of One Ixim/One Hunahpu. The Franciscan priest Andrés de Avendaño y Loyola (1987) made two trips to Lake Petén in A.D. 1695 and A.D. 1697 to convert the Itza' Maya. He noted that these Maya had an idol in the form of a stone column called *Yax Cheel Cab. Yax Cheel Cab* literally means "blue/green tree of the world," but Avendaño translated *yax* as "first," another meaning of *yax*, because he was aware that the Maya thought of this tree as the first tree in the world, which was set up after the flood ending the last era. Prescott (1979:159) suggests that the Maya transferred their devotion from the cross-shaped yaxche to that of the Christian cross, but contemporary beliefs about crosses indicate that these two symbols were merged. Blom (1936:76) and Vogt (1969:587) have noted that most contemporary crosses found in the landscape are thought of as trees. Even in some areas where the identification is directly made with Christ's cross, the cross is still conceived to be a tree (Sosa 1985:242).

In addition to his commonalities with One Ixim/One Hunahpu, Christ was endowed with the qualities of One Ajaw/Hunahpu, the child of One Ixim/One Hunahpu and his wife One Moon/Lady Blood. The primary function of One Ajaw/Hunahpu was as the sun of the new era, and Christ's identification with the sun is widespread in the Maya area. The Virgin Mary acquired many of the attributes of One Ajaw/Hunahpu's mother (One Moon/Lady Blood), most notably, her association with the moon and fertility. The Virgin also acquired the characteristics of the elderly and wise Ix Chel/Xmucane (the mother of One Ixim/One Hunahpu). In Christian mythology, other holy women also played a prominent role in the story of Christ's crucifixion and resurrection. It is stated in the book of John (19:25) that Mary of Cleophas (the Virgin's sister) and Mary Magdalene stood at the foot of the cross with the Virgin Mary. Three Marías, who are thought to be sisters, appear in a variety of contemporary Maya stories that are not thematically related to the role of these women in Christian mythology. There is, however, a triad of young goddesses who were involved in the restoration of One Ixim, and it is apparent that these pre-Columbian goddesses were the precursors of the Three Marías in these particular stories.

## THE CALENDAR SYSTEM

The Maya calendar was an intricate system of interlocked cycles, aspects of which are still in use today in some areas. The following is a brief overview of its structure and function. A formal calendar date in Classic Period inscriptions typically includes a series of notations including the Initial Series Introductory Glyph (ISIG), the Long Count, the *tzolk'in*, the Supplementary Series, the Lunar Series, and the *haab*.

The Maya counted in units of twenty, and the solar calendar known as the haab was composed of eighteen periods of twenty days (360) plus five days known as the *wayeb'*. The months were *Pohp, Woh, Sip, Sootz', Tsek, Xul, Yaxk'in, Mol, Ch'en, Yax, Sak, Keh, Mak, K'ank'in, Muan, Pax, K'ayab,* and *Kumk'u*.

The tzolk'in cycle was 260 days long and ran concurrently with the 365-day solar cycle of the haab. Each day in the tzolk'in had a name composed of a number and a day name. There were thirteen numbers (1–13) and twenty day names (*Imix, Ik', Ak'b'al, K'an, Chikchan, Kimi, Manik', Lamat, Muluk, Ok, Chuwen, Eb, Ben, Ix, Men, Kib, Kab'an, Etz'nab, Kawak,* and *Ajaw*). Both the number and the day name changed each day; thus, a sequential series of names would be *1 Imix, 2 Ik', 3 Ak'b'al, 4 K'an, 5 Chikchan, 6 Kimi, 7 Manik', 8 Lamat, 9 Muluk, 10 Ok, 11 Chuwen, 12 Eb, 13 Ben.* Following *13 Ben* would be *1 Ix, 2 Men, 3 Kib, 4 Kab'an,* and so on. Because thirteen (the number of coefficients) and twenty (the number of day names) do not have a common denominator, the same number and day name only occurred together every 260 days. It has long been argued that the 260-day cycle originated in the region located at latitude 15° north (Nuttall 1928; Merrill 1945; Malmstrom 1973; Aveni 1980). In this region, it is 105 days from the first zenith passage on April 30 to the second zenith passage on August 13. From August 13 to the next zenith passage on April 30 is 260 days. Because of the mathematics, the beginning of the solar year (*0 Pohp*) could only begin on four day names of the tzolk'in. These four day names (*Ik', Manik, Eb,* and *Kaban*) were called the yearbearers. Again, because of the mathematics, the same tzolk'in date and haab date appeared together only after fifty-two haab years or seventy-three tzolk'in cycles.

Another calendar cycle was represented by Glyph G of the Supplementary Series. Glyph G is composed of nine different glyphs, which have been nicknamed G1, G2, G3, G4, G5, G6, G7, G8, and G9. The cycle represented by these glyphs was nine days long, and Glyph G changed each day. All *bak'tuns, k'atuns,* and *tuns* ended on a Glyph G9 day. Because 9 and 260 (the number of days in the tzolk'in cycle) have no common denominator, it takes 9 cycles of the tzolk'in (2,340 days) before the same tzolk'in position and Glyph G appear together again. The Glyph G cycle has been equated with the Nine Lords of the Night series found in Aztec culture because of their structural similarity, but what this cycle actually represents is not yet known (Thompson 1950:208). The Lunar Series, which usually follows the Glyph G Series, gives information concerning the moon, including the number of days since the new moon, the number of the lunar half-year, the regent of the lunation, the name of the lunation, and the length of the lunar month (Thompson 1950; Lounsbury 1978; Aveni 1980).

On Classic monumental art, most formal narratives include what is called a Long Count date. At its most basic level, the Long Count date gave the number of days (k'in) that had transpired since a zero base date. These days were grouped into larger cycles of twenty days (winals), 360 days (tun), twenty tuns (k'atun), and 400 tuns (bak'tun). A Long Count date of 9.12.9.8.1 indicated that nine b'aktuns, twelve k'atuns, nine tuns, eight winals, and one day (k'in) had expired since the zero base date. According to the Thompson correlation, the zero base date used to calculate dates during the Classic Period occurred on 13 August 3114 B.C. The zero base date of the Long Count began on a day named 4 Ajaw. Because of the mathematics, this means that all bak'tuns, k'atuns, and tuns began on Imix days and ended on Ajaw days. It also means that all k'atun endings occurred with the same Glyph G.

If the Maya were merely interested in calculating the number of days since the beginning of the era, one would expect the length of the tun to be 400 days (20 × 20), not 360. In the beginning of Maya studies, it was postulated that the Maya chose 360 days because it was the closest multiple of twenty to the solar year of 365. Christopher Powell (1997) presents a much better explanation. He notes that a period of 360 days would make the haab and tzolk'in cycles commensurable with the cycles of Venus, Mars, and Mercury. They were also commensurable with the Glyph G cycle.

## THE FORTUNE OF THE TIME PERIOD

Each of the twenty day names of the tzolk'in was ruled by a different deity with a unique personality. This day lord was thought to affect the events that occurred on his day and sometimes even determine what those events would be. Although it is impossible to reconstruct the personality of each day lord, the situation was more complex than a simple formula of good, bad, or indifferent. It is likely that the full-figure hieroglyphic variants of the day names are portraits of the day lords. For example, on the Hauberg Stela, an Early Classic full-figure variant of the day name Kan is the deity One Ixim.

The coefficient of the tzolk'in also affected the fortune of the day. During the Classic Period, a different deity represented each of the numbers from 1 to 13. This concept of number deities is found in the calendar system recorded in the Ixil area, where "the 13 numbers and 20 day names are both regarded as sacred beings or deities who are worshipped and petitioned in prayer" (Lincoln 1942:106). Each twenty-four-hour period was thus jointly ruled by its number deity and day lord as well as by the sun god, who presumably came into power every morning at dawn. In order to ensure the optimum outcome, planned events were scheduled to occur when the appropriate deities were in power. It is likely that the power of the sun god was affected by his position in the annual cycle. For example, the sun at summer solstice is stronger (hotter) than it is at winter solstice.

The importance of the 260-day tzolk'in cycle in divination is well documented. The Maya believed that one's character and destiny were determined by the tzolk'in day of one's birth. There is some evidence that an individual's co-essences were also determined by the tzolk'in day on which the person was born (Bunzel 1952; Vogt 1976; B. Tedlock 1982). The significance of the tzolk'in in calculating a person's fate is reflected in the custom of naming babies according to their birth date in the 260-day calendar.

The belief in the divinatory nature of the tzolk'in impacted all calendar cycles, for the character and events of any given time period were established by the tzolk'in day name on which that time period began. Landa records the Late Postclassic belief that *K'an* or *Muluk* years would be basically fortunate, while *Ix* or *Kawak* years would be disastrous. Landa's account of New Year ceremonies and the *Dresden Codex* New Year pages illustrate that in addition to the day lord yearbearer, each of the four years also had another regent. Landa names these year regents as Bolon Dzacab, K'inich Ajaw, Itzamnaaj, and Uac Mitun Ajaw. In the *Dresden Codex* New Year pages, similar year regents are named God K, God G, God D, and God A1. Each of the eighteen months of the year also had a regent. These regents are recorded in the Initial Series Introductory Glyph that frequently begins the Long Count date.

Although k'atuns (periods of twenty tuns) end on the day name *Ajaw*, it takes thirteen k'atun periods before the same coefficient and day name appear again. A full k'atun cycle was, therefore, thirteen k'atuns long. It is known from Postclassic sources that each of the thirteen k'atuns had predetermined characteristics that impacted the events of the k'atun and that each k'atun was ruled by a different regent (Roys 1933:184). Each k'atun had its own idol, priest, and separate prophecy of its events.

The *Paris Codex* illustrates a series of k'atuns. Although some pages are missing and others badly eroded, this series gives us some understanding of these time periods (Love 1994). Each page represents one k'atun. The upper section details the events that occurred during the various tun and winal periods of the k'atun. The center section of each page illustrates the inauguration of the new k'atun. In these scenes, a deity stands in profile and holds a God K head. The text to the left begins with a "change of rulership" sign followed by the deity's name or title (Love 1994:21). In front of each of these k'atun regents is an individual seated on a throne. The throne suggests that these individuals were also being seated into an office. The only individual whose image is still intact looks like a human. He is wearing a headdress associated with priest/diviners. Bruce Love (1994:20) has suggested that these *Paris Codex* diviners were human priests in charge of the k'atun and its prognostications. It is also possible that they were supernatural priests who were the role models for the human k'atun priests. This is similar to the deities in the *Dresden* New Year pages, who provided the model for human New Year ceremonies. In either case, the *Paris Codex* scenes illustrate the k'atun regent and the priest/diviner of the k'atun.

The importance of the moon in timing activities, from sexual intercourse to planting and harvesting, is well attested. In the modern Tzotzil area, the phase of the moon on the day of birth is an important sign of the newborn child's future (Nash 1970:312). Given these practices, one would expect that the Maya had lunar regents ruling the various lunar periods. As noted above, the Lunar Series, which is frequently given after the Long Count date, gives information about the nature of the moon on the day in question. Glyph E and Glyph D indicate the phase of the moon by stating that the moon is not visible (new moon) or by giving the number of days since new moon or first appearance of the waxing crescent moon. Glyph C of the Lunar Series is composed of a coefficient, a verb in the form of an extended hand (flat hand), and a deity name above the hand. The coefficient in Glyph C can range from one to six, and this number indicates whether the date of the event is in the first, second, third, fourth, fifth, or sixth month in the lunar half-year. Glyph X and Glyph B give the name of the lunation, while Glyph A gives its length (either twenty-nine or thirty days). The fourteen-odd names for the moon that have been recorded in Glyph X and the patterns in which they appear indicate that the Maya were not naming their moons according to their relationship with the solar cycle. Instead, the distribution shows that the name of the moon was dictated first of all by the Glyph C deity and then by the number in the lunar half-year (Schele, Grube, and Fahsen 1992).

Three different deity names can appear in Glyph C: One Moon, Seven Moon, and Ten Moon. Schele and others have shown that these deities alternate in each new lunation and that the pattern is One Moon, Seven Moon, and Ten Moon. How these deities are related is unknown. It has been suggested that the deities of Glyph C are a "graphic reference to images the ancient Maya saw on the moon" (Schele, Grube, and Fahsen 1992:4), but the alternation of deities from lunation to lunation and the association of the flat-hand verb found in Glyph C with accession suggests that these three deities might have been the deities who ruled the lunation. Just as a day, a night, a month, a year, and a k'atun had a regent who ruled that particular period, so did the lunar month.

The Venus cycle also had regents who ruled its various intervals. Venus's average synodic period of 583.92 days is composed of four intervals: morning star, superior conjunction (disappearance), evening star, and inferior conjunction (disappearance). At each sunrise during its morning-star interval, Venus is found in a different location in the sky. The path Venus makes over its morning-star interval can have configurations like a loop or arch (Aveni 1990). The same is also true for the evening star. It takes five Venus cycles before Venus makes a similar loop or arch again. This greater Venus cycle averages 2,919.6 days—close to the interval of eight solar haab cycles (2,920 days). Because each of the five Venus cycles was divided into four intervals, the greater Venus cycle contained a total of twenty intervals. The greater Venus cycle is represented on *Dresden Codex* pages 46 to 50 (Thompson 1972). These five pages clearly indicate that a different deity ruled each of the twenty intervals. The Venus interval regents include God A, God E, God K, God N, and God S, as well as lesser-known characters such as Ulum, "turkey," Sinan, "scorpion," and Great Rabbit.

It is apparent from this brief overview of calendar components that the sun, moon, and Venus ruled the time periods when they were in the sky, but there were also other deities in power during these times, such as the number lords, day lords, lunation regents, and Venus regents, all of whom influenced the events of these periods. In addition, there were month regents, year regents, and k'atun regents. It is likely that other cycles and influences also impacted the events of the day, such as those of Jupiter, Mars, and Mercury. Divination was at the heart of the Maya calendar system. Maya divination, however, was not a simple calculation of good and bad days, but rather a complex system based on many interrelated factors.

# 2

# CORN

The corn cycle is intrinsically important to the Maya; beliefs about the spirit and nature of corn are paramount in their mythology. The Maya categorize their wide variety of corn types according to habitat, maturing time, plant size, ear size, kernel shape, and color (Tozzer 1907:51; Wisdom 1940:41; McBryde 1947:21; Bunzel 1952:50; Vogt 1969:61; Baer and Merrifield 1971:174; Butler and Arnold 1977; Sosa 1985:74; Breedlove and Laughlin 1993:235). The basic colors of corn are white, yellow, red, and black, and the Maya plant the different colors separately to limit cross-pollination. The primary crop is usually a late-maturing type with large ears, but corn with an early or intermediate maturing time and smaller ears is often planted to supplement the main supply. Kaufman and Norman (1984) have reconstructed three proto-Ch'olan corn terms: *ajän*, "roasting corn" (green corn); *nal*, "ear of corn"; and *ixim*, "grain corn." The term *ixim* is often used to refer to corn in general. Seed corn is often given a separate name from stored corn that is for consumption (Laughlin 1975:420; Butler and Arnold 1977:188).

The Maya believe that corn has a spirit or soul, although how that essence is perceived or categorized varies slightly from region to region (Thompson 1930:48; Wisdom 1940:391; Siegel 1941:66; Bunzel 1952:54; Aulie 1979:24; Johannessen 1982:86). The Maya go to great lengths to ensure that the spirit of corn is not harmed, because they believe that without a strong soul the harvested corn and even the subsequent harvests will be diminished. They treat kernels of corn with respect, and every kernel is held in high esteem (Redfield 1941:121; Siegel 1941:66; Steggerda 1943:217; Bunzel 1952:45; Vogt 1969:35; Nash 1970:44; M. Wilson 1972:98; Carlson and Eachus 1977:47–48; Johannessen 1984:94; Breedlove and Laughlin 1993:108, 231).

## THE DEVELOPMENT OF CORN

Once planted, corn seed will sprout in about eight days if there is enough moisture. The plant grows from a needle-like sprout to a seedling with small leaves. As
the broader leaves and stalk develop, the tassel appears at the tip of the stalk. The
broadening of the leaves and the flowering of the corn plant is an important step in
development. In the Tz'utujil area, the cornfield is called *awes,* "young maize plants,"
before this development, and *awän,* "mature corn plants," afterward (Arnold and
Butler 1977:188). Following the tassel development, one or perhaps two ears grow
from buds on the sides of the upper stalk. In the initial development of the ear,
many leaf-like husks grow from the bud; then the cob begins to take form inside
the husk, and the silks emerge from the end. When the plant has almost reached its
maximum height, the pollen from the male tassel is shed over a five-to-eight-day
period and is dispersed by the wind. Corn pollen has the appearance of fine white
dust, and the Maya refer to it as "its ash" (Atran 1993:679; Breedlove and Laughlin
1993:470). The white pollen lands on the silks of the female ear and fertilization
occurs. The kernels of the corn ear are underdeveloped at this stage, but the darkening
and drying off of the corn silks is an indication that the green corn kernels inside
the husk are growing larger.

The Maya are known to harvest some of the lower ears on the stalk at the earliest
stage of ear development, but they do the main harvesting of green corn when the
ears are more developed. The green corn can be boiled, grilled over the fire, baked in
an underground oven, or ground into dough. Only a limited number of green ears are
harvested, while the rest is left to further mature.

During the period of internal ripening and yellowing, the farmer bends the cornstalk over, cutting off the food supply from the roots and causing the corn seed to
harden. Bending the stalk also prevents rainwater from entering the husk, makes the
kernels less accessible to birds, and lessens wind damage. It also allows more sunlight to
reach the crops growing interspersed with the corn. A stalk with a single ear produces
a larger ear, with better quality seed, than a stalk with multiple ears. Harvesting lower
ears at the green stage allows the upper ear to develop into a better product.

Occasionally a corn plant will develop ears of corn that have unusual forms, and
the Maya view such ears as both good and bad omens. The cobs of bad omen are
destroyed after shelling to nullify their influence. The types that are consistently seen
as good omens are an ear of corn with multiple tips; two ears of corn growing
inside one husk; two ears of corn in separate husks, but growing from one node; and
one large ear of corn in its own husk with several smaller ears growing around its
base. Two ears of corn in one husk or growing from the same node are often called
twins and played a vital role in ancient beliefs (see chapters 10 and 11).

Because good-quality seed is a prerequisite for a successful crop, choosing the
seed for the next planting is an important task during the harvest. The largest ears
of corn are chosen because the Maya recognize from experience that large seeds

give the best results. In some areas, seed ears are chosen from the center of the field, which is called *corazón del maíz*, or "heart of the corn" (Kelsey and Osbourne 1961:45). While harvested corn is frequently stored in granaries near the field, seed corn is usually hung from the rafters of the house or kitchen or on the house wall where it can be protected (Blom and La Farge 1927:339; La Farge and Byers 1931:47; Stadelman 1940:112; Wisdom 1940:49; Wagley 1941:41; 1949:127; Hermitte 1964:59; Carter 1969:105; Vogt 1969:45; Baer and Merrifield 1971:179; Berlin, Breedlove, and Raven 1974:117; Carlson and Eachus 1977:47).

## GUARDIANS OF THE SPIRIT OF CORN

A common belief is that the patron saints or deities of a community protect the spirit of corn. For example, in the Tzeltal town of Pinola, it is believed that the deity Thunderbolt is the guardian of the maize spirits and that he hides the spirits under his foot (Hermitte 1964:60). To explain a drop in agricultural productivity, it is said that he once absentmindedly raised his foot, and part of the maize spirits were stolen by the ancestral spirits of neighboring Amatenango. This also explains why Amatenango is thought to have better harvests. Holland (1961:109) records a Tzotzil story at San Andrés Larráinzar in which the patron saint prevents a man from taking the spirit of corn to a neighboring community.

In addition to the protection of the patron saint, the Maya perform rituals to ensure the safety of the corn and its spirit. They place crosses, small idols, ritually prepared ears of corn, or unusual ears of corn with their harvested corn. The presence of these spiritually strong guardians is thought to protect the corn and even make it increase. Twin ears of corn are frequently placed in the granary for this purpose. In the *Popol Vuh*, the hero twins plant green corn in their house before journeying to the underworld, and they tell their grandmother that this corn is an omen of their fate. The corn of the hero twins is the prototype for the twin ears of corn that the Maya use to guard the harvested corn.

In the Kaqchikel town of San Antonio Palopó, twin ears of corn are hung in a pine grove near the milpa at the beginning of the harvest (Redfield 1945:224, 226). At the end of the harvest, the ears are placed in the granary and are not eaten until all the corn has been consumed. In Chichicastenango, the K'iche' place a corn ear, still on the stalk, with the harvested corn (Rodas, Rodas, and Hawkins 1940:66). A piece of wood is fastened to the stalk to form a cross. In other areas, cornstalks with their tassels removed are tied to a piece of wood to form a guardian cross. In Tzeltal Pinola, little wooden crosses are put on top of the corn, and two of the first ears of corn are hung from the house altar (Hermitte 1964:60).

In the Ch'orti' zone, four effigy corn ears made from copal are wrapped in white cloths and placed with the corn to guard the spirit of maize against the evil spirit *cicimai* (Wisdom 1940:403, 447). When the corn is completely stacked in the crib, a cross is erected in the center. Prayers are made to the spirit of the earth to protect the corn (Fought 1972:508–509). The Q'eqchi' place a pair of smoked ears in each corner of the storage loft as guardians (M. Wilson 1972:104).

The role of ears of corn as guardians is not restricted to the stored corn. Lacandon women rest in their hammock to regain their heat and strength after giving birth (Baer 1952:18). An ear of corn is tied to each end of the hammock to protect mother and child from evil spirits. During the Lacandon renewal rites for their god pots, an ear of corn is placed on the north and south sides of the board that contains the incense nodules for the ceremony (Tozzer 1907:128). The corn is thought to guard the incense from evil spirits who might steal it. A similar practice is found in Jacaltenango, where they place an ear of corn on each side of the baby if it is to be left alone (La Farge and Byers 1931:86).

## THE GENDER OF CORN SEED

In the vast majority of communities, ears of corn, kernels, and the spirit of corn are thought to be female. This belief reflects the observation of all corn growers that the female ear is impregnated by the white, powdery pollen that spills from the male tassel. In the Proto-Ch'olan list proposed by Kaufman and Norman (1984:121), the words for corn and female are similar. The term for dried corn kernels is *ixim*, the word for shelled corn is *ix*, and the words for female and woman are *ix* and *ixik*, respectively.

Corn is most frequently referred to by the Maya as "our mother corn" or "our holy mother corn" and represented as a young woman (Siegel 1941; Mendelson 1957:444; Valladares 1957:196; Saler 1960:52; Guiteras Holmes 1961:218; Paul and Paul 1962:783; Nash 1970; Shaw 1971; Hunn 1977; Cook 1981:111–12; Tarn and Prechtel 1986; Montejo and Campbell 1993; Preuss 1993). Evidence that corn ears and kernels are viewed as female can be seen in many contexts. In the riddles of the *Chilam Balam of Chumayel*, an ear of corn (*nal*) is referred to as a beautiful maiden:

> Son, go and bring me here (the girl) with the watery teeth [corn ker-
> nels]. Her hair [the silk] is twisted into a tuft; she is a very beautiful
> maiden. Fragrant shall be her odor when I remove her skirt [husk]
> and her (other) garment. (Roys 1933:130)

The concept that corn silk is like hair is also found in the Ch'ol, Q'eqchi', and Tzotzil areas (M. Wilson 1972:42; Attinasi 1973; Breedlove and Laughlin 1993:491).

The Tzotzil believe that each kernel of corn, like a person, has a soul that resides in its heart (Vogt 1969:37). The spirit of corn is manifested as one of the daughters of the mountain lord, and she is called X'ob (Guiteras Holmes 1961:40, 192, 216, 218, 268, 291; Laughlin 1977:165–67, 238–46). In the Ch'ol region, the spirit of abundance found in corn, beans, and chickens is called *ña'al* (Aulie 1979:24). The term *ña'* means mother, and *ña'al* means female animal. *Ña'al* is thought to have the form of a triple ear of corn.

In Santiago Atitlán, the phrase "the spirit of corn" may refer to the specific spirit in a kernel or ear of corn, the spirit of a class of corn such as yellow corn, or the spirit of all corn (Douglas 1969:69, 78). The San Juan cofradía house in Santiago Atitlán formerly contained two stone fetishes called "hearts of the corn" that represented the female spirits of corn (Mendelson 1958:409; Douglas 1969:69, 78). María was the spirit of dark and multicolored corn, and Juana was the spirit of white and yellow corn. In the same cofradía house, a box contains a ritual cloth with ribbons and two bags attached to it (Tarn and Prechtel 1986:175–76; Christenson 2001:121). This bundle is said to belong to the creator grandmother Yaxper. The ritual cloth has three faces sewn on it that represent "three corn girls." Yamri (María) is the spirit of yellow corn, Yachón (Concepción) is the spirit of white corn, and Yaxuan (Juana) is the spirit of dark or speckled corn. The ribbons are thought to be umbilical cords and plant tendrils, and the two bags represent the first father and mother. The bags are said to contain dried lumps of corn dough. The Atiteco cloth reflects the pre-Columbian belief that the first humans were created from corn. Three girls who represent three kinds of colored corn are also found in the Achi' region (Shaw 1971:48–51).

Further examples of female corn are found in San Lucas Tolimán, where to dream of beautiful women foretells a good harvest (Woods 1968:214), and in San Pedro Sacatepequez, where unmarried Kaqchikel girls dance with female corn dolls during the Dance of the Ears of Corn (Thompson 1970:286). In the Tzotzil area, an unborn child is said to be inside its corn husk—which suggests that an ear of corn is like a pregnant woman (Rosenbaum 1993:77). Also in the Tzotzil area, the stage of growth when the young plant has just produced its ears is called *muk'tik me? yi* (Vogt 1969:50), which can be translated as "large mothers of little corn" (Robert Laughlin, personal communication). The Achi' place a corncob in the coffin of a child to represent its mother (Carlson and Eachus 1977:45).

## Corn as Bones and Teeth

The Maya metaphorically refer to kernels of corn as bones or teeth (Thompson 1930:54; Roys 1933:130; Bunzel 1952:55; Nash 1970:204; Shaw 1971:179; Barrera Vasquez 1980:710; Laughlin 1988:377). In many Mayan languages, a corncob is also referred to as a bone or white bone. In the Tz'utujil region, corn seed is referred to as *jolooma,* "little skulls" (Carlsen and Prechtel 1991:28). The equation of corn seed with teeth is found in a Q'eqchi' myth that tells how a young girl planted her teeth in place of corn seed and ended a famine (Preuss 1993). Bone and teeth are all that remain after flesh has decomposed. In several stories, corn is said to be the remains of a woman or goddess: "It (the corn seed) was blessed, also that it might not cease until the judgment, until the end of the age. Years have passed, and this body of our mother has never ceased" (Shaw 1971:209). The likening of corn seed to female bones is also found in the Tzeltal town of Amatenango, where the bones of Santa Teresa are thought to be corn seeds (Nash 1970:204).

Divination practices also associate females, corn, and bone. In Yucatan, the crystal used in divination is thought to contain a virgin. When no crystal is available, eighteen kernels of corn are used (Tozzer 1907:163–64). The close relationship between corn seed and bone is found in the pre-Columbian custom of using both corn kernels and bones as divination lots (Tozzer 1907:163; 1912:505; Saville 1921:206; Edmonson 1971:59). The belief that corn kernels are bones is also found in the *Popol Vuh,* where the teeth of Seven Macaw are replaced with "ground bone," also referred to as white corn (Edmonson 1971:42, D. Tedlock 1985:93). In a Tzotzil myth, the teeth of a gopher are created from corn stubble (Breedlove and Laughlin 1993:231). The Itza' Maya of the Petén compare white corn kernels to the teeth of dogs (Reina 1967:6). In a Mopan Maya story, the protagonist drills holes in seven grains of red corn, which causes his opponent to have a toothache (Shaw 1971:178–79).

The discovery of corn seeds in a mountain is a well-documented Maya belief (Burkitt 1920:213; Wagley 1941:20; Redfield 1945:36; Oakes 1951:244; Valladares 1957:196–200; Mayers 1958; Miles 1960; Vogt 1969; Thompson 1970; Edmonson 1971:146; Shaw 1971; Montejo and Campbell 1993; Preuss 1993). In many of the ancient and contemporary stories, the white corn seed is hidden in a crevice on a white cliff or under an immovable rock in a cave. The prominent role of leaf-cutter ants in accessing this corn is an indication that a nest of these creatures lives near the cave. A variety of small animals initially takes the corn from the ants to use as food, but the defining act is that the crevice or stone is eventually split open by a deity using a lightning bolt in the form of an ax. Many of the corn stories indicate that when the lightning strikes, it singes and burns some of the white corn, which results in the creation of the other three colors of corn: yellow, red, and black. I have presented evidence that this corn is the remains of Lady Bone Water (One Hunahpu's first wife), and that she was parallel to the Classic Period corn goddess (Bassie-Sweet 2002; see also chapter 8).

## The Annual Corn Cycle

The ancient Maya are known to have used a variety of agricultural strategies to increase the productivity of their land, such as terraces, raised and drained fields, and so forth, but I am only concerned with a discussion of the slash-and-burn technique. This type of corn production is similar throughout the Maya domain despite the area's diverse altitude, topography, drainages, soil composition, and weather patterns. Certain aspects of slash-and-burn production are central to understanding the Maya world view and deities. Although many of these topics are addressed more thoroughly later in the book, a brief overview of the yearly corn cycle and the natural phenomena associated with it is in order.

In the Maya region, the year is divided into a wet and dry season that sets the basic rhythm of life and dictates the planting cycle. The principal corn crop is planted at the beginning of the rainy season. In the lowlands, a smaller second crop may be planted either later in the wet season or during the dry season, in low-lying areas where there is enough moisture. In the highlands, a second crop of corn suited to the high altitude is planted in March.

The specific dates of the rainy season vary slightly from zone to zone as well as from year to year, but generally the season begins with light rains in late March and early April. These rains trigger the blossoming of various plants, and honey production soars. In the Yucatan, this *man ha' che'* period is also called by the descriptive term *nik che'*, "flower tree." This is followed by a short dry spell with distant thunder and hailstorms and then the heavier rains of late April and May. These two months are the hottest of the year. Although some rain usually falls every month of the year, the precipitation of the rainy season is intense and frequent. The true rainy season begins with afternoon and evening lightning storms and torrential downpours brought by the prevailing east wind. The heaviest rainfall is usually in June.

A short dry period referred to in some areas by the Spanish term *canícula* occurs anywhere from late July to late August for about seven to twenty-one days (Wagley 1949:107, Guiteras Holmes 1961:, Merrill-Sands 1984). The Ch'orti' believe that the canícula officially begins on July 25 with the feast of Santiago, while in Yucatan the period ends on September 15 and 16 (Girard 1962:251–52, de Jong 1999:156). As will be discussed in chapter 10, a female feathered serpent is thought to grind corn dough during the canícula and place it in the ears of corn in the fields. When this feathered serpent flies across the sky on September 15, her shadow causes particular animals to metamorphose into other animals (Villa Rojas 1945:157; de Jong 1999:156–61). It is believed that deer, agoutis, peccaries, rabbits, and foxes turn into various kinds of snakes; turtles turn into parrots; bats turn into mice; and armadillos turn into vultures. Conversely, snakes turn into deer, agoutis, peccaries, rabbits, and foxes; parrots turn into vultures, and so forth.

In Latin, "canicula" refers to Sirius, the dog star. During these "dog days" of summer, Sirius rises in the southeast near dawn; hence the name. Although the ancient Maya name for the canícula is unknown, this time period is vitally important, for if it lasts too long, the harvest will be diminished or destroyed. The corn tassel will not release its pollen in dry conditions, so it is imperative that the canícula not coincide with this phase of corn production (Merrill-Sand 1984:70). The rains again reach a high volume in September and then decline. As the dry season progresses, the temperature drops. The driest months are February through April, with March usually being the driest of all.

The success of the corn harvest depends on a regular and adequate amount of rain throughout the growing season. Too much can be as damaging as too little. The timing and volume of rainfall varies greatly and is quite unpredictable. In addition, rain does not fall consistently over the entire area, so one milpa might receive enough rainfall while another located just a short distance away may not.

## Storms, Drought, and Fires

The rainy season is occasionally marked by storms reaching hurricane status that sweep across the region. Areas outside of the immediate path of the hurricane still receive high volumes of rain. Even when hurricanes pass to the north, they often create heavy rainfall that causes widespread flooding and destruction. During the months from October to March, frequent cold fronts from the north are the most significant factor in the weather and rainfall patterns of the dry season. These *nortes*, called *xaman ka'an* (north sky) in Yucatec Maya, begin with a dark cloud bank rolling across the sky out of the north, followed by high winds that can reach hurricane force, rain, and a sudden drop in temperature. The dominance of these north storms is reflected in the practice at San Pedro Chenalhó of referring to any rain during the dry season as a norte (Guiteras Holmes 1961:7). The *Relación de Merida* (A.D. 1579) states that the cold weather of the nortes was unhealthy and caused many deaths, and that the winds often uprooted large trees and demolished the thatched-roofed houses of the Maya (Garza et al. 1983, vol. 1, 69–70). In addition, hurricanes and strong nortes damage and destroy beehives and reduce the honey harvest. The nortes are beneficial in one regard: their moisture can contribute to the success of the second corn crop that is planted later in the season. This dry-season moisture can also trigger the production of flowers and increase honey volume (Merrill-Sands 1984:70).

Inadequate rainfall during any part of the growing season can be disastrous for the quality of the harvest. When drought conditions prevail for any length of time, the immediate crop is obviously affected, but there are other, equally dangerous, long-term consequences. Prolonged drought weakens or kills forest vegetation and sets the stage for wildfires that can spread over large areas. The destructive winds of hurricanes and nortes do similar damage. As the season progresses, the trees become desiccated, and the dried-out foliage can ignite and fuel massive fires when lightning storms arrive at the beginning of the next rainy season. If the fires burn over too large an area, they damage the ecological balance between fields and forest by destroying the wooded areas that are necessary for future milpas and for the regeneration of fallowed milpas. On a positive note, the fires from drought and storm conditions are a natural regeneration cycle of the rain forest, and, like the fires of the milpa, they create nutrient-rich ash. It seems likely that the technique of slash-and-burn agriculture evolved from watching this natural destructive cycle and the resulting regeneration of the forest.

## Labor and Scheduling

The corn cycle requires intensive labor during the crucial periods of corn planting and harvesting. While a farmer may plant by himself or with the assistance of his young sons, it is more common and more efficient for a group of farmers to form a planting party and help each other seed the field. A farmer may also hire labor, although this is less common. Hired laborers for the harvest can be paid with surplus corn, but during the planting season, resources are at their lowest and additional expenses are avoided. Reciprocal labor and cooperative activities are a time of bonding with close kin and neighbors. The ritual foodstuffs exchanged at this time also create positive relationships and a sense of community participation and well-being. Unlike house construction and repair, which can take place anytime during the dry season, coordinating the planting parties is a major organizational task because everyone is planting within a very brief period.

## Making the Field

Field locations are chosen in the dry season based on soil type, drainage, slope, vegetation cover, topography, and access. In hopes of minimizing crop failure, several different types of field site are often chosen to turn into milpa. In addition, the farmer will also be replanting fields that were cleared and planted in previous seasons. These second- and third-year milpas will not be as fruitful as a first-season field, but the time and labor expended in cutting the vegetation in these kinds of fields is obviously much less.

The square or rectangular field is often measured out using a rope or string as a guide, and its corners are sometimes marked with poles, trees, or small piles of stones (Redfield and Villa Rojas 1934:43; Wisdom 1940:40; Carter 1969:42; M. Wilson 1972:90; Love and Peraza Castillo 1984:291; Schackt 1986:35; Hanks 1991:357; Hostettler 1996:274). In the community of Oxkutzcab, five stones are ideally used to mark the corners of the fields, with the first three that are put in place said to be like the three hearthstones of the kitchen fire (Hanks 1991:357). It may take weeks or even months to cut a new field or fallowed field, and it is a dangerous undertaking given the number of poisonous and deadly animals such as snakes, scorpions, spiders, centipedes, and caterpillars. Injuries and even death from falling trees are not uncommon. Vegetation is not removed from the designated field; rather, it is stacked across the field to prepare it for burning. Useful trees that might survive the burning are left standing (for example, copal, cedar, *zapote*, rubber, and palm), as are very large trees that are too difficult to cut.

As the season progresses, the cut vegetation gradually dries into a combustible state. The burning of the vegetation is beneficial; it clears the slash, loosens the soil, lowers the rate of herbaceous and ligneous plants, reduces animal pests, and produces nutrient-rich ash (Carter 1969:57). It also releases lime from the surface rock that improves the pH value of the soil (Stadelman 1940:109). To take advantage of the prevailing winds, the fire is usually started on the eastern side of the cornfield using a long, burning stick or a bundle of burning cornstalks. The right wind velocity is vital. Not enough wind may result in an incomplete burn, but too much can cause excessive combustion with a subsequent loss of nutrients or cause the fire to spread to adjoining areas. The smoke from the burning fields creates a haze across the landscape, and the heat adds to the already scorching temperature of the dry season.

## The Planting

To maximize the benefit of the burn, the corn seed should be planted the day after the firing or soon thereafter, and the rains must arrive immediately after that or corn will not germinate well. Determining the correct day for the burning and the subsequent planting is difficult but critical (Villa Rojas 1945:77). Across the Maya region, the standard method of planting corn requires only a seed bag and a planting stick. The planting of corn is seen as a sexual act that only men are allowed to perform (Wilson 1995:111; Faust 1998:131; Sieber 1999). In K'iche', the term *awexibal,* "sowing," is used only for human sexual intercourse and planting corn. The farmer splits the earth open with the stick and creates a hole three to five inches deep by working the stick side-to-side and back-and-forth. With his other hand, the farmer extracts the correct number of seeds from the bag and drops them as a group into the hole with a downward flick of his wrist. He then moves on to make the next hole. The number of seeds planted in each hole varies from region to region, but Stadelman (1940:113) notes that ideally there should be five corn plants per mound. The rows of corn plants are offset from one another. Corn planted in this pattern is more resistant to wind damage, retains rainwater better on slopes, and impedes soil erosion. Later, the farmer may pile earth around the sprouting plants to create mounds or hillocks. The corn holes are sometimes left uncovered to trap dew (Butler and Arnold 1977:192; Wilks 1991:93). The need for dew is reflected in a Mopan Maya myth in which the first person to plant corn took the sweat from his brow and put it in the corn hole (Thompson 1930:145). The farmer weeds his field several times during the season and attempts to protect it from marauding animals and pests.

Beans and squash as well as a variety of other crops are sown with the corn. The Lacandon plant as many as eighty different kinds of plants, such as sweet potatoes, taro, manioc, chile peppers, cotton, tobacco, and cacao (Nations 1981:4). In the rain forest of the Petén, the Itza' Maya create a separate, secondary garden of useful plants on the east side of the milpa (Atran 1993:679). The opening of the forest canopy or the secondary growth of a fallow field allows a variety of wild plants to regenerate, and the Maya harvest many of these for food, medicine, and firewood. The flowers from some of these plants as well as those from the secondary garden at the edge of the field provide nectar and pollen for bees, which, in turn, provide honey. The hollow trees of the burned milpa are colonized by wild bees. Honey was and still is an important commodity. Thus, the milpa is a rich source of a variety of foods and useful plants.

## Harvest and Storage

In the dry region of northern Yucatan, corn can be left in the field during most of the dry season and gathered when needed. The remaining corn is stored in March in anticipation of the rainy season. In many other areas, however, corn is immediately harvested and stored. Often, some harvested corn is kept in the house, but the majority is kept in small granaries near the field or close to the main house. The building of corn storage structures precedes the harvest. A farmer who is producing a surplus of corn for sale must have adequate storage facilities that will allow the corn to be stored for the maximum amount of time, for he will attempt to sell his surplus when regional supply is low and the market price is high.

In many communities, corn is harvested by simply tearing or cutting the ears from the stalk. Huskers, traditionally made of deer bone, are also employed (Vogt 1969:51–52). The remainder of the plant (the bent-over, dried stalk; foliage; and tassel) is left in the field to be burned the following season, although some corn plants may be used for fuel or building materials. The ears of corn are transported to the storage place in large net bags that the Maya carry using a tumpline.

In drier regions of the northern peninsula and the cooler southern highlands, corn in its husk can be stored for up to three years, but in the heat and humidity of the southern lowland rain forest, corn may only last a year (Alfonso Morales, personal communication). The kernels must be thoroughly dry or they will rot in storage. If not completely dry, the harvested ears can be laid out and further dried in the sun for several days. In some areas, corn is smoked to preserve it and make it less susceptible to weevils (M. Wilson 1972:103; Reina and Hill 1980; Johannessen 1982:89). Corn is smoked by placing the ears on a rack of saplings suspended on the house rafters. A smoky fire is kept burning underneath until the corn has become thoroughly dried and coated in smoke. Reina and Hill (1980) report that natives in Alta Verapaz used this method at the time of the conquest and that smoked corn could last an entire year in the hot lowlands, while untreated corn only lasted four months. The longevity of smoked corn allows it to be sold to other communities later in the season when demand and prices are most advantageous to the seller.

An important concept is that a cornfield does not exist until it is planted, and that it ceases to exist once the corn has been harvested. The milpa reverts to being just earth when the corn is removed (Butler and Arnold 1977:187; John Fought, personal communication). Still, harvested fields or those in fallow are not physically abandoned but continue to produce. The fields contain useful plants whose roots, leaves, wood, sap, fruits, and seeds are continually harvested, and some plants such as chile peppers and manioc will even survive the next cycle of burning and regenerate (Carter 1969:47, 60, 130; Nation and Nigh 1980:15). Fallow fields are often planted with trees such as fruit, cacao, and rubber that will not only regenerate the soil, but that can be harvested. Plant density and diversity is high in the fallow fields, and these plants attract animals that are hunted for their meat and skins.

## Processing of Corn

The corn a family eats must be prepared daily because it is susceptible to mold and souring. Women are in charge of processing corn into many different kinds of food, including tortillas, tamales, gruels, and drinks, using a variety of techniques. To transform dried corn kernels into usable dough, they must have pots, bowls, strainers, grinding equipment, and large supplies of lime, firewood, and water. The lime is produced by burning limestone or freshwater snails in a large pyre (Tozzer 1907:51).

The different types of corn have unique tastes and textures. While white and yellow corn are commonly used for everyday meals, black corn is frequently prepared for ritual meals (Reina 1967:6). A woman begins the corn processing by removing the dried corn from the cob using the heel of her hand, a second ear, or an awl. The kernels are put in a container along with water and lime and placed over a fire to boil. The addition of lime increases the food value of the corn by releasing nutrients. Alternatively, the corn can be boiled without lime to produce a different flavor, or it can be boiled, once with and once without lime. The softened corn, or *nixtamal*, is rinsed in fresh water until the hulls and lime have washed away. This usually takes five to seven rinses. Because the washing uses a good deal of water, it is done outside in a designated part of the yard. If there is a nearby water source such as a river, the corn is rinsed there, a process that attracts fish that come to nibble at the debris.

Traditionally, the nixtamal is then ground with a *mano* (cylindrical stone) on a metate (stone slab) until it has the desired texture. The metate and mano are made rough for better grinding by pecking them with a flint (Baer and Merrifield 1971:187), and these grinding tools are often passed down from mother to daughter. The ancient Maya used a variety of metate types including a flat stone, a tripod stone, and a stone in the form of a turtle. The *masa* dough is ground from three to five times to obtain the correct consistency. While grinding, the woman wets her hands and the soft dough with water to prevent it from sticking (La Farge and Byers 1931:50; Baer and Merrifield 1971:186). At the end of grinding, she again sprinkles the dough with water, kneads it into a ball, and wraps it in a leaf. The process of grinding corn by hand is labor intensive and requires that the woman rise well before dawn.

Tamales are made from corn dough and various fillings wrapped in leaves and then baked or boiled. Common fillings are beans, squash seeds, and the meat from wild or domestic animals. Spices and seasonings are also added. Tortillas are made by patting the dough into a round, flat shape and grilling it on a flat cooking surface called a *comal* that has been seasoned with ash to prevent the dough from sticking. A meal usually consists of ten to twenty tortillas per person. Toasted tortillas are made from corn seeds that have been first boiled in lime water and then in plain water. After cooking on the comal, they are propped up beside the fire to dry. It is also possible to grind up a tortilla into a paste and then re-grill it. Such tortillas do not get as hard as regular tortillas. Tortillas can be eaten individually, or stacked with fillings in between. Tortillas are often used to scoop up other food such as stewed meat.

Each of the different kinds of corn drinks or gruel is prepared in a slightly different way across the Maya area. *Atole* (*ul*) is made from corn that is boiled in lime, ground into dough, and mixed with water and boiled again. It can be sweetened and spiced. The drink called s*akha*, "white water," can be created by two methods. The corn seeds can be partially boiled and ground, or soaked for three days and ground. Because no lime is used, sakha retains a white color; hence its name. The sakha corn dough is then mixed with more water and either drunk as is or boiled before drinking. It can also be flavored with spices, honey, or chocolate. The drink *pozol* is created from corn that has been boiled twice and ground just once. The dough is wrapped in leaves or corn husks. When needed, it is mixed with cold water as a drink. A drink called *pinole* or *maatz* is made from corn kernels roasted on the griddle and then ground to a powder. This drink may also have *Theobroma cacao* or *T. bicolor (pataxte)* and spices mixed with it. The Maya make many other drinks that incorporate corn. In particular, fermented drinks from corn are used extensively in rituals.

Food and drink such as toasted tortillas, reground tortillas, pozol, and pinole are suitable to take on journeys because they last much longer than fresh foods and are easily transported. In the Ch'orti' area, pilgrims walking to the festival of Esquipulas take enough reground tortillas and pinole to last until their return home (Fought 1972:451). Pozol can be quickly prepared at any water source.

The ancient Maya processed corn much like their modern counterparts. Tamale offerings of turkey, deer, iguana, turtle, and fish are illustrated in Maya art, and this food category appears to be the dominant food eaten by the ancient Maya (Taube 1989). Numerous Classic Period bowls are labeled as dishes for the corn gruels called *ul* and *sa'* (Houston, Stuart, and Taube 1989:722).

## Summary

There is an almost universal belief among the Maya that the spirit of corn is female. The physical act of preparing, planting, maintaining, and harvesting cornfields requires considerable knowledge about soil types, plant and animal ecology, and weather patterns. Although the length of time varies, corn can not be stored indefinitely, and surpluses not needed for local consumption eventually have to be traded for other goods or services. Ideally, this surplus is held until supplies in other areas are low in order to obtain the highest price. Surplus corn is also consumed during feasts that establish goodwill and reciprocal obligations with other groups.

The success of the corn crop is uneven in the Maya region. While some communities may experience bumper crops, adjacent communities may suffer shortages during the same season. This imbalance stimulates positive trade and exchange between areas that might not otherwise have occasion to interact. The negative effect is that imbalances always give rise to conflicts. Competition for agricultural lands is also a basic source of discord and disputes.

In Alta Verapaz, Reina and Hill (1980) note that smoked corn is traded to areas where conditions are less favorable for corn production, but where the environment allows for abundant cacao and cotton crops. Taube (1996) suggests that Olmec corn surpluses were also smoked and that these surpluses were converted into high status commodities such as quetzal feathers and jade. He notes that corn was symbolically represented by quetzal feathers and jade in Mesoamerican art. This relationship will be explored in later chapters.

# 3

# AGRICULTURAL EVENTS
# AND CEREMONIES

The precautions, both practical and ritual, that the Maya take to ensure an adequate food supply are complex. They perform many agricultural ceremonies during the corn cycle to appease the deities and guarantee a successful season. A number of factors come into play to gauge the timing of such ceremonies, including the day of the religious calendar, the observation of plant and animal behavior, and celestial and meteorological events.

It must be kept in mind that the signs used to time activities and rituals are often subjective and require a certain amount of interpretation and adaptation. In addition, circumstances may prevent an activity from occurring at the ideal time, but the Maya have numerous techniques and rituals to handle these conditions. For instance, the Tzotzil believe that corn planted during the new moon will not sprout, but if they are obliged to plant at this time, they carry with them three miniature tortillas with three holes in each (Guiteras Holmes 1961:41). The tortillas metaphorically represent the surface of the earth, and the holes allow the seeds to sprout.

## TRACKING THE SUN

The Maya are keenly interested in signs that the rainy season is coming, because they must time their corn planting to coincide with adequate moisture. Like most cultures, the Maya use the rising and setting points of the sun to establish the basic time frame for seasonal and climatic changes that impact their crops. The Ch'orti' watch to see where the sun rises and sets in relation to certain mountains in the vicinity of their community (Fought 1972:386), and the use of natural landmarks for such purposes is well known in Mesoamerica (Aveni 1980).

A unique feature of the tropics is that twice a year the sun passes directly overhead. The latitude of the observer dictates the exact day. In the extreme southern zone of the Maya region, the first zenith passage occurs around April 29. For the next fifty-four days, the sun moves farther north each day until the June solstice, when it begins to move south again. After fifty-four more days it reaches its second zenith passage on about August 12. In the northern region of Yucatan, the zenith passage occurs on May 20 and again on July 22. The approach of the first zenith passage of the year coincides with the start of the rainy season. In the *Popol Vuh*, the climax of the creation cycle occurs when Hunahpu in his sun manifestation rises on zenith passage and initiates the corn cycle (see chapter 11).

## THE MOON

The Maya also watch the moon, the Milky Way, and certain stars to time events. On the first night that the waxing moon is visible, it appears at sunset as a sliver near the sun. The next night and on every subsequent night of its cycle, the crescent moon appears slightly fuller and higher in the sky at sunset. About thirteen days from when it is first visible, the full moon is seen rising in the east as the sun sets. Each night after full moon, the moon rises a little later and its disk is narrower. Finally, the waning moon rises just before dawn as a slim crescent near the rising sun. On the next night it is too close to the sun to be seen and remains unseen for several days before beginning its cycle again.

The Maya time a host of activities to coincide with specific phases of the moon. Aulie (1979:24) notes that the phases of the moon control the timing of planting and the cutting of trees for construction. The cutting of wood for house posts, lumber, and thatch is done during the full moon, as is the clearing of the fields (Steggerda 1943:205; Redfield 1945:211; Guiteras Holmes 1961:35, 153; Woods 1968:209; Nash 1970:312; Gossen 1974:334; B. Tedlock 1985:85; Atran 1993:678; Breedlove and Laughlin 1993:106). The Maya believe that wood for construction must be cut at full moon or its resin will seep through the cut and attract insects that will attack the wood (Atran 1993:678). Even the log hives used for domesticated bees are cut at full moon (de Jong 1999:167). Wood cut at other times will rot more easily. The presumed decrease in the flow of liquids at full moon is also reflected in the Tzotzil belief that flesh wounds that occur at full moon bleed less and heal more rapidly, while those occurring at new moon bleed profusely and take much longer to heal (Holland 1961:105). Menstruation is also associated with the new moon (Milbrath 1999:32).

The phases of the moon that seem to be bad for planting corn, harvesting, and woodcutting are the latter stages of the waning moon, the new moon (when the moon is not seen), and the early stages of the waxing moon (Guiteras Holmes 1961:35, 45, 153, 175, 287; B. Tedlock 1985:85; Atran 1993:678; Breedlove and Laughlin 1993:504). The Maya ideally plant corn at full moon (Mayers 1958:38; Guiteras Holmes 1961:35, 175, 287; Holland 1961:105; Reina 1966:190; B. Tedlock 1985:85; R. Wilson 1990:81; 1995:63). The K'iche' plant yellow corn during the full moon and perform other agricultural rituals on subsequent full moons (B. Tedlock 1985:85). The Itza' Maya living in the Petén believe that crops should be planted at full moon to grow properly (Atran 1993:678) as do the Poqomam of highland Guatemala (Reina 1966:190) and the Maya of northern Yucatan (Pérez Toro 1942:17–18, 204). The Tzotzil plant corn when the moon is full or slightly waning (Breedlove and Laughlin 1993:106). In the Tzotzil town of San Andrés Larráinzar, the full moon is thought to be the best time for planting and harvesting. Crops planted at other times will grow poorly and yield little (Holland 1961:150).

In many areas, the doubling-over of the cornstalk and final harvest are done at full moon or completed by that time (Guiteras Holmes 1961:35, 45, 153; Gossen 1974:334; B. Tedlock 1985:86; Breedlove and Laughlin 1993:106; Vogt 1997:112). In Quintana Roo, it is believed that insects will attack the bent corn if it is not bent during the full moon (de Jong 1999:223). At San Lucas Tolimán, there is a belief that a corn crop harvested at any other time will simply not yield enough food for a family's needs (Woods 1968:210).

The full moon is also thought to have a positive influence on human conception; women are considered to be most fertile at full moon (Holland 1961:105, Atran 1993:678). This accords with the belief that the act of corn planting is like sexual intercourse. In Quintana Roo, the later phases of the waxing moon and the full moon are thought to have great influence in inducing the delivery of babies, so these phases of the moon are taken into account when predicting the birth date (Villa Rojas 1945:136, 141). The Tzeltal believe that a child born at full moon will mature more readily and that the phase of the moon is an important sign of the newborn's future (Nash 1970:312).

The moon is also thought to influence the productivity of plants (Thompson 1939:144). The Tzotzil say that "those who work the land watch the moon," and that the presence of the moon keeps the earth "open" so corn can sprout (Guiteras Holmes 1961:175, 286). The Q'eqchi' believe "the moon watches over and protects the growing crop, as well as furnishing fertility," and that its role is to "help the plants grow" (R. Wilson 1990:81, 1995:63, 106). In the *Book of Chilam Balam of Tizimin* it is said that the moon germinates the plants (Makemson 1951:41). The Ch'orti' associate the moon with plant growth in general and with the productivity of useful trees, which they believe the moon owns (Wisdom 1940:400). The waxing moon is particularly associated with growth, and this extends to humans as well. In San Antonio Palopó, the waxing moon is thought to make wounds heal more quickly, make adult teeth appear in children, and make the body grow (Redfield 1945:211).

A relationship between rainfall and the phase of the moon was noted by Landa, who stated that the only time it rained during the dry season months of January and February was during a new moon (Tozzer 1941:4). The contemporary K'iche' believe it rains more at new moon and full moon (Remington 1977:81). In other areas, it is the full moon or a change in the moon's phase that is thought to bring the rains (Redfield 1945:213; R. Wilson 1990:81; 1995:63; Milbrath 1999:29)

Numerous Maya groups believe that the vertical tilt of the "horns" of the crescent moon also affects rainfall (Girard 1962:134; Fought 1972:387; Laughlin 1975:262, 101; Neuenswander 1981:147; Tarn and Prechtel 1986:176; Breedlove and Laughlin 1993:504). Many of these same groups also believe the moon contains water. The Cubulco Achi' and Tz'utujil believe that this water spills out during the rainy season. They envision the crescent moon as being like a bowl or water jar that when tipped in a vertical position spills its water onto the earth. The Ch'orti' also see the moon as a water container. A similar concept is reflected in the Tzotzil term *pachal,* used to describe the crescent moon of the dry season with its horns perpendicular to the horizon (Laughlin 1975:262, personal communication). The root of this word is *pach,* meaning to hold a basket or bowl. The adjective used to describe the tilt of the crescent moon when it indicates the arrival of the rains is *c'e?el,* "tilted." The same word in verb form is used to describe the action of tipping over a water jar (Laughlin 1975:101). The association of the moon with a water container is reflected in the Tz'utujil belief that the moon goddess is the lady of stored water such as that found in the household water container (Tarn and Prechtel 1986:176). In explaining why the Maya would relate the vertical tilt of the waxing crescent moon to rainfall, Milbrath (1999:29) notes that the first visible crescent moon is tipped over from June to November, which roughly corresponds to the rainy season.

Although it is visually much easier to count lunar periods by full moons, Landa noted that the Maya counted the lunar cycle "from the time at which the new moon appeared until it no longer appears" (Tozzer 1941:133). This counting is also reflected in some examples of the Classic Period Lunar Series. Many Classic public monuments begin their narrative with a date and a reference to the lunar cycle. Glyph E and Glyph D of the Lunar Series record the age of the moon on the given date. In some examples from Palenque, the count begins at the first appearance of the waxing moon. Other examples suggest a particular count begins on the new moon.

In order for agricultural ceremonies to be successful, the participants have to be prepared mentally and physically. Sexual abstinence before planting is a near-universal Maya practice (Sapper 1895; Rodas, Rodas, and Hawkins 1940:65; Stadelman 1940:124; Wisdom 1940:441; Tozzer 1941:103; Wagley 1941:34; Thompson 1954:274; Villa Rojas 1969:199; Johannessen 1982:93; Preuss 1993:122–25; R. Wilson 1995:63–67). The Maya invariably fast before planting, as well. In many areas, the average length of time for planting is about two weeks (Thompson 1954:274; R. Wilson 1995:63), approximately the length of time from new moon to full moon. Given that the Maya plant on a full moon near the time of the zenith passage, it is highly likely that the Maya watched for the first crescent moon near the zenith passage to start their ritual fasting and abstinence, and this explains why they counted their lunar cycle from new moon/first crescent.

## THE MILKY WAY

The Milky Way was also associated with rain. This celestial body appears as a band of mist or clouds with various stars along its path. It is a continuous band, but only a section of it is visible at any given time.

The ecliptic is an imaginary line tracing the apparent annual path of the sun across the sky. While the path of the ecliptic is not as obvious as the Milky Way, the moon and planets are always within five degrees of this celestial road, and a careful observer of the night sky soon recognizes the constellations along the ecliptic. Due to precession, the solstice and equinox positions of the sun along the ecliptic shift from one constellation to another over time. The sun, however, continues to rise and set at the same points along the horizon, and the stars that rise at the winter and summer solstice locations on the horizon only shift one degree along the horizon over a five-hundred-year period. The Milky Way and ecliptic intersect at two places in the night sky. Despite the shift from precession, the Maya from the Preclassic to the Postclassic era would have seen these two celestial crossroads rising and setting near the solstice horizon locations.

The first crossroads of the Milky Way and ecliptic occurs near the constellations of Gemini and Taurus, while the second crossroads is in Sagittarius. These two crossroads rise and set on the horizon at the same locations where the sun rises and sets during the solstices. At sunset on the summer solstice, the Gemini crossroads of the Milky Way is in conjunction with the setting sun in the northwest, while the Sagittarius crossroads of the Milky Way is seen rising on the southeast horizon where the sun rises on the winter solstice.

The path of the Milky Way at summer sunset follows the rim of the horizon from the northeast all the way around the southern horizon and back up to the northwest. Due south is marked on the Milky Way by the Southern Cross, which stands at its apex position. This constellation rises and sets in a tight arc centered on due south, and it is a visual pivot point of the Milky Way. As the night progresses, the Southern Cross pivots to its setting position, and the section of the Milky Way that rimmed the northeastern horizon rises higher in the sky. This section has a distinctive rift that the Maya characterized as the open mouth of a crocodile. The tip of the crocodile's mouth is on the celestial equator and always rises and sets due east and due west. At midnight, the Sagittarius/Milky Way crossroads and the tip of the crocodile's mouth have reached their apex positions. The Southern Cross has set by this time, and on the opposite end of the Milky Way in the northeast is the constellation Cassiopeia, which has just risen into the sky. By sunrise, the Sagittarius/Milky Way crossroads and the tip of the crocodile's mouth are setting in the west, Cassiopeia is near its apex position, and the Gemini/Milky Way crossroads is rising with the sun in the northeast.

The opposite sections of the Milky Way dominate the sky on the winter solstice. At sunset, the same constellations visible at sunrise on the summer solstice are in the sky. The Sagittarius/Milky Way crossroads is setting with the sun in the west, the crocodile's mouth is setting due west, Cassiopeia is near its apex in the northern sky, and the Gemini/Milky Way crossroads is rising on the northeast horizon at the summer solstice sunrise location. By midnight, the Milky Way is arching across the sky from the southeast to the northwest. Cassiopeia is nearing its setting position in the northwest, and the Gemini/Milky Way crossroads is now at its apex position near the center of the sky. Although there are no prominent stars on the southern section of the Milky Way, the Southern Cross will rise in the southeast about two hours later just as Cassiopeia sets in the northwest.

The modern Ch'orti' say that the rainy season begins when the Milky Way rises in the east, and they call the section of the Milky Way that rises at this time and dominates the sky for the entire night the "black rift" (Fought 1972:267, 431, 435; personal communication). The Tzotzil divide the Milky Way into two sections. The black rift section that is overhead during the rainy season is the *be vo'*, "road of water or rain," while the section overhead during the dry season is the *be taiv*, "road of frost" (Laughlin 1975:469). The moist nature of the Milky Way is reflected in the Jakalteko term for the Milky Way, "road of dew" (*s-be lente'y'u;* La Farge and Byers 1931:130).

In the Yucatec Maya community of Yalcoba, the Milky Way is called the white road (Sosa 1985:430). The K'iche' also describe the Milky Way as the white road, but they refer to its black rift or mouth as the road of the underworld (D. Tedlock 1985:38, 334). They consider the Milky Way the ultimate source of mist and fog (B. Tedlock 1985:81). They indirectly associate the Milky Way with rain, for they believe that the migratory birds who are "the openers of the rainy season" lift the Southern Cross above the horizon, which brings the rains. As noted above, the Southern Cross is the pivot point of the Milky Way, and the rising of this constellation is immediately followed by the rising of the Milky Way rift along the eastern horizon. Lifting the Southern Cross lifts the Milky Way rift into the sky.

The association of the Milky Way with water is also found in pre-Columbian imagery. A crocodilian creature found in Maya art has been identified as a representation of the Milky Way (Schele 1992:136; Freidel, Schele, and Parker 1993:151; Stuart 2003a). The Milky Way crocodile appears in numerous contexts, but it is most frequently seen arching over a scene or doorway. It is likely based on *Crocodylus acutus,* a crocodile with a wide distribution that lives in rivers, lakes, and brackish coastal habitats and hunts at night.

The Milky Way crocodile has a long, upturned snout that frequently has water flowing from it, and a star sign or crossed bands mark its eye. Its feet often appear like those of a crocodile, but occasionally it has deer hooves. On the tail of the Milky Way crocodile is a motif that has been nicknamed the Quadripartite Badge Monster. This motif is the headdress of the storm- and thunderbolt-deity nicknamed GI (see chapter 6). In many examples, water pours out of this motif.

In some examples, the body of the Milky Way crocodile is shown as a sky band or clouds. A sky band is a long band divided into cartouches that contain symbols associated with celestial objects. In many contexts, these sky bands are conflated with or replaced by the body of a serpent. Because "serpent" and "sky" are homonyms in Mayan languages, it has been argued that these serpent-sky bands represent the sky. I believe that they specifically represent a pathway across the sky or along the horizon. For example, the *Paris Codex* sky band, which has animals hanging below it, represents the ecliptic with its accompanying animal constellations.

The open mouth of the Milky Way crocodile's head is specifically identified with the black rift of the Milky Way, and the star sign in its eye is the bright star Deneb of the constellation Cygnus. The water that pours from the mouth of the Milky Way crocodile is clearly related to the beliefs concerning the Milky Way's wet nature. The association between the water falling from the Milky Way crocodile's mouth and rain is demonstrated on *Dresden Codex* 74. This scene shows the world being flooded by torrential rain pouring from the mouth of the Milky Way crocodile. It is apparent from this imagery and from modern beliefs that the Milky Way was envisioned as a misty river with a supernatural crocodile floating in it. In the *Paris Codex*, the sky band of the ecliptic also has a band of water beneath it, which suggests that, like the Milky Way, it was thought to be a river.

The body of the Milky Way crocodile begins above Cygnus, so its tail must be located somewhere farther along the Milky Way river. If we follow that continuous path, we encounter the constellations of Cassiopeia, Perseus, Auriga, Gemini, Monoceros, Vela, the Southern Cross, Scorpius, and Sagittarius before returning to the mouth of the Milky Way crocodile. Schele associates the Quadripartite Monster with those zones where the ecliptic crosses the Milky Way, that is, at the Gemini/Milky Way crossroads and also at the Sagittarius/Milky Way crossroads (Freidel, Schele, and Parker 1993:86–87). In chapter 14, I present evidence that the Southern Cross is the tip of the crocodile's tail.

### The Morning Star

It is important to conduct agricultural rituals at the correct time of day, and dawn is a particularly auspicious time. The pilgrimage the Q'eqchi' make to the cave of the mountain lord to ask permission to plant is scheduled so that the participants arrive at the mouth of the cave at dawn (R. Wilson 1990:89, 1995:71). In Chichicastenango, the closing of important prayers should coincide with the rising sun, and all-night vigils should end at dawn (Bunzel 1952:300). The Ixil have similar beliefs (Colby and Colby 1981:40). The appearance of the morning star in the east is one of the indications the Maya use to tell when dawn is approaching. In the *Popol Vuh*, the first humans go to their sacred mountains to await the first rising of Hunahpu (sun) and Xbalanque (full moon). This event is preceded by the first appearance of Venus as the morning star (Christenson 2003a:225).

Venus is visible in the east before dawn for only 263 days of its approximately 584-day cycle. During the other phases of Venus, whatever bright star is seen in the east before dawn is referred to as the morning star. The morning star plays an important role in some modern planting ceremonies (Wagley 1941:34; 1949:86, 98; R. Wilson 1995:100–103). In these rituals, the farmer goes to his cornfield before dawn with the morning star still in the sky. He plants the first corn and makes offerings to various deities to ensure the success of the planting. Then the other workers arrive to help plant the rest of his field. I present evidence in chapter 15 that the morning star was one of the manifestations of One Hunahpu/One Ixim.

## THE PLEIADES

The Pleiades, which are adjacent to the Gemini-Taurus crossroads, are another prominent celestial body that many cultures, including the Maya, use to time events (Aveni 1980:30–35). The Lacandon say that the field must be burned and planted before the Pleiades reach the top of the trees at dawn (Baer and Merrifield 1971:136). The Ch'orti' also use the Pleiades to help determine the coming of the rains and to fix the day for planting (Girard 1979:77). In the *Popol Vuh*, a group of male deities called the Four Hundred Boys are identified as the Pleiades, and they first rise into the sky when the hero twins ascend as sun and full moon. Like many cultures, the Maya associated constellations with episodes from their creation mythology, and some of the Maya names for other constellations have survived. More will be said on this subject in later chapters.

## ATMOSPHERIC CHANGES

The Maya take note of atmospheric conditions that are harbingers of the rainy season. The rains of May are frequently preceded by April hailstorms, so the Maya say that the hail is announcing the rains (Hester 1954:18; Guiteras Holmes 1961:36). Rain is also preceded by the sound of distant thunder and a buildup of clouds in the east. The color and shape of clouds, rainbows, and the rings around the sun and moon are all used to predict rain (Redfield 1945:216; Villa Rojas 1945:157; Mendelson 1957:557, 560–61; Fought 1972:267; Hull 2000).

## ANIMALS

The Maya pay particular attention to biological changes that herald the beginning of the rainy season. They recognize a variety of plant and animal behavior that is directly connected to changes in the seasons and coordinate their agricultural activities to coincide (Steggerda 1943:201; Baer and Merrifield 1971:174; Nation 1981:4; Hanks 1991:355; Patterson 1992:45–46). Toads, in particular, are associated with the rainy season, and these amphibians are also beneficial to the corn. In many Mayan languages, the specific name for the Mexican burrowing toad (*Rhinophrynus dorsalis*) is "*uoh*," which mimics the toad's call (Thompson 1970:258). The uoh toad uses its hind legs to dig deep into the earth, where it feeds on ants and termites. It is rarely seen above ground except following the first heavy rains of the season. At this time, the uoh toads emerge from the ground in great numbers to breed in the pools of water created by the annual downpour. The toads are most frequently encountered in cultivated fields during periods of heavy rain (Janzen 1983:419). They eat vast quantities of insects that would otherwise damage garden and field crops.

Another important toad is the giant *Bufo marinus,* called "*totmuch*" in reference to the toad's call of "to-to-to." The totmuch is nocturnal and thrives in areas disturbed by agriculture. The loud mating croaks of these two toad species fill the night air, and the Maya believe that such toads are announcing the rain or calling the rain to come (E. H. Thompson 1932:64, 69; Redfield and Villa Rojas 1934:142; Mendelson 1957:561; Thompson 1970:251; Laughlin 1975:45, 232; Sosa 1985:381; Hanks 1991:355; Hostettler 1996:277; Lee 1996:426; Faust 1998:104, 133; de Jong 1999:141). During the rain ceremonies in Yucatan, young boys are tied to the altar in the cornfield, and at the appropriate moment in the ceremony, they make croaking sounds like the uoh and totmuch.

Birds, both migratory and resident, are also associated with the change in the seasons. In the highlands, such birds as Swainson's hawks, broad-winged hawks, and turkey vultures form what is described as an aerial river of birds as they pass over the highlands on their northern migration from South America to North America in March and April and back south in October and November. Their northern migration coincides with the onset of the rainy season, so their appearance is viewed as an omen of rain (Redfield 1945:30, 58, 192; B. Tedlock 1985:81). Conversely, their southern migration is seen as a sign that the rains will stop. Non-migratory birds are also viewed as omens of rain. In particular, the call of the resident laughing falcon (*Herpetotheres cachinnans*) is associated with rain. The paramount importance of this bird of prey is discussed in chapter 7.

## THE ANCIENT CALENDARS

Although the Maya were keen observers of nature who used their practical knowledge to time events, they also employed their calendars and divination system to assist in choosing auspicious days. Spanish priests in the Alta Verapaz region observed that the Maya used the 260-day calendar and divination to establish when to sow and harvest, and in an Ixil calendar myth it is said that the Ixil were given the ancient 260-day calendar so that they could calculate the proper time for sowing and harvesting (Lincoln 1942:109; Colby and van den Berghe 1969:98). The 260-day calendar is used for similar purposes in the Mam, Chuj, K'iche', Q'eqchi', and Poqomchi' regions (La Farge and Byers 1931:224; Rodas, Rodas, and Hawkins 1940:65; Wagley 1941:34; Mayers 1966:99; R. Wilson 1990:88; 1995:69).

Many of the ancient ceremonies were timed to occur at the moment an agricultural action happened or at certain times in the corn's development, and some were incorporated into major festivals. For example, the purpose of the Postclassic New Year ceremonies was to install into office the set of creator deities who would rule the upcoming haab period. Offerings were made to these deities during the ceremony to guarantee an abundant harvest (Tozzer 1941). The New Year ceremonies continue to have an agricultural purpose in areas where this calendar has survived. In Q'anjob'al-speaking San Miguel Acatán, rain prayers are said during the New Year ceremony that occurs in March (Siegel 1941:73). Rain petitions are begun three days later and continue every five days until the rains begin in April or May. Four other rain ceremonies are performed during the first four heavy rainstorms. In Mam-speaking Santiago Chimaltenango, the New Year ceremony includes petitions for good crops, and the May rain ceremony is timed according to the ancient calendar (Wagley 1949:112–14).

The close association between the New Year ceremonies and the agricultural cycle is seen in the prognostication by the Chuj ritual specialist, who makes a pilgrimage to a sacred cave during the New Year ceremonies. If he finds ample water in the river of the cave, the year will have abundant rain (Mayers 1966:222). Similar prophecies are made in the neighboring Q'anjob'al community of Santa Eulalia (La Farge 1947:123, 127) and the Jakalteko community of Jacaltenango (Blom and La Farge 1927:444).

In K'iche' Momostenango, the consecutive days 7 *Quej* (Manik) and 8 *K'anil* (Lamat) in the 260-day calendar are days for celebrating an abundant harvest, no matter what time of year these dates occur (Rodas, Rodas, and Hawkins 1940:15; Bunzel 1952:55–56; B. Tedlock 1982:80). On this date, the seed corn is blessed by censing it. If *8 K'anil* falls close to planting, the ritual specialist prays for good crops, but if it occurs closer to harvest, he gives thanks. If the date falls soon after planting, the ritual specialist also makes a pilgrimage to the eastern sacred mountain and petitions for rain. In addition, rituals are performed on the *K'anil* day nearest to planting and again at harvest. A series of four rain rituals timed according to the ancient Maya calendar is also performed (Bunzel 1952:59; Cook 1986:150). The officials and shaman go to their four yearbearer mountains to perform rituals on four specific days.

When the Maya were converted to Spanish Catholicism, agricultural rituals often became identified with festivals in the Catholic calendar that coincided with those activities. For example, the Day of the Holy Cross, May 3, commemorates the day in the second century when Saint Elena is said to have found the original cross on which Jesus Christ was crucified. In Mesoamerica, pre-Columbian rain rituals became merged with this Catholic spring festival because it occurs at the start of the rains. Despite the Vatican's removal of the celebration from the church calendar in 1960, the Day of the Cross has remained a central event for the Maya. From the earliest times, the Roman Catholic celebration of Easter incorporated agricultural-based rituals, so it is not surprising that the Maya would also time corn ceremonies to occur during this great festival. In Santiago Atitlán, the five dates used for sowing are timed according to the Catholic feasts (Mendelson 1957:146). In addition, most festivals for patron saints include agricultural rites regardless of the time of year.

Pilgrimages to locations outside of the community are also an important aspect of the ceremonial cycle. One of the most popular pilgrimages is made to the festival of the Black Christ in Esquipulas, Guatemala, on January 15. Although this festival attracts tens of thousands of Central American Catholics, the Maya living near Esquipulas have their own beliefs and practices concerning this shrine (Fought 1972:439–78, 521–26). Ch'orti' pilgrims from adjacent communities make the two-day walk to Esquipulas by way of an ancient path. They stop en route at other sacred locations, and on their return they hold an elaborate ceremony in honor of the spirit of the earth.

## THE CEREMONIES OF THE CORN CYCLE

In many areas of the Maya region, rituals are performed before clearing, burning, sowing, weeding, harvesting, and storing corn. The contemporary Mam of highland Guatemala believe that every step in the corn cycle requires some type of ceremony, and many of the Yucatec Maya communities hold the same conviction (Wagley 1941:27, 44; Villa Rojas 1945:111). Not all Maya adhere to such an elaborate sequence, but they all have some essential rituals. The most elaborate and consistent rituals are those performed to ensure that the planting at the beginning of the rainy season is successful, that rains arrive on time, and that the seed germinates. Special ceremonies are carried out when the crop is threatened by too little or too much rain, strong winds, or pests.

Petitions, offerings, and expressions of gratitude are made to the supernatural beings who are thought to own the earth and who send the winds and rains. They ensure the safety of the farmer and the success of the crop. Some of these rituals are performed by the individual farmer and his family, but many are community-wide functions led by ritual specialists. Pilgrimages for rain and good crops are also undertaken to sacred locations outside of the community and district. During these long journeys, petitions are made at shrines along the way as well.

The offerings made to the deities and the settings in which these payments are made are fairly consistent across the Maya area. Ritually prepared foods, birds, blood, incense, tobacco, liquor, and flowers are the most common gifts. A key component in the offerings is the presence of fire. Cook (1981:114) notes that K'iche' rituals always begin with lighting fire. This fire can be an offering fire, the fire of a candle, or the burning of splinters of pine pitch and incense.

During the agricultural rituals themselves, the participants are usually given rich food, or they dine on the remainder of the food offerings after the deities have been given their portions. While this nourishment gives participants added energy to carry out the labor-intensive activities of cleaning, planting, or harvesting, it is also intended to place the participants in a state of contentment, considered necessary for the crop to be productive.

Obtaining the necessary foodstuffs for these various rituals often entails hunting expeditions to the forest to procure wild meat. When it is a village-wide ceremony, these hunts are conducted by groups of men. The most esteemed meat is from deer and peccary. As in the production of corn, men are the procurers, but it is the women who transform these raw materials into ritual food.

## FIELD-MAKING RITUALS

One of the first rituals to be performed in the agricultural cycle is an offering to the supernatural owner of the earth to obtain his permission to create a field and to disturb the wild plants and animals that live there (Wagley 1941:32; Villa Rojas 1945:70, 111; Mayers 1966:23, 113; Carter 1969:39; M. Wilson 1972:90; Colby and Colby 1981:122–23; Johannessen 1982:93; Hanks 1991:363; Breedlove and Laughlin 1993:57; Faust 1998:120; Siebers 1999:67). In the highlands, these ceremonies include pilgrimages by individuals and entire communities to important mountains and caves. In the Q'eqchi' area of El Estor, site selection begins with prayers to Jesus, the saints, and the mountain spirits that inhabit all the important mountains in the region (Carter 1969:42–43). The farmer and his wife go to the site of a new field at dawn and erect a small cross in the middle of the field. They then scatter two bottles of water mixed with the blood from a sacrificed chicken around the cross and in the four directions. They also offer burning incense to the four corners. The area around the center cross is called the heart of the milpa. It is cleared of brush, and offerings of blood, incense, and candles are made. The sides of the field are then measured out. Similar clearing rituals are conducted in other areas (Thompson 1930:45, 115; Wagley 1941:32; Hanks 1991:363; Breedlove and Laughlin 1993:57; Preuss 1993:126–27; Faust 1998:119; de Jong 1999:223).

During the latter part of the nineteenth century, the Yucatec Maya living near Chichén Itzá worshipped an agricultural deity called Zactalah (Le Plongeon 1889:88–91). The statue of this deity was a pre-Columbian stone sculpture of a bearded man with upraised arms, a common motif in the art of Chichén Itzá. The idol was housed in a small *sac cab* cave near the ruins, and petitions were made to Zactalah when the field was burned, when the seeds were planted, and again at harvest. Before harvesting, the entire hamlet went to the cave and gave offerings to the deity. In the Q'eqchi' area, a petition to the mountain/valley gods is made in the center of the milpa before the burning, as well as at the family altar (R. Wilson 1990:110). God and the mountain/valley gods are asked for their permission to burn the field, and they are petitioned to prevent wildfires. Offerings to the gods to prevent the spreading of the fire are common (Faust 1998:126).

To help with the burning, prayers and offerings are also made to the winds. The milpa fires create small whirlwinds that dance across the field as they pick up ash, smoke, and flashing sparks. In Yucatan, they are called *kakal mozon ikob,* "fiery whirlwinds," and are thought to carry the flame across the field and create a good burn (Tozzer 1907:162; Gann 1918:415–16; Redfield and Villa Rojas 1934:119, 133; Villa Rojas 1945:88, 104, 112; Hostettler 1996:278). An altar is often erected at the southeast corner of the field, and an offering is made to these whirlwind spirits just before the field is fired.

The farmer will also whistle for the whirlwinds to come and fan the flames of the fire. In a Mopan Maya prayer said before the burning of the field, these winds are called a red wind and a white wind (Thompson 1930:47). This may refer to the white ash and red sparks of these whirlwinds, or it may indicate their directional association, because the dominant winds come from the east and north (red = east; white = north). The association of red and fire with the burning season is reflected in the Tzotzil belief that the red sky at dawn during this time of year is the fire of the Old Possum (Guiteras Holmes 1961:196–97, 206, 292). The concept that whistling will bring the winds is found all over the Maya area. Spirits associated with whirlwinds caused by fire are also found in Lacandon mythology (Bruce 1977:195). At the start of burning, the Lacandon are known to signal the snakes in the field with a whistle. It is thought that the snakes help ignite the field as they slither through it (Baer and Merrifield 1971:178). In Oxkutzcab, the fiery whirlwinds are thought to sweep the field clean just as any socially constituted space is swept clean (Hanks 1991:364). This is reminiscent of the belief that the morning star sweeps the path for the rising sun.

## PLANTING CEREMONIES

Planting is universally seen as a crucial time to perform rituals, though the specifics vary across the Maya area (Brinton 1883:252; Redfield and Villa Rojas 1934; Stadelman 1940:112, 123; Villa Rojas 1945:79, 112; Bunzel 1952:56; Johannessen 1982:93). Generally speaking, petitions associated with planting are made in a number of locations including the house, the field, the church, and the shrines and caves on the sacred hills and mountains of the community. Prayers are directed at the rain, wind, sun, moon, and the gods who are thought to own the earth and control the rain. Types of offerings include candles, pine boughs, flowers, incense, maize gruel, corn foods, chocolate, poultry (particularly turkey), liquor, and blood. People in many areas take corn seed to the community church to be blessed, and they hold rituals to prepare it for planting.

As discussed above, the corn seed is metaphorically referred to as bone—the Tz'utujil refer to the planted seeds as *muk*, "interred ones" (Carlsen and Prechtel 1991:28). The Lacandon also view the corn seed as dead (Bruce 1979:101). This notion is found in a number of concepts. In Yucatan, a crystal used for divination must be awakened to consciousness by placing it in a bowl of liquor. When corn seeds are substituted for the crystal, offerings must be given to the guardian deities so that the seeds come alive. The Maya liken the planting of the corn/bone to a burial (Carlson and Eachus 1977:48; Bruce 1979:101; Carlsen and Prechtel 1991:28; R. Wilson

1990:120; 1995:100). Because the seed is considered dead, it must be ritually heated in order for it to germinate, just as sick people must be ritually heated to regain their lost souls. The use of candles in corn-planting rituals is common. The night before planting, there is often an all-night festival that has the characteristics of a funeral wake (Thompson 1954:238, Carlson and Eachus 1977:48, R. Wilson 1995:94–103).

In the Q'eqchi' region, the planting party gathers at the house of the farmer to begin the vigil, overseen by a community elder who is considered the master of ceremonies (R. Wilson 1990:116, 1995:96). If the farmer's father is alive, he fulfills this role by burning incense and leading prayers directed to God, the mountain/valley gods, the sun, the moon, and Venus. At dusk, the seeds are placed in a basket on the family altar. A large, lit candle that represents or replaces the fading sun is placed in the center of the seeds: "During the planting vigil, the seeds are 'being born' (*yolaak*). They must have light for this because 'the seed cannot be born in the darkness.' The vigil is a critical time for the seed, and it must be guarded all night. The host stays awake until dawn, sitting next to the altar wrapped in a blanket. If not cared for, the seed may 'take fright,' lose its spirit, and not germinate" (R. Wilson 1995:94–95). The categories of hot and cold play an important role in the planting. Richard Wilson notes that before planting, the prevalent state is cold and that during the planting process, the state is changed through the use of hot items such as liquor, cigarettes, candles, and blood. Siebers (1999) notes that chocolate drinks and blood from a sacrificed turkey are poured on the seeds. As is the case with most Maya ceremonies, music and dancing are also performed during the planting ceremony.

An important element of the Q'eqchi' planting process is that the first ceremonial planting occurs before sunrise. The farmer proceeds by himself to his cornfield: "He aims to arrive before the sun breaks. It is important that the *chapok k'al* be performed at a certain conjuncture of celestial bodies—before the sun rises, but while the moon and the morning star still shine in the sky" (R. Wilson 1995:101).

In many areas, the center of the milpa is referred to as its heart or navel. The Q'eqchi' planter erects a tree/cross or an altar in the center of the field and places a large, white candle in front of it. He places food and beverage offerings to the mountain lord beside the cross or on the altar and then swings a burning incense holder toward the four directions, the sun, the moon, and Venus. He may also dig a shallow hole in front of the altar and deposit turkey pieces in it for the mountain/valley gods. While facing the rising sun, he makes his petition to these guardian deities, the sun, the moon, and Venus to protect his field, and then he plants the first corn seeds.

> With a single plunge of his planting pole, he opens a hole about five inches deep in front of the cross or altar and drops three, four, six or seven seeds into it. People of different communities customarily sow different numbers. The hole is then covered with earth. He repeats this four more times within a few feet of the cross in the four cardinal directions. He places a lit candle by each one of the five groups of

planted seeds. A candle may be located in each of the four corners of the field, "to form a corral so the animals can't get in." Part of the meaning of this ritual is containment and classification, defining the borders of cultivated fields versus wild forest. (R. Wilson 1995:103)

Richard Wilson (1995:63) also writes that "Some informants plant only during a full moon, when the maize 'will come out strong and in abundance.' . . . Like the female mountains, the full moon is said to 'send the rain.'" After the sun rises, the farmer is joined by others who help him plant the rest of the field. The warmth of the sun completes the heating of the corn seed.

Another similar planting ritual is found in the Mam community of Santiago Chimaltenango (Wagley 1941:34, 40). The farmer and his wife begin their ceremony when the morning star first appears in the predawn hours. They place the corn seed on a blanket in the middle of their house and burn two candles before it. The farmer then cuts the throat of a chicken over a pile of copal and mixes the blood and copal together. After kindling a small fire in front of the seed, the bloody copal is burned. While these activities are taking place, the farmer prays to God, Father Paxil (the god of Paxil Mountain, who owns maize), to the Day Lord, and to Señor Santiago (patron saint and owner of planted corn). He asks Father Paxil to send enough rain for the crop, but not damaging rains and whirlwinds. Just before dawn, the farmer goes alone to the milpa. In the center of the field he erects a cross, lights two more candles, and burns more of the bloody incense while repeating his earlier prayer. The planting party then arrives and the men spend the day planting the field. At the end of the day, when the others have left, the farmer burns another candle at the center cross. After returning to his house, he and his wife go to the church and burn the remainder of the incense and pray again to God, Father Paxil, the Day Lord, and Señor Santiago. The church ceremony is repeated a week later, during which the farmer also burns candles for Señor Santiago and asks for his protection. Later in the season, the farmer and his wife will go again to the field to hold another ceremony. This time, they place four candles at the center of the milpa in the form of a square to represent the milpa. Again they burn their incense and recite their prayers.

Making offerings in the center and four corners of the milpa is one of the most common rituals. Just after the Spanish conquest, such a planting ritual was recorded by Francisco Ximénez (Christenson 2001:117–18), who noted that the farmer placed fire and incense at the center (heart) and four corners of his field. He also sacrificed chickens and sprinkled their blood on the ground. In the Tz'utujil area, the planting ceremony includes setting up a colored candle in each corner of the field. In the center of the field, a hole called a navel is dug and offerings are placed in it. These include quantities of incense, drinks, chocolate, sugar, honey, and sacrificial turkey blood as well as the ash from twin ears of corn that have been blessed and burned.

In the Tzotzil area of Zinacantan, the planting ceremonies are directed by a ritual specialist and include a circuit to the cross shrines that mark the corners and center of the milpa (Vogt 1976:55). A visit is also made to the water hole where the farmer draws his water. In San Pedro Chenalhó, the planting ceremony begins at sunrise when the farmer goes to the center of the field and offers incense to the Earth Lord, the Holy Earth, the God/Sun, the Virgin, and San Pedro asking these deities to protect X'ob (the daughter of the Earth Lord and soul of maize) and to prevent any calamities that would harm the crop (Guiteras Holmes 1961:43, 151). The directional nature of these rituals is reflected in the four candles and four pine boughs used in the ceremony.

In addition to the food offered during the night vigil and planting, it is customary to provide a ritual meal at the end of the planting day to all who have participated. The night vigil and this meal are times of relaxed interaction and conversation as elders retell stories about local history and encounters with supernatural forces that demonstrate and reinforce the traditional values of the community.

The K'iche' believe that that a lightning bolt splits open the corn seed at germination (Christenson 2001:74, 134). Lightning is said to charge the earth with life-giving powers so that whatever is buried within it can rise from the dead. The role of lightning as an essential life element will be discussed more fully in later chapters, but suffice it to note here that the planting period is one of intense lightning storms. Thunderbolts have a natural association with the milpa, since the large trees left standing in the cleared field act like lightning rods.

## RAIN RITUALS

As noted above, communities frequently perform rain rituals during their festival of the Day of the Cross. The prominence of this festival underscores the critical importance of rain (Blom and La Farge 1927:252; Thompson 1930:55; La Farge and Byers 1931:97; Redfield and Villa Rojas 1934:84, 239; Wisdom 1940:447; 1951:223; Bunzel 1952:57; Mayers 1958:49; Holland 1961:129; Mace 1970:31; Aulie 1979:33, 49; Breedlove and Laughlin 1993:49, 74, 106; Faust 1998:86). In many areas, the festival includes masses, dances, and pilgrimages to caves, springs, and lakes. The numerous crosses the Maya use are decorated with plants and renewed during this time period. In Tumbala, the Ch'ol believe that the raising of a cross during the festival will cause the water to flow again from its source in the mountain (Whittaker and Warkentin 1965:78). In the Ch'ol village of Joloniel, the Day of the Holy Cross ceremony is centered on a pilgrimage to the caves at Jolja' (Jolja' Cave Project field notes). An image of the Virgin who is the patron saint of the village is taken to the cave and bathed in its waters. Don Juan, the deity who inhabits the cave, is petitioned to send rain and a bountiful harvest. The Ch'ol of Tila make a pilgrimage to a cave on their sacred mountain on the Day of the Cross to ask for rain and good crops. This cave contains a stalagmite idol that is thought to represent the Black Christ in their church. The Tzotzil of San Andrés Larráinzar perform their Day of the Cross ceremonies deep within the caves that are the main source of their water (Holland 1961:130). They petition the earth lord who is thought to release the waters. Tzotzil from Chamula go to the mountain Tzontevitz, where at a cave near the summit they petition the earth lord for rain (Gossen 1974:317; 2002:1047, 1067).

At Lake Amatitlán, pilgrims from all over Guatemala and Chiapas come to the lake on the Day of the Cross to ask the Virgin and a Christ figure to provide rain (Berlo 1980:304). There is a belief that the Virgin herself leaves the church and goes to the lake and a nearby volcano to petition the cloud-gathering mountains for rain. Pilgrimages are made to sacred locations around the lake and on the mountainside, and offerings are cast into the lake. Archaeological evidence at the lake indicates a long history of ritual activities dating to at least the Early Classic. The pre-Columbian offerings recovered from the lake indicate that pilgrims came to this location from great distances.

In the Ch'orti' community of Jocotán, a rain ceremony is held on April 25 during the festival for the patron saint, which is thought to bring the rains on the Day of the Cross (Wisdom 1940:393, 437–41). The day before the ceremony, young children are sent to a sacred spring to obtain virgin water. The women of the village use the water to make the food for the ceremony. On the morning of the festival, the people of the village make a pilgrimage to the nearest sacred hill or spring to petition the earth lord and rain deities for rain and abundance. They carry out the planting in the morning after the Day of the Cross. The same is true in the Mopan town of San Antonio (Thompson 1930:55).

When the young plants first emerge from the ground, the Ch'orti' also conduct a petition to the wind gods in which they ask the gods to bring the rains but not the damaging evil winds (Wisdom 1940:444–45). The farmer attaches an eight-inch wooden cross to the top of a cane that is six or seven feet high. Smaller pieces of cane are attached to the crossbar of the wooden cross to form smaller crosses. The big cross is called San Pedro, said to be the chief of the wind gods, and the smaller crosses are his companions. The San Pedro cross is placed in the middle of the cornfield. Smaller crosses are also set up in each corner of the field, and water from a sacred source is sprinkled in each location. A four-day celebration follows this ceremony.

The Itza' of the Petén plant their corn between the feasts of San Marcos on April 25 and Santa Cruz on May 3 (Atran 1993:679). A milpa ceremony may be performed near the other saints' days of May (San Isidro on May 15, Santa Rita on May 22, and San Augustín on May 28). In northern Yucatan, the days from the feast of San Marcos on April 15 to the feast of San Isidro on May 15 mark the coming of the rains (Villa Rojas 1945:77, 100). It is said that these saints celebrate their day by sending rain.

At Chichicastenango, the feast of Corpus Christi, held in May or June, is a time for rain ceremonies in the mountains surrounding the community (Bunzel 1952:58). The villagers hold processions to the mountain shrines at dawn on the day before the church ceremonies begin. On July 25, the feast day of their patron saint, Santiago, they perform rituals at the mountain shrines for the protection of the cornfield from wind.

In the Tojolab'al village of Jotana, the rain ritual is called the Fiesta of the Cave; it involves a February pilgrimage to make petitions to the saints of the towns of Oxchuk and Venustiano Carranza, who are well known in the region for providing rain (Brody 1987). The festival concludes in the inner recesses of a local cave with a ceremony that includes dancing and burning incense. The villagers believe that the dripping stalactites of the cave will provide rain, and if their festival is done correctly, it will ensure that the moisture from the cave will be transferred as rain to the cornfields.

Despite the rain rituals and Day of the Cross festivals, there is often insufficient moisture, and additional rain ceremonies must be initiated. The Yucatec Maya perform a *ch'a chaac,* "bring rain," ceremony to petition the rain gods (Gann 1918; E. H. Thompson 1932; Redfield and Villa Rojas 1934:138–43; Villa Rojas 1945:115; Hanks 1991:369; Faust 1998:95–99). This three-day affair often begins with the erection of an altar in an isolated location on the outskirts of the community or in a field. A pilgrimage to obtain virgin water from a distant cenote is undertaken, and the gourd water containers are hung beside the altar. Special foods are baked in an underground oven called a *pib,* and ritual drinks are prepared. As was the case in ancient times, some of the petitioners imitate the gods of the rains and their animal assistants during the ceremony.

In Momostenango, the ritual specialists petition the saints in the church and then make pilgrimages to the mountains of the four yearbearers. The four saints from the church are also carried in processions. If the rains have not arrived, the Ch'ol of Tumbala lower the image of San Miguel on his feast day (May 8) and wash his feet (Aulie 1979:33). If this fails, he is taken to the Hidalgo River in the valley below Tumbala and bathed. In other Ch'ol areas, rain petitions are made at special ritual caves where the owner of the earth is thought to live (Jolja' Cave Project field notes). Saints are also taken to these caves and bathed. In the mid-twentieth century, the Tzeltal of Amatenango performed rain rituals in a cave associated with their ancestors (Nash 1970:142). It was thought that a spring in the cave was the source of rain.

In the Ch'orti' region, the ritual specialist in charge of the ceremony has an arbor the size of a house constructed some distance from the village (Fought 1972:410–22). His assistants prepare the arbor and ritual paraphernalia while he stays secluded in his house, praying and waiting for a sign. At the appropriate moment, he goes to the arbor to make offerings of incense, liquor, and chicken, and he beseeches God, the angels, and all the mountains in the region to send rain and save the spirit of corn and beans.

In Santiago Atitlán, a sacred cave called Paq'alib'al southwest of the community is thought to be where clouds and rain originate (Christenson 2001:84–85). The cofradía house of San Juan replicates this cave, and in addition to making pilgrimages to Paq'alib'al cave, ceremonies are conducted in the house to petition for rain (see chapter 14). A sacred bundle belonging to the deity Diego Martín is placed on the cofradía house altar, followed by a procession of various saints to bring the rain. In former times, the saint images were dressed in green capes with a thin yellow border at the bottom that were called "cloaks of rain" (Mendelson 1957:460, 476).

## PREVENTION AND THANKSGIVING CEREMONY

The farmer regularly inspects his field and often makes offerings to the gods to ensure the ongoing health of the crop. In the Mam area, the ritual specialists are called upon to perform offerings almost every day (Wagley 1941:39). The offerings are made at the field and at several mountain shrines.

During the period of green corn, the Maya frequently perform a ceremony to give thanks to the gods for providing sustenance (Thompson 1930:118; Redfield and Villa Rojas 1934:143–44; Stadelman 1940:115; Wisdom 1940:422, 445; Wagley 1941:41; Villa Rojas 1945:79; Carter 1969:102; Aulie 1979:34; Merrill-Sands 1984; Faust 1998:133). The first-fruits ceremony is a joyous occasion with great celebration and sharing of food. Offerings are made to the various spirits who are thought to be responsible for the success of the crop. Relatives and neighbors are given gifts of green corn in the form of boiled ears of corn, tamales, and atole.

In the Ch'orti' region, a ritual is performed in the field when the corn is yellowing, to thank the female spirit of the earth (Fought 1972:510–14, 518). The ritual specialist and the owner of the field make three holes in the milpa and light a fire. After saying a prayer of thanksgiving, the ritual specialist cuts the throats of two chickens and a tom and hen turkey, and pours the blood into one of the holes. A ritual assistant takes the bodies of the fowl back to the owner's house to be made into tamales. Liquor is poured in the second hole, and the remaining amount is consumed by the ritual specialist, the owner of the field, and other participants. Coals from the fire are placed in the third hole with a dish, and large quantities of incense are placed in the dish and burned. The ritual specialist and the owner of the field remain in the field until all the incense has been consumed by the fire, at which time they return to the owner's household and eat the turkey tamales. The Mam thanksgiving rituals involve a ceremonial circuit in which the ritual specialist, the farmer, and his wife make offerings of candles and blood-soaked copal at the church, plaza, and three mountain shrines (Wagley 1941:41).

## HARVEST FESTIVALS AND STORAGE RITUALS

If the corn is to be stored adjacent to the milpa, a granary must be built. As with any structure, the Maya perform ceremonies to ensure its successful building and maintenance. Harvest festivals and storage rituals are indispensable elements in the corn cycle. In Santiago Chimaltenango, the farmer and his wife go alone to the field first thing in the morning before harvest help arrives (Wagley 1941:41). The farmer clears a square space at the center of the field, leaving two tall stalks of corn standing. He lights a candle and sacrifices a chicken over a pile of copal before these plants. As he burns the bloody offering in his censer, he announces to the deities that he has come to harvest the field. The harvesting party then arrives and begins removing the ears of corn, row by row. As the harvest progresses, the ears are piled in the center space in front of the two remaining stalks. These two stalks are reminiscent of the twin ears of corn used in storage rituals in other areas. After the corn is carried to the house and placed in the corn bin, two candles and the remaining bloody copal are burned before it. The farmer and his wife pray to God and Father Paxil (the mountain deity who owns corn) to protect the corn. Later in the evening, the farmer and his wife take two ears of corn and place them on the church altar as an offering to Señor Santiago, the patron saint.

In Tzeltal-speaking Pinola, the harvested maize is piled into four heaps in the milpa (Hermitte 1964:59). A hole is created in the center and a statue of the patron saint, Michael/Thunderbolt, is placed in the hole. Four candles are placed around the image and lit as an offering to Thunderbolt. Incense is burned in the four corners of the field, firecrackers are set off, and liquor and chocolate are served. It is believed that without this ritual, Thunderbolt will decrease the corn and it will not last until the next crop. In Tzeltal Amatenango, offerings are made to the spirit of corn so that the next harvest will also be good (Nash 1970:38).

Making sure that the spirit of corn is contained in the granary or storage area is a vital part of the harvest process. Some ears of corn may have been overlooked during the gathering and left in the field. In addition, the spirit of corn that was contained in the ears eaten by animals or destroyed in other ways must be induced to reside in the granary (Guiteras Holmes 1961:46). Prayers are said to entice the soul from these ears to come to the granary. Offerings to the spirit of corn in the form of candles, incense, liquor, turkey blood, and chocolate are made (Carter 1969:104). In the Q'eqchi' area, a calling ritual is performed a week after the harvest (R. Wilson 1995:152). The farmer burns incense around the stored corn and asks the mountain/valley god who is the owner of corn to allow the spirit of corn to come join its body (the ear of corn). As noted in chapter 2, crosses, idols, and guardian ears of corn are placed with the stored corn to protect it. More offerings may be made at the household altar.

Thanksgiving ceremonies are not always timed to coincide with the harvest, but are frequently part of the patron saint festival (Carter 1969:112). In Yucatan, a thanksgiving ceremony in February is performed to express gratitude to the fiery whirlwinds that burned the field during the previous season (Villa Rojas 1945:116). The offerings ensure that the evil heat left by these winds is removed from the milpa. It is followed the next day by another thanksgiving ceremony dedicated to the rain gods.

## PROTECTION RITUALS

During its growing cycle, the corn is susceptible to damage from a number of sources. Windstorms and hail can damage or flatten the field, heavy rains can flood the field, disease can impair the quality of the corn, people can steal the corn, and animals can attack and eat the various parts of the plant. The farmer must guard against a number of destructive animals. Insects such as earworms, locusts, and ants are also harmful, while moths and weevils attack the stored corn. Smut and root rot also affect corn.

Regular rituals are performed to petition the gods to prevent these various calamities (Wisdom 1940:397; Wagley 1941:38; La Farge 1947:77; Breedlove and Laughlin 1993:74). In the Mam area, these rites are performed on the *Kan* and *Imix* days of the 260-day calendar, for these days are thought to be favorable for maize. The ceremonies include pilgrimages to several mountain shrines to make offerings. Whenever the corn is threatened, ceremonies are immediately performed. For example, near the turn of the twentieth century, a locust plague swept across the Mam region (Oakes 1951:245). As the swarms neared Todos Santos, all of the ritual specialists went to the sacred mountains and prayed to the mountain god to halt the destruction. He responded by sending a strong wind- and rainstorm that drove away the locusts, sparing the corn. E. H. Thompson (1932:73) notes that Yucatec Maya villagers responded to a locust infestation near Chichén Itzá by firing guns, beating on tin pans, and ringing the church bell. These same measures are taken to ward off an eclipse.

Exceptional events also require ceremonies. In April of 1982, the volcano El Chichón exploded and covered a large part of Chiapas in ash. Houses, livestock, and cornfields in the Ch'ol region were destroyed. The ritual specialists of the communities went to their sacred caves and petitioned the mountain lord for rain. Their prayers were answered, as the strong rains of May washed away the ash (Domingo Pérez Moreno, personal communication 2001).

## Summary

The information that I have presented in this chapter has covered many topics related to agricultural events, including different kinds of ceremonies, scheduling, and ecological concerns. Despite the contrasting environments in the Maya region, some beliefs and practices regarding corn are universally shared by Maya people. Corn farming is the basic foundation of Maya society, and it is no exaggeration to say that everything hinges on the success of the corn cycle. The integral role corn production plays in the world view of the Maya will be explored in the following chapters.

# 4

# WORLD VIEW

The primary purpose of a world view is to give a sense of order and control to life. At its most basic level, world view explains the creation of life and provides a means for maintaining and renewing it. The intent of this chapter is to give a general description of Maya world view and the organizing principles behind their cosmology. Later chapters will expand on these basic descriptions and examine their underlying meaning.

## THE PLACE OF DUALITY

In Mesoamerican culture, creation began at a place of duality. The *Popol Vuh* opens by describing the place of duality before the appearance of the earth and the creation of human beings. It is characterized as a dark pool of water with a dark sky above (Christenson 2003a:67–68). In these waters lived a sexually dualistic, primordial, generative power that was personified as a bisexual deity or an elderly couple who exemplified the male/female principle of complementary opposition. In the *Popol Vuh*, this primal husband and wife, Xpiyacoc and Xmucane, were also the first parents and grandparents. In Maya culture, grandparents are valued and consulted for their knowledge, wisdom, and experience. Though physically weaker than younger members of the society, they are considered spiritually stronger. The creator grandparents were the original priests, diviners, healers, and artisans. The Maya lowlands do not have any single document with the scope of the highland *Popol Vuh*, but numerous sources refer to a pair of aged deities known as Itzamnaaj and Ix Chel who have many of the same roles and characteristics as Xpiyacoc and Xmucane.

The respect that the Maya give the elderly members of their community is reflected in the use of the Tzotzil world *mool,* glossed in a colonial-period dictionary as "old man" (Laughlin 1988:260; personal communication). The contemporary

Tzotzil term *mol* used as an adjective means "old" or "large," but used as a noun, it means "elder," "husband," or "man" (Laughlin 1975:239). It is the term used for old men in general and for the highest-ranking elders in the religious hierarchy (Vogt 1976:254). The Lacandon use the title *t'o'ohil*, "great, venerable," to describe an old community leader who is spiritually powerful, has divination skills, cures diseases, and guards the order of things. A Classic Period glyph for *mam*, grandfather, has been identified, and it consists of the portrait of an old man with a hank of hair on his forehead (Stuart 2006).

The *Popol Vuh* lists a host of paired titles and animal manifestations for Xpiyacoc and Xmucane, such as Framer and Shaper (*Tz'aqol* and *B'itol*); Protector and Shelterer (*Matzanel* and *Chuqenel*); Patriarch and Midwife (*Mamon* and *I'yom*); Hunahpu Opossum and Hunahpu Coyote (*Junajpu Wuch'* and *Junajpu Utiw*); Great White Peccary and Great White Coati (*Saqi Nim Aq* and *Saqi Nima Sis*); Sovereign and Quetzal Serpent (*Tepew* and *Q'ukumatz)*; Heart of Lake and Heart of Sea (*U K'ux Cho* and *U K'ux Palo*); Creator of the Blue/Green Plate, Creator of the Blue/Green Bowl (*Aj Raxa Laq* and *Aj Raxa Sel*); Jeweler and Worker in Precious Stones (*Aj K'uwal* and *Aj Yamanik*); Sculptor and Wood Worker (*Aj Ch'ut* and *Aj Tz'alam*); and Incense Maker and Master Artist (*Aj Q'ol* and *Aj Toltecat*). They were also called K'ajolom, "He Who Has Begotten Sons," and Alom, "She Who Has Borne Children" (Christenson 2003a:68–69). Framer and Shaper, the most frequently used titles for Xpiyacoc and Xmucane, refer to the creator grandparents' role in ordering and shaping the earth and the first human beings. The paired titles Heart of Lake and Heart of Sea are references to the fact that these creator gods were specifically identified with the center and with the essence of these places. The creator grandparents are described as:

> the Mother and the Father of life and all creation, the giver of breath and the giver of heart, they who give birth and give heart to the light everlasting, the child of light born of woman and the son of light born of man, they who are compassionate and wise in all things—all that exists in the sky and on the earth, in the lakes and in the sea. (Christenson 2003a:66)

The breath and heart were thought to contain the soul or essence of a person; thus, the couplet "the giver of breath and the giver of heart" appears to refer to the role of the creator grandparents as the source of human souls.

Las Casas noted (1967, vol. 3, pt. 124, p. 650) that the highland Maya worshiped as their principal gods "the Great Father and the Great Mother that were in heaven," clearly referring to the creator grandparents. The concept of powerful creator grandparents is also found in the Tzeltal and Tzotzil areas, where colonial dictionaries refer to a creator couple with the names Patol, "maker," and Alaghom, "bearer, goddess with children" (Calnek 1988:45; Laughlin 1988:153). This couple created the earth, the sky, and mankind, and they were said to be the head and beginning of all the other gods of each town. In some contexts, Alaghom is paired with the title *naom,* which means to spin, and the creator grandmother was the first goddess to spin cotton (Robert Laughlin, personal communication).

In addition to being the home of the creator grandparents, the place of duality was also inhabited by three powerful lightning-bolt gods who dwelled in the sky. The *Popol Vuh* text first introduces an entity called the Heart of Sky and says that his name was Huracan. Then it rather cryptically states that Thunderbolt Huracan was first, Ch'i'pi (youngest child) Thunderbolt was second, Raxa (sudden or blue/green) Thunderbolt was third, and together they were the Heart of the Sky. In council with one another, the creator grandparents and Heart of Sky decide to create human beings who will honor and respect them. Their first act is to make a place for these humans to live:

> Then the earth was created by them. Merely their word brought about the creation of it. In order to create the earth, they said, "Earth," and immediately it was created. Just like a cloud, like a mist, was the creation and formation of it.
>
> Then they called forth the mountains from the water. Straightaway the great mountains came to be. It was merely their spirit essence, their miraculous power that brought about the conception of the mountains and the valleys. Straightaway were created cypress groves and pine forests to cover the face of the earth. Thus Quetzal Serpent rejoiced: "It is good that you have come, Heart of Sky—you, Huracan, and you as well, Youngest Thunderbolt and Sudden Thunderbolt. That which we have framed and shaped shall turn out well," they said. First the earth was created, the mountains and the valleys. The waterways were divided, their branches coursing among the mountains. Thus the waters were divided, revealing the great mountains. For thus was the creation of the earth, created then by Heart of Sky and Heart of Earth, as they are called. They were the first to conceive it. The sky was set apart. The earth also was set apart within the waters. Thus was conceived the successful completion of the work when they thought and when they pondered. (Christenson 2003a:71–73)

The paired couplet "Heart of Sky and Heart of Earth" also appears in the passages referring to the creation of animals and the first humans by the creator grandparents and Heart of Sky (Christenson 2003a:76, 201).

In the scene on K7750 and K2796 is a list of deity names that Stuart has identified as categories of deities rather than individual gods (Stuart, Houston, and Robertson 1999). Given the couplet and triplet structure of Maya narratives, it is also quite possible that these six names refer to just two or three sets of gods. In this list are references to sky gods and earth gods that are reminiscent of the Heart of Sky and Heart of Earth titles found in the *Popol Vuh*. Sky gods and earth gods are also paired in several texts such as the Palenque Temple of the Inscriptions tablets, Copan Stela 2, and Tikal Stela 31. Stuart interprets the Classic Period couplet as a general reference to the gods of the universe, but it may be specifically naming the creator deities.

As the *Popol Vuh* story progresses to the time after the creation of the earth, it is revealed that Xpiyacoc and Xmucane had two sons named One Hunahpu and Seven Hunahpu who lived in a house on the surface of the earth. Seven Hunahpu was a childless bachelor, but One Hunahpu fathered two sets of twin boys with his two wives (Lady Bone Water and Lady Blood). The eldest twins were One Batz and One Chouen (the monkey twins), while the second set of twins was Hunahpu and Xbalanque (the hero twins). As noted in chapter 1, there is a Maya concept that children and grandchildren are the embodiment and replacement of their parents and grandparents. Such was the case with the children and twin grandchildren of Xpiyacoc and Xmucane, for they were also skilled in the occupations of the creator grandparents. One Hunahpu and Seven Hunahpu were wise diviners like their parents:

> They were great thinkers, for great was their knowledge. They were seers here upon the face of the earth. They were good by their nature, and in their birth as well. (Christenson 2003a:113)

The text emphasizes that they were the epitome of proper behavior. One Hunahpu and Seven Hunahpu taught the monkey twins to be diviners as well as musicians, singers, writers, sculptors, jade workers, and metalsmiths. The *Popol Vuh* specifically says that One Batz and One Chouen were the *k'exel,* "replacements," for One Hunahpu, although they were eventually subjugated by their younger brothers for their inappropriate behavior and turned into monkeys. As will be discussed in later chapters, the monkey twins became the patron gods for the secondary lords who practiced their arts, while the hero twins became role models for young rulers and warriors. The importance of offspring continuing the skills of their forefathers is emphasized in the speech One Hunahpu gives after impregnating his second wife, Lady Blood, with the hero twins:

> If his son becomes a lord, or a sage, or a master of speech, then nothing will have been lost. He will go on, and once more become complete. The face of the lord will not be extinguished nor will it be ruined. The warrior, the sage, the master of speech will remain in the form of his daughters and his sons. (Christenson 2003a:129)

In later episodes of the *Popol Vuh* story, a variety of supernatural beings are said to have dwelled on the surface of the earth. Their origins are not stated, but because they challenge the supremacy of the creator gods, they are subordinated by Heart of

Sky and the hero twins. For example, the supernatural called Zipacna claims to be the creator of a number of volcanic mountains (Chigag, Hunahpu, Peculya, Xcanul, Macamob, and Huliznab), and he goes on to falsely boast that he is the creator of the earth and all the mountains. Heart of Sky then sends the hero twins to defeat this impostor.

## THE UNDERWORLD

The *Popol Vuh* tells of a region below the earth called Xibalba, "place of fright," that was home to a large array of death-related supernatural beings. Although it does not indicate when or how Xibalba was created or whether it always existed, the *Popol Vuh* does say that this place of death was ruled by two gods called One Death and Seven Death who were adversaries of the creator gods. One Hunahpu and Seven Hunahpu played ball at the Nim Xob' Karchaj ballcourt that was located on the surface of the earth at one of the gateways to the underworld. This intrusion into their territory angered the lords of death, who issued a challenge to One Hunahpu and Seven Hunahpu to come to the ceremonial center of Xibalba to play ball at the Puk'b'al Cha'j ("Crushing Ballcourt") located there. Their route followed a descending passageway by or through various canyons; rapids; rivers filled with scorpions, pus, and blood; and a crossroads before finally arriving at the Death Lords' council house beneath the earth. Also at the center of Xibalba were a number of buildings known as Darkness House, Shivering House, Jaguar House, Bat House, Blade House, and Fire House that no ordinary being could enter without dying. Later in the story, the hero twins Hunahpu and Xbalanque went to the underworld along the same pathway as their father and uncle.

One Death and Seven Death presided over twelve secondary death gods whose names and offices reflected the manner in which they brought disease and death to people. The death gods had wives and children, feasted, conducted business, and played ball at the Crushing Ballcourt. One of the higher-ranking secondary lords of the underworld was named Gathered Blood (*Kuchuma Kik'*), whose daughters (Lady Bone Water and Lady Blood) were the wives of One Hunahpu. As the maternal grandfather of the twins, Gathered Blood was the complementary opposite of the paternal grandfather Xpiyacoc.

A good portion of the *Popol Vuh* involves the conquering of One Death and Seven Death by the creator gods and their offspring. The epic struggle between the creator gods and the death lords was a role model for foreign marriage alliances and territorial warfare. After the defeat and death of One Death and Seven Death, Gathered Blood became the leading lord of the underworld. In contemporary K'iche' stories, Gathered Blood is still known as a cruel lord of the underworld who gathers the blood that falls to the ground when a person is injured so he may serve it to his fellow lords at a banquet (Christenson 2003a:116).

## Layers of the Sky and Underworld

A number of Mesoamerican sources refer to the sky and underworld as being composed of stacked, hierarchical levels. Each layer or plane had a specific name and was associated with particular phenomena, deities, and supernatural animals. It is highly likely that each region in Mesoamerica conceived of these layers in slightly different ways, just as each region has different genesis myths. The colonial *Codex Ríos (Vaticanus A)* manuscript from Central Mexico illustrates thirteen upper levels and nine lower levels, with the earth representing the first level in each domain (Nicholson 1971:407). While it is often assumed that this configuration was standard in the Maya area as well, it is not known how the Maya thought the layers of the universe were created and demarcated or what specific supernatural beings and natural phenomena were thought to inhabit each layer. Evidence for a layered sky is found in a reference to the *yoxlahun taz caan,* "the 13th layer of the sky," in the *Chilam Balam of Chumayel* (Roys 1933:99). It is very likely that the Maya, like other Mesoamerican groups, identified the place of duality with the uppermost level of the sky directly above the center of the world. As will become apparent in later chapters, the place of duality was a flowery celestial paradise closely associated with the zenith passage of the sun at midday as well as with a constellation in the night sky called the Three Hearthstones, located in Orion. The ruling elite were thought to ascend to this zenith paradise after death. This is apparent in many scenes that show the parents of the ruler situated in the sky above the ruler's head (for example, Yaxchilan Stela 12). In his description of Lacandon afterlife beliefs, Tozzer (1907:156) notes that men who died in war and women who died in childbirth were thought to ascend to a paradise in the highest level of the heavens. As will be discussed below, the center of the surface of the earth was also identified with the place of duality.

## The Surface of the Earth

The *Popol Vuh* indicates that the creator deities and their offspring prepared the surface of the earth for human habitation and the cultivation of maize by creating the celestial and meteorological cycles and by creating a quadrilateral space on its surface. Humans could safely live in the quadrilateral world if they made the proper petitions to the gods. The points where the sun rises and sets at solstice defined the corners of the quadrilateral world, while the zenith passage of the sun defined its center (fig. 4.1).

On each side of the quadrilateral world was a mountain (Bassie-Sweet 1996). The sides were also envisioned to be a rope or path that formed a protective perimeter that kept supernatural forces from entering and harming humans. Access to each of the four directional mountains was through a cave opening aligned with the cardinal directions. These caves constituted breaks in the perimeter of the quadrilateral world through which both destructive forces and essential elements could enter. The directional mountains and caves were also metaphorically related to houses and house doorways.

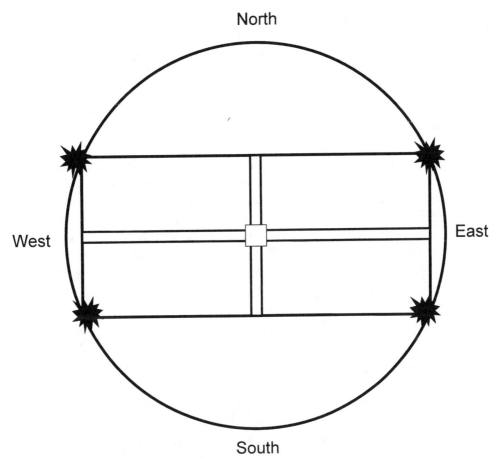

North

West

East

South

Figure 4.1. The four world roads

The K'iche' describe the earth using the merismus phrase *juyub'-taq'aj,* "mountain valley" (Cook 2000:75). Although mountain/valley appears to be a simple description of the hills and valleys that make up the majority of the earth's surface, it is used in contexts where the contrast is between mountain as a wild, dangerous, supernatural space and valley as a cultivated, safe, human space. In virtually every culture there is a need to create territorial boundaries to demarcate a safe human space from the wild. The inhospitable nature of mountains made them a logical choice for wild, supernatural space. At first glance, the idea of mountain versus valley seems to be a highland concept because the distinction between valley and mountain is so pronounced in this region. However, in the lowlands the traditional agricultural practice is to leave the natural vegetation on hilltops (Atran 1993). When the field is returned to fallow, these small mountains of wild vegetation regenerate the lower slopes and fields. The distinction between wild and human space, between planted and unplanted land, and between mountain and valley is sustained.

The idea for a quadrilateral human world originated in the action of making a cornfield, for it was during this annual practice dictated by the sun's cycle that wild space was first turned into human space. The introductory passage in the *Popol Vuh* makes reference to the quadrilateral world:

> Great is its performance and its account of the completion and germination of all the sky and earth—its four corners and its four sides. All then was measured and staked out into four divisions, doubling over and stretching the measuring cords of the womb of sky and the womb of earth. Thus were established the four corners, the four sides, as it is said, by the Framer and the Shaper, the Mother and the Father of life and all creation, the giver of breath and the giver of heart, they who give birth and give heart to the light everlasting, the child of light born of woman and the son of light born of man, they who are compassionate and wise in all things—all that exists in the sky and on the earth, in the lakes and in the sea. (Christenson 2003a:65–66)

While translating the *Popol Vuh* with Dennis Tedlock, the K'iche' ritual specialist Andrés Xiloj recognized that the "four divisions" referred to the gods measuring out the surface of the earth as though it were a cornfield being laid out for cultivation (D. Tedlock 1996:220).

The Maya believed that the deities created and destroyed the quadrilateral world several times and that they would eventually destroy and re-create it again. This cycle of destruction and re-creation was also rooted in the corn cycle, for each year, the wild space is destroyed by cutting and burning, and then it is transformed into cultivated human space with the planting of corn. The notion that the perimeter of the quadrilateral world was a protective rope or path was also related to the cornfield, for the field was often measured out using a rope, and it frequently had a fire path cut around it. Each year when the Maya burned the dried vegetation, planted a new cornfield, and performed their rituals to ensure a good harvest, they were validating and reinforcing their quadrilateral world model.

## The Quadrants of the World

Each quadrant of the world was associated with a particular color: east-red, north-white, west-black, and south-yellow (Thompson 1934). As numerous authors have noted, these are also the colors of corn. The division of the earth's surface into colored quadrants is reflected in the quadripartite forms of various deities such as Itzamnaaj, Ix Chel, Chahk, and Bakab. Deities associated with the colors and directions are also found in the calendar cycle called the 819 Day Count (Berlin and Kelley 1961). The *Chilam Balam of Chumayel* refers to ceiba trees, plants, animals, flints, and deities with directional and color designations (Roys 1933:64).

The Maya cosmogram comprised four roads radiating from the center of the world to each of the four directional mountains. The east–west road represented the daily passage of the sun across the sky; the north–south road represented the sun's annual path. These roads were also identified with the roads that the Maya saw in the night sky (the Milky Way and the ecliptic), and with the four major rivers of central highland Guatemala (see chapter 12).

The color associations of the directions are closely related to the sun's daily and annual cycle. The red of east is naturally associated with the red of dawn and the rising sun. A former Tzotzil president of Chenalhó described this red as the fire of the Old Man Possum, and he explained how it lit up the landscape: "When I was a child, my father and my mother said to me, 'The fire of the 'Uch (Old Man Possum) has manifested itself.' I was in my house on the mesa, and I woke up when it was still night and the roosters crowed, and I saw that the heavens were red. The leaves of the corn were red; the sky toward the northeast was red" (Guiteras Holmes 1961:206).

The black of the west is related to the setting sun and resulting black of night. In addition, it is related to the color of black corn. The milpas in the Petén contain a variety of secondary crops. In order to keep corn pollen from covering and blighting these plants, the secondary crops are planted on the east edge of the milpa in the direction of the prevailing wind. Because black corn is the worst offender, it is planted on the far west side of the milpa (Atran 1993:679). This directional association is reflected in a variety of black corn called *chik'in ts'ono'ot,* which literally translates as "west cenote" (Tozzer 1907:51, Barrera Vásquez 1980:99). This suggests that color and direction were, at least in part, also the result of corn production practices.

The north–south axis of the cosmogram represents the annual path of the sun as it moves from the December solstice in the south to the June solstice in the north. It has long been argued that the relationship between yellow and south may have been based on the fact that during the dry season when ripe cornfields are yellow, the sun is in the southern part of the sky. The association of white with north is also likely related to corn (Bassie-Sweet 2003). As noted in chapter 3, the Maya use the first zenith passage of the sun in late April or early May as an indication that the rains are coming and that it is time to burn the field. The cleared fields are all turning from dried yellow to ash-white just as the sun is moving into the northern sector of the sky. In addition, the atmosphere at this time is filled with dense white smoke.

## THE CENTER

In the metaphorical relationship between the earth's surface and a cornfield, the center is defined by the center planting mound and its altar or hole for offerings. The Maya often refer to the planting hole as a cave, and the sign used to represent it and other cave entrances is a quatrefoil. In mountain imagery, these symbols mark the cave as the entrance to the center or heart of the mountain. The shape of the quatrefoil may have originated in the action of making the planting hole, for the digging stick is often rocked back and forth and from side to side to enlarge the hole. In contemporary world view, the center is often marked by a cross, but in pre-Columbian times, the center was marked by a tree, just as the center area of the milpa frequently contains a large tree.

Other metaphors to describe the surface of the earth include the human body and a house, with the center described as a heart or navel and as a fireplace, respectively (Siegel 1941:66; La Farge 1947:112, 127; Guiteras Holmes 1961:26, 159, 203, 217, 287, 289; Hermitte 1964:45; Carter 1969:37; Vogt 1969:297; Nash 1970:2l; Nicholson 1971:403; Gossen 1974:18, 37; Rosenbaum 1993:77). The axis connecting the center of the earth to the place of duality in the heavens was pictured in many forms, such as a tree, an umbilical cord, a cotton spindle, and a fire-drilling stick. The center axis was associated with a circling, whirling motion such as the spinning of the cotton spindle, the fire drill, and the drill used to carve precious stones. Communication or movement between the heavens and earth often took the form of a circling or whirling motion (López Austin 1988:209; Furst 1995:70).

Tozzer described the Yucatec Maya belief that a ceiba marked the center of the world and created an axis to heaven:

> According to the natives of Yucatan, there are seven heavens above the earth, each of which has a hole in the center, one directly above the other. According to one idea, a giant ceiba growing in the exact center of the earth, rears its branches through the successive holes in the heavens until it reaches the seventh, where "El Gran Dios" of the Spaniards lives. It is by means of this tree that the dead spirits ascend from one world to the other until they reach the topmost one, where they finally remain. Another explanation is that there is a ladder made of vines running from the earth up through the holes in the heavens to the seventh, and it is by this vine that the souls ascend. (Tozzer 1907:154)

The position of the place of duality (heaven) above the center of the earth is reflected in a Yucatec ritual altar. The surface of this altar replicates the quadrilateral world (Sosa 1985:139–40). Tree branches are arched over the altar to create a dome that represents the sky. A small platform is hung from the arches above the center of the table to mark the location in the sky called *u hol gloryah,* "the hole in the sky." The ritual specialist places offerings on this platform and directs his prayers to it. The axis between the center of the table and *u hol gloryah* is thought to be a conduit between these two locations just like the center tree. It is apparent that *u hol gloryah* parallels the pre-Columbian concept of the place of duality at the center of the heavens.

## THE K'AN CROSS AS A SYMBOL FOR THE CENTER

In the context of the directional colors, the center is usually associated with *yax,* "blue/green," while the south is associated with *k'an,* "yellow." The sign for k'an, however, was also used to designate the center in certain contexts (Taube 2000:313). The k'an sign is composed of a cross that frequently has a circle at its center. This sign is thematically parallel to the architectural form of a pyramid platform with four radial staircases. Such a structure represents the surface of the earth; the staircases of the radial pyramid represent the four directional roads that radiate from the center of the world.

The same configuration is found in *huipil* (blouse) designs that represent the world. In some examples, the road designs radiate from the neck hole of the garment (Morris 1987). Wearing the garment places the woman at the center of the world. The same is true at Santiago Atitlán, where the center hole of the huipil explicitly represents the center of the world (Christenson 2001:97). The center of the quadrilateral world was thought to be a replication of the place of duality (López Austin 1988:59).

In addition to meaning "yellow," the word *k'an* is also used as a metaphor for abundance, richness, and health—concepts associated with the place of duality (Thompson 1950:275; Bunzel 1952, 55, 282; B. Tedlock 1982: 114; Christenson 2003a:138). The Tzotzil, for example, use the four colors of corn to describe famine and scarcity of corn (Guiteras Holmes 1961:287); white, red, and black in this case are related to famine, but yellow is associated with abundance. The K'iche' day name *K'anil*, "yellowness," is used to refer to the yellow of the ripe maize field and to the fruitfulness of the earth. The Mam also associate the color yellow with abundance during their pilgrimages to their sacred corn mountain (Miles 1960:433). At a water shrine on the mountain, the diviners look into the water to predict the nature of the coming harvest. If the water is pure yellow, it will be an abundant year.

Christenson's description of a diviner sitting before his divination table echoes the configuration of the k'an cross:

> A prominent K'iche' *aj q'ij* priest, named Don Vicente de León Abac, described his work to me in this way: "When I am seated at my table, I am *aj nawal mesa* [of, or pertaining to, the spirit essence of the table]. My body is in the form of a cross just like the four sides of the world. This is why I face to the east and behind me is the west. My left arm extends out toward the north, and my right arm points to the south. My heart is the center of myself just as the arms of the cross come together to form its heart. My head extends upward above the horizon so that I can see far away. Because I am seated this way I can speak to Mundo [the gods]." (Christenson 2003b:65)

This description suggests that the k'an cross should symbolize Xpiyacoc, the first diviner, and that the surface of the earth (the divination table) should represent his body.

## The Earth Turtle

The turtle shell was used as a metaphor for the surface of the earth, with the k'an sign marking its center (Taube 1988a). The name Xpiyacoc is difficult to translate, but *kok* is a term for turtle in both highland and lowland languages, and the term *piyakok* is the name for a slider turtle (*Trachemys scripta elegans*) and for a turtle design in the weavings of Rabinal (Akkeren 2000:207, 261–64; Christenson 2003a:63). The Classic Period parallel of Xpiyacoc was Itzamnaaj/God N. This god had a turtle manifestation with a k'an sign on the middle of his back. I suggest that when the surface of the earth was first brought forth from the waters of the place of duality, it was this turtle form of the creator grandfather that appeared. The earth is characterized in many metaphors as a house, and several Maya terms for a house describe it as though it were a turtle (Carrasco and Hull 2002; Hull and Carrasco 2004). These descriptions certainly fit with the turtle form of Itzamnaaj, for the shell of the turtle is his house. The K'iche' term for the pack frame that merchants carried on their back was *kok* (Carmack 1981:89). Many scenes show Itzamnaaj/God N walking with his shell on his back like a *kok* pack frame.

Itzamnaaj/God N also had four mountain manifestations, one for each direction, and each mountain symbolized one quadrant of the world (Thompson 1950:133; Taube 1986, 1992a:92–99). These four mountains, which demarcated the sides of the quadrilateral world, were the focus of the annual New Year ceremonies. Itzamnaaj/God N was the first calendar priest, and it is highly appropriate that these New Year mountains should be associated with him.

A supernatural being called Itzam Kab Ayin, "Itzam earth crocodile," is mentioned in association with the flooding of the world in the colonial Chilam Balam books of northern Yucatan. In these enigmatic passages, Itzam Kab Ayin is said to have arisen after the destruction of the world by floods and to have had his throat cut. These texts imply that the body of the slain Itzam Kab Ayin formed the surface of the earth. In *Dresden Codex* 4b–5b, a double-headed crocodile is shown with the head of Itzamnaaj emerging from its mouth. Taube (1989; 1992a:128–31; 1993), following earlier interpretations by Seler, Martínez Hernández, Roys, and Thompson, has suggested that this beast may represent a caiman form of Itzamnaaj called Itzam Kab Ayin. These authors have also suggested that Itzam Kab Ayin was parallel to the Aztec Cipactli/Tlaltecuhtli. Cipactli was a monstrous caiman/fish who lived in the primordial waters and was later transformed into the earth (Tlaltecuhtli, "earth lord"). Although some sources indicate Cipactli/Tlaltecuhtli was male or dual-sexed, the *Histoyre du Mechique* relates that Tlaltecuhtli was a female who was torn in half by Quetzalcoatl and Tezcatlipoca (Jonghe 1905). In this version, the upper portion of her body became the earth and the lower portion was thrown into the sky to become the heavens. While there is ample evidence that the turtle form of Itzamnaaj represented the surface of the earth, there is little Classic Period evidence to suggest that Itzamnaaj had a crocodile form or that the earth was thought to be represented by a crocodile.

## THE CENTER HOUSE OF THE CREATOR GRANDPARENTS

Because the center of the earth replicated the place of duality, it is logical to conclude that the house used as a metaphor for the quadrilateral world was that of the creator grandparents. In the Palenque Temple XIX platform text, the creator grand-father Itzamnaaj is referred to as Yax Naah Itzamnaaj, "first house Itzamnaaj" (Stuart 2005b:66), which I believe probably alludes to this fact.

The *Popol Vuh* mentions the house of the creator grandparents in the episodes concerning the birth and early life of the hero twins and describes this house at the center of the world as a thatched structure like that of an average corn farmer. At this point in the story, One Hunahpu, Seven Hunahpu, the monkey twins, and Xmucane live together in the house. Little is said about the monkey twins' mother (Lady Bone Water) except to say that she died. Xpiyacoc is also said to be dead at this time, despite being an active participant later in the story.

There is circumstantial evidence from contemporary practices that Xpiyacoc and Xmucane were the original owners of the house. Male children learn how to grow corn from an early age by working side-by-side with their father. They will continue to work with him and live in his house even after they marry. It is the custom in some areas for a newly married man to pay part of his bride price with labor, so the man lives with and works for his father-in-law for a specified period. The young couple will later reside with his parents until they establish their own house-hold. When the father dies, the eldest married son still living at home will inherit his father's house, and the widow and unmarried children will continue to reside with him. It would, therefore, have been unusual for the bachelor Seven Hunahpu to be living in his married brother's household, but it would be expected if the house originally belonged to their father, Xpiyacoc.

## The Center Fire as the Creator Grandfather

In some contexts, the center was thought to be like a mirror or a pool of water (Taube 1992b), both metaphors for the waters of the place of duality. In house metaphors, the center of the earth was thought to be marked by a fire surrounded by three stones like those found in Maya houses (Freidel, Schele, and Parker 1993; Taube 1998). The yellow of the k'an sign likely refers to this yellow fire. As noted above, the Maya also had a constellation called the Three Hearthstones, formed by the stars Alnitak, Saiph, and Rigel in Orion. The center of this celestial fireplace was the Orion Great Nebula M42, which appears in the sky like a smoky fire (B. Tedlock 1985:86; 1992:29). The K'iche' Maya referred to the three stars of Orion's belt as the *je oxib' chi q'aq' ajaw,* "the tail of the three fire lords" (B. Tedlock 1992:29). This name suggests that the three hearthstones were thought to be deities. Such a concept is found in the Aztec *Annals of Cuauhtitlán,* where the old fire god Xiuhtecuhtli is guarded by three deities (Mixcoatl, Tozpan, and Ihuitl) who are said to be the three hearthstones (Bierhorst 1992:23).

The old fire god Xiuhtecuhtli was a manifestation of Ometeotl and was also known as Huehueteotl (Nicholson 1971:413). In Central Mexican mythology, the principle of duality was manifested by a bisexual deity called Ometeotl ("two god") who also took the form of Ometecuhtli ("two lord") and his wife Omecihuatl ("two lady"). In Aztec healing incantations, the fire is specifically called the old man and the smoke is the old woman (Coe and Whittaker 1982:229). Xpiyacoc has many of Xiuhtecuhtli/Huehueteotl's attributes. For example, the *Florentine Codex* describes Xiuhtecuhtli/Huehueteotl in his hearth at the navel of the earth as being enclosed "with the waters of the lovely cotinga, enclosed with clouds" (Sahagún 1959–63, book 6, 88–89). The appearance of the cotinga in water also occurs in the *Popol Vuh* in the description of the creator grandparents as Sovereign and Quetzal Serpent:

> All alone are the Framer and the Shaper, Sovereign and Quetzal Serpent, They Who Have Borne Children and They Who Have Begotten Sons. Luminous (*saqtetoj*) they are in the water, wrapped in quetzal feathers and cotinga feathers. Thus they are called Quetzal Serpent. In their essence, they are great sages, great possessors of knowledge. (Christenson 2003a:68–69)

Another manifestation of Xpiyacoc that is related to fire is his role as Hunahpu Opossum. The intimate relationship between the opossum and fire is well known in Mesoamerica (López Austin 1993), and as noted above, the Tzotzil call the red light before dawn the fire of Old Man Opossum. In the *Popol Vuh*, the light of dawn appears on the horizon before the hero twins are ready to rise up as sun and full moon, and Old Man Opossum (Xpiyacoc), who is also called *mam*, "grandfather," is asked to darken the sky again (Christenson 2003a:173–74). The role of Xpiyacoc as a fire god is also seen in his role as the fire of the sweat bath and of the volcano.

Fire is a generating and transformational force in Mesoamerica. The burning volcano spews ash across the landscape, and the following season there is a bumper crop. The fire burns the field or forest, and abundant life springs forth from the ashes. Stuart (1998) notes the widespread Mesoamerican belief that heat is a reflection of one's strength or soul. In the *Popol Vuh*, the K'iche' term for power is *q'aq'al*, "fiery-ness" (Allen Christenson, personal communication). As discussed in chapter 1, the corn seed must be ritually heated for it to germinate. The notion that heat is the generating element of the soul is reflected in the belief that a lightning strike in the cornfield causes the bone/corn seed to come to life. It is also seen in Sahagún's statement that the soul of a fetus is drilled like fire into the child by the creator grandparents (López Austin 1988:208). Two common expressions used to describe the dedication of buildings are "fire entering" and "house censing" (Stuart 1998). Stuart suggests that placing a fire in a new building figuratively makes it a home by creating a hearth, thus investing the building with heat and strength. In other words, this action gives a house its soul. If this concept is applied to the metaphors where the world is thought to be a house, it seems apparent that the heat and soul of the earth was the creator grandfather in his fire manifestation.

The center of the place of duality and the center of the earth were marked by the three hearthstones, but the fire itself was the creator grandfather in his manifestation as the old fire god. All fire ultimately originated from this center god and his fire. Manmade fires can be produced by twirling a hard wooden stick on a softer piece of wood and tinder. The friction generated between the soft and hard wood creates heat that ignites the tinder. A cord can be twisted around the drilling stick and pulled to facilitate the spinning of the stick. Fire can also be made by striking flint. The resulting sparks are used to ignite combustible material. Whether drilling fire or striking flint, the resulting fire was a manifestation of the creator grandfather. The creator grandmother also played an important role in regard to the center fire. The most common scene encountered in a Maya home is the woman of the house kneeling beside the three hearthstone fire. While women do not ignite the fire, it is their job to tend and maintain it. The ultimate role model for these women was the creator grandmother.

The glyph for the three stones of the hearth has been identified as being composed of three T528 *tuun* "stone" signs clustered together (MacLeod, cited in Schele 1992:125; Freidel, Schele, and Parker 1993:67). In some examples, plumes of smoke billow up above the stones (Taube 1998). A number of Classic Period texts refer to the renewal of three hearthstones by gods at the Period Ending ceremony that ended the thirteenth b'aktun in B.C. 3114 (Schele 1992; Freidel, Schele, and Parker 1993). As noted, the making of a new fire was an important part of house dedication ceremonies and calendar festivals (Furst 1995:68, Stuart 1998). It is, therefore, not surprising that the 13.0.0.0.0 Period Ending ceremony would involve the act of making fire.

## THE WORLD TREES

Numerous sources refer to trees located at the center, corners, and midpoints on the sides of the quadrilateral world. Landa describes four Bakab deities who were set up after the last destruction of the world by floods. They were intimately related to the world trees: "Among the multitudes of gods which this nation worshiped they worshiped four, each of them called Bacab. They were four brothers whom God placed, when he created the world, at the four points of it, holding up the sky so it should not fall" (Tozzer 1941:135–36). Recent hieroglyphic decipherments suggest that the term Bakab should be translated as *ba,* "first," and *kab,* "world," with a meaning of "first in the world" (Houston and Stuart, personal communication 2001). Each Bakab also had an individual name (Hobnil, Can Tizic, Sac Cimi, and Hosan Ek) and was addressed by the titles Xib Chahk and Pawahtun. For example, the Bakab named Hobnil, who was associated with the color k'an, "yellow," was addressed as K'anal Bakab, K'an Pawahtun, and K'an Xib Chahk. As will be discussed in chapter 8, these gods were manifestations of One Ixim.

A passage in the *Chilam Balam of Chumayel* says that after the Bakabs were set up, a colored bird and an *"imix yaxche"* were set up in each of the four directions (Roys 1933:15). Both Roys and Thompson (1951:70–72) gloss the word *imix* as "abundance" by relating it to the supposed association of the day name *Imix* with abundance, but it is unclear what the meaning of *imix* is in this context. Another passage in the *Chilam Balam of Chumayel* as well as passages in the *Chilam Balam of Maní* and *Chilam Balam of Tizimin* describe colored directional trees but simply refer to them as the red *imix* tree in the east, the white *imix* tree in the north, the black *imix* tree in the west, and the yellow *imix* tree in the south (Roys 1933:99–100; Makemson 1951:41–42; Craine and Reindorp 1979:119). These three passages end by saying that a *yax*, "blue/green," *imix* tree was set up at the center of the world.

In his discussion of the *Chilam Balam of Chumayel*, Roys (1965:xii) notes that people were assigned a tree and an animal called *mut* according to the day on which they were born. Although there were many different kinds of fauna, *mut* literally means bird. The practice of assigning a tree and bird to each person suggests that the colored birds set up in the four directions belonged to One Ixim in his role as the Bakab deity.

The caption texts in the four *Dresden Codex* New Year pages refer to four directional trees. The *Dresden Codex* almanac represents the fifty-two years of the sacred calendar round as a four-year cycle repeated thirteen times. It is divided into units of four because only four of the day names can begin a new year. The day on which a time period begins establishes the nature of the time period; thus, there are only four kinds of years. Each of the four pages illustrates a number of gods performing a series of three events honoring the outgoing yearbearer and ushering in the new year. The final event is performed before a world tree corresponding to the appropriate direction for that yearbearer (fig. 4.2). Landa states that the New Year ceremonies performed by the Maya were in honor of the four Bakabs, and the parallels between his descriptions of these events and the *Dresden Codex* New Year scenes are well established (Tozzer 1941; Thompson 1972). In other words, the four-year festival cycle conducted by the gods that created the four quadrants of the world and set up the four world trees was celebrated by humans who annually reenacted these divine ordering ceremonies.

In Postclassic Yucatan, the town layout replicated the quadrilateral world model. On each side of the community was a ritual entrance marked by a pile of stones. Each pile represented one of the directional mountains. Four ritual roads led out from the center of the community to these symbolic mountains. In addition to these man-made locations, the Maya believed that the mountains and caves in the vicinity of the community also represented the four directional mountains. These mountains and their deities defined the safe space of the community. In the highlands of northwestern Guatemala, the New Year ceremonies are still conducted on such mountains (B. Tedlock 1982).

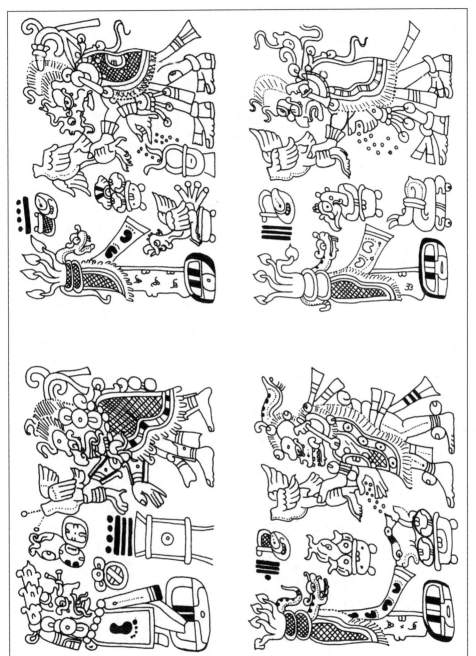

Figure 4.2. *Dresden Codex New Year pages 25, 26, 27, and 28* (after Villacorta)

The New Year ceremonies recorded by Landa began at the start of the wayeb' period (the five days before the new year began). At this time, a statue of the appropriate wayeb' god was placed on one of the ritual mountains. A statue of the patron deity for the new year was set up in the house of a town leader at the center of the community. The road leading from the center of town to the mountain was cleaned and decorated with arches and greenery. The ruler, the priests, and all the men of the community formed a procession and traveled down this forested path to the mountain. After giving various offerings to the wayeb' idol, they placed it on a standard and danced with it to the center of town, where it was set beside the patron deity. At the end of the wayeb', the patron deity was placed in the town temple for the year, and the wayeb' idol was taken to the ritual entrance that would be used in the New Year ceremonies the following year. The next year, a similar series of events would be performed, but oriented toward a different direction. Although the four wayeb' ceremonies were structurally identical, the amount of offerings and the kinds of dances that were performed were specific for each of the four years. Dancing in the four directions to re-create the world is a common theme in Maya festivals (La Farge 1947:50–57; Christenson 2001).

Numerous images on public monuments and pottery illustrate One Ixim—or a ruler in his guise—performing a dance (Coe 1978; Reents 1985; Reents-Budet 1991; Houston, Stuart, and Taube 1992). The placement of his feathers indicates that he is costumed as a bird. Such scenes often show One Ixim dancing beside a wooden frame or carrying it on his back. As noted by Coe (1978:14), this back rack is decorated with a witz monster with a supernatural being seated on it. One Ixim is often portrayed dancing two, three, and four times on the same vessel, indicating that he is performing his dance at least four times or in the four directions. These dances are thematically related to the four dances in the wayeb'/New Year ceremonies, and his back rack is reminiscent of the standards on which the wayeb' idols were carried. The dance that One Ixim performs at the center of the world will be discussed more fully in later chapters, but for the moment, it is sufficient to say that this dance is related to the first planting of corn at the center corn mound and to the establishment of the center tree.

The antiquity of ordering rituals such as the *Dresden Codex* New Year ceremonies is attested to by parallels in Preclassic imagery. The Preclassic west mural at San Bartolo illustrates five world trees (Stuart 2004). A Preclassic deity is shown standing before these trees, which have offerings beneath them. As Taube notes (cited in Stuart 2004), three of these offerings parallel those in the *Dresden Codex* New Year ceremonies. The bird form of Itzamnaaj is perched on the top branches of four of the San Bartolo trees, and he carries a double-headed serpent in his mouth. The serpent is thematically parallel to the snake illustrated in the *Dresden Codex* New Year trees. The association of the Itzamnaaj bird with the world tree was described by the Spanish priest Andrés Avendaño y Loyola (1987), who noted that the *Yax Cheel Cab,* "first/blue-green tree of the world" of the Petén Itzá, had a stone mask at its base that represented a deity called *Ahcocáhmut*. *Yax Cheel Cab* was another name for the *Yax Cocah Mut* deity who was worshipped during the New Year ceremonies and who was parallel to the Classic-Period Itzamnaaj bird.

Many dance festivals include the erection of a ceremonial pole representing the world tree in the center of a ritual space (Thompson 1930:111; Redfield 1936; Rodas, Rodas, and Hawkins 1940:80–82; Villa Rojas 1945:127; Girard 1948; 1952:358; Termer 1957; Hill 1992:98–100; Akkeren 2000; C. Beekman 2003). In some of the festivals, participants climb the tree, as in the Dance of the Voladores that is still performed in the central highlands (Rodas, Rodas, and Hawkins 1940:80–82; Girard 1948; 1952:358; Termer 1957). In this festival, a procession goes to a sacred mountain and searches for a tall tree with a straight trunk. Two monkey imitators who also perform later in the festival play an important role in the procurement of the tree. For thirteen nights, one of these monkeys sleeps at the base of the tree while the other maintains a period of sexual abstinence. After prayers and offerings are made at the base of tree, it is cut down and the branches and bark removed. A great number of men then carry the tree pole to the center of the plaza while the monkeys cavort along the trunk. After a deep hole is dug in front of the church, the head ritual specialist descends into the hole and hollows out a side chamber where he places offerings and burns incense for the sky and earth gods. The base of the pole is inserted into the hole, and the pole is raised with much difficulty while one of the monkey imitators clings to the top. After the base of the pole is firmly packed with rocks and dirt to secure it, a square frame, constructed so that it can rotate around the pole, is placed at the top of the tree. Four ropes are tied to the top of the pole, wound around it, and looped over the frame.

Four men dressed in bird costumes enter the plaza, climb the pole, and tie the ends of the ropes around their waists. With the monkey imitators clowning around on the top and making music with a flute, the four bird men fly headfirst off the tree. They maintain this position by keeping the rope between their legs. The weight of their bodies and centrifugal force cause their ropes to unwind from around the pole as they descend in ever-widening circles around the pole. When their heads approach the ground, the four flyers right themselves and touch down. Each flyer is supposed to make thirteen revolutions for a total of fifty-two turns around the pole—the sacred number of years in the calendar round.

In ancient times, this pole ceremony was a centering ritual that demarcated the four quadrants of the world and symbolically began the celestial cycles of the calendar round. The four bird men reenacted the thirteen cycles as they flew around the pole. Each of the thirteen revolutions represented one of the four-year cycles of the year-bearers. The pole performance condensed the four-year cycle that is repeated thirteen times in the *Dresden Codex* New Year pages into a single performance. In the contemporary Dance of the Voladores, the bird men are most often identified as eagles that represent the sun, so each revolution also represents the yearly cycle of the sun.

## The Ceiba

In many sources, the world trees are specifically identified as *yaxche* (ceiba). It is a common belief in the Maya area that trees have spirits. Before cutting a tree down for use in a ceremony, one must obtain its permission through prayers and offerings. There is also a belief that the spirit of the tree can take the form of an animal. The ceiba marking the town cenote at Valladolid had a hawk as its spirit. According to Tozzer:

> The *ceiba* tree (Bombax ceiba) plays a great part in the mythology of the Mayas. One was supposed to have grown in Valladolid. It was cut down, but it grew again and had four branches, one for each of the cardinal points. A cenote was directly beneath the tree. A hawk lived in the topmost branch, the spirit of the tree. The bird's cry was "suki, suki" and this was the name given to the town, which later was changed by the Spaniards to Valladolid. (Tozzer 1907:154)

An interesting association between a hawk and the ceiba is found at Seibal. This site was named for the large number of ceiba trees that grew there, but the indigenous name for the site was *Sac Tan Kiki,* "white fronted hawk" (Maler 1880:27). In the Poqomam community of Palin, the ceiba tree of the plaza is said to have a huge snake living in its upper branches. It is believed that if the snake were killed, the tree would dry up and die (Maynard 1963:8, 91).

Two types of ceiba trees are common in the Maya region: *Ceiba pentandra* and the smaller *C. aesculifolia.* The most common name for the ceiba is *yaxche,* "blue/green tree," which directly relates to the green color of the tree. Although it is deciduous, a ceiba that is not flowering sheds and regains its foliage in a period of about two weeks during the dry season, so it is green for most of the year. In addition, ceibas retain water in the cortical cells of their trunks and are able to maintain their green leaves even through periods of extreme drought. Their tender, green trunks are covered in small conical spikes that protect the bark from herbivores. The trunk stays bright green for about the first twelve years before gradually turning gray-green and becoming less spiky. The color yax is also used to describe gray tones, so the term *yaxche* is an appropriate description of either a young or old ceiba trunk.

Ceibas are fast-growing trees that can increase by a dramatic twelve feet a year and attain a mature height of 120 to 130 feet, making them one of the tallest trees in the region. The foliage of a mature ceiba is concentrated in a massive, spreading crown at the top of the tree. The high crown permits the tree to thrive in the dense canopy of the rain forest. Ceiba branches are often covered with grasses and epiphytes such as bromeliads and orchids. Diverse insects inhabit this environment, and some species of frogs even raise their tadpoles in the tiny pools that collect in the bromeliads. The canopy of the ceiba also hosts a number of other animals including opossums, coatis, squirrels, weasels, snakes, and a wide variety of birds. Although there are few jaguars in the forests near Yalcoba in northern Yucatan, it is common knowledge in the region that these animals rest in ceibas and wait for their prey (Sosa 1985:244). A mature trunk has wide buttresses at its base to support its colossal height and crown and to protect it from strong winds that damage and uproot many of the other trees of the forest. Ceibas are often found beside cenotes, rivers, and lakes; thus they are good indicators of underground sources of water. In fact, the ceiba is one of the signs used to select a site for drilling a well for water in arid parts of Africa.

The tree does not flower until at least its fourth year of growth, and then it only flowers once every two to three years on average (Zotz and Winter 1994). A flowering ceiba remains leafless for three months as it blossoms and fruits. The flowering period comes at a time when other nectar sources are quite low. The night-blooming flowers are pollinated by bats, but they are also visited by bees and numerous nectar-seeking birds in the early morning hours. During the cool weather of a norte, these visits can extend well into the day. In addition, large flocks of birds such as orioles, tanagers, and blackbirds are often seen descending on the flowering ceiba to feast on nectar and the swarming insects (Dickey 1938:534). The mature seed pods are filled with white cotton-like floss called kapok. At the start of the rainy season, the seedpods burst open while still on the tree, and the wind disperses the seed and cotton widely.

Ceibas are frequently left standing when a milpa space is cleared. Young ceibas require a significant amount of sunlight, so the new trees from these ceibas readily grow in and around the opened field. The rapid growth of young ceibas allows them to out-compete slower-growing trees not only in cleared agricultural areas, but in areas that have been damaged or leveled by storms and wildfires.

The Maya used the ceiba in a variety of ways. Its high, spreading crown makes it an ideal shade tree when the forest is removed. This shaded location is a natural spot for the farmer to rest and take his midday meal while working in the field. In a second- or third-year milpa, the shed leaves of the ceiba provide additional ash around the base of the tree and increase the fertility of the soil. The ceiba's shade also makes it an ideal choice for town plazas and marketplaces (Roys 1931:299; Thompson 1958:204). In the late seventeenth century, Núñez de la Vega noted the common practice of having a ceiba on the town plaza (Thompson 1950:71), a tradition that continues today in many areas (Blom and La Farge 1927:444). In A.D. 1519, Cortez encountered stiff opposition from a community at the mouth of the Grijalva River in Tabasco. After winning a fierce battle, he marked the community's ceiba with three cuts of his sword and declared the town to be a possession of the Spanish crown.

As ceiba wood is soft and easily cut, the trunk was used to construct dugout canoes (Standley 1923:791). In A.D. 1677, the Spanish priest Joseph Delgado lost his boat during his expedition through the Petén (D. Stone 1932:267). It took his native expedition members a day to find a ceiba in the forest and another ten days to transform the tree into a dugout. In A.D. 1535, the Spaniard Gonzalo Fernández de Oviedo y Valdés described how ceibas growing beside rivers were felled to use as bridges across wide rivers in Central America (Standley 1930). The Lacandon use the bark of a young ceiba to wrap around their bows and arrows (Tozzer 1907:61). Some other reported uses of the tree are medicinal. The bark is applied to wounds and taken orally for its emetic, diuretic, and antispasmodic properties. The oil from the seeds is used for lamp fuel and soap. Young fruit, seeds, and shoots are eaten (Steggerda 1943: 201; Breedlove and Laughlin 1993:178). The seeds are said to resemble kernels of corn.

Before the pods disperse their seeds, the cotton-like kapok is often harvested by the Maya and used for stuffing. The numerous pillow thrones illustrated in Maya art were likely filled with kapok, and Oviedo raves about its softness in comparison with feathers, wool, and cotton. The floss from *C. aesculifolia* was used in woven cloaks in the Uman area (Roys 1931:276). Ceiba cotton is too short to be spun by itself, but it is likely that Maya women interwove it with other fibers. The floss was also used as tinder (Standley 1930:352). Steggerda (1943:201) records a Yucatec Maya belief about ceiba cotton. It is believed that the cotton that is blown by the wind is set on fire by the sun at noon. If this "burning" cotton falls on a thatch roof, it will set it on fire. Ceiba cotton is dispersed at the start of the rainy season, which is associated with the first zenith passage of the sun.

As noted in chapter 2, the opening of the forest canopy permits the regeneration of a host of wild plants, the flowers of which provide nectar for honeybees. As bees frequently make their hives in the adjacent ceibas, there are numerous stories of gods and culture heroes climbing the ceiba to obtain honey.

In a Ch'ol story, the young sun is tormented by his older brother and sets out to destroy him (Whittaker and Warkentin 1965:22). The sun asks his mother (the moon goddess/Virgin Mary) to clean cotton seeds for him to plant, which he places in a tree, thus creating the *sajajal te'*, "the whitening tree," or ceiba. This cotton grows and is transformed into honey. When the young sun returns home, he tells his elder brother about the honey. The next day at dawn, the two brothers go to the tree to collect the honey. After the elder brother climbs up to the top, the young sun, who has shrewdly stayed at the bottom, chops the ceiba down, killing his brother.

In a Lacandon myth, T'uub (the youngest son of the creator god) is also associated with a ceiba that contains honey (Boremanse 1982:81–83). His elder brothers want to kill him, but he gets them drunk on *balche* (an alcoholic drink made from honey), takes away all their power, and banishes them to the edge of the world. T'uub is able to replace the fruit on the ceiba so its cotton then belongs to him.

The choice of the ceiba as the tree that marks the center of the world was based on its properties such as its speedy growth, its association with water, and its use as a central gathering place. An obvious reason why the Maya would choose a yaxche to be the first tree set up after the destruction of the world lies in the ceiba's swift regeneration both after the burning of the cornfield and after severe wind- and rainstorms.

Directional trees mark the borders of the quadrilateral world, just as young ceibas grow around the borders of the milpa. The tree can be used to establish directions when other celestial or landscape features are not visible because the largest buttress of the tree usually faces the prevailing east winds (Guest 1995:47). Another interesting aspect of the ceiba is that if cut down, its trunk will regenerate in a four-branched form, one for each direction (Tozzer 1907:154; Guest 1995:47). These features make the ceiba a good choice for the directional world trees that mark the four world roads extending out from the center of the world.

The tradition of a ceiba tree marking the central gathering place of the town is based on more than just its shade. One of the most important factors in choosing the location of a new community is access to fresh water. As noted above, ceibas are markers of water. In terms of the world model, the ceiba at the center of the world marked the pooled water at the place of duality—the ultimate source of the community's water. The contemporary Maya still link the ceiba with standing water in their creation stories. For example, in the Q'anjob'al community of Santa Eulalia, Christ/the Sun God is thought to have created a lake at the base of a ceiba (La Farge 1947:51–56). A parallel myth from neighboring San Miguel Acatán describes this water as a lagoon (Siegel 1943:123). In the Tzotzil region, ceibas are thought to be sources of water and therefore should not be felled (Breedlove and Laughlin 1993:177). Abundant flowers and fruit on a ceiba are said to be an indication of a bountiful corn harvest to come (Guest 1995:56).

Ceibas are closely associated with clouds, rain, and lightning. As noted, there is a Tzotzil belief that the Earth Lord's daughters spin cotton to make clouds, but the lightning god has to strike the cotton with a bolt to transform it into rain clouds. It is believed that the corn will also not germinate without this bolt of lightning. At the start of the rainy season, a fruiting ceiba is covered in seedpods that burst forth with white floss. Its canopy looks like a hovering cloud. The beginning of the rainy season is characterized by violent lightning storms, and the lone ceiba trees of the milpa are natural lightning rods.

The association of ceibas with rain rituals is found in a ceremony Edward Thompson recorded (1932:55) during a severe drought near Chichén Itzá. He noted that the rite was performed in the bush at the base of a ceiba. All of the vines hanging from the ceiba were stripped from the tree except for those on the east side. The surface under the ceiba was cleared, and an altar for the ceremony was constructed. A deer, a peccary, and wild turkeys were placed in an underground oven to cook. In the morning, the altar was laden with offerings of food and drink. Four young boys were tied to each of the legs of the altar and one placed under the center. At the appropriate time, the boys began to croak like the toads that are thought to call for the rain. Another ritual participant, called the "Bringer of the Winds," pulled the vines on the ceiba to create the sound of the great wind that brings the rain, while the participant called "Keeper of the Lightning" struck together two pieces of wood in imitation of thunder. After an hour of invocation, a rainstorm descended on the area. A ceiba was also the central focus of an agricultural dance festival (Thompson 1930:111; Redfield 1936; Villa Rojas 1945:127).

In addition to the New Year pages, several almanacs in the *Dresden Codex* illustrate the directional world trees. *Dresden Codex* 30c–31c shows four sequential scenes of a chahk sitting in a directional tree. The caption text denotes the west and south trees as black and yellow, respectively. The east tree is prefixed with a red sign, but the main sign of its hieroglyphic name has not been deciphered. The north tree is named using the corresponding white color and a T548 *haab* sign. Both of these latter trees appear to have buttressed trunks, suggesting that they are large, mature trees. On *Dresden Codex* 29a–30a, another series of four trees containing chahks is illustrated. Although the text is damaged, enough remains to show that each tree was associated with one of the directional colors. The yellow tree of the south has the conical spikes of a young ceiba.

The caption texts in the four New Year pages of the *Dresden Codex* name four trees, each associated with a direction. Each name consists of a color, a bird head, and the *che*, "tree," sign (Stuart, cited in Zender 2004b). Stuart has suggested that the bird head is a direct reference to the bird form of Itzamnaaj. The first tree is said to be *chak*, red, but the remaining three names are prefixed with *yax*, blue/green, signs. The red tree of the east is illustrated as a chahk. The south, west, and north *yaxche* trees are each illustrated with a straight trunk that terminates in four leafy branches. These four branches are reminiscent of the ceiba that grew from the cenote at Valladolid noted above. The elements from the T528 *tuun* "stone" sign decorate the trunk.

Numerous researchers have suggested that T528 elements placed on objects indicate that they are made from stone, and that these New Year trees are stone trees like the effigy *Yax Cheel Cab* of the Petén Itzá. T528 elements do appear on stone objects such as ax blades, the mountain symbol, and so on, but I am inclined to believe that they indicate more than just stone. Rather, they indicate that the object is similar in nature to the quintessential stone that hid the corn used to make humans. The most important feature of this corn stone is that it was struck by lightning and became imbued with this engendering force. The association of the ceiba with lightning is very direct: as noted above, the ceiba is a lightning rod.

In the late seventeenth century, Núñez de la Vega described the prominent role of ceibas in Chiapas (Thompson 1950:71). He noted that the Maya elected their leaders under a ceiba tree located on their main square, and that their lineage originated through the roots of the tree. The association of lords and founding ancestors with a tree is common in Mesoamerica. In 1656, Coto (1983:385) noted that the Kaqchikel described their lords as being like a ceiba tree that provided shelter at its roots. The concept of the founding ancestor as a tree is evident in the illustration of the Xiu family tree from northern Yucatan. Here the lineage founder is shown as the roots and trunk of a tree growing from a cave. The various descent lines are shown as branches, and the latest descendants are illustrated as blossoms (Bassie-Sweet 1996, fig. 60). In many contemporary myths, ancestors are manifested as trees. For example, in the Tzotzil hamlet of Paste', an important water hole is located in a limestone sink to the south of the community (Vogt 1969:174, 1976:99). In the myth concerning the discovery of this water source, the first residents of the hamlet noticed a great tree at this location. The residents dug beside the tree without success. Returning the next day, they saw an ancestor standing in place of the tree. As they approached, he was changed into a stump (the tree equivalent of an old man). They interpreted the appearance of the ancestor as a message to keep digging. They did and eventually found the water source.

In Santiago Atitlán, Atitecos build a mound of earth on top of graves and plant a tree there, which is said to represent the soul of the dead who has been reborn as this tree. Christenson notes that the practice is ancient:

> The community cemetery has long rows of graves bearing trees, giving the appearance of a great orchard or grove. Ximénez described a similar practice in highland Guatemala at the beginning of the eighteenth century and noted that persons were frequently buried in the maize fields, an indication that the dead were reborn as maize (1929–1931, I, 100). This is particularly significant with regard to Atiteco traditions of one of their principal culture heroes, Francisco Sojuel, who is believed to have set the pattern for many of the contemporary ritual practices observed today: "When Francisco Sojuel was being persecuted by his enemies they tried to kill him by cutting him into little pieces and sprinkling them with lemon juice and salt. But when they came back the next day they found that his coffin was empty and from it grew a giant zapote tree filled with fruit. People plant zapote trees over the graves of their family in memory of Francisco Sojuel because he did not die." (Christenson 2003a:126–27)

The association of Maya lords and ancestors with the ceiba tree strongly suggests that these community leaders were identified with the Bakab deities, and in fact, the most common title for rulers during the Classic Period was "Bakab." There is a Maya belief that the deceased leaders live on in the caves surrounding the community and continue to look after their people. The ancestral leaders also care for the souls of the departed. The interpretation that the Maya lords were identified with the ceiba tree sheds light on a comment Landa makes about the afterlife. He states that after death the virtuous Maya were destined to rest under the shade of a ceiba (Tozzer 1941:131, 220). In other words, they rested under the care of the Bakabs and the ancestral leaders. This comment also suggests that the paradise of the afterlife was modeled after the role of the ceiba as the shade tree of milpa and town.

## OTHER TREE SPECIES

Although world trees are specifically identified as *yaxche* (ceiba) in many sources, other species appear. The five world trees illustrated in the San Bartolo murals, for example, are clearly five different species. The same is true in Central Mexico, where the *Codex Fejérváry-Mayer* and the *Codex Borgia* illustrate different species of directional trees. This raises the possibility that the world trees of the Maya were metaphorically thought to be *yaxche* trees, but that each was a different species. Regional variations in the environment probably contributed to these differences, but the diverse metaphors used to describe the quadrilateral world may also have been a factor (see chapter 13).

*Ficus* trees were also very significant to the Maya, and some of the beliefs about this tree are similar to those of the ceiba. It is thought that the felling of *Ficus cotinifolia* will cause the rain to stop because it is the source of water (Breedlove and Laughlin 1993:178). If such trees are found near the milpa, the cornfield offering is placed before them. A holy fig tree that informant Nicolás Chávez describes near the sacred Tz'utujil cave called Paq'alib'al is remarkably similar to the world trees, as Christenson notes:

> Near the cave in a small ravine is a giant *po'j* tree (wild fig) where angels rest when it rains, and inside the branches are clouds. The branches are covered with squirrels and birds. A peccary circles the trunk when it is about to rain because clouds and the first rays of dawn begin at this tree. Tremors shake the earth every five minutes there because this is where the *nuwals* (ancestors) live when they leave Paq'alib'al. My great grandfather did not believe in this tree and wanted to use its wood to build a cayuco (canoe) and to burn for firewood. When he began to cut the *po'j* tree, it bled. Immediately he had a stroke and he remained half-paralyzed for the rest of his life. Another man, who didn't believe in the tree, tried to climb it and became a monkey. During the rainy season people gather leaves from the tree at full moon because they are good for medicine. (Christenson 2001:84–85)

Chávez stated that rain clouds came from this tree because it was the birthplace of life and all good things. The tree was also associated with the ancestor named Francisco Sojuel, a powerful rainmaker who was thought to still live in the cave and make rain clouds there (Christenson 2001:98). In another source, this deified tree is said to be the original father-mother who existed before the creation of the world, and that given appropriate offerings, this ancestor would continue to renew and regenerate the world (Carlsen and Prechtel 1991:27). Ceiba trees do not grow well at the high elevations found around Santiago Atitlán, and this may account for the role of the fig tree in this mythology (Allen Christenson, personal communication).

## The Creation of Humans

In the creation story portion of the *Popol Vuh*, the deities struggle with the task of producing beings that will honor them. They begin by making animals, but these creatures are not capable of speech and, therefore, can not make petitions and offerings to them. They then try to make beings of earth, but these mud people simply dissolve. Next they use wood and reeds, but these beings are also dismal failures and have to be destroyed. The wooden people are attacked by their animals and tools, devoured by supernatural beasts, and drowned in a flood sent by Heart of Sky.

The flooding of the world is a common theme not only in Mesoamerica, but around the world. A flood is illustrated in a scene in the *Dresden Codex* (Thompson 1972; Taube 1988b). In this scene, rain pours from the mouth of the Milky Way crocodile and from eclipse signs that hang from its body. An old jaguar goddess creates more rain by pouring water from her jar, and God L is seen brandishing his weapons at the base of the scene. The eclipse signs suggest the flooding occurred during an eclipse, and the Maya still view eclipses as signs that the world is coming to an end. In Quintana Roo, the Yucatec Maya believe that an eclipse will cause all the household tools to attack their owners, much like the destruction of the wooden people in the *Popol Vuh* (Villa Rojas 1945:156). Following the *Dresden Codex* flood scene are the four New Year pages that illustrate the reordering of the world into quadrants (Thompson 1972; Taube 1988b). As discussed above, Bishop Landa also refers to this flood as well as the quadrilateral ordering of the world.

After the flood, the creator deities again try to make humans. This time they decide to use a special corn hidden in a mountain called Paxil, "split," and Cayala, "lime water, bitter or stagnant water." Four wild animals (fox, coyote, parakeet, and raven) are said to have led them to this extraordinary cave:

> These were the names of the animals that obtained their food—fox and coyote, parakeet and raven. Four, then, were the animals that revealed to them the yellow ears of maize and the white ears of maize. They came from Paxil and pointed out the path to get there. Thus was found the food that would become the flesh of the newly framed and shaped people. Water was their blood. It became the blood of humanity. The ears of maize entered into their flesh by means of She Who Has Borne Children and He Who Has Begotten Sons. Thus they rejoiced over the discovery of that excellent mountain that was filled with delicious things, crowded with yellow ears of maize and white ears of maize. It was crowded as well with pataxte and chocolate, with countless zapotes and anonas, with jocotes and nances, with matasanos and honey. From within the places called Paxil and Cayala came the sweetest foods in the citadel. All the small foods and great foods were there, along with the small and great cultivated fields. The path was thus revealed by the animals. (Christenson 2003a:193–94)

The *Annals of the Cakchiquels* version has only two animals: a coyote and a raven (Recinos and Goetz 1953:48). In the contemporary stories referring to the discovery of corn, an array of animals including ants, foxes, and ravens is involved in the discovery. The ants first bring the corn seed out of a small crack in the rock, and then the other animals begin to eat it. The creator grandmother had a coyote manifestation, and it would seem likely that her coyote form was one of the animals that first found the corn seed. The raven appears in corn stories in the Tzotzil and Achi' regions (Vogt 1969:311, 379; Shaw 1971:41; Laughlin 1975:199). In Tzotzil myths from Zinacantan, after the flood, the raven brings humans four colored ears of corn from a mountain called *Na Hoh,* "House of the Raven," located northeast of the community. During the fiesta of San Sebastián, the men who impersonate the raven carry corn ears in their beaks (Vogt 1969:542). These ravens are called *k'uk'ulchon,* "quetzal serpent." Given that the creator grandparents had a quetzal serpent form, the raven of Paxil Mountain may have been one of the avian forms of the creator grandparents.

The corn seed found at Paxil/Cayala was not the first corn the deities used. Prior to the discovery of corn at Paxil/Cayala, corn was being grown in the monkey twins' field, the hero twins planted green corn in their house, and the creator grandparents were using corn kernels as divination lots. I have argued that the Paxil/Cayala corn seeds were the buried remains of Lady Bone Water, One Hunahpu's first wife. This goddess and her Classic Period counterpart, Ixik, represent the ear of corn and its seed (Bassie-Sweet 2002; see also chapter 8).

As noted in chapter 1, many of the contemporary stories indicate that a lightning god had to break open either the mountain or the stone under which the corn was hidden with a thunderbolt (Burkitt 1920; Oakes 1951:244; Thompson 1954:273, 1970:354; Mayers 1958; Miles 1960; Vogt 1969; Edmonson 1971:146; Laughlin and Karasik 1988:203; Montejo and Campbell 1993; Preuss 1993; Christenson 2001). Humans were made specifically from the white corn and yellow corn. Xmucane ground the lightning-struck corn into fine dough and mixed it with water, and from this material the first human beings were modeled. The role of lightning in creation is akin to the belief that a cornfield must be struck by lightning to be able to germinate.

A creation myth told in the *Leyenda de los soles* from Central Mexico has thematic parallels with Maya creation stories (Bierhorst 1992:146–47). In this myth, Quetzalcoatl goes down to the underworld and retrieves the bones of the humans from the previous creation. After he delivers the bones at Tamoanchan, the goddess Quilaztli/Cihuacoatl grinds them and places them in a jade bowl. Six gods, including Quetzalcoatl, bleed onto the bones, which gives life to the new humans. Queztalcoatl then goes to find food for the new humans and sees a red ant carrying corn seeds. The ant tells him that he obtained the seeds from inside Tonacatepetl (Sustenance) Mountain. Quetzalcoatl transforms himself into a black ant, and together the ants enter the mountain, retrieve the seeds, and carry the grains back to Tamoanchan. The gods chew the grains and place them on the mouths of the newly formed humans to give them strength. Quetzalcoatl attempts to move Tonacatepetl but fails. The diviners Oxomoco and Cipactonal then perform a divination and ascertain that the thunderbolt Nanahuatl should be the one to strike open the mountain so that humans would have corn to grow and eat.

Divination is closely linked to seeing; the *Popol Vuh* stresses that the vision of the first fathers gave them powers of divination.

> They had their breath, therefore they became. They were able to see as well, for straightaway their vision came to them. Perfect was their sight, and perfect was their knowledge of everything beneath the sky. If they gazed about them, looking intently, they beheld that which was in the sky and that which was upon the earth. Instantly they were able to behold everything. They did not have to walk to see all that existed beneath the sky. They merely saw it from wherever they were. Thus their knowledge became full. Their vision passed beyond the trees and the rocks, beyond the lakes and the seas, beyond the mountains and the valleys. Truly they were very esteemed people, these Balam Quitze, Balam Acab, Mahucutah, and Iqui Balam. (Christenson 2003a:197–98)

When the creator gods realized that these first humans had perfect sight, they decided to withdraw some of this divination power so that the humans would not surpass them:

> Their knowledge of everything that they saw was complete—the four corners and the four sides, that which is within the sky and that which is within the earth. But this did not sound good to the Framer and the Shaper: "It is not good what they have said, they that we have framed and shaped. They said, 'We have learned everything, great and small.'" Thus their knowledge was taken back by She Who Has Borne Children and He Who Has Begotten Sons: "What now can be done to them so that their vision reaches only nearby, so that only a little of the face of the earth can be seen by them? For it is not good what they say. Is not their existence merely framed, merely shaped? It is a mistake that they have become like gods. But if they do not multiply or are increased, when will the first planting be? When will it dawn? If they do not increase, when will it be so? Therefore we will merely undo them a little now. That is what is wanted, because it is not good what we have found out. Their works will merely be equated with ours. Their knowledge will extend to the furthest reaches, and they will see everything." Thus spoke Heart of Sky and Huracan, Youngest Thunderbolt and Sudden Thunderbolt, Sovereign and Quetzal Serpent, She Who Has Borne Children and He Who Has Begotten Sons, Xpiyacoc and Xmucane, the Framer and the Shaper, as they are called. Thus they remade the essence of that which they had framed and shaped. Their eyes were merely blurred by Heart of Sky. They were blinded

like breath upon the face of a mirror. Thus their eyes were blinded. They could see only nearby; things were clear to them only where they were. (Christenson 2003a:199–201)

The newly created humans reproduced and populated the world, but they did so in darkness, for Hunahpu and Xbalanque, who would become sun and full moon, had not yet risen into the sky. The first leaders journeyed to a city called Tulan Zuyva, Seven Caves and Seven Canyons, to obtain their political legitimacy and patron gods. From this city, they carried their patron gods and migrated to new locations. After setting up their patron guardians in the surrounding landscape of their new communities, they waited for the rising of the sun (Hunahpu). After Venus rose as morning star, the sun finally rose in the east and the annual rhythm of life began. The latter sections of the *Popol Vuh* detail the journey of the sons of the founding fathers to Tulan to obtain more symbols of authority, describe the migrations and victories of the various K'iche' lords, and explain how the K'iche' came to dominate the other groups of central highland Guatemala.

Mesoamericans had a long history of obtaining symbols of political legitimacy and authority from a foreign polity (for example, see A. Stone 1989; Byland and Pohl 1994; Ringle 2004). In many instances, this polity was explicitly named the Place of Reeds (Tollan, Tullan, or Tulan). While there has been much debate over where Tulan of the *Popol Vuh* was located, there is consensus among researchers that many cities were at various times identified as the Place of Reeds, such as Teotihuacan, Tula, Tenochtitlan, Cholula, Chontalpa, Mayapan, and Chichén Itzá. Stuart (2000a) has proposed that the Place of Reeds for the Classic Maya was Teotihuacan. Schele and Mathews (1998:39) have argued that the concept extended back into Olmec times, and that the original model for the Place of Reeds was Lake Catemaco in the Tuxtla Mountains of Verapaz.

Postclassic accounts of the Place of Reeds describe it as a paradise of abundance and a source of great knowledge and artistry. It was full of wonderful foods and cotton of multiple colors, and all the birds with precious feathers lived there, including the quetzal and cotinga. It is apparent that the Place of Reeds replicated the house of the creator grandparents at the center of the world, which, in turn, replicated the place of duality in the heavens. I will argue in later chapters that Maya concepts concerning the place of duality were based on the features found in the region around Lake Atitlán in highland Guatemala.

## REPLICATION OF THE WORLD MODEL

In order to create a safe human space, the Maya replicated the quadrilateral world model or parts of that model. As noted above, the Postclassic Yucatan town was a quadrilateral space with four ritual locations representing the directional mountains on each side of town. Idols representing the gods of the four directions were found on top of these symbolic mountains, and annual New Year ceremonies were conducted there. In addition to man-made locations, the Maya believed that mountains and caves in the vicinity of the community also represented the four directional mountains. These mountains and their deities defined the safe space of the community. In the highlands of northwestern Guatemala, the New Year ceremonies are still conducted on such mountains.

The narrative on Quirigua Stela C that describes the mythological placement of three hearthstones on the 13.0.0.0.0 Period Ending indicates that each was placed adjacent to an altar. This action is highly evocative of a ceremony Landa described in which travelers created a ritual space by placing three small stones on the ground (Tozzer 1941:107). They then placed a flat stone in front of each stone to make a small altar on which to make offerings. The Maya also replicate the world model when they create a cornfield. In his discussion of replication, Christenson (2003a:65) notes: "By laying out the maize field, or setting up a ritual table, the Maya transform secular models into sacred space. With regard to the maize field, this charges the ground with the power of creation to bear new life." By replicating the place of duality and the directional mountains in their towns and milpas, and designating sacred sites in the natural landscape, the Maya created locations where offerings could be made to the creator deities to ensure the safe continuation of life. This ritual activity was not only structured according to the cosmological model, but constantly validated that model (Sosa 1985).

# 5

# WATER, WIND, AND DIVINATION

Our understanding of the place of duality and the creator deities who originated there can be amplified by examining Maya concepts associated with water, wind, and divination. The Maya often depicted water naturalistically. In the codices, they represented both rain and standing bodies of water with wavy black lines on a blue background. On sculpture and pottery, they depicted water as lines, dots, and beads with shells and water plants floating in it (fig. 5.1).

Water scrolls indicate turbulent or flowing water. In some examples, such as the rain flooding the world on *Dresden Codex* 74, falling water is shown with a scroll shape (fig. 5.2). These water scrolls often have a beaded edge. Similar falling liquid is depicted on several Yaxchilan stelae, where it pours from the hands of a ruler performing a Period Ending–renewal ceremony (fig. 5.3a). Beaded liquid also occurs in the God C *k'uh/k'ul*, "god, holy," sign (fig. 5.3b). A number of signs may appear infixed in the liquid, including the k'an "yellow" sign, the yax "blue/green, fresh" sign, a shell sign, a water lily sign, and a T24 jade sign, all of which directly relate to water.

Most of the early researchers concluded that this beaded liquid represented water, and Thompson (1950) nicknamed the liquid in the God C sign as "the water group." Schele (in Schele and Miller 1986) and Stuart (1988), on the other hand, identified the beaded liquid of the *k'uh* sign as blood rather than water. They believed that in the Yaxchilan contexts, the ruler was letting blood from his genitals and collecting it in a container, and they concluded that all beaded liquid was blood. However, based on a phonetic decipherment for the T683 sign as *muyal*, "cloud," Stuart later revised his interpretation and concluded that beaded scrolls that appear to float in the air refer to clouds (fig. 5.3c; Stuart and Houston 1994:44). Stuart (2003b:4) has since deciphered another sign that has the value of *k'ik'*, "blood." Given the clear use of the beaded-liquid motif to represent rain in the *Dresden Codex*, I believe that the liquid of the *k'uh*

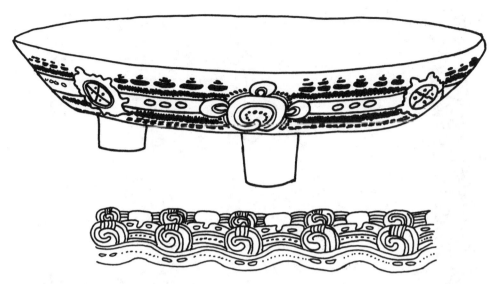

Figure 5.1. Standing water (after Hellmuth)

Figure 5.2. *Dresden Codex* 74 (after Villacorta)

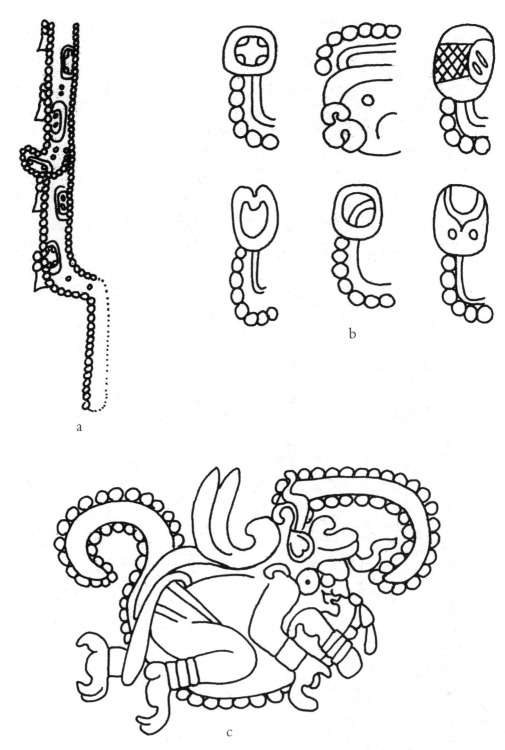

Figure 5.3. Water and cloud symbols: a. Yaxchilan Stela 1 liquid; b. emblem glyph prefixes; c. paddler god riding a beaded scroll that represents a cloud

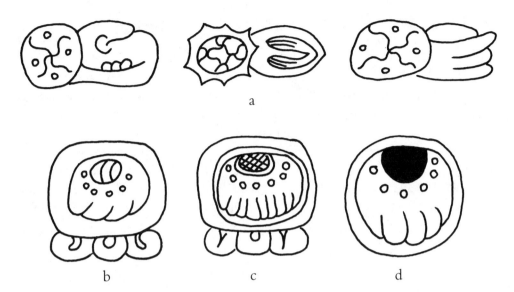

Figure 5.4. a. Water lily signs; b.–d. T501 *Imix* signs

## The Water Lily

sign represents water. Clouds are illustrated with the same beaded edge because they are full of rainwater.

### THE WATER LILY

In the Maya area, still bodies of water are frequently covered with water lilies, and these plants were used as a symbol for water (Rands 1955). The tzolk'in day name *Imix* is represented by the T501 sign—a water lily blossom. In the hieroglyphic texts, the blossom and root of a water lily represent the word *nahb*, "sea, still water," while the blossom by itself (T501) represents the word *ha'*, "water" (Fox and Justeson 1984; Stuart and Houston 1994:19), and is used to form the word *ha'al*, "rain" (fig. 5.4 a–b; Houston, Robertson, and Stuart 2001; Lacadena 2004). The turtle that represents the surface of the earth is often illustrated with water lilies attached, a symbol that evokes the earth floating on the waters of the place of duality. Some examples of the T501 water lily sign have a crosshatched circle (fig. 5.4c). Cross-hatching on stone monuments is a convention often used to indicate the color black, and in painted examples of the T501 sign, the infix is frequently painted black (fig. 5.4d). The place of duality was described as a dark place.

The symbols found in many Classic Period ritual scenes indicate they took place at water shrines that replicated the waters of the place of duality. These scenes often incorporate the water lily in their hieroglyphic place name and in the basal register (Bassie-Sweet 1996:69–80). Numerous scenes illustrate gods at watery locations that also likely represent the waters of the place of duality. A scene on a Tikal ceramic vessel illustrates a god filling his jar from such a body of water (fig. 5.5a). The jar takes the form of a serpent. The interior of the jar is marked with the T504 *ak'bal,* "darkness," sign, which means "night" in almost all Mayan languages. *Ak'bal*-marked jars are common in Maya art and were used by the gods to dispense rain. Although it has been suggested that the *ak'bal* sign is used in these contexts to refer to dark rain clouds (Taube 2004:77), I think the *ak'bal* sign may also refer to the dark water of the place of duality—the ultimate source of this dark rainwater. Herman Beyer (1928) has identified the T504 *ak'bal* sign as a pictograph representing the markings found on the body of a feathered serpent. The feathered serpent on Copan Altar O illustrates this observation (fig. 5.5b). The crosshatched circles on the body are mirror signs (Taube 1992b). The relationship between a mirror and the reflective surface of water is obvious.

## THE CONCH SHELL AS WATER AND WIND

Conch shells (*Strombus* sp.) were used to indicate both water and wind. An element composed of stacked rectangles that represents the tapering point of a conch shell appears in many depictions of water. It is frequently juxtaposed with a water lily sign to indicate water (see fig. 5.1a; Hellmuth 1987). Three conch shells appear in the T143 sign that represents the word *ha'al,* "rain," again reinforcing the conch's close identification with water (Lacadena 2004:91). God N is often illustrated carrying a conch shell on his back, emerging from a shell, or juxtaposed with it. The conch form of God N demonstrates Itzamnaaj/God N's intimate relationship with the waters of the place of duality. A close association between a conch shell and water is found in the depictions of San Gregorio at Santiago Atitlán (O'Brien 1975:119). It is believed that when a person drowns in the lake and the body is not recovered, the soul goes to live at the bottom of the lake. San Gregorio, who also lives in the lake, is thought to rule over these souls. A conch shell is found on the statue of this saint in the church and is thought to signify his habitation in the lake and his rule over these lost souls.

The logograph for wind or breath is T503, the T-shaped *ik'* sign. Wind or breath is often represented in Maya art by a pair of symmetrical scrolls curving outward from the source of the wind or breath, and the T shape of the *ik'* sign may be a stylized form of the double scroll (Houston and Taube 2000:270; Taube 2001:108–109; 2003). Wind or breath also takes the form of a serpent who blows wind scrolls from his mouth (Looper and Kappelman 2001; Taube 2003). The conch shell was used as a wind instrument in Mesoamerica. The blowing of a conch shell to announce the beginning of a ceremony was common in the Maya region, and Robert Redfield (1936:241) noted that conch shells were used in modern times to announce fiestas. The conch shell has long been recognized as a symbol of wind—in particular, the whirling, howling wind of a rainstorm. The close association between wind and water is also seen on the Palenque Temple XIV tablet where the young lord Kan

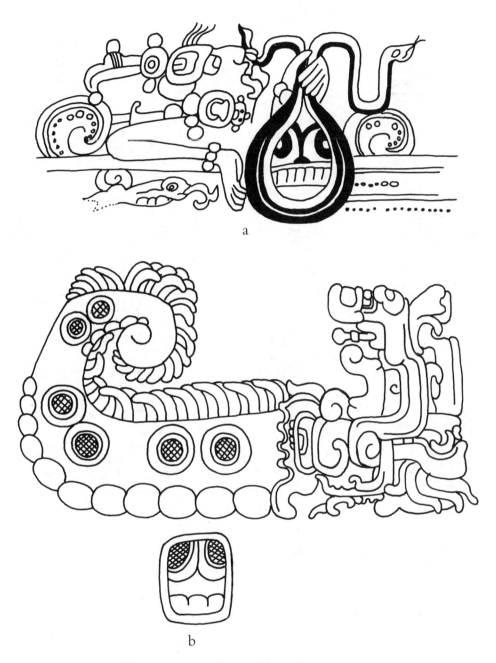

Figure 5.5. a. vessel from Tikal Burial 160; b. feathered serpent from Copan altar

B'ahlam is illustrated performing a pre-accession ritual with his mother (Bassie-Sweet 1991:223). They stand beside a body of water that is marked with T503 *ik'* wind signs and T501 *ha'* water signs.

In the San Bartolo murals, the Preclassic version of One Ixim/One Hunahpu blows wind in the form of a conch shell, and on Kaminaljuyu Stela 9 (500 B.C.), a

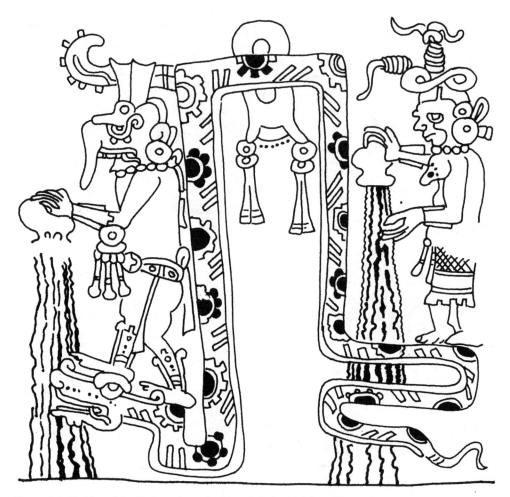

Figure 5.6. Chahk and Ix Chel creating rain, *Madrid Codex* 30 (after Villacorta)

male who is likely also a version of One Ixim/One Hunahpu stands on top of a crocodile's back with the conch shell/wind emanating from his mouth (Houston and Taube 2000:265; Saturno, Taube, and Stuart 2005:1). The close association of One Ixim/One Hunahpu and wind will be discussed in chapters 8 and 15.

## WATER SERPENTS

The ancient Maya often represented water as a serpent, and the spirit of water is still represented by a serpent (Bassie-Sweet 1996:81). Examples of water serpents are found on *Madrid Codex* 30a, where Chahk and Ix Chel pour water from their jars and dispense rain. They stand on a serpent that represents the path of rain across the sky (fig. 5.6). Ix Chel's headdress represents a serpent that is related to the making of rain-filled clouds. In numerous Classic pottery scenes, Chahk's *ak'bal* rain jar hangs

Figure 5.7. a.–c. Water bird serpents (after Hellmuth)

upside-down on his chest with water serpents emerging from it (Bassie-Sweet 1991, fig. 43).

Many of the serpents illustrated in Maya art are decorated with a row of feathers running down their backs or a crest of feathers on their snout and body. A supernatural bird wearing a water lily headdress is illustrated moving through water in several pottery scenes. The bird also appears as the Number 13 Deity and as one of the birds used to represent the tun period. The bird has a long, hooked beak, the body of a serpent, and a crest of feathers on its back. In several examples of this water lily bird, the serpent body is decorated with water and shells or marked with large circles representing mirrors (figs. 5.7a–b). In other illustrations, a T501 water sign surrounded by layered water replaces the serpent body (fig. 5.7c). The conflation of water symbols and mirrors with the serpent body indicates that the body represents water. The use of a feathered serpent to symbolize water is not limited to visual imagery. As noted, the creator grandparents were manifested in the waters of the place of duality as Sovereign and Quetzal Serpent. The blue and green feathers of Quetzal Serpent were a metaphor for the shimmering light reflected off the water's surface.

## DIVINATION

The ancient Maya consulted diviners in all aspects of their lives, from the mundane to the sacred. The waters of the place of duality were intimately associated with divination. The first diviners were the creator grandparents, who were called upon to perform a number of divinations during the creation of humans and the ordering of the earth. The 260-day tzolk'in calendar was the organizing principle behind prognostications. In the Maya system of reckoning time, each day also had several interrelated designations that referred to its position in such cycles as the haab, the k'atun, the Supplementary Series, the Lunar Series, and the greater Venus cycle. The Maya believed that a different deity or combination of deities ruled each period within these cycles and that these deities influenced the fortune of the events that occurred during these periods. The messages that the diviners received during their prognostications apparently came from the deities in power on the day in question. Messages could also be sent in dreams or when the diviner was in trance. In order to be effective, the diviner had to understand these various cycles, how they were interconnected, and who the ruling deities were. Divination provided a means for foreseeing the future as well as analyzing a current crisis and developing a suitable solution. Divinations facilitated the resolution of conflict and could be used as a tool for adaptive change. It is important to stress that the Maya were not fatalistically resigned to the predetermined nature of the time period. The Postclassic Maya, for example, attempted to modify or nullify the negative characteristics of the coming year by making petitions and offerings to Itzamnaaj and four deities known as Chi Chahk Chob, Ek Balam Chahk, Ah Canuol Cab and Ah Buluc Balam (Tozzer 1941:139–48). The divination system was not rigid and inflexible, but an innovative method of bringing a sense of control and order to life.

Prognostication was accomplished using several different techniques. A prominent method was the casting of lots. The diviner most frequently used corn kernels, but bones, seeds, rock crystals, or small stones were also used (Tozzer 1907:163, 1912: 505; Saville 1921:206; Edmonson 1971:59; Orellana 1987:54). The Tzotzil use corn kernels as counters in many ritual procedures (Vogt 1969:63). In the *Popol Vuh* and in modern K'iche' practice, divination lots are referred to metaphorically as corn kernels (Rodas, Rodas, and Hawkins 1940:68; Edmonson 1971:22; B. Tedlock 1982; D. Tedlock 1996:70). Originally, 260 seeds were used, one for each day in the calendar.

One of the descriptions from the sixteenth century describes a Tz'utujil prognostication in which the community elders threw corn seeds on "some ancient paintings by which they used to count the months and year" (Orellana 1987:54). Where the seeds landed dictated the date of the coming event. In all likelihood, these ancient paintings were a divination codex like the books illustrated in Classic Period art. Barbara Tedlock (1982:153–71) describes the modern K'iche' process of casting lots as mixing, grabbing, choosing, and arranging piles of seeds. Although this is a complicated affair involving many steps, the casting action involves the diviner blowing into his right hand and then grasping a handful of his divining seeds. He sorts these seeds into units of four and then uses the day names to count out these arrangements. The diviner repeats this sorting and counting process several times. Through "the lightning in his blood," he receives messages as he counts, and he interprets these messages according to the day name on which they occur. The day name's "face" or nature establishes the fortune of the event. These day names reveal to him any problems or issues related to the client's question or problem and provide him with an answer or solution. In pre-Columbian divination, the "face" of the day name and the "face" of the k'atun were said to determine the nature of the time period. A divination method that is related to the lightning in the blood is called pulsing. This technique involves the ritual specialist feeling either his own pulse or that of his client.

Tzotzil curing ceremonies also use corn seeds for divination purposes. Thirteen kernels from each of the four colors of corn are placed in a "soul-calling" gourd that holds salt water (Vogt 1969:422; Breedlove and Laughlin 1993:580). The ritual specialist counts the positions of the kernels and interprets what this means in terms of the patient's soul. A Tzotzil term for corn kernels is *ssat,* "its face" (Breedlove and Laughlin 1993:491). The modern Atiteco ritual cloth that represents the three kinds of corn has divination qualities as well: "An ajkun [daykeeper] can place the cloth on the belly of the female client, face downward. Whatever looks at the navel will give the child its 'face.' The cloth will give the child the propitious 'face' of one of the three corns" (Tarn and Prechtel 1986:175).

A second method of divination was scrying, the study of reflective surfaces (Taube 1983, 1992b; Furst 1995:94). This technique involved interpreting the light or movement seen on reflective surfaces such as natural pools of water, rock crystals, the liquid in a bowl, or a circular mirror placed in the bottom of a bowl. In addition, the lots used in divination casting were sometimes placed in a bowl of liquid. Pre-Columbian mirrors were often constructed from many small pieces of reflective material, such as pyrite, attached to a backing. Such a mirror did not produce a clear image but one full of reflections suitable for divination (Taube 1983, 1992b).

Brinton (1883:245) describes the prevalent practice in Yucatan of using a divination crystal. In the Yucatec Maya community of Yalcoba, the ritual specialist places his divining stones in a small cup of water or liquor and makes predictions according to what he sees (Sosa 1985:309). In Santa Eulalia, the ritual specialist is said to look into a pool of blood or water in the sacred cave and make the prophecy for the new year (La Farge and Byers 1931:183).

As noted, the first K'iche' humans were created with perfect vision that gave them powerful divination skills. The K'iche' verb *iloh* means both to see and to divine: the crystals used in divination are called *ilobal,* and the principal crystal is called *ilol,* "seer" (Edmonson 1965:46; B. Tedlock 1982:159). The vision of these first fathers was later blurred in order to diminish their divination skills; the *Popol Vuh* text says that Heart of Sky blurred their vision like breath on a mirror. It is likely that the importance of mirrors in pre-Columbian times was related to the tradition of gazing at reflective surfaces for divination purposes. The reflective surfaces of these circular divination tools represented the pooled water of the place of duality. Divination knowledge was therefore linked to the waters of this sea and, by extension, to the creator grandparents who lived there.

The continuing, fundamental role of water in divination is found in the world view, initiation rituals, and divination methods of the modern K'iche' of Momostenango, who have four sacred lakes, one for each direction (Atitlán, Lemoa, Pasocop, and Pachi'ul; B. Tedlock 1982:54, 139, 157). They believe that the "clear light" of divinatory knowledge is transferred from the four lakes via chilly, moist air, and they describe this air as the breath, the chilly wind, the cloud, and the mist from the four directions. Certain illnesses and dreams are viewed by the Maya as an indication that the person is being called upon by the gods to become a diviner (B. Tedlock 1982: 54). The association between water and divination knowledge is evident in the dreams a diviner has before he begins his career. Dreaming of a lake is one indication that the ritual specialist is ready to receive divination knowledge; the lake is described as a mirror (B. Tedlock 1982:54, 139). Snakes also play a role in these dreams. In an Ixil dream, the dreamer thought he was walking on the waters of Lake Atitlán when a snake entered his left foot, traveled up his body, through his head, down his right side and out his right foot (Lincoln 1942:121). This was a clear sign he must become a diviner. "Snake illness," characterized as sudden body cramps, is one of the main illnesses that afflict people destined to be diviners.

The nature of some K'iche' ceremonies also indicates that water contains divination knowledge. The ritual specialists of Momostenango bring back water from the four lakes and place it in their local springs. This water both purifies the spring and adds divination information to it (B. Tedlock 1982:139). During the initiation ceremony of a diviner, water from the spring is sprinkled on his bundle that contains his divining tools (B. Tedlock 1982:65). This act adds divination knowledge to these objects.

Lightning also plays a key role in divination. Sheet lightning is the bright flash of light seen in the sky when the lightning bolt occurs inside or behind a cloud. It can also be observed as a reflection on the surface of water. Sheet lightning is usually called heat lightning when it occurs so far away that no thunder is directly associated with it. The bright flash of lightning is called *coyopa* in a number of highland Maya languages (B. Tedlock 1982:138) and *sak tzeul* in Tzotzil (Laughlin 1975:302). K'iche' diviners believe that they have a kind of soul in their blood in the form of sheet lightning. When a diviner experiences tingling or twitching in his muscles, it is thought to be the movement of the lightning in his blood, and these movements provide him with the answer to whatever question he has posited (B. Tedlock 1982: 53, 110, 138). As noted, the regents of a particular day are ultimately thought to convey these answers. The intimate relationship between the lightning in the blood and the prognostications using the 260-day tzolk'in calendar may explain the Classic Period convention of showing the day names in a cartouche, which Stuart (2005a: 92) has identified as a sign for blood. In painted versions of these signs, the cartouche is painted red. These day glyphs literally show the day regents in blood.

People who are destined to become diviners often experience dreams that symbolize that the Mundo (earth lord) wants them to begin their vocation (B. Tedlock 1982:54). As noted above, to dream of a lake indicates that the lightning in their blood is ready to move and give them answers to their divination questions. Tedlock's informant described the relationship like this: "A lake is like a mirror, not moving until one's day comes, and then it begins to move with the lightning." The association of mirrors and lightning is seen in the term *lem,* which means brilliant, shiny, or flashing, in many Mayan languages, but it is also used to refer to mirrors, lightning, and sheet lightning (Schele and Miller 1983:13).

This lightning in the blood is related to the waters of the place of duality, for it is equated with the sheet lightning that occurs over the sacred lakes (B. Tedlock 1982: 138). The diviners describe the sensation of the lightning in the blood to be "as if air were rapidly moving through their flesh in a flickering or undulating manner, similar to the pattern of exterior sheet lightning as it moves at night over the lakes" (B. Tedlock 1982:53). The undulating manner of the sheet lightning is reminiscent of the movement of snakes.

In addition, when the diviner casts his divination lots, he specifically says that he is receiving his divination knowledge not only from the moist air, but also from the sheet lightning from the sacred lakes (B. Tedlock 1982:155). The crystals used in the divination process are also associated with lightning, and they are thought to draw the lightning from the four directions (B. Tedlock 1982:160). During their divinations, K'iche' diviners study the refracted light in their crystals and refer to this light as lightning (Allen Christenson, personal communication).

Sheet lightning is also used by the Momostecan diviners to predict rain. When it is seen at night coming from the direction of the north or east sacred lakes, the rain will stop, but if it comes from the west or south sacred lakes, the rain will come (B. Tedlock 1982:139). The association of sheet lightning with the sea is also found in the Tzotzil and Tzeltal region. In the Tzotzil area, heat lightning is thought to be sea-foam cast into the sky by the ocean (Laughlin 1975:302). The Tzeltal say that heat lightning is the older brother of the lightning bolt who fell into the sea (Hermitte 1964:43).

This overview of divination practices suggests the central role that wind, water, and lightning played in transmitting knowledge from the creator deities to humans. As noted, the *Popol Vuh* describes the creator grandparents in the sea of duality as luminous beings covered in quetzal and cotinga feathers. The term *saqtetoj,* used to describe their luminosity, is glossed in a colonial dictionary as "the brightness that enters through cracks" (D. Tedlock 1996:222). Given the K'iche' beliefs about divination, sheet lightning, wind, snakes, and the sacred lakes, it seems reasonable to conclude that this brightness in the waters of the sea of duality was sheet lightning, and that Feathered Serpent was a manifestation of the creator grandparents as sheet lightning. The serpent portion of this name is directly related to their role as wind, water, and lightning deities because there was a prevalent Maya belief that the spirit of wind, water, and lightning could take the form of a serpent.

### The Divination Skills of Itzamnaaj

Itzamnaaj's name suggests an affiliation with divination and the waters of the place of duality because *itzam* is defined as "magician of the waters" (Barrera Vásquez 1980:272). Like Xpiyacoc and Xmucane, Itzamnaaj and Ix Chel were the deities of medicine whom the priests and healers invoked in their prayers (Thompson 1939; Tozzer 1941:153–55; Taube 1992a). They are also mentioned in the *Ritual of the Bacabs* incantations for curing certain diseases (Roys 1965). Itzamnaaj was considered to have been the first priest and the role model for human priests (Tozzer 1941: 153–54). In Yucatan, the high priest wore a costume similar to one worn by Itzamnaaj in the codices, and both priest and deity wore this costume while dispensing dew (Tozzer 1941:105; Taube 1992a:34). The high priest was called *Ah K'in Mai* and *Ahau Can Mai. Ah K'in,* "he of the day," refers to his role as a daykeeper, while *Ahau Can* (a name for the rattlesnake) may refer to his role as a dispenser of dew. Like the creator grandfather, who gave advice to the other deities through his divinations, the high priest was a sage who gave advice to the lords (Tozzer 1941:27). The calendrical knowledge and literary skills of the high priest echoed those of the creator grandfather, who, in addition to being the quintessential daykeeper, was credited with the invention of writing. He was also the role model for the hereditary descent of the high priest's office, for the children and grandchildren of the creator grandfather also possessed his literary and divination skills.

### The Work of the Diviner

Diviners guided individuals and the community by means of their prognostications. Diviners were supposed to adhere to the highest moral and ethical principles, to use their skills in a positive and socially responsible fashion, and to be role models for proper human behavior. The most important attribute of the diviner was a spiritually strong soul. It was thought that a strong soul allowed diviners to direct their co-essences to carry out many supernatural duties. The superior spiritual power of the diviners also allowed them to withstand the dangers of communicating with supernatural beings.

Diviners did not simply pull their revelations out of thin air. To be effective in their occupation, they had to have their finger on the pulse of the community and understand its political, economic, and social relationships. They also had to understand the natural cycles of the world and the role of the deities in creating and maintaining these cycles. This required an awareness of the structure and function of the calendar cycle and its effect on human existence. A diviner's comprehension encompassed all of the celestial cycles as well as important events such as eclipses. Another essential skill was the ability to create, read, and revise the divination almanacs. The initial education of a diviner, therefore, included a wide range of subjects such as mythology, history, calendars, astronomy, writing, and healing arts.

A description of the initial training of a K'iche' diviner in the early twentieth century details this extensive preparation:

> The education of a chuch kahau requires at least three years. His instructor is an older chuch kahau, his spiritual father. The young man has to learn the cholomkih (calendar) thoroughly and the art of seed-sorting (divination). He must learn to interpret dreams, for the ancestors give certain instructions in dreams. He must know when and where and how to make offerings and pray to the gods and the ancestors; and he must know the signs of whether his prayer is accepted or not. He must be instructed in the conduct of his relations with his clients or patients and in all the customs, beliefs, and ethical principles of his people. (Rodas, Rodas, and Hawkins 1940:71)

Diviners were repositories of cosmological information as well as teachers and maintainers of a community world view. The numerous texts and depictions of elite activities found in Maya art indicate a great deal of visiting and exchange between diviners of different communities. They were also prominent members of pilgrimages. These journeys were ideal opportunities for the dissemination of knowledge.

Diviners also played an important role in maintaining affiliations with groups that had migrated from the original community. An example is the highland Guatemalan town of El Palmar, which was founded in the mid-nineteenth century by people from Momostenango (Saler 1960). As would be expected, the locations chosen to define the sacred landscape of El Palmar were modeled after those of Momostenango. Despite having their own ritual sites, some El Palmar diviners occasionally go to Momostenango and perform their renewal rituals at the even more powerful ancestral altars. Momostenango daykeepers working on the coast who can not make the long pilgrimage back home to renew their divination tools go to the altars at El Palmar. There are no longer any economic or political ties between these communities, but a connection is maintained through the interactions of the diviners.

## LEVELS OF OFFICE HELD BY THE DIVINER

Despite having a strong soul, a contemporary diviner begins his career in a spiritually weak state in comparison with more mature diviners. He gains strength from a lifetime of the various religious and political offices he attains. This upward movement through the community hierarchy provides experience, wisdom, and prestige. The following discussion of modern Tzotzil diviners emphasizes the importance of holding office and its relationship to supernatural power:

> A man acquires supernatural power and prestige through holding office. The rank of office holder, like the status of old age, is based on supernatural power, which implies authority and control over others. A man and his wife holding or having held office are qualified as pan-wil—"they have heated their souls." Those in office are called by their office title. . . . The prestige and power accorded the office holder is cumulative, and related to his ascension to higher positions in his service to the community and the saints. . . . He who serves the people and the saints is uplifted, enhanced, exalted: he becomes greater and "sees the world in an ever clearer light." (Guiteras Holmes 1961:72)

In Momostenango, a K'iche' area, modern novices begin their career by acquiring the office of *poronel,* "burner" (B. Tedlock 1982). The training for this office involves learning how to burn incense at public shrines and recite the proper prayers to invoke the deities. This initial training also includes education in cosmology, astronomical observations, curing, and proper ritual behavior. After obtaining the office of poronel, diviners progress through a second training period, at the end of which they acquire the office of *ajk'ij,* "he of the day," also known as daykeeper. This title refers specifically to the diviner's ability to cast lots and receive messages from the day regents. These diviners can then go on and acquire other offices such as healer (midwife or bonesetter), singer, marriage broker, or spiritualist. A diviner may also become the head diviner for his lineage, thus acquiring the office called mother-father. He may then go on to become the mother-father of the canton and then the town. The power and duties of these senior diviners are cumulative, and they are obligated to train the novice diviners. The offices in the traditional civil hierarchy of the Momostenango municipality (the Auxiliary Organization) are also available to him. The highest post in this organization is that of mayor, called *ilol katinimit,* "seer of our town."

Suzanna Miles (1955) observes that entries in the Morán dictionary indicate that the Postclassic Poqomam had a hierarchy of divination-related offices. The lowland Maya had a number of offices related to divination as well. For example, the *aj k'in,* "he of the day," title appears in the inscription of Xcalumkin (Stuart, cited in Schele and Miller 1986:138). As noted above, the Postclassic priests in northern Yucatan also held the office of *aj k'in.* Like the K'iche' *ajk'ij,* "he of the day," title, this title refers to the priest's use of the 260-day count in prognostications. Landa's comments concerning the highest-ranking *aj k'in* priests indicate that their duties involved attending to the major festivals, divining for the lords, healing, teaching and initiating novice priests, and producing and distributing the divination almanacs (Tozzer 1941: 27). The title of *ajk'uhuun* was one of the most common offices held by secondary lords and royal women during the Classic Period, and Zender (2004b) has argued that it was parallel to the Postclassic *aj k'in* office.

The duties of the Postclassic priest also included the preparation, distribution, and burning of incense as offerings for the gods. In modern K'iche' society, the acquisition of the poronel, "burner," office entitles the novice diviner to invoke a deity or deities and make offerings to them at public shrines. It implies that he knows which deity to invoke, which prayers to use, and the correct amount and kinds of offerings. During the Classic Period, there was an office called *ch'ahom.* This title is composed of a stylized fist prefixed to a pictograph of a ball of incense. The full-figure variant shows a man putting incense into a burner (Schele, Stuart, and Grube 1989). The *ch'ahom* office was held by a ritual specialist who knew how to make offerings of incense, and like the modern office, it is implied that this specialist was trained in the fundamentals necessary to invoke the deities.

Another modern K'iche' office with a pre-Columbian parallel is that of spiritualist. The ancestors and sacred mountains speak through spiritualists while they are in a trance (B. Tedlock 1982:74). The Postclassic *chilam,* whose duty "was to give the replies of the gods to the people" had a similar role (Tozzer 1941:112). In the *Chilam Balam of Tizimin,* the prophecy of the *chilam* was produced in a trance state: "He retired to a room in his house where he lay prostrate in a trance while the god or spirit, perched on the ridgepole of the house, spoke to the unconscious chilan [*sic*] below" (Roys 1933:182).

The Classic Period parallel of the *chilam* was the *ti'sakhuun,* who was a prophet, oracular priest, and spokesman for the ruler (Zender 2004b).

Another office that appears frequently in the Classic Period texts is that of *ah ts'ib* (Stuart, cited in Schele and Miller 1986; Stuart 1987). The word *ts'ib* refers to writing, painting, engraving, and similar acts that created figures, such as embroidery and brocade work, and the *ah ts'ib* title has been glossed as scribe, writer, artist, and painter (Stuart 1987, 1989; Reents-Budet 1994). A pictographic version of this sign shows a hand drawing or writing with an implement. In the upper text of a Classic Period pottery scene, the phonetic rendering of the *ah ts'ib* title is followed by a portrait of a scribe writing in a codex (K6020). A motif associated with divination has been nicknamed the "computer printout" (Coe 1973, 1978). It represents a sheet of paper inscribed with numbers. The *ah ts'ib* has one of these "computation papers" emerging from under his arm. Like the bar-and-dot notations in the codices, this sheet of paper likely represents a counting of days or an inventory. On *Madrid Codex* 73, Chahk has this computation paper emerging from his mouth. He holds a brush and inkpot for writing. Most examples of the computation paper are drawn like vegetation, in reference to the tree from which the paper was made.

It is likely that the various divination-related offices held by Classic Period lords were organized into a formal hierarchy. The presence of a hierarchy within a single Classic Period office has been noted in the inscriptions (Schele 1990). For example, the title *ch'ok,* which has the meaning of unripe, immature, young child, and sprout, is found in the name phrases of many Maya lords (Schele 1990, 1992:45). On the Palenque Cross Group narrative, the climax of the young Kan B'ahlam's three pre-accession rituals included the acquisition of the office of *ba ch'ok. Ba* has the meaning of "best, first, and top-ranking." The Palace Tablet contains a narrative concerning Kan B'ahlam's younger brother K'an Joy Chitam, who succeeded him as ruler. K'an Joy Chitam's birth passage names him as a *ch'ok*. A later passage in this narrative states that on the occasion of Kan B'ahlam's accession, K'an Joy Chitam was seated in the office of *ba ch'ok*. The implication appears to be that Kan B'ahlam vacated this first-ranking position in the *ch'ok* office when he became ruler, and then his younger brother acquired it.

## Divination by the Ruler

The majority of scenes illustrated on Classic Period public monuments are Period Ending ceremonies related to tun and k'atun endings. During the Postclassic Period, the prognostications for these time periods were an essential part of the ceremonies. A comparison of the Period Ending ceremonies found in the *Paris Codex* and the Piedras Negras niche scenes suggests that during the Classic Period, the ruler performed such divinations. Although Proskouriakoff (1960) identified the Piedras Negras niche scenes as accession ceremonies, I have pointed out that the text that frames many of these actions refers to Period Ending events (Bassie-Sweet 1987, 1991). The accession event of the ruler appears earlier in the narrative, often on the side of the monument. If one accepts the theory that the text in proximity to an actor and an action names that actor and action (and virtually all epigraphers accept this general assumption), then it must be concluded that many of the Piedras Negras niche scenes are Period Ending events. Furthermore, on Stela 11, which represents the k'atun ending 9.15.0.0.0 *4 Ajaw 13 Yax*, the ruler clutches a bag in his left hand that is decorated with the day name *4 Ajaw*. In the Piedras Negras niche scenes, the ruler sits on a throne framed by the Milky Way crocodile with a supernatural bird sitting on top of it. A headless animal appears at the base of the throne. As Hellmuth

(1987) has pointed out, this same kind of throne also appears in the k'atun ceremonies found in the *Paris Codex* (pages 2–11). In these scenes, the k'atun diviner sits on the throne while the regent of the k'atun stands before him (Love 1994:17–25). The parallel position of the k'atun diviner and Piedras Negras ruler strongly suggests that the ruler had the same function, that is, he was responsible for the divinations performed during the Period Ending ceremony.

## Summary

This chapter has reviewed some of the beliefs concerning divination knowledge and ability and has explored the water imagery related to divination. Water was illustrated as streams, layers, or beads of liquid; a pool of water or dew; a mirror; or a serpent. These forms could also be combined, as with the beads of water around the feathered serpent sign. Signs that functioned to further qualify the sacred nature of the water were frequently added to these water motifs. These include the yax, "blue/green, fresh"; k'an, "yellow, center"; and *k'uh,* "sacred," signs as well as quetzal feathers and water lily flowers. It is likely that the water group affix was pronounced *k'uh,* "sacred," because it represented the most sacred of natural elements, water from the place of duality. Divination knowledge was intimately associated with water from the place of duality and with the creator grandparents who lived there. The creator grandfather was the first diviner. He taught the calendrical arts and was said to be the inventor of writing, which was a necessary tool for the creation of divination tables and almanacs. Lightning also played an essential role in divination.

# 6

# THE THUNDERBOLT TRIAD

Three male thunderbolt gods appear in both the *Popol Vuh* and Classic Period art, and there is significant evidence that they were parallel deities. In this chapter, I explore the nature and manifestations of this triad. I argue that they were specifically identified with the three hearthstones that define the center fire, and that they were manifestations of One Ixim/One Hunahpu.

### The Heart of Sky Thunderbolt Triad

In the *Popol Vuh*, the sky at the place of duality is inhabited by a being called Heart of Sky who is described first as a single entity and then as a triad of gods:

> Thus surely there is the sky. There is also Heart of Sky, which is said to be the name of the god. Then came his word. Heart of Sky arrived here with Sovereign and Quetzal Serpent in the darkness, in the night. He spoke with Sovereign and Quetzal Serpent. They talked together then. They thought and they pondered. They reached an accord, bringing together their words and their thoughts. Then they gave birth, heartening one another. Beneath the light, they gave birth to humanity. Then they arranged for the germination and creation of the trees and the bushes, the germination of all life and creation, in the darkness and in the night, by Heart of Sky, who is called Huracan. First is Thunderbolt Huracan, second is Youngest Thunderbolt, and third is Sudden Thunderbolt. These three together are Heart of Sky. (Christenson 2003a:69–70)

They are always named in this order. The Heart of Sky thunderbolt gods are central actors in the *Popol Vuh* story who perform such deeds as flooding the world, destroying the wooden people, and dimming of the eyesight of the first lineage heads so they will not be as powerful as the creator deities. They also direct the hero twins to defeat Seven Macaw and his sons, and assist them in various endeavors.

Núñez de la Vega indicates that a Tzeltal master sorcerer always taught his skills to three individuals at a time. He notes that "No one of the three disciples is permitted to practice any of these arts without previously informing the other two, and also the Master, by whom the three have been taught" (Brinton 1894:19). The consultation of the three disciples with the master sorcerer is highly evocative of the three Heart of Sky thunderbolt gods, who consult with the creator grandfather in order to form the earth and create humans.

## Huracan, the Eldest Thunderbolt God

The eldest thunderbolt god was Huracan, which in K'iche' literally means "one-footed" (*jun raqan*). The homophonous Spanish word *huracán* (hurricane) is believed to be a loanword from Taino, and in the cultures of the Caribbean and north coast of South America, many of the words for hurricane are also homonymous with "huracán." It has been suggested that the people of the Caribbean had contact with the Maya and that "Huracan" and "huracán" are cognates (Hunt 1977:242; D. Tedlock 1985:343, 1996:223). Although some researchers doubt a semantic connection between these words, lame or one-legged gods are associated with hurricanes in Mesoamerica, and Huracan has been identified as such.

Winds (*ik'*) in general are an important subject for the Maya, with different types of winds thought to be manifestations of different gods. The most powerful of the windstorms are the hurricanes that frequently originate in the eastern Caribbean Sea. The hurricane season extends from June to November. Accompanied by thunderbolts and torrential rains, they usually sweep across the Maya lowlands from the east and northeast. Even the hurricanes that bypass Yucatan can cause heavy rains that descend on the peninsula from the north. Dry-season storms also come from the north. In the highlands, the heavy rains can cause landslides that destroy the vegetation of the mountain slopes. In addition to the immediate devastation and deaths caused by wind, rain, and flooding, hurricanes flatten large tracts of forest, and the entire area becomes a fire hazard during the dry season when this uprooted vegetation dries out (Konrad 1985). Either through lightning strikes or careless human activity, uncontrolled fires can then sweep across the landscape. These conditions imitate on a massive scale the annual burning of the cornfield.

It is appropriate that the most senior of the *Popol Vuh* thunderbolt gods should be identified with a hurricane, because hurricanes are the most powerful storms and are accompanied by thunderbolts. The name Thunderbolt Huracan conjures up the image of a deity who could destroy the entire world, exactly what Huracan does when he floods the world of the wooden people with a black rain that falls day and night (Christenson 2003a:85). The K'iche' phrase *jun raqan* is a well-known expression for large drops of rain (Allen Christenson, personal communication), and the first drops of rain at the beginning of a storm are huge.

The Maya closely identify hurricanes with whirlwinds. The Yucatec Maya terms *keh ik'* and *mozon ik'* refer to a fleeting hurricane or strong whirlwind (Barrera Vásquez 1980:309, 490). Whirlwinds are frequently created during the burning of the cornfield. Their swirling winds take on a dark shape when they move across the field, picking up ash, smoke, and fire, not unlike the dark conditions associated with hurricanes. In Yucatan, a whirlwind—called *k'ak'al mozon 'ik'*, "fiery whirlwind"— is viewed in a positive way as it is thought to fan the fire of the milpa and create a good burn (Redfield and Villa Rojas 1934:119). In the Tzeltal town of Pinola, there is a triad of gods known as Whirlwind (*Sutu 'iki'*), Thunderbolt (*Chaguk*), and Meteor (*Paslam*), and this Whirlwind is also closely associated with fire. A man with Whirlwind for his nagual, or animal counterpart, can eat live coals and can create a whirlwind by blowing on fire (Hermitte 1964).

In the colonial period documents of the Tzeltal it is noted that a person could have thirteen naguals, of which whirlwinds and thunderbolts were the most powerful (Calnek 1988:56). In the lore of Tzeltal Pinola, Whirlwind is thought to be less powerful than either Thunderbolt or Meteor in the triad of animal counterparts (Hermitte 1964). However, in the adjacent Tojolab'al area, Whirlwind is considered equally powerful, and evil as well. The Tojolabal believe there are three evil deities who can take the lives of people and animals: Bitus (tornado or whirlwind), Chakaxib (hurricane), and Takin Chawuk (dry lightning; Spero 1987). In the Ch'orti area, Whirlwind is seen as the head of all the evil beings and is identified with the devil (Wisdom 1940:397).

The most important Lacandon deity is called Nohotsakyum or Hachakyum, "our true lord." Nohotsakyum's assistant, Ah K'uklel, is manifested as a fiery whirlwind who is thought to bring Nohotsakyum the ashes from the burning milpa and from the firing of the clay idols (Perera and Bruce 1982:31). Nohotsakyum is also called Yurika'an (Davis 1978:78). The similarity of this name to "hurricane" is reinforced by Nohotsakyum's nature. He makes the wind that brings the lightning, thunder, and rain. It is said that at the end of the world, Nohotsakyum will wear a snake as a belt, and that this snake will suck people to it with its breath and then kill them (Tozzer 1907:94). In another myth recorded by Bruce and interpreted by McGee (1989), Nohotsakyum destroys the world with a hurricane and flood.

The southern Lacandon refer to Nohotsakyum as *U Yolika'an*, "the heart of the sky." Other names recorded for him are Humbrikam (Cline 1944:109), Yumbirihka'an, (Davis 1978:78) and Yumbilika'an (Bruce 1977:191). Bruce translates this latter term as "lord of heaven (sky)" or "lord heart of heaven (sky)." Bruce identifies Nohotsakyum with Huracan of the *Popol Vuh*, who is also called Heart of Sky, and notes that both deities were powerful sky gods involved in the creation of the earth. Nohotsakyum directs the water gods to bring the rain, thunder, and lightning, and as noted above, he is associated with whirlwinds and hurricanes. The Milky Way is said to be the road of Hachakyum (Nohotsakyum; Duby and Blom 1969:295).

## Youngest Thunderbolt and Sudden Thunderbolt

Youngest Thunderbolt (Ch'i'pi Kaqulja) and Sudden Thunderbolt (Raxa Kaqulja) are the other two members of the thunderbolt trio. *Ch'ip* is a term referring to the youngest child in a family, which suggests that the Heart of Sky deities were a triad of brothers.

The portrayal of thunderbolts as small children or dwarfs is found across highland Guatemala. Saki C'oxol is described in colonial dictionaries as a dwarf who moves like lightning (B. Tedlock 1986:134). He is also briefly mentioned in the *Popol Vuh* and in the *Annals of the Cakchiquels,* where he is characterized as the keeper of animals and the spirit of volcanic mountains. In the latter account, he has the appearance of a small boy dressed in red. After the conquest, Spanish priests wrote dance-dramas to use in the conversion of the natives and to replace the well-established pre-Columbian dance-dramas that were important components of every festival. Dances similar to the colonial-era ones are still performed in some highland towns. One of the main characters in the drama called the Dance of the Conquest is a character called Ajitz, who is a native diviner (Bode 1961:213). He is also called C'oxol, Saki C'oxol ("white C'oxol"), Quiakacoxol ("red Coxol"), and Tzitzimit. Ajitz is dressed all in red and carries an ax. A smaller version of Ajitz who is characterized as his younger brother also appears in the drama. In contemporary Momostenango, the C'oxol is a red, dwarf thunderbolt god who appears in creation stories. It is said that he struck the first K'iche' elders (father-mothers) with his ax and awakened the sheet lightning in their blood, and that he "whipped knowledge" into them (B. Tedlock 1982:147; 1986; D. Tedlock 1985:305). Cracking a whip is also associated with lightning in contemporary beliefs. Given their similar form and associations with lightning, it is highly likely that the red dwarf C'oxol was one of the manifestations of Ch'i'pi Thunderbolt.

Christenson (2003a:71) translates the name of the third Heart of Sky thunderbolt as Sudden Thunderbolt (*Raxa Kaqulja*); Thomas Coto's 1651 vocabulary lists the term as "the flash of the lightning." *Raxa* also means green/blue. In the *Popol Vuh,* Youngest Thunderbolt (Ch'i'pi Kaqulja) and Sudden Thunderbolt (Raxa Kaqulja) are referred to as Ch'i'pi Nanavac and Raxa Nanavac (Christenson 2003a:207). It has been proposed that Nanavac is a cognate of Nanahuatl, the deity who split open the corn mountain in Central Mexican lore (Schultze-Jena 1944:187; Edmonson 1971:159; see also chapter 15). Some of the contemporary Maya tales that recount this core Mesoamerican event indicate that a series of thunderbolt gods tried but failed to break open the stone enclosing the corn. In the Tzeltal village of Bachajón, it is said that the red thunderbolt god broke open the rock after two other thunderbolt gods failed (Slocum 1965:5). In the Poqomchi' area, the smallest or youngest thunderbolt was the one who was finally able to do it (Montejo and Campbell 1993). This suggests that Youngest Thunderbolt, rather than Sudden Thunderbolt, was the deity responsible for the ultimate success. In the hierarchy of lightning gods found in the Ch'ol and Tojolabal areas, the green/blue thunderbolt is invariably the weaker one (Spero 1987; Jolja' Cave Project field notes).

The appearance of a young, red thunderbolt god associated with corn is not restricted to highland Guatemala. In Tzeltal Pinola, the thunderbolt god has red, black, and white forms (Hermitte 1964). Thunderbolt is characterized as a young, very small boy identified with Saint Michael, patron saint of the town, who has a sword like a thunderbolt with which he protects the community. He is the leader of the ancestors (mother-fathers), and the most powerful naguals of the mother-fathers past and present take his form. Thunderbolt is also the owner of corn. It is said that he had the spirit of maize hidden under his foot, but the mother-fathers from the neighboring town of Amatenango stole part of it when he raised his foot, which explains why Amatenango is more prosperous. The Ch'ol of Joloniel have two kinds of thunderbolt gods: red and green/blue. Red Thunderbolt is the most powerful, and he also has the form of a small boy (Jolja' Cave Project field notes; Felipe Pérez Montejo and Domingo Pérez Morenos, personal communication 2001). In Yucatan, X Thup Chahk is said to be the smallest but most important of the thunderbolt gods (Redfield and Villa Rojas 1934:114–15, 137). The word *thup* means smallest in a series and youngest of a number of brothers and sisters. He dwells in the east and is the guardian of the species of corn called *x thup nal,* which matures early. The smallest of the guardian deities who protect the village and the cornfield is also called Thup. He, too, dwells in the east and stands ready to assist the other guardians if they are not strong enough to overcome a harmful animal or evil wind.

## WOK, THE BIRD MESSENGER OF HEART OF SKY

Birds as messengers are a common theme in Mesoamerica. An avian god named Pax is referred to as one of the *ebeet* messengers for Itzamnaaj (Houston 2001; Miller and Martin 2004:28–29, Houston, Stuart, and Taube 2006:229–51). The phrase *y ebeet,* "his messenger," appears in the Classic Period texts. Humans who carried the *ebeet* title appear to have functioned as messengers for their lord (Stuart, cited in Houston 2000). The Popol Vuh mentions four warrior lords of the underworld called Arrow Owl, One Leg Owl, Macaw Owl, and Skull Owl, who served as messengers (*samajel* in K'iche') for the rulers One Death and Seven Death.

When the *Popol Vuh* first describes the ball playing of One Hunahpu, Seven Hunahpu, and the monkey twins at the Nim Xob' Karchaj ballcourt, it states that a swift-flying bird called Wok, who was a messenger for the Heart of Sky deities, would arrive at the ballcourt and guard them as they played (Christenson 2003a:114). Later in the story, when the hero twins are playing ball at this same court, another messenger bird called Wak arrives with a message from the creator grandmother, Xmucane. Wak is a laughing falcon whose name mimics the sound of his call (see chapter 7). It is likely that Wok's name was similarly onomatopoeic. It is reasonably certain that Wok is modeled after another bird of prey, the collared forest falcon, *Micrastur semitoguatus.*

The forest falcon may be confused with the laughing falcon because of their similar songs, but Smithe (1966:42) states that the call of the forest falcon has a slower tempo and a shorter duration, and that it falls off "toward the end into a quavering, human-like moan." Sutton (1951:125, 140) characterizes this second part of the forest falcon's call as "an astonishingly human cry, almost a moan"—"how startlingly human were those loud, slightly quavering moans." Although the proto-Ch'olan word for hawk is *lik lik* (another hawk sound), *muwaan* is found as a word for hawk in Mopan, Ch'olti', and Ch'orti' (Grube and Schele 1994), and it is specifically used to describe the collared forest falcon in Yucatec Mayan and Itza' Mayan (Steggerda 1943:237, Atran 1999:191).

The *Popol Vuh* describes Wok as a swift bird that could fly from the earth to Huracan in the sky in an instant. The laughing falcon is a slow, clumsy flier that hunts for its snake prey while sitting in a tree, but the collared forest falcon flies with great agility as it hunts. It darts through heavy forest in a flash. In the Classic Period texts, the sign that represents the word *muwaan* is a hawk in the process of swallowing a large bird (fig. 6.1a). The muwaan bird sign was initially thought to be an owl because of its features (Thompson 1950:11). Indeed, the indigenous people in Vera-cruz consider the collared forest falcon to be a kind of owl because of its large eyes and love of shade. It also has a facial ruff like an owl to aid its hearing. The collared forest falcon primarily eats birds, and often the birds are bigger than it is. Hawks, by contrast, do not swallow their prey whole; they strip away parts of the flesh with their beaks. The depiction of the muwaan swallowing a bird whole may be a convention for indicating its predatory nature. All this points to the identification of Wok with the muwaan and the collared forest falcon.

A Late-Classic king at Bonampak was called *Yajaw Chan Muwaan,* whose name literally means "the vassal of the Sky Hawk" (Zender 2004b). This Sky Hawk must surely be a reference to Wok. The close association between the muwaan bird and the sky is further seen in the art of Yaxchilan. On Stela 4, the muwaan bird is used as the head variant for the word *chan,* "sky" (Martin 2004:2).

## The Classic Period Thunderbolt Triad

An important triad of Classic Period thunderbolt brothers is known by the nick-names GI, GII, and GIII, also known as the Palenque triad. Their attributes are similar to those of the Heart of Sky thunderbolt gods. The Palenque Cross Group is composed of three temple/pyramids that flank a small plaza. A small, radial pyramid platform marks the center of the plaza as the center of the world (Taube 1998:441). Each of the three Cross Group temple/pyramids focuses on one member of the Palenque triad. GI is featured in the Temple of the Cross, GII in the Temple of the Foliated Cross, and GIII in the Temple of the Sun.

Inside each temple is a small sanctuary, and on the back wall of each sanctuary is a tablet that describes the birth and activities of its respective god. Each tablet also illustrates two ceremonies performed in that god's honor by the ruler Kan B'ahlam (Bassie-Sweet 1991). The narratives focus on Kan B'ahlam's historical actions as well as providing a mythological charter for his ceremonies.

The Palenque Cross Group inscriptions refer to each sanctuary as a *pib'naah*. Houston observes that the Yucatec Maya term *pib*, which is most frequently used to refer to the underground pits used to bake food, was also used to refer to sweat baths associated with birthing, and he argues that the Cross Group sanctuaries were the sweat baths of the deities. In contrast, Stuart (2006) has recently rejected this interpretation and has proposed that the term *pib'naah* is simply describing these sanctuaries as underground houses. He notes that the Cross Group pyramids are symbolic mountains, and he equates the sanctuaries with mountain caves that are also viewed by the Maya as the houses of deities. Given that caves are often characterized as sweat baths, I do not think that these two interpretations are mutually exclusive.

The texts found in the temples of the Palenque Cross Group and the adjacent Temple XIX give a series of events, the earliest being GI's accession into lordship on 12.10.1.13.2 *9 Ik' 5 Mol* (10 March 3309 B.C.) under the authority of the creator grandfather Yax Naah Itzamnaaj at a sky location (Stuart 2005b, 2006). A series of events follows involving the Milky Way crocodile on 12.10.12.16.18 *3 Etz'nab 6 Ch'en* (30 March 3298 B.C.). These actions, said to be the work of GI, include an ax event that likely refers to the decapitation or defeat of the Milky Way crocodile. A parallel crocodile deity in the *Popol Vuh* is called Zipacna. Under instructions from Heart of Sky, the hero twins defeated Zipacna.

The next chronological event was the birth of a deity called Muwaan Mat on 12.19.13.4.0 *8 Ajaw 18 Tsek* (7 December 3121 B.C.). Although this deity was initially given the nickname Lady Beastie or First Mother, it is now apparent that the deity was male (Stuart 2000b, 2005b, 2006; Martin and Grube 2000). A slight digression is in order to discuss his name. The word *mat* is represented in the hieroglyphic text by syllabic signs representing *ma* and *ta* or by a logograph of a crested bird with an upturned, bulbous beak (Bowen and Anderson 1994). The *mat* bird is the main sign of an emblem glyph found in the Palenque texts and elsewhere (fig. 6.1b). Other emblem glyphs found at Palenque have a bone or skull as the main sign. Based on the assumption that these main signs were all equivalent and that they represented the word *bak*, "bone," it was argued that the *mat* bird was either a heron or a snowy egret because the term for these birds was *bak ha'*, "bone water." However, the three emblem-glyph main signs are not equal, and that identification has been discredited (Stuart and Houston 1994:73–77). Stuart (2000b, 2005, 2006) identifies the *mat* bird as a cormorant, based on the Yucatec Maya cognate *mach*, "cormorant." Cormorants have hooked beaks, and when paddling in the water, their bills are angled upward much like the *mat* bird's.

The deity Muwaan Mat's complete name glyph is composed of two parts (fig. 6.1c). The first part, which has not been deciphered, includes a T1000a sign that

Figure 6.1. a. *Muan* month sign used to represent the word *muwaan*; b. Matwiil emblem glyph; c. Muwaan Mat name phrase

Stuart (2005b) has demonstrated is a portrait of One Ixim. The last part of his name phrase is most often represented by a *mat* sign in the form of a cormorant, conflated with a *muwaan,* "hawk," sign. In one example of Muwaan Mat's name, the muwaan bird is followed by a phonetic *mat* sign, which confirms that the reading order of these two conflated signs was Muwaan Mat (Simon Martin, personal communication).

The birth of Muwaan Mat was followed by the Period Ending event on 13.0.0.0.0 *4 Ajaw 8 Kumk'u* (13 August 3114 B.C.) that involved the changing or renewal of the three hearthstones, followed by GI descending from the sky and conducting a dedication event for his Six Sky house that was said to be located in the north (5 February 3112 B.C.). The house dedication is followed by the creation of three deities: GI, GIII, and GII, on 1.18.5.3.2 *9 Ik' 15 Keh* (21 October 2360 B.C.), 1.18.5.3.6 *13 Kimi 19 Keh* (25 October 2360 B.C.), and 1.18.5.4.0 *1 Ajaw 13 Mak* (8 November 2360 B.C.), respectively, at a place called Matwiil. As Stuart (2005b, 2006) has shown, there was likely only one GI, and the GI born in 2360 B.C. was probably a new manifestation of the earlier GI. Stuart (2006) notes that their births are also characterized as "arrivals" and as "earth-touching," although the meaning of this latter phrase is not well understood. The narrative also states that they were the creation (offspring) of Muwaan Mat, and that Muwaan Mat was a holy lord of Matwiil. The Period Ending on 2.0.0.0.0 *2 Ajaw 3 Wayeb* (17 February 2325 B.C.) is followed by Muwaan Mat taking an office on 2.0.0.1.2 *9 Ik' 0 Sac* (7 September 2325 B.C.).

## THE TRAITS OF GI

GI is a Roman-nosed deity often shown with a shark's tooth protruding from his mouth (fig. 6.2a–c); Hellmuth 1987:99–104). He also has a mouth curl similar to those found on lightning gods, and what has been termed a fish fin above the curl. Early Classic vessels show GI surrounded by water symbols, which fits with his water-related traits. GI's eyes are formed by water scrolls like the ones shown in illustrations of turbulent water.

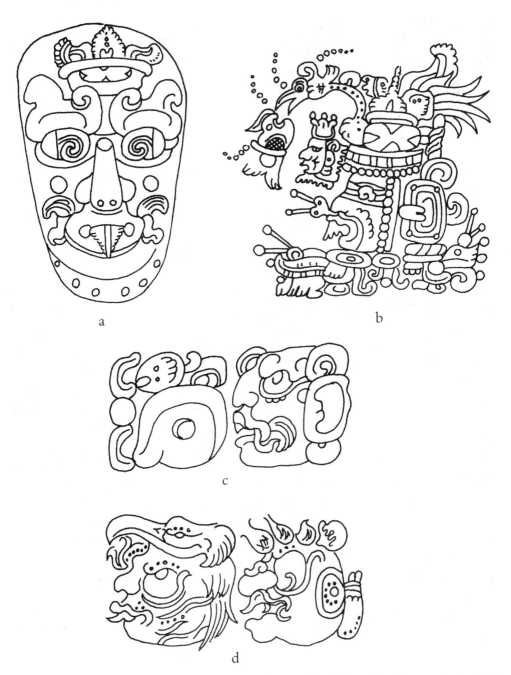

Figure 6.2. a. GI mask (after Hellmuth); b. GI incense burner (after Hellmuth); c. GI name glyphs; d. GI name glyphs, Palenque Creation Tablet.

Because GI is usually illustrated wearing Chahk's shell earring (fig. 6.2c), he has been associated with the Chahk thunderbolt deities (Coe 1973). This Chahk earring is, in fact, one of the keys to GI's identification. I take this as evidence that GI is a thunderbolt deity. As noted, Maya scribes frequently combined two separate words into one sign that still represented two words. The names of numerous Classic Period lords include the name *Chahk,* "lightning bolt" (Martin and Grube 2000). When the scribes combined the two parts of the ruler's name into one sign, they took the shell earring of Chahk and placed it on the other sign. The name of the Tonina ruler B'aaknal Chahk, for example, is composed of the signs for *b'aaknal* followed by a Chahk portrait glyph. However, on Tonina Monument 29, his name is represented by a skull (*b'aak*) wearing the shell earring of Chahk. I suggest that this is the same convention used with GI's name. Evidence for this interpretation is found on the Palenque Creation Tablet, where the name phrase of GI is composed of his portrait followed by the full form of the Chahk sign (fig. 6.2d). Although we do not know what word the portrait of GI represents, it was followed by the word *chahk,* "thunderbolt"; hence, GI was a thunderbolt deity.

GI frequently wears a headdress composed of the Quadripartite Badge Monster, and the Temple of the Inscriptions text states that this motif was the headdress of GI. The Tablet of the Cross, which features GI in its main text, has the Quadripartite Badge Monster at the base of its central icon (fig. 6.3). The Quadripartite Badge Monster is composed of a zoomorphic creature with an incense burner on top of its head (Houston, cited in Taube 1998:439). The bowl of the incense burner is marked with a *k'in,* "sun," sign, and inside the bowl are a stingray spine, a shell, and a variable element. Based on this sun glyph, many researchers have identified GI with the sun, but I believe this is incorrect; rather, GI was a thunderbolt deity.

In many of the Early Classic depictions of GI, his Quadripartite Badge Monster headdress includes a fish-eating water bird with a long neck and a sharp, pointed beak (see fig. 6.2b; Hellmuth 1987). This bird has been identified as a manifestation of GI. On the Palenque Temple XIX platform, the ruler Akhal Mo' Nahb reenacts the accession of GI as part of his own accession ritual (Stuart 2005b). The caption text states that he has taken on the guise of GI. Although most of Akhal Mo' Nahb's headdress was destroyed by the collapse of the building, the fish-eating water bird was not damaged, and it is juxtaposed immediately in front of GI's name.

GI is also associated with the Six Sky place. The name of this location, mentioned in many inscriptions, is composed of the number six, a yet-undeciphered sign, and a sky sign (Stuart 2006). This Six Sky place also appears in name phrases in which deities, rulers, and their consorts are called lords of the Six Sky place (Martin 2001). GI's *pib'naah* temple in the Palenque Cross Group is called the Six Sky. In the Temple of the Inscriptions text, the Six Sky place is referred to as GI's seat, and thus it has long been recognized that GI was a lord of the Six Sky place (Schele 1992:186). On the Tablet of the Cross, GI is said to have descended from the sky for the events on the 13.0.0.0.0 Period Ending at the three hearthstones and then ascended to the Six

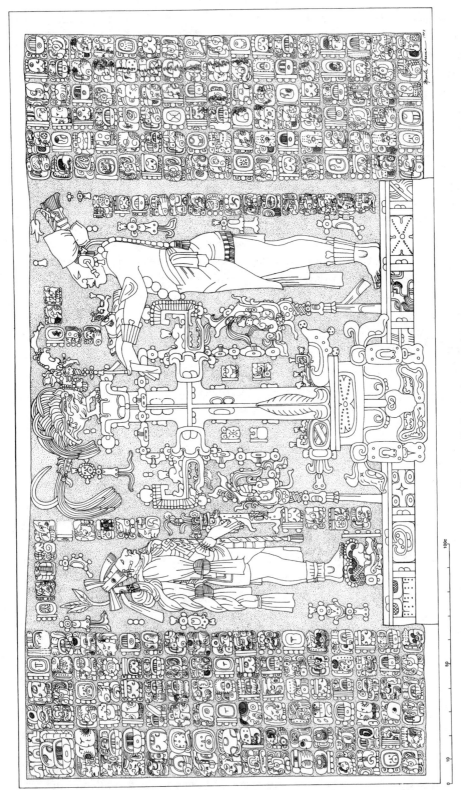

Figure 6.3. Palenque Tablet of the Cross (drawing courtesy Merle Greene Robertson)

112

Sky place (Zender 2005). On Quirigua Stela C, the setting up of the three hearth-stones on the 13.0.0.0.0 Period Ending was done under GI's authority as the Six Sky lord.

Some of GI's traits, like those of Huracan of the *Popol Vuh*, are associated with wind, storms, and hurricanes. The orientation of the Temple of the Cross and the inscriptions in this building indicate that GI was associated with the north, the direction of heavy rainstorms. Texts in Temple XIX and the Cross Group indicate that GI's accession and arrival at Matwiil occurred on the date *9 Wind,* as did the accession of Akhal Mo' Nahb. This tzolk'in date is also the name of the wind god Ehecatl/Quetzalcoatl, and GI's association with this deity has long been proposed (Kelley 1965). In the *Codex Vaticanus A*, Quetzalcoatl is said to cause hurricanes. The association of GI with the north and with the northern storms that descend on the Maya region during the dry season may explain GI's identification with the fish-eating water bird. The Maya observe that when the north wind begins to blow, the waterfowl return (Escobar 1841:91).

Part of GI's complete name phrase includes a name or title composed of three signs that have yet to be completely deciphered (see fig. 6.2c). The first sign represents the word *hun,* "one." Although the last two signs have been translated as *ye nal* (Schele 1992; Freidel, Schele, and Parker 1993:61), Stuart (2005b, 2006) has recently suggested that these readings are incorrect. While the meaning of the *hun* title or name is unclear, the word *hun* appears in the Yucatec Maya phrase *hunyecil* used by Diego López Cogolludo in 1688 in referring to "an inundation or hurricane which they (the Yucatec Maya) call *hunyecil* or submersion of the forest" (Tozzer 1941:41).

## The Traits of GII

GII was the third born of the Palenque triad brothers, but whenever the triad is named as a group, he appears in the second position; hence his nickname GII. This order is like Youngest-Born Thunderbolt, who is always named second despite being the youngest.

GII is one of the God K deities. Although the chahks dispensed lightning bolts by throwing their axes, God K deities are those identified with the lightning bolt ax itself. In the ax versions of God K, the body forms the handle of the ax and one of his legs often has the form of a serpent (fig. 6.4a). Many illustrations of God K show smoke emanating from the ax blade in reference to the fire caused by a lightning strike. God K's name is usually represented by a portrait with phonetic complements and substitutions that indicate it represents the word "K'awiil" (Stuart 1987). Although there are variations, God K has the same type of zoomorphic face as the chahks, but he has a celt sign in his forehead and an ax blade protruding from his head. Some God K deities also have cigars or torches in their foreheads. GII's portrait glyph is composed of a God K with phonetic *u* and *ne* prefixes (fig. 6.4b). In other contexts, the reclining pose, baby proportions, and phonetic complements displayed by GII

a

b

Figure 6.4. a. God K with a serpent leg; b. GII name glyph

have the meaning of *unen,* "baby, child" (Stuart, Houston, and Robertson 1999; Martin 2002). As Martin has demonstrated, GII's name is a conflation of *unen,* "baby, child" and God K, "*K'awiil.*" Baby K'awiil is an appropriate designation for GII, youngest of the Palenque triad of brothers.

GII was also a red dwarf, *chac ch'at,* as we know from the Tablet of the Foliated Cross (Houston 1992; Houston, cited in Schele 1992:161). The association of dwarfs with lightning is found on the Yaxchilan hieroglyphic stairs in front of Structure 33. In this scene, the ruler Bird Jaguar is illustrated playing ball accompanied by two dwarfs with star signs under their arms. The first dwarf wears the shell earring of Chahk, indicating he is a thunderbolt god. Dwarfs are found in a number of Period Ending scenes in the eastern lowlands. These human dwarfs may have been viewed as the living embodiment of GII. The parallel nature of the red dwarf

C'oxol and the red dwarf GII has been noted (Freidel, cited in Schele 1992:161; Freidel, Schele, and Parker 1993:201).

The Temple of the Foliated Cross at Palenque is the pib'naah of GII. The central image on the tablet is a personified corn plant with a zoomorphic head at its base (fig. 6.5). The head is infixed with a *k'an*, "yellow," sign. The hieroglyphic name of this plant is *k'an nahb' ixiimte*, according to Stuart (2006), and he translates this name as "the precious pool, maize plant" (though *ixiimte* is more correctly translated as corn tree). Unlike a normal stalk of corn, which has two ears growing from an upper and lower node, the *k'an nahb' ixiimte* corn tree has two personified ears of corn growing from the same node. As noted in chapter 2, the Maya categorize such ears as twins. Because the word *k'an* can also mean ripe, it is tempting to view the *k'an* sign in this context as an indication of a mature corn plant, but its stalk is not bent over like mature, ripe corn. The two ears of corn have the youthful characteristics of the Classic Period hero twins One Ajaw and Yax Bolon. As will be discussed more fully in chapters 10 and 11, the hero twins of the *Popol Vuh*, Hunahpu and Xbalanque, plant two ears of green corn in their house before they descend into the underworld, and these green ears of corn become omens of their fate. The creator grandmother names these effigy ears of corn Center House, Center Ancestral Plot, Revitalized Maize, and Leveled Earth (Christenson 2003a:189). The *k'an* sign can be used to represent the concept of the center, and in the Tablet of the Foliated Cross it appears to designate these twin ears of corn as a center plant in a manner similar to the two ears of green corn of the *Popol Vuh*. The center house of the creator grandparents where the green corn is located is the place of duality at the center of the world. This leads me to conclude that the *k'an nahb'*, "precious pool," likely refers to the pooled water of the place of duality.

The ruler K'an B'ahlam is illustrated on the left side of the Tablet of the Foliated Cross standing on a witz monster whose eyes contain two glyphs that can be read as *yaxhaal witznal* (Stuart 2006). Corn foliage emerges from the cleft head of the witz monster. Because of the split and the corn imagery, most researchers have assumed that this place name represents Paxil Mountain, where corn was first found. Although I have agreed with that interpretation in the past, I now suggest that *yaxhaal witznal* is simply the name of GII's particular mountain, and that the witz monster is the generic representation of the word "mountain." On the right side of the tablet, the young Kan B'ahlam stands on a shell with two glyphs inscribed on it that identify it as the k'an shell of the place called Matwiil. The Tablet of the Foliated Cross indicates that GII was identified with the center of the world and that one of the names for the center was Matwiil.

## THE TRAITS OF GIII

In many examples, GIII has the same face and *k'in* infixes as the sun god, a square-eyed deity with *k'in*, "sun," signs infixed on his face. But unlike the sun god, GIII

Figure 6.5. Palenque Tablet of the Foliated Cross (drawing courtesy Merle Greene Robertson)

116

Figure 6.6. GIII name glyphs

has jaguar features and a looped cord, sometimes in the form of a serpent or marked with water signs, over the bridge of his nose. Thompson (1950:11, 134; 1954:175, 213, plate 19) suggested that the sun took on jaguar characteristics when it passed through the underworld at night, and he proposed that GIII was a jaguar manifestation of the sun. He nicknamed him the Jaguar God of the Underworld. There is, however, no evidence that the Maya believed that the sun was transformed into a jaguar at night, and despite the general acceptance of Thompson's identification, I consider it highly unlikely. GIII's personal name in the texts at Palenque is composed of three parts: a *k'inich* title, a T1008 sign in a day-sign cartouche, and a T594 shield sign (fig. 6.6). Although GIII's *k'inich* title has been translated as "sun-faced," Wichmann (2004) has argued that it represents the word *k'ihnich,* "hot one," while Stuart (2006) translates it as "radiant one." The T1008 sign appears to mean "youth." The central icon on the Tablet of the Sun is a portrait of GIII emblazoned on a war shield with two crossed spears behind it (fig. 6.7). Such shields frequently appear in Maya art, underlining GIII's association with war. It is likely that GIII's three-part name is also the name of this shield.

GIII appears in a number of contexts outside of the Palenque triad. He is the Number 7 Deity, the patron of *Woh* and the day regent of *Kib*. GIII has been identified as a god closely associated with fire (Stuart 1998:408), and Taube (2000) notes that GIII's looped cord is a twisted cord used in fire drilling. On Naranjo Stela 30 and Sacul Stela 9, the ruler impersonating GIII holds a ceremonial fire-drilling stick (Stuart 1998:404). Most of GIII's titles are not securely deciphered, but he is called *yajawk'ahk',* "its lord fire," (Stuart 1998), an office held by secondary lords during the Classic Period. Zender (2004b) has pointed out that the term *ajaw,* "lord," actually

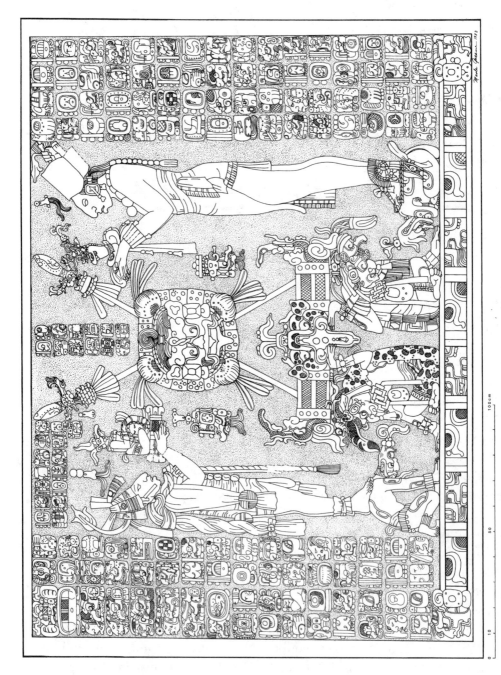

Figure 6.7. Palenque Tablet of the Sun (drawing courtesy Merle Greene Robertson)

means "vassal" when it is stated in a possessed form such as *yajawk'ahk'*, and thus he translates GIII's title as "fire's vassal." In other words, GIII was the vassal of the fire god. One of GIII's names has been translated as Great Sun Torch (Stuart 2006).

Taube has shown that in Mesoamerican culture, the sparks given off by meteors were associated with the drilling of fire, and that meteors were viewed as arrows, darts, and spears. He has also demonstrated the pan-Mesoamerican association of meteors with warfare and that they were omens of death. As Stuart observes (cited in Taube 2000), the so-called "star war" glyphs are likely meteors. GIII's warlike nature has long been recognized and is reflected in the numerous depictions of Maya rulers holding both a spear and a GIII shield (Coe 1973:15, 83, 107). GIII's war paraphernalia is found in close association with the *waxakla juun u'baah kaan* serpent and Tlaloc imagery, both of which are associated with warfare, fire serpents, and meteors (Taube 1992c, 2000). On Dos Pilas Stela 2 and Aguateca Stela 2, Ruler 3 wears these GIII war accoutrements as well as an owl necklace. Another kind of owl is associated with GIII on K758. In this scene, GIII emerges from the mouth of the owl, who also wears GIII's twisted cord over his nose. Owls are frequently viewed as omens of death in Maya culture. On the Tablet of the Sun, the young Kan B'ahlam is pictured holding up a personified flint (*took'*) and another kind of shield called a *pakal* (see fig. 6.7). The *took' pakal* emblem has been identified as another important war-related object (Houston 1983; Stuart 1995:301–304) that is directly related to GIII (Bassie-Sweet 1991, 1996).

In brief, GIII was a vassal of the fire god and has the fire-drilling cord looped over his nose. This suggests that the fire stick is actually a manifestation of GIII. He was associated with war and meteors, specifically with two kinds of war shields. Unlike the chahks, who threw thunderbolt axes, GIII's weapon appears to have been the flint spear. Given that flint produces sparks when struck, it is likely that this spear was a metaphor for the flaming meteor. In Tzotzil, *ch'ob* means both torch and falling star; GIII's torch title may have been another metaphor for a meteor (Laughlin 1975:137). Because meteors range from brief flashes of light to flaming fireballs, it is not surprising that different metaphors would be associated with them.

Images of GIII are frequently found on tall clay cylinders that were used as idols. An incense brazier was placed on top of the cylinder. An association between these cylinders and meteors is seen in the Tojolab'al area, where a nagual called *k'ak chob* (literally "fire jaguar") is described as having either a fireball on his forehead or a brazier tied to his forehead (Ruz 1982:57). The fireball relates him to GIII's meteor identification, and the brazier relates him to GIII's frequent appearance on incense cylinders. The notion that the looped cord over GIII's nose was used to drill fire and that it also referred to the sparks created by a meteor may explain a Tz'utujil belief about babies born with their umbilical cords looped around their shoulder or neck. This is viewed as a sign that the child's spirit is a meteor (Paul and Paul 1975:709).

It can be assumed that GIII, like his older and younger brothers, was viewed as some kind of thunderbolt. His position as the third in the trio may indicate that he was a less powerful flash of light than his brothers. Flashes of light in the sky that are weaker than thunderbolts are meteors. The association of lightning with meteors is found in the Tojolab'al area, where the *tzantzewal* are thought to be either lightning, falling stars, or lights that appear at night in the hills (Spero 1987:172). In addition to being flashes of light, big meteors share other characteristics with lightning bolts. Both can be accompanied by a tremendous boom, and both are associated with fire (Taube 2000:325). Meteors are considered to be omens of death, and lightning bolts usually bring death to any living being they hit. Both lightning bolts and meteors are associated with obsidian and flint, and both are considered to be weapons of the thunderbolt gods.

GIII's ranking after his younger brother GII has a parallel in the Tzeltal meteor god Paslam, who is said to live in the same locations as Thunderbolt but is second to him in rank (Hermitte 1964). Sixteenth-century Tzeltal and Tzotzil dictionaries also refer to a meteor deity called Pazlam, Pozlom, or Poxlon. Núñez de la Vega describes him as a ball of fire that traveled in the sky in the form of a star with a tail like a comet—in other words, a meteor. He equates him with a deity called Tzihuizin, the Pipil form of *xihuitl,* "turquoise." The Central Mexican deity Xiuhtecuhtli was a fire and war god, and Taube (2000) has shown that the Xiuhcoatl, "turquoise snake," was a Postclassic version of the *waxakla juun u'baah kaan* serpent that was closely identified with GIII. In Tzotzil Zinacantan, Poslom is still considered a meteor or a ball of fire (Vogt 1969:305; Laughlin 1975:284, 513). In Tzotzil Chenalho, he is called Poslob (Guiteras Holmes 1961:292–93). His animal manifestation is the jaguar, reminiscent of GIII with his jaguar traits. Poslob is also associated with the barn owl, screech owl, and the other night prowlers (Guiteras Holmes 1961:249); GIII is likewise associated with an owl.

Meteors may appear as white streaks across the sky, or they may flame in red, yellow, blue, or green hues. In Tzeltal-speaking Pinola, the meteor deity Paslam has green/blue, red, and white forms, while in Tzeltal-speaking Oxchuc, he has green/blue, red, and yellow forms (Hermitte 1964, Villa Rojas 1947). In Tzotzil-speaking San Andrés, diseases sent on the wind by witches are called *poslom.* They take green/blue, red, yellow, white, and black forms and are described as *yash tsanam ik',* which can be translated as "green/blue burning wind" (Holland 1961:189–96, 207; Robert Laughlin, personal communication). They have a close relationship with whirlwinds. The consistent association of Poslom with green/blue is reminiscent of Sudden Thunderbolt (Raxa Kaqulja), the third member of the Heart of the Sky triad. As noted above, *raxa* means both "green/blue" and "sudden," and both these meanings are consistent with meteors. Although the major meteor showers occur regularly from May to December, meteors can appear in the night sky with little warning. They are sudden flashes of light in the sky. As noted, the green/blue lightning bolt is frequently the weakest. It is conceivable, then, that a meteor might have been classified by the Maya as a kind of sudden lightning with a weaker nature than a lightning bolt. Although GIII is never directly named as a chahk, it seems reasonable from this evidence to conclude that he was a thunderbolt god.

## The Palenque Triad as Three Planets

The Cross Group narrative at Palenque tells of some event that occurred on 9.12. 18.5.16 *2 Kib 14 Mol* (23 July A.D. 690). Stuart (2006) has recently argued that the event was the creation of three ceramic effigy figures representing the Palenque triad of GI, GII, and GIII. Because Jupiter, Mars, and Saturn appear in the same area of the night sky in the months before and after this date and their paths interweave, it has been suggested that the Palenque triad of gods represented these planets (Lounsbury 1989:248). Whether these identifications are correct remains to be seen, but such associations do not negate the identification of the Palenque triad of brothers with storms, lightning bolts, and meteors. Rather, they may enhance our understanding of the role these planets played in Maya world view.

## The Three Hearthstones and the Palenque Cross Group

It is well established that pyramids represented mountains and that the Maya believed that mountains were manifestations of their gods. In other words, each Cross Group building represents the mountain aspect of one member of the Palenque triad. In a Belizean myth collected by Thompson (1930:123), mountains are identified with hearthstones. In this myth, a grandmother goddess asks her grandson a riddle: What are three hills with something flat on top? The correct answer is the three stones of the hearth with the comal (griddle) on top. Several researchers have suggested that the triad building arrangement of the Palenque Cross Group represents the three hearthstones (Hansen 1992; Freidel, Schele, and Parker 1993; Taube 2002). I would expand this interpretation to say that the three hearthstones are manifestations of the three thunderbolt gods GI, GII, and GIII. As noted in chapter 4, the identification of three gods with the hearthstones is also found in the Aztec area (Bierhorst 1992:23).

As will be discussed in chapter 13, the Palenque Cross Group buildings replicate three specific volcanoes in highland Guatemala that mark the center of the Maya world. In the *Popol Vuh*, the three thunderbolt gods are most often referred to as simply "Heart of Sky," but they are also named with the paired title "Heart of Sky and Heart of Earth." Heart of Earth is a reference to the center of the quadrilateral world, and in house metaphors, these three gods represent the three hearthstones that mark this location. The striking parallels between the three Heart of Sky thunderbolt gods and the Palenque triad indicates that these deities represented core beliefs about gods of storms, lightning, and fire and their role in creation.

The building of complexes such as the Palenque Cross Group established more than just a central location to worship deities. These sites likely became destinations for pilgrims from the hinterland as well as other far-flung regions. The ruling elite had a vested interest in creating, promoting, and maintaining these pilgrimage destinations because they generated significant prestige and economic gain.

## ONE GOD, THREE MANIFESTATIONS

The three Heart of Sky thunderbolt gods are portrayed in the *Popol Vuh* as one god with three manifestations (Huracan, Youngest Thunderbolt, and Sudden Thunderbolt). It makes sense that the parallel Palenque triad of thunderbolt gods were also thought to be manifestations of one god. The Heart of Sky deities play a major role in creation, they collaborate with the creator grandparents, they direct the hero twins in many episodes, and they assist them at critical moments. Despite these active roles, their relationship with the creator grandparents and the hero twins is ambiguous. A clue to the identity of the Heart of Sky deities may be found in a statement the hero twins make to their father, One Hunahpu, that human beings would worship him first:

> The child who is born in the light, and the son who is begotten in the light shall go out to you first. They shall worship you first. Your name shall not be forgotten. (Christenson 2003a:191)

Later, a prayer that the leaders of the K'iche' make to the gods indicates that the first god called upon by humans was Heart of Sky (Christenson 2003a:289–90). The creator grandfather Itzamnaaj/Xpiyacoc has numerous manifestations, so we should also expect his son One Ixim/One Hunahpu to have numerous forms.

Some authors have proposed that One Ixim and GI (Huracan's Classic Period counterpart) were aspects of the same god (Schele, Mathews, and Lounsbury 1990; Schele 1992; Freidel, Schele, and Parker 1993:61), and they coined the term "first father" for this god. They based this interpretation partly on the idea, now disproved (Wichmann 2004), that GI's *hun* title and One Ixim's name were the same.

However, there is evidence that One Ixim and all three members of the Palenque triad were closely associated. The birth date for both GI and Ehecatl/Quetzalcoatl is *9 Wind*, and Kelley (1965) has demonstrated their parallel characteristics. One Ixim and Ehecatl/Quetzalcoatl also share many attributes and characteristics, and it has been convincingly argued that these two deities were parallel (Florescano 1999). The overlapping attributes between these three gods suggests that GI and One Ixim were different forms of the same deity. Martin (2006a) has suggested that One Ixim and GII were synonymous. In numerous Classic scenes, One Ixim is shown with the axhead of GII protruding from his head (Taube 1992:49). The Palenque Temple of the Inscriptions sarcophagus lid shows K'inich Janab' Pakal dressed in the jade costume of One Ixim, but he has GII's cranial axhead. Conversely GII frequently has the elongated head of One Ixim.

GIII was a meteor deity who played a dominant role in war. As noted above, there was a sixteenth-century Tzeltal and Tzotzil meteor deity called Pazlam, Pozlom, or Poxlon with traits similar to GIII. In addition to being a meteor, this deity was closely associated with the breath of the human sorcerers who used their breath to send illness. In Tzotzil San Andrés, diseases sent on the wind by sorcerers are still called *poslom*. As will be discussed in chapter 8, One Ixim in his Wind God manifestation was identified with this breath or wind. Thus, GIII may be an aspect of One Ixim.

## THE BIRD OF THE TABLET OF THE CROSS

Bardawil (1976) has grouped together a number of supernatural birds that he refers to jointly as the Principal Bird Deity. The birds appear in a number of contexts, perching on trees, serpents, sky bands, or the Milky Way crocodile. While these birds exhibit several common features, such as wings in the form of serpents and the talons of a bird of prey, they also exhibit subtle but distinct characteristics that indicate they were not all the same bird. On the Tablet of the Cross, one of these so-called Principal Bird Deities perches on top of the tree (see fig. 6.3). While most researchers have assumed that the bird is the avian form of Itzamnaaj, it lacks the *ak'bal* headdress that the Itzamnaaj bird consistently wears, as well as the snake that the Itzamnaaj bird frequently holds in its mouth. The unusual feature of the Tablet of the Cross bird is a motif hanging from its mouth composed of a shell and braided strips of cloth. This kind of bird is not restricted to Palenque. The same bird with the braided strips in his mouth perches at the top of the back rack on Copan Stela H, where the ruler Waxaklajuun Ub'aah K'awiil is shown dressed as One Ixim.

Given the parallels between the Heart of Sky thunderbolt gods and the Palenque triad, a logical parallel for the Tablet of the Cross bird is the falcon Wok, which I have argued was a muwaan falcon. The many depictions of the Itzamnaaj bird that are found in Maya art indicate that this supernatural bird was thought to be a manifestation of Itzamnaaj rather than just his messenger. This raises the possibilities that Wok, likewise, was not just the messenger of the Heart of Sky thunderbolt gods, but one of their manifestations, and that the Tablet of the Cross bird was a manifestation of a member of the Palenque triad. In the passage concerning Wok in the *Popol Vuh* mentioned at the beginning of this chapter, Wok is said to return specifically to Huracan Thunderbolt, whom I have equated with GI. Given that the Tablet of the Cross is in the *pib'naah* of GI and that the bird is perched on the tree with GI's Quadripartite Badge Monster as its base, I propose that this bird was one of GI's avian manifestations.

Another supernatural bird perches on the central icon of the Temple of the Foliated Cross. This bird is distinguished from the Tablet of the Cross bird in that it has an upturned beak rather than a hooked beak, and the object hanging from its mouth is not braided (see fig. 6.5). I speculate that this bird is an avian form of GII.

## THE DEITY MUWAAN MAT

Although the texts in the Temple of the Cross relate the birth of GI, the main text of the Tablet of the Cross focuses on the deity Muwaan Mat. The Initial Series date of the text begins with Muwaan Mat's birth and moves forward to a *"k'almay* event" eight years later (Carrasco 2005:451). The young K'an Joy Chitam also underwent a *k'almay* event when he was seven years old, according to the Palenque Palace Tablet, an event that appears to refer to his first shedding of blood as an offering to the gods. It seems reasonable to conclude that Muwaan Mat's event set the precedent for this kind of early childhood ritual (Carrasco 2005:452). The Tablet of the Cross narrative then moves forward to the 13.0.0.0.0 Period Ending event involving the three hearthstones (3114 B.C.), the Six Sky house event with GI two years later (3112 B.C.), and the birth of GI on *9 Wind* (2360 B.C.). The story then relates the accession of Muwaan Mat (2325 B.C.) on another *9 Wind* date and concludes with a series of accessions for the mythical, as well as historical, Palenque rulers who followed Muwaan Mat. On the Temple XIX platform, which also refers to these mythological events, Muwaan Mat's accession is stated to be the first of a series of accessions (Stuart 2005b).

While numerous examples of Itzamnaaj and the Palenque triad appear in Maya art, no portrait of Muwaan Mat has been identified. The appearance of the muwaan bird in his name suggests the possibility that this deity was manifested as a bird. I tentatively suggest that the bird who sits atop the tree on the Tablet of the Cross was not only the avian form of GI, but also Muwaan Mat. Stuart (2006) has suggested that Muwaan Mat was a manifestation of One Ixim, presumably because of the *ixim* glyph that occurs in the part of his name that is not yet completely deciphered. These two seemingly different identifications are reconcilable if we accept the notion that One Ixim, like his father Itzamnaaj, had multiple manifestations. In summary, I believe that the three Heart of Sky thunderbolt gods and the bird Wok were all manifestations of One Hunahpu, and that the three Palenque thunderbolt gods and Muwaan Mat, who were parallel to these *Popol Vuh* deities, were all manifestations of One Ixim.

# 7

# THE PATERNAL GRANDFATHER

The creator grandparents—the first parents, priests, diviners, healers, and artists—were role models for their children and grandchildren as well as for the humans who practiced their arts and sciences. The complementary nature of the creator grandparents, who also had numerous animal manifestations, is well known. This chapter focuses on the creator grandfather, Itzamnaaj/Xpiyacoc, and the complementary functions he shared with his wife, Ix Chel/Xmucane. This creator couple were the paternal grandparents of the hero twins. A more detailed examination of the creator grandmother is found in chapter 10.

## Patriarch and Midwife

The *Popol Vuh* describes Xpiyacoc and Xmucane as extraordinary sages and possessors of great knowledge. Xpiyacoc was called *mamom* (literally, grandfather), which Christenson (2003a:62) has translated as patriarch. In contemporary K'iche' society, he notes a mamom is the head of a patrilineal group who conducts family-oriented rituals. He is required to be a wise diviner and shrewd marriage negotiator with eloquent speaking skills, who can convince the bride's family of the worthiness of the groom and formalize the arrangements. Similar matchmakers, often accompanied by their wives or an elderly woman who fills the role of assistant, are found throughout the Maya region (Tozzer 1941:218; Miles 1955:81; Laughlin 1962; Orellana 1984:87). Diviners gain insight from dreams and also interpret the dreams of others. No direct evidence exists in the *Popol Vuh* that the creator grandparents interpreted dreams, but their role as the first diviners suggests that they did, and they were likely considered to be the source of divine messages sent to humans in their dreams.

Xpiyacoc's title of patriarch is paired with Xmucane's title of *iyom*, "midwife." Midwives often work in unison with a male healer and diviner to perform complementary tasks during the pregnancy and labor of their client. Both pregnancy and childbirth are hazardous, and the Maya consider a woman to be ill and very vulnerable during this period. The midwife provides prenatal care, supervises the labor and delivery, and conducts postpartum treatments. Midwives are usually older women well past their reproductive age, and they are sometimes referred to by the honorific of "grandmother." Pregnant women may be given prenatal sweat baths; they often give birth in the sweathouse, especially if the delivery is difficult; and they and the new infants are given postnatal sweat baths (Groark 1997). The midwife prepares the sweat bath and accompanies her patient inside, where she washes and massages her. There is a practical aspect to this birthing tradition because heat can speed the delivery, and the warmth of the sweat bath helps the mother and child regain their central core of body heat lost during the birthing (Furst 1995:96–102).

Maya women traditionally squat on a mat to give birth, but when labor is prolonged and difficult, they are known to hold on to a cord or shawl that is tied to the rafters of the house (Redfield 1945:480; Taube 1994). The midwife kneels or stands behind the woman and supports her with her arms. A skilled midwife can rotate a fetus that is in the wrong position and administer massages and potions to expedite the process. Protracted labor or other problems can end in the death of the mother, child, or both. In a successful birth, the midwife cuts the umbilical cord and collects and deposits the placenta in an appropriate location. One of the key tasks after the baby and mother are washed and redressed is to help initiate breast-feeding and ensure that there is adequate breast milk. The contemporary midwife performs important ceremonies to protect the health and welfare of the mother and child. It is also her job to recognize the "signs" that appear on the newborn (Paul and Paul 1975). The midwife thus plays a key role in interpreting the destiny of the individual. By their very nature, these various duties of the midwife require her to be a diviner and healer just like the creator grandmother.

Given the birthing functions of the sweat bath, it is not surprising to find that the interior of a sweat bath was identified with a womb. In the Tz'utujil region, the sweat bath is called *retit tux,* "mother–sweat bath." Although the births of Xmucane's children are not described in the *Popol Vuh,* it is not unreasonable to suggest that One Hunahpu and Seven Hunahpu were born in a sweat bath that metaphorically represented Xmucane's womb. Given her husband's association with fire, it also seems reasonable to assume that the fire of this sweat bath was one of his manifestations. As she was the first goddess to give birth, hers should be the quintessential sweat bath. A connection between the paternal grandparents and a sweat bath is found in a Kaqchikel myth in which the grandfather is placed in a sweat bath and is transformed into a coati (Redfield 1945:27).

The creator grandparents of the Classic Period were also associated with the sweat bath. Child (2006) has presented convincing evidence that God N (also known as the creator grandfather Itzamnaaj) and Ix Chel were identified with this structure. He reached this conclusion based on the role of the sweat bath in healing and birthing rituals, and using comparisons with other Mesoamerican groups. The theme of God N emerging before a young, voluptuous goddess appears on a number of pottery scenes that refer to birth (Taube 1994). In the Tz'utujil region, the *mam* (grandfather) healer is summoned during labor to ease the pain and duration of the delivery, and Taube has suggested that God N in these scenes has been summoned to assist in the birth. In some of these scenes, God N touches or stares at the breast of the young goddess. Although it has frequently been characterized as sexual fondling, I believe it may be related to the production of breast milk. One of the critical duties of the mother immediately after the birth is to suckle her child. When this ability is lacking, a healer immediately provides potions and rituals to stimulate lactation. On K2067, God N extends a cup to the goddess.

## Animal Manifestations of the Creator Grandparents

The Great White Peccary and Great White Coati manifestations of the creator grandparents act as healers who repair teeth and set bones during the hero twins' defeat of Seven Macaw. The pairing of a peccary and a coati is found in the underworld ball game episode when Xbalanque petitions the animals of the world to bring food with which to create a replacement head for his decapitated brother:

> Then Xbalanque summoned all of the animals—the coati and the peccary, and all the animals both small and great—while it was still dark, early in the morning . . . the coati arrived last of all bringing a chilacayote squash. She came rolling it along with her nose. This was to be transformed into the head of Hunahpu. (Christenson 2003a)

This pairing of the coati and peccary also occurs in the miraculous restoration of the hero twins' milpa, indicating the high position of the coati and peccary in the animal hierarchy. The role of the coati manifestation of the creator grandmother will be deferred until chapter 11.

Like Xpiyacoc, the creator grandfather Itzamnaaj was also closely associated with peccaries. In several pottery scenes (K1991, K8622), Itzamnaaj rides a peccary, and he emerges from the mouth of a peccary on *Madrid Codex* 39. Itzamnaaj also had a rattlesnake form. In the transformation of the animals that occurs at the end of the canícula period, rattlesnakes are said to turn into peccaries and peccaries into rattlesnakes (Redfield and Villa Rojas 1934:208–209). This belief may stem from the fact that the two animals were both manifestations of the creator grandfather.

In his opossum form, Xpiyacoc was identified with fire and with the darkness before dawn, when the eastern sky begins to lighten and glow red (see chapter 4). In their role as Hunahpu Opossum and Hunahpu Coyote, Xpiyacoc and Xmucane are asked to perform a counting of the divination seeds to discover whether making people from wood and reeds will be successful. The human-like characteristics of

the opossum are well known, and the Tzotzil believe that the opossum was originally a person because it has five fingers on each paw (Blaffer 1972). The hands of
such an animal are well suited for counting out the lots used in divination. The
opossum form of Xpiyacoc was associated with healing; its ground-up tail was used
as a potion in childbirth (Sahagún 1959–63, book 11, 11; Hunn 1977:202).

When Xpiyacoc and Xmucane are asked to perform their joint divination for
the creation of the wooden people, the text states:

> For this was the Grandfather, the Master of the Tz'ite, Xpiyacoc by
> name. And this was the Grandmother, the Mistress of Days and Mis-
> tress of Shaping who is at the foot, who is called Xmucane. (Christen-
> son 2003a:82)

The phrase "at the foot" has been interpreted to mean that Xmucane was positioned
at the feet of the petitioners, as contemporary diviners are today and as a midwife is
when assisting at a birth (D. Tedlock 1996, 234n70; Christenson 2003a:82). This
certainly fits with the position of the creator grandmother Ix Chel seen on K6020,
where she sits at the foot of her patient whom she is in the process of healing. Divinations performed in the presence of the diviner's wife are thought to be the most
accurate, and the phrase "at the foot" may also refer to Xmucane being at the foot
of Xpiyacoc during the casting of the lots.

In the *Popol Vuh*, a coyote, a raven, a fox, and a parakeet bring the corn used to
create humans to the attention of the creator gods, while in the *Annals of the Cakchiquels*, it is just the coyote and raven (Recinos and Goetz 1953:48; Christenson
2003a:193–94). Given that the creator grandmother had a coyote manifestation in
the *Popol Vuh*, one wonders if the raven might be a manifestation of the creator
grandparents as well. Coyotes and ravens play important roles in the discovery of
corn in contemporary Poqomchi', Kaqchikel, Ixil, Mam, and Tz'utujil stories as well.
In a Tzotzil variation on the theme, a man and his family survive the primordial
flood that kills everyone else by climbing to the top of a high mountain (Laughlin
1977:254–59). In the aftermath of the disaster, they have nothing to eat, but a holy
raven brings them two ears of corn for seed from the mountain called Hol Na Joj,
"head of Raven House." This mountain is located northeast of Zinacantan center
and is thought to contain two bins of corn, yellow and white. In the festival for San
Sebastián, two participants are thought to represent the raven who brought corn to
man (Vogt 1969:542; Laughlin 1975:199). Each wears a bird mask with an ear of corn
stuck in its beak. Their formal name is *k'uk'ulchon,* literally "quetzal serpent" (feathered
serpent) in Tzotzil, which is also one of the names of the creator grandparents.

## Itzamnaaj and Ix Chel

Las Casas tells us that in the Alta Verapaz region of Guatemala, Itzamnaaj and Ix
Chel were considered to be a divine husband and wife (Miles 1955:38); they are

Figure 7.1. Itzamnaaj/Ix Chel, *Dresden Codex* 9 (after Villacorta)

paired in the Poqomam dictionaries of Zúñiga and Morán (Miles 1955:39). Although the sources from northern Yucatan do not specifically refer to Itzamnaaj and Ix Chel as husband and wife, they are repetitively paired in an incantation from the *Ritual of the Bacabs,* a series of prayers for the cure of certain diseases (Roys 1965:23–28). As discussed in chapter 4, the Central Mexican creator grandparents called Ometecuhtli and Omecihuatl were manifested as a single bisexual deity called Ometeotl (two god). Evidence that Itzamnaaj and Ix Chel were also viewed as a bisexual deity parallel to Ometeotl is seen in several scenes in the codices, where a deity is illustrated with the head of God D (Itzamnaaj) and the body of his wife, Ix Chel, such as *Madrid Codex* 30. On *Dresden Codex* 9, this deity is named in the caption text as God D (Itzamnaaj) (fig. 7.1).

Itzamnaaj's omnipotence is indicated in a number of colonial documents. The Yucatec Maya *Relación de Valladolid* states that "they worshipped one god alone who had the name Hunab and Itzamna which means only one god" (Tozzer 1941:146). An entry in the Yucatec Maya Vienna dictionary reads:

> Principal idol (god), which these Indians of this land had, from which they said all things proceeded and who was incorporeal; hence they made no image of him: *Colop-u-uich-kin.*
> Idol said to be of the preceding: *Hun Itzamna, Yax-cocah-mut.*
> Another idol, who was a man and whom they worshipped for having discovered the art of the letters (writing) of this land: *Itzamna, Kinch ahau.* (Roys 1933:100)

The quadripartite form and directional associations of Itzamnaaj and Ix Chel are found in the incantations in the *Ritual of the Bacabs* (Roys 1965:23–28). The Maya believed that disease was caused by evil winds. These winds originated in the water found in the caves of the guardian deities. In the healing ceremony, the ritual specialist created a quadrilateral space around the patient and swept the area with a broom. The sweeping motion was directed at "holes" on the sides of the quadrilateral space that represented the caves of the guardians. This action drove the winds and, by extension, the disease back to the caves. Each *Ritual of the Bacabs* incantation describes the caves of the Pawahtuns, in which the disease was born, and demands that the four Bakab guardians take back the disease-carrying wind. An incantation for the cure of asthma also refers to a red, white, black, and yellow Ix Chel as well as a red, white, black, and yellow Itzamnaaj. The association of color with the four directions in Maya ritual indicates that each Ix Chel and Itzamnaaj was identified with a particular direction. As noted, Itzamnaaj was also called Yax Cocay Mut. A reference to an Ek Cocay Mut in the *Chilam Balam of Chumayel* also implies an association between color and direction (Tozzer 1941:145).

## GOD D AND GOD N AS MANIFESTATIONS OF ITZAMNAAJ

God D and three other gods (God A, God K, and God G) appear in the *Dresden Codex* New Year pages engaged in putting the quadrilateral world in order (Thompson 1972; Taube 1988b). God D was first identified as Itzamnaaj because he appears in these scenes performing the New Year functions that Landa indicated were performed by Itzamnaaj. The latter was also active in Classic Period ordering rituals. God D is recorded on Quirigua Stela C as one of the deities involved with setting the three

Figure 7.2. God D glyph and portraits

hearthstones during the 13.0.0.0.0 *4 Ajaw 8 Kumk'u* Period Ending ceremony (Schele 1992; Freidel, Schele, and Parker 1993; Stuart 2005b).

God D is illustrated as an old man with receding gums and wrinkles around his mouth (fig. 7.2). His eye may be round or square, and he most often wears an *ak'bal* flower headdress and a shell ornament. Seashells were widely traded in Mesoamerica and are a common item found in tombs. Given their aquatic origins, it is expected that shells would be associated with the waters of the place of duality. In the hieroglyphic text, God D's shell represents the word *yax,* a term that includes a color range from green to blue.

A bird form of God D is illustrated in the *Paris Codex* in the series of pages relating to the k'atun ceremonies (Bardawil 1976:195; Love 1994). In each scene, a bird representing the omen for the k'atun hovers before the participants. On page 4, which represents the k'atun *11 Ajaw,* the bird of omen has the face of God D. As noted, Bardawil grouped together several different kinds of supernatural birds which he called the Principal Bird Deity. One of these supernatural birds wears the ak'bal flower headdress of God D, and he has been identified as a bird manifestation of God D based on this diagnostic trait (fig. 7.3a–c; Bardawil 1976; Hellmuth 1987; Taube, cited in Houston and Stuart 1989:14; 1992:36). The Itzamnaaj bird had a wide geographical distribution during the Preclassic Period, with examples found at highland Kaminaljuyu (Altars 9 and 10, Stela 10) and the lowland site of El Mirador (Stela 2). In the Preclassic San Bartolo murals, the Itzamnaaj bird is pictured landing in each of the four world trees (Saturno 2006). I stress that I am only discussing the supernatural bird that wears the ak'bal flower headdress and carries a snake in its beak. I am excluding, for example, birds in the art of Izapa and the Palenque Cross Group birds that other researchers equate with the Itzamnaaj bird, which do not have these traits.

Five illustrations of God D in the *Dresden Codex* show him wearing the ak'bal flower headgear, but he is most frequently shown without it. His name in the caption texts is, however, composed of the ak'bal flower element (T152) prefixed to either the bird head or to his portrait as seen in the first example in figure 7.2. Both the bird and his portrait have the same large eye decorated with a curl. As Stuart notes, evidence indicates that God D and God N were manifestations of the same god. Before discussing this evidence, a brief description of the various manifestations of God N is in order.

God N is the designation given to the set of old gods who frequently wear a net bag headdress or water lily headdress. The T1014 sign is a portrait of God N wearing his net bag headdress (fig. 7.4a). There are many examples where the full form of the T1014 portrait glyph is reduced to just the net bag (David Stuart, personal communication). This net bag sign is designated as T64. When God N is illustrated in the codices, he has an almond-shaped eye like that of a human being, and he lacks the eye curl found with God D. In Classic Period images, he also has almond-shaped eyes, in contrast to God D's large, square eye.

Figure 7.3. a. Itzamnaaj bird, K3863; b. Tonina monument; c. Itzamnaaj bird with serpent, K2131

a

Figure 7.4. a. God N portrait, T1014; b. T64:528 sign, T64:548 sign; c. Number 5 Deity

Coe suggests that the T64 net bag represents the word *pauah,* and that God N's name was Pawahtun. The name Pawahtun is given by Landa as an alternate name for the Bakabs, and it appears in the *Ritual of the Bacabs* incantations. In the codices, God N's name is usually composed of a number (three, four, or five), the T64 net sign, and either a T528 or T548 sign (fig. 7.4b). The Yucatec Motul dictionary gives the word *pauo* for a net bag. In the hieroglyphic texts, a number of crosshatched signs represent the sound *pa.* Because of the close similarity between *pauah* and *pauo* and because the net bag has cross-hatching, Coe has suggested the Pawahtun name for God N. Stuart, however, has noted that neither T1014 nor T64 ever substitutes for any of the numerous examples of the syllabic *pa* signs, so this is an unlikely reading. Furthermore, *pauo* does not appear in Ch'olan languages as a term for net bag.

Scribes often took two signs representing two separate words and merged them into one glyph block. On *Dresden Codex* 56, God N's portrait is conflated with the T528 sign. This manifestation of God N appears in a number of Classic Period scenes, such as K1485 and Copan Structure 22. His diagnostic traits are a water lily head-dress and T528 "stone" elements on his body. K1485 illustrates four of these God N water lily headdress deities in the upper register, while three God N deities in their net bag manifestation are pictured in the lower register.

God N in his water lily headdress manifestation appears as the Number 5 Deity, and in this context he wears the T548 drum sign on top of his headdress (fig. 7.4c). T548 is a picture of a wooden drum that was used throughout Mesoamerica, although it is not used to represent the word for drum. The T548 sign is a logo-graph representing the tun period (*ha'b'*) in the Long Count, and it also appears as part of the logograph for the k'atun period (*winikha'b'*).

In Classic Period art and in the *Dresden Codex,* the T64 net sign is prefixed to a portrait of an opossum—another of the animal manifestations of God N (fig. 7.5; Stuart 1998:404). God N was also represented as a turtle (fig. 7.6a–c; Taube 1992:94). On *Dresden Codex* 37, his turtle shell is marked with a k'an, "yellow," infix, and this old man turtle appears in many contexts. Numerous members of the Classic Period elite were named after deities, and the name God N Yellow Turtle is found at a variety of sites (David Stuart, personal communication).

The manner in which this name is presented contributes to our understanding of God N. On Copan Stela C, the God N Yellow Turtle name phrase is presented as two separate words (fig. 7.6d). This example is composed of God N's portrait followed by syllabic signs representing the word *ak,* turtle. The k'an sign appears in God N's earring. In an example from Piedras Negras, the T64 net sign and a turtle shell with a k'an infix are employed (fig. 7.6e). In a third example, the T64 net bag representing God N and a turtle head representing the word *ak* are used (fig. 7.6f). The turtle wears the k'an sign as an earring. In a final example, the God N portrait is conflated with the turtle (fig. 7.6g). In this case, God N is represented by the net bag, nose, and "old mouth" elements, while the turtle is represented by the "water lily" eye, mouth curl, and k'an earring.

Figure 7.5. God N opossum (after Taube)

Figure 7.6. a. God N, Lower Temple of the Jaguar, Chichén Itzá; b. God N, Quirigua Zoomorph P; c. God N, *Dresden Codex* 37; d. God N and *ak* "turtle" sign; e. T64 and turtle shell; f. T64 and yellow turtle head; g. conflation of God N and yellow turtle, Lintel 3, Piedras Negras

The occasional appearance of God N's name in the name phrase of God D has raised the possibility that God N and God D were manifestations of the same deity (David Stuart, personal communication). This conjunction occurs on a panel at the site of Xcalumkin and on a Late Classic vessel, where God D's name phrase is composed of a God N portrait followed by the ak'bal flower and bird head (fig. 7.7a–b; see also K7727). The bird has a T617 sign, which frequently appears on the bodies of deities, infixed on its forehead. On Quirigua Stela C, the T64 net bag appears as a superfix above the ak'bal flower and bird (fig. 7.7c). In this example, the God N portrait is represented by the T64 sign. Several examples of God D in the *Madrid Codex* also suggest that these two gods are the same. *Madrid Codex* 94a and 106b illustrate God D, while the associated caption text refers to God N. On *Madrid Codex* 96, God D is illustrated wearing a headdress with the cross-hatching of God N's net bag. God D is also shown on K1196 wearing the God N net bag headdress (Taube 1992a:36).

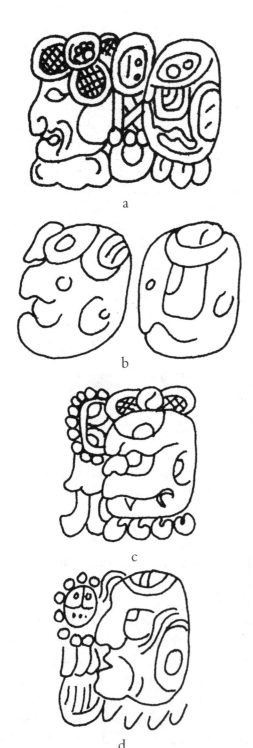

Figure 7.7. Itzamnaaj name glyphs: a. Xcalumkin panel; b. Late Classic vessel, American Museum of Natural History; c. Quirigua Stela C; d. Palenque Temple XIX

Another example of the conjunction of God D with God N is seen on the Palenque Temple XIX platform, where God D is named with a portrait of his square-eyed form and the ak'bal flower (fig. 7.7d). No God N sign seems to appear in this name. However, I believe that this name is a conflation of an almond-eyed God N with a square-eyed bird head, in the same manner that the God N portrait is conflated with his turtle manifestation (see fig. 7.6g). The old-man nose and mouth represent God N, and the square eye, T617 sign, and ak'bal flower headdress represent the bird—that is, the bird manifestation of God D. When the old man God N wears the flower headdress, he becomes this square-eyed bird or takes on the traits of this bird.

A recently discovered Classic Period carving at Tonina illustrates this point (see fig. 7.3b). It shows the God D bird with the head of the almond-eyed God N, who wears the ak'bal flower as a headband. The manner in which the name of an Early Classic ruler at Yaxchilan is written also suggests that the ak'bal flower is specifically identified with the bird. On the hieroglyphic staircase, the ruler's name is composed of the ak'bal flower and a jaguar head, but on Lintel 47, at B7, the ak'bal flower has been replaced with just the bird head (Martin and Grube 2000:118–19). Although its meaning is unclear, a syllabic *ji* sign appears as a subfix on most examples of God D's name.

The most logical explanation of the appearance of the God N net bag in the name phrase of God D is that God N with his net bag headdress and the God D bird with its ak'bal flower headdress represent two separate words. Stuart (2005b, 2006) has concluded that the portrait of God N with his T64 net bag represents the word "Itzamnaaj" and that the God D bird represents the word *mut,* "bird." In contrast to Stuart's interpretation, Martin (2006b) has suggested that the portrait of God N represents the word "Itzam" and that the name for the bird might be related to one of Itzamnaaj's Postclassic avatars, Yax Cocah Mut. In the absence of a clear decipherment of these two names, I will continue to refer to God N as Itzamnaaj, and I will refer to the bird as the Itzamnaaj bird.

The T64 net bag headdress should symbolize some specific office or primary function of God N/Itzamnaaj. Net bags were created with either closely spaced knots to contain small items or widely spaced knots to accommodate bulky loads. In the *Dresden Codex*, the opossum manifestations of the creator grandfather use net bags to carry deities on their backs. A female opossum has a pouch to carry her young, and once the young have matured, they migrate from the pouch and cling to her back. Opossums carry their young just like the *Dresden Codex* opossums carry the deities. It is possible that the net bag was a metaphor for the pouch of the opossum.

In colonial-period Yucatan, an avian manifestation of Itzamnaaj was called Ahcocáhmut, Yax Cocah Mut, Ek Cocah Mut, Yax Kok Ahmut, or Ahkok Ahmut (Tozzer 1941:145; Boot 2004). Boot suggests that the name refers to the Tzeltal term *kokmut,* which means the rare harpy eagle (*Harpia harpyja*). The etymology of nominal phrases is a difficult topic, but if this name can be divided into two parts it may represent the names *ah coc* and *ah mut,* "he of the turtle, he of the bird"; *yax coc* and *ah mut,* "blue/green turtle, he of the bird"; or *ek coc* and *ah mut,* "black turtle, he of the bird." In addition to meaning "bird," *mut* also means "messenger" (Houston, Stuart, and Taube 2006:229). The following overview of the Itzamnaaj bird will demonstrate that he was the archetypal messenger bird and that he was based on a laughing falcon.

## THE ITZAMNAAJ BIRD

As a primary manifestation of the creator grandfather, the Itzamnaaj bird exhibits some of the key traits of this paramount god. In several pottery scenes, such as K4546 and K1226, the hero twins One Ajaw and Yax Bolon shoot at the Itzamnaaj bird with their blowguns (fig. 7.8). Numerous authors have equated these scenes with the *Popol Vuh* episode of the hero twins Hunahpu and Xbalanque shooting Seven Macaw (Robicsek and Hales 1981:147–48; Cortez 1986; Taube 1987; Freidel, Schele, and Parker 1993:69–71; D. Tedlock 1996:78; Houston, Stuart, and Taube 2006:236). This identification is highly unlikely. Seven Macaw was a supernatural bird who lived during the era of the wooden people (Christenson 2003a:91). The hero twins of the *Popol Vuh* climb up into Seven Macaw's nance tree and hide in its leaves. When Seven Macaw arrives to eat the fruit, Hunahpu shoots him with his blowgun and breaks his jaw. This loosens his teeth and causes him great jaw pain. The bark from the nance tree is used as a remedy for loose teeth (Breedlove and Laughlin 1993:151), and if Seven Macaw had healing skills, he would have known that and cured himself. Instead, he has to employ Great White Peccary and Great White Coati to perform a healing and is thus tricked into giving away his insignia, without which he is powerless. This eventually results in his defeat and death.

Although both stories involve shooting an avian deity, the similarity ends there, for Seven Macaw was not a manifestation of the creator grandfather (see chapter 14 for a further discussion of Seven Macaw). Depictions of macaws are common in Maya art, and they are distinguished from other birds by a macaw-like beak and circles around the eyes. The portrait of a macaw represents the word *mo',* "macaw," in hieroglyphic texts. Hellmuth (1987:166, 196) observes that the features of the Itzamnaaj bird are those of a bird of prey, not a macaw, and he notes that the Itzamnaaj bird is frequently illustrated with a serpent clutched in its beak (see fig. 7.3c). Given that macaws do not eat snakes, he suggests that a better parallel for the Itzamnaaj bird would be Wak of the *Popol Vuh,* who was a snake-eating bird and who was also shot by the hero twins. A slight digression is in order to discuss this episode of the *Popol Vuh.*

The trespassing by the hero twins when they play ball at the eastern ballcourt on the road of the underworld annoys the underworld rulers. They send their four owl messengers to the household of the hero twins to demand that the twins come to the underworld. When the owls arrive, only the grandmother, Xmucane, is at home, so they give her the message. She, in turn, sends a louse from her head to give the

Figure 7.8. K1226 (after Kerr)

message to her grandsons. On the road to the ballcourt, the slow-moving louse meets a young toad called Tamazul who volunteers to carry him. Tamazul eats the louse and continues the journey. The toad then meets a great snake named Saqi K'as who volunteers to take him at a faster rate of speed. Saqi K'as swallows the toad and again the journey continues. Then the snake encounters a bird called Wak, who swallows him.

When Wak arrives at the ballcourt he alights on its rim and calls out. The twins grab their blowguns and shoot the bird in the eye because they want to know what his message is. Wak whirls around and falls to the ground, where the twins seize him. Wak promises to give the twins their message on the condition that they first restore his eyesight. They do so by rubbing his eye with black rubber resin from their ball. Wak vomits up the snake, who in turn vomits up the toad. In the teeth of the toad, the twins find the louse, who finally delivers the message.

Although he does not identify the type of bird of prey Wak is, Hellmuth correctly concludes that this bird is parallel to the Itzamnaaj bird. There are, however, more reasons for identifying the Itzamnaaj bird with Wak than just the snake eating and the blowgun.

Recinos notes that an eighteenth-century K'iche' dictionary recorded "Wak" as the name of a hawk that eats snakes (Goetz and Morley 1950:137). When Wak of the *Popol Vuh* arrives at the ballcourt, he calls out "wak-ko," the call of *Herpetotheres cachinnans,* also known as the guaco or laughing falcon (D. Tedlock 1985:132, 282, 336; 1996:270, 346). The laughing falcon is so named because it makes two kinds of calls: a "wa-ko" sound and a "ha-ha-ha" sound like laughter. It is most often found in open areas rather than deep forest. Unlike other falcons and hawks, it is frequently seen conspicuously perched on top of trees for long periods (Janzen 1984:583). This bird of prey is also called a snake hawk because it feeds almost exclusively on snakes that it kills and takes up into trees to eat. For humans, the presence of deadly snakes is one of the hazards of living in a tropical environment, especially during the field-clearing season. The laughing falcon often eats venomous snakes, and his presence in a cornfield is of great benefit. To eat a snake, the laughing falcon bites off the snake's head and flies into a nearby tree to devour the body. This is evident in one of the

San Bartolo murals, which illustrates Itzamnaaj birds sitting in the four world trees with double-headed serpents in their mouths. In one of the trees, the double-headed serpent has had one of its heads ripped off.

Dennis Tedlock notes that Wak was a messenger bird and that from Central Mexico to Brazil the laughing falcon is viewed as an omen. Throughout Mesoamerica, the call of the laughing falcon is specifically an indication of the coming of the rains. Other, migratory hawks are said to bring the rains and take them away, but the laughing falcon is "the local forecaster, and when he becomes especially vociferous rain is not far away" (Dickey and Van Rossem 1938:131). In Veracruz, it is said that if a laughing falcon calls from a dead tree it will not rain, but if he calls from a green tree it will (Lowery and Dalquest 1951:555). The Itzaj Maya also believe in this omen, and they consider the laughing falcon to be one of the main predators necessary for the survival of the forest (Atran 1999:191; 2003). They refer to the laughing falcon as *ajpäy ja'*, "announcer of rain," and *ajpäy k'in*, "announcer of summer" (Hofling and Tesucún 1997:123). The Ch'orti' also believe the call of the laughing falcon brings the rain, and they characterize the bird as a *padrino* (Fought 1972:388). In the Ch'orti' area, the padrino is the prayer maker in the village who conducts the ceremonies for rain. The laughing falcon's "ha-ha-ha" sound resembles the Maya words for water and rain: *ha'* and *ha'al*. When the guaco is calling for rain, he is literally saying, "water, water, water" (Alonso Méndez, personal communication).

Several contemporary Maya groups view the laughing falcon as a healer, one of the principal occupations of the creator grandfather. The Tzotzil associate the laughing falcon with curing. It is believed that if a person can return the call of this bird without tiring, he will become a bonesetter (Laughlin 1975:362). The Ch'ol of Joloniel believe that the laughing falcon can kill poisonous snakes because it knows how to cure itself if bitten (Jolja' Cave Project field notes; Domingo Pérez Moreno and Felipe Pérez Montejo, personal communication 2001). It is said that the first woman to spin cotton (the Virgin Mary/moon goddess) was bitten by a poisonous snake, but a laughing falcon came and cured her (Jolja' Cave Project field notes; Felipe Pérez Montejo, personal communication 2001). This may also be related to the role of the laughing falcon as a rainmaker, for there is a common belief that the spinning of cotton creates rain clouds. The healing abilities attributed to the laughing falcon contrast with Seven Macaw's powerlessness as a curer.

In summary, the attributes of the laughing falcon match those of Itzamnaaj and his bird manifestation. Both birds are snake-eating birds of prey as well as birds of omen. The ability of the laughing falcon to kill poisonous snakes must have been viewed by the Maya as an indication of enormous spiritual power. He is thus an appropriate manifestation of the powerful Itzamnaaj. The laughing falcon is viewed as a healer with the ability to cure snake bites. Itzamnaaj was the first curer. Healers begin their careers by first healing their family members. In the Joloniel myth, the laughing falcon heals the first woman to spin cotton, and Ix Chel, wife of Itzamnaaj, was the first woman to spin cotton. The favorite perch of the laughing falcon is the tops of trees in clearings, and the Itzamnaaj bird is illustrated perched at the tops of trees. From his treetop location, the laughing falcon calls for rain. Itzamnaaj was the first priest, and one of the primary functions of these ritual specialists was rain petitions. This evidence indicates that the Itzamnaaj bird was based on the laughing falcon.

A proposed identification of the snake in the mouth of the Itzamnaaj bird as an indigo snake (*Drymarchon corais*) supports the conclusion that the bird was a laughing falcon. The snake Saqi K'as in the *Popol Vuh* is described as a fast moving, terrestrial snake that eats the slow-moving toad named Tamazul. "Tamazul" is derived from the Nahuatl word *tamasolli* (toad), and based on its description in the *Florentine Codex,* it can be identified as the *Bufo marinus* (Sahagún 1959–63, book 11, 72). The *Bufo marinus* is an enormous, nocturnal toad that thrives in areas disturbed by agriculture. Toads are a staple for many predators, but the adult *B. marinus* is not frequently preyed upon because of the toxicity of its white parotid secretion. Through muscle control, this toad can squirt poison a distance of up to thirty centimeters. It does not have to move fast because it has few enemies. The *Florentine Codex* compares a lazy messenger to this toad (Sahagún 1959–63, Book 11, 72).

Varea identifies the *saqiq'as* as a snake of great size that makes a lot of noise in fleeing, while Guzmán (*Compendio de nombres en lengua cakchiquel*) says it is a black snake (Christenson 2003a:156). The word *k'as* can be translated in a number of ways. Edmonson and Christenson translate it as "life," but *k'as* is also a K'iche' term for a raccoon. The Tzotzil term for a raccoon is *me'el chon* (old woman snake), and this term is also applied to the indigo snake. This close linguistic association suggests that Saqi K'as was an indigo.

If we assume that the Saqi K'as of the *Popol Vuh* and the snake that the Itzamnaaj bird is holding are the same species, it would have to have a wide distribution throughout the Maya area, as the indigo snake does (it is found from sea level to 1,900 meters; Campbell 1998:212). The indigo snake has the characteristics of Saqi K'as: dark color and a black tail (one of its indigenous names is "black tail"). When the indigo snake is disturbed, it hisses loudly, vibrates its tail, flattens its neck, and hurries away. In other words, it makes a lot of noise when fleeing. The indigo is a primarily terrestrial snake, fast-moving and large (only the boa and tiger tree snake are longer). This snake rushes to seize its prey, which it swallows alive, as Saqi K'as swallowed the toad. The indigo is at the top of the snake food chain in that it eats other snakes, including boas and venomous snakes, but it especially likes toads. It is known to eat the *Bufo marinus.*

Some of the attributes of the indigo snake are similar to those of the double-headed versions of the serpent held by the Itzamnaaj bird. The long, thin form of this serpent may be more suggestive of a vine snake, but a passage in the *Florentine Codex* indicates that the indigo becomes long and thin at times (Sahagún 1959–63, book 11, 70–71). The codex describes the indigenous belief that the indigo lives in the water and likes to drown people. If it fails at that endeavor, the snake builds a pit at water's edge and deposits fish in it as bait. When a man removes the fish, the snake emerges from the water and pursues him. After coiling around him, the indigo inserts its forked tail into the nostril of the man and squeezes him to death. To outsmart the snake, a man must first dig a hole at the foot of a tree. When the serpent pursues him, he must run to the tree and hide in the hole. When the indigo arrives at the tree, it will coil around the tree. "And this tlilcoatl then wraps itself about the tree; it coils itself many times, it stretches itself well. It stretches so much that it becomes very thin; its spine is broken up. Thus this serpent dies there" (Sahagún 1959–63, book 11, 70–71). This description of an indigo snake is consistent with the thin, coiled form of the doubled-headed serpent. The indigo snake loves water, and in Miguel Álvarez del Toro's *Reptiles de Chiapas* (1960:157–58), he notes that the indigo is thought to be the owner of springs. In some examples of the double-headed serpent, the body is marked with water signs. These various ethnographic sources provide overwhelming evidence that the Itzamnaaj bird and his snake are based on the laughing falcon and the indigo snake.

The group of supernatural birds labeled as the Principal Bird Deity shares the feature that their wings are conflated with snake heads. These conflated snakes/wings also appear in the costumes worn by rulers when they dress as these birds. The following behavior of the laughing falcon likely explains the conflation of the snake and wing. The laughing falcon's wing feathers are stiff, and when the bird hunts, it alights near a snake and spreads one wing toward the snake to fend off a strike until it can grasp the snake's head with its talon (Wetmore 1965:262).

The greatest concern for the Maya was the timely arrival of the rains. The Itzamnaaj bird was the messenger who announced the rainy season with its "ha-ha-ha" call. Given that Itzamnaaj was the paramount god of the Maya, it is apparent that the Itzamnaaj bird was the quintessential messenger bird. Many concepts in Maya culture were derived from the Olmec, but what is most interesting about the laughing falcon/ Itzamnaaj bird is that its origin had to have been Mayan, because only in this language does its call mean "water, water, water."

## DEW AND THE AK'BAL HEADDRESS OF THE ITZAMNAAJ BIRD

Dew, essential for the germination of the corn seed, is collected for rain ceremonies in many areas of the Maya region. The proto-Ch'olan word for dew is *tij* (Kaufman and Norman 1984:151). Itzamnaaj is associated with dew in the *Madrid Codex* and in the Santa Rita murals, where he is shown dispensing dew from a container with the form of a bearded serpent (Tozzer 1941:105; Taube 1992a:34). In the codex examples, the serpent container holds two or three rattlesnake tails. This parallels the Postclassic "baptism" ceremonies where the priest (in the role of Itzamnaaj) used a carved stick topped with rattlesnake tails to dispense dew (Tozzer 1941:105). The priest was called *Ajaw Can*, "lord serpent," which is one of the names for the rattlesnake in most Mayan languages.

Perhaps because dew appears overnight, the Tzotzil refer to it metaphorically as *'ik' 'ak'abal,* which can be translated as either "the black of the night" or "the dark of the night" (Laughlin 1988:144). The waters of the place of duality in the *Popol Vuh* are also described as dark. The Itzamnaaj bird wears a flower with an ak'bal, "dark," sign placed in the bowl of the flower. Sometimes the flower bowl is shown in profile, but most often the viewer looks directly into the bowl. The ak'bal sign is a reduced form of the feathered water serpent that has mirror signs on its body. The reflective water that pools inside the bowl of a flower is dew. It is likely that the ak'bal sign in the bowl of the Itzamnaaj bird's flower is a reference to dew, and by extension, to the dark waters of the place of duality.

Evidence for such an interpretation is found in the uses and depictions of mirrors, which also represent the waters of the place of duality. When a diviner gazed into a mirror to perform his divination, he was looking into these waters. As Taube notes (1992a:33, 1992b:184), the rims of many Mesoamerican mirrors are depicted as flower petals, while the mirror itself corresponds to the inside of the flower bowl. In other words, looking into one of these mirrors was like looking into the bowl of a flower. In some examples, the ak'bal flower of Itzamnaaj's headdress looks more like a pendant with fringe. Various deities and humans wear similar circular pendants attached to their belts, and Taube has identified these objects as circular mirrors. Stuart (cited in Schele 1992) notes that the jade earrings worn by the elite were stylized flowers. The death mask of a Calakmul lord had jade flower earrings with a pyrite mirror inside the bowl of each flower (Piña Chan 1992:154).

Divination mirrors were frequently placed in the bottom of a clay bowl, which relates them visually to the reflective dew in the bowl of a flower. In fact, the Tzotzil refer to the bowl formed by the petals of a flower as *spoketal snich* "its bowl, its flower" (Breedlove and Laughlin 1993:470). Just as Chahk's jar is marked with the ak'bal sign to indicate it contains dark water, so is the bowl of Itzamnaaj's flower. By looking into the bowl of Itzamnaaj's flower, we see not just dew, but the dark, reflective waters of the place of duality. When the diviner looked into his mirror or the liquid of his divination bowl he saw this same water. In most examples of Itzamnaaj's flower, the bowl is edged with a circle of beads, which I believe indicates a pool of dew.

## THE RAINMAKER

Itzamnaaj's costume and actions as himself and as his laughing falcon manifestation were intimately associated with the water necessary for the germination of corn seed. In the Postclassic, Itzamnaaj was the principal deity to whom petitions were made to avert agricultural disasters. Offerings were made to him during the New Year ceremonies of *Kan, Muluc,* and *Ix* years to prevent drought, locust infestations, and famine (Tozzer 1941:144–47). The oldest people in the community also conducted an annual rain festival in order "to obtain a good year of rains for their grains"

(Tozzer 1941:163). The first act of the festival was the burning of a great bundle of sticks into which the hearts of many different animals were thrown. Chahk imitators then doused the fire with water from their jars. This paralleled the burning of the cornfield (during which many animals were consumed by the fire) and the subsequent arrival of the rains. The final act of the festival involved offerings to Itzamnaaj and the Chahks.

## Itzamnaaj/God N as the Mountain God of Thunder

In his k'an turtle form, Itzamnaaj represented the earth. The quadripartite forms of Itzamnaaj/God N marked with T528 *tuun*, "stone," elements are his manifestation as the great mountains of the four directions (Taube 1992a:92–99). The turtle, conch shell, and mountain manifestations are all shown as bearers holding up serpent-sky bands, just as mountains reach up for the sky. Although he was not the only deity associated with thunder, God N's role as a thunder deity is well documented (Taube 1992a). On K5164, a lightning bolt is illustrated as K'awiil/God K, and his left leg is a long serpent representing a lightning flash. God N emerges out of this serpent's mouth. In this scene, God N appears to be the thunder that occurs immediately after a lightning bolt strikes.

God N is found in a number of contexts wearing the T548 drum sign on top of his water lily headdress. On Copan Hieroglyphic Stairs Step K, the k'atun glyph, which normally only illustrates the T548 sign in the central position, also includes the portrait of God N, indicating this deity's close association with the T548 drum sign and with the period of 360 days. The wooden drum mimics the sound of thunder, and like thunder, it can be heard at great distances (Tozzer 1941:104; Thompson 1970:266; Bassie-Sweet 1991:118). There is a belief that thunder is the voice of the thunder gods shouting to each other—in other words, thunder was the voice of God N. The juxtaposition of God N and the T548 drum suggests that the drum not only belonged to God N, but was a manifestation of his thunder voice.

A number of scenes suggest that Itzamnaaj/God N was also responsible for earthquakes. Vessels K2772 and 2068 show vivid scenes of Itzamnaaj apparently causing an earthquake. On K2772, three goddesses are pictured sitting in a stone house with the hero twins kneeling before them (fig. 7.9). Behind the hero twins is a slab shaped like a small stela. Inside this slab is a pile of stones stacked in seven rows of three stones each. The first goddess, who wears a distinctive circular flower headdress, leans forward and touches Yax Bolon's hand. Above the heads of the goddesses is a cartouche containing a Xib Chahk deity. In his right hand he holds an object that has been identified as a stone cudgel (Zender 2004a). A logogram of a hand holding this stone cudgel represents the verb "to strike," used in the contexts of striking flint to create fire and the striking of opponents in the ball game. In his left hand, the Xib Chahk holds his ax behind his head, ready to throw, and his mouth emits a sound scroll that likely refers to thunder. Behind the Xib Chahk and the three goddesses,

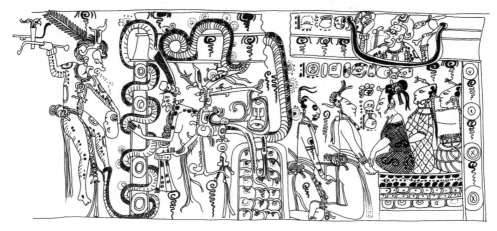

Figure 7.9. K2772 (after Kerr)

another Xib Chahk stands with his ax raised in the air. In his left hand he also holds a personified stone cudgel, positioned in front of the corner post of the house. His left foot is represented by a long lightning serpent that snakes up the corner post, across the roof, and down through a split in the ceiling. From the mouth of the lightning serpent emerges Itzamnaaj/God N, whose hand is positioned over the corner post of the house.

A similar structure appears on vessel K2068. In this scene, One Ixim dances in front of the house while a bound captive sits to the right. Only one Xib Chahk appears in the scene, and he stands with his ax raised in his left hand, while his right hand is behind the corner post. A personified T528 sign is seen in the split of the house roof and appears to represent the stone cudgel used to break open the roof. On the other side of the house, the lightning serpent emerges from behind the corner post, and Itzamnaaj/God N comes forth from its mouth. The corner posts of a house shake violently during an earthquake and cause the roof to collapse. The presence of the stone cudgels, the serpent wrapped around the corner post, and the position of Itzamnaaj/God N's hand over the corner post suggest that the scene shows an earthquake and that Itzamnaaj/God N played a major role in this event.

## The Bird Serpent

A bird serpent is associated with God N and his drum (see fig. 5.7). As discussed in chapter 5, this bird serpent has the hooked beak of a bird and a water lily flower and lily pad tied around its forehead. Its snake body is decorated with a row of blue/green feathers, water signs, and mirrors. In one example, the serpent's body is replaced by a pool of water and the T501 water sign, indicating its close association with water (see fig. 5.7c). This bird serpent deity appears as the Number 13 Deity and is also used to represent the 360-day period in the Long Count. Elites are frequently illustrated dressed as this deity. Its name phrase has been identified (Houston and Stuart 1996:299; Stuart, Houston, and Robertson 1999:55, 56) and is composed of three parts. The first can securely be read as *Yax Chit,* although the meaning is unclear. The second is the number one prefixed to a portrait of the bird serpent's head. The last part of its name is the glyph for *kan,* "snake," prefixed with a sign that has been tentatively read as either *nah,* "house," or *noh,* "great." Stuart has suggested that the phonetic complements on the portrait glyph of the bird serpent indicate that it is a logogram representing the word *witz',* "water spray, waterfall," and he speculates that the bird serpent represented coursing water in rivers and streams. He also suggests that the bird serpent was the antecedent for the contemporary Ch'orti' Chicchan deities—thunder and rain deities characterized as half-man and half-feathered-serpent. The Chicchan deities also create landslides and earthquakes (Wisdom 1940:392–97).

When the bird serpent is used to represent the tun period of the Long Count, it frequently wears the T548 drum sign like a headdress. In some examples, the bird serpent wearing the drum sign is also used as the headdress for God N in his manifestation as the Number 5 Deity. The role of the bird serpent as the Number 13 Deity and his association with the thunder drum are reminiscent of the Postclassic Tzotzil god called Thirteen Water Snake (Laughlin 1988:216). He was thought to be an old man who walked through the clouds at night and made thunder. It is possible, then, that the bird serpent was the Classic Period parallel of Quetzal Serpent, and that he was a manifestation of the creator grandfather. Sovereign and Quetzal Serpent are paired titles for the creator grandparents in the *Popol Vuh,* but which grandparent was associated with each title is unclear. Feathered serpents are ubiquitous in Mesoamerica, and consequently, it is difficult to identify a Classic Period parallel for Quetzal Serpent.

Today in Quintana Roo, a female supernatural known as Xkukikan (feathered or quetzal serpent) is thought to exist, whose traits are remarkably similar to those of the creator grandmother. Although the modern Maya of Quintana Roo no longer weave, they do embroider, and Xkukikan supervises their activities (Morris 1994). Xkukikan lives in a mythological cenote far to the east below the earth, where all the cenotes join in a single source (an apt description of the pooled waters of the place of duality). Xkukikan has five young corn goddesses who assist her: Huch Vilan, who grinds the corn; Xpat Vilan, who makes the corn dough; Tox Vilan, who distributes the corn; Tzol Vilan, who puts the corn in rows; and Xpiki Ka Vilan, who is the wind that fertilizes the corn. During the dry, hot break in the rainy season (the canícula), Xkukikan and the corn goddesses grind corn, but unlike normal grinding, this produces whole kernels. The goddesses then fly to the cornfields and fill the ears of corn with these kernels. The myths concerning Xkukikan are not conclusive evidence that Quetzal Serpent was a manifestation of the creator grandmother, but it raises the possibility that she was.

## SUMMARY

The complex duties and functions of the creator grandparents included divination, marriage negotiations, medical treatments, agricultural rituals, and rain production. One of the essential duties of the priest/diviner was to perform ceremonies to ensure the arrival of the rains and adequate rainfall, and the role model for this ritual specialist was Itzamnaaj. Perhaps the most interesting aspect of the creator grandfather was his bird manifestation based on a laughing falcon. The contemporary beliefs about this bird's rainmaking and healing abilities are likely so widespread and consistent in the region because of the dominant role played by the creator grandfather in Maya religion.

# 8

# THE SONS OF THE
# CREATOR GRANDPARENTS

The *Popol Vuh* recounts that the creator grandparents had two sons, One Hunahpu and Seven Hunahpu, who were born "in the darkness, in the night" (Christenson 2003a:113). The Classic Period equivalents of these deities were called One Ixim and Seven Ajaw (Taube 1985, 1992a; Stuart 2003, Zender 2004a). The following is a brief review of this first generation of male deities and One Ixim/One Hunahpu's first wife, Ixik/Lady Bone Water. I will also discuss the evidence that the triad of the thunderbolt gods and the Bakab, Xib Chahk, and Pawahtun deities were all manifestations of One Ixim/One Hunahpu.

The attributes of One Ixim/One Hunahpu were not unique. All across Mesoamerica, other deities who were thought to be the sons of the creator grandparents had the same characteristics and aspects (Florescano 1999). In central and southern Mexico, these sons were known by such names as Centeotl, Xochipilli, Tezcatlipoca, Quetzalcoatl, Nine Wind, Ehecatl, and Mixcoatl. They represented a fundamental Mesoamerican stereotype for young males of all professions and social standing to emulate.

## One Hunahpu and Seven Hunahpu

Deities and humans were often named for the day in the 260-day calendar on which they were born. The twentieth day name in the 260-day calendar is *Hunahpu* in K'iche' and Ixil; *Ajpu'* in Awakateko and Poqomam; and *Ajaw* in most other Mayan languages. The description of the birth of One Hunahpu and Seven Hunahpu seems to indicate that they were twins, yet they have different calendar names. The text actually names Seven Hunahpu as the servant of his brother, One Hunahpu (Christenson 2003a:113). A parallel of this hierarchy is found in contemporary Tz'utujil ceremonial life, where the ritual specialist has an assistant who must accompany him as he conducts any ritual (Tarn and Prechtel 1981:119).

One Hunahpu and Seven Hunahpu live on the surface of the earth in their father's thatched house along with their mother Xmucane; One Hunahpu's first wife, Lady Bone Water; and their sons, the monkey twins, One Batz and One Chouen. Each day One Hunahpu, Seven Hunahpu, One Batz, and One Chouen play dice and ball by pairing off and opposing one another. Following the death of Lady Bone Water, One Hunahpu, Seven Hunahpu, and the monkey twins play ball at the Nim Xob' Karchaj ballcourt located in the east on the road of the underworld some distance from their home. The noise from the ball playing annoys and threatens the principal lords of the underworld, who send their owl messengers to summon the brothers to account for their actions. The underworld gods One Death and Seven Death want the brothers' ball-game equipment, and they specifically tell the owls to have the brothers bring their gaming paraphernalia. Before leaving for the underworld, the brothers tell the owls that they must return to their house to give instructions to their mother, Xmucane.

When they arrive at the house to inform Xmucane of their travel plans, One Hunahpu and Seven Hunahpu tie their ball-game equipment up in the rafters in direct defiance of the underworld gods. The brothers instruct the monkey twins not to play ball, but to continue with their writing, carving, singing, and music making. To get to the council house of the underworld, One Hunahpu and Seven Hunahpu return to the road of Xibalba, and the owl messengers guide them down the descending pathway to the palace of the death lords. When they arrive at the court, the underworld lords subject them to a series of challenges that they fail, and the brothers are promptly sacrificed before they even have a chance to play ball. One Hunahpu and Seven Hunahpu are buried at the Crushing Ballcourt of Xibalba, but the severed head of One Hunahpu is placed in a nearby tree adjacent to a road. Suddenly the tree sprouts gourds, and this is how the first calabash tree (Crescentia cujete) comes into being (Allen Christenson, personal communication 2001; 2003a:126–27). It is impossible to tell the difference between the gourds and One Hunahpu's skull. The lords of the underworld greatly fear this magical act and order that no one cut any gourds from the tree or stand underneath it.

One of the secondary lords of the underworld, named Gathered Blood, tells his daughter Lady Blood about the gourd tree, and she can not resist going to see it:

> Thus she went alone beneath the tree that was planted at Crushing Ballcourt: "Ah! What is the fruit of this tree? Is not the fruit borne by this tree delicious? I would not die. I would not be lost. Would it be heard if I were to pick one?" asked the maiden. Then spoke the skull there in the midst of the tree: "What is it that you desire of this? It is merely a skull, a round thing placed in the branches of trees," said the

head of Hunahpu when it spoke to the maiden. "You do not desire it," she was told. "But I do desire it," said the maiden. "Very well then, stretch out hither your right hand so that I may see it," said the skull. "Very well," said the maiden. And so she stretched upward her right hand before the face of the skull. Then the skull squeezed out some of its saliva, directed toward the hand of the maiden. When she saw this, she immediately examined her hand. But the saliva from the skull was not in her hand. "My saliva, my spittle, is merely a sign that I have given to you. This head of mine no longer functions, for it is merely a skull that cannot work. The head of a truly great lord has good flesh upon his face. But when he dies, the people become frightened because of his bones. In like manner, his son is like his saliva, his spittle. He is his essence. If his son becomes a lord, or a sage, or a master of speech, then nothing will have been lost. He will go on, and once more become complete. The face of the lord will not be extinguished nor will it be ruined. The warrior, the sage, the master of speech will remain in the form of his daughters and his sons. Thus may it be so, as I have done to you. Climb, therefore, up there to the face of the earth. You will not die, for you have entered into a promise. Thus be it so," said the skull of One Hunahpu and Seven Hunahpu. Now in this they merely carried out the thoughts and words of Huracan, Youngest Thunderbolt, and Sudden Thunderbolt. Thus the maiden returned again to her home, having been given many instructions. Straightaway her children were created in her womb by the mere saliva. Thus was the creation of Hunahpu and Xbalanque. (Christenson 2003a:128–30)

The Maya do not eat the fruit of the gourd tree, but for the K'iche', the eating of fruit is a common metaphor for sexual intercourse, which suggests that Lady Blood was well aware of the consequence of her actions (Allen Christenson, personal communication). The K'iche' believe that sexual intercourse heats the menstrual blood in the womb and creates the lifeblood of the infant (Earle and Snow 1985: 243). In this episode, the spittle of One Hunahpu is like semen that heats the blood of Lady Blood and creates the hero twins. One Hunahpu's spittle/semen transfers the essence of One Hunahpu to his sons.

The newly impregnated Lady Blood returns to the home of her father, where she remains for six months until her father notices that she is with child. Although she denies having sexual intercourse with a man, the lords of the underworld assume she has committed fornication and condemn her to death. Her father instructs the owl messengers to take her to a faraway location, sacrifice her, and take the lords of the underworld her heart in a bowl. The owls fly off with Lady Blood, the offering bowl, and the sacrificial flint knife called *saq toq'*, but Lady Blood convinces them that she has only visited the tree of Hunahpu and that she has not had sexual intercourse. To create a fake heart for the owls to take back to the underworld lords,

Lady Blood cuts a croton tree, collects its red sap, and forms the sap into a heart. The owls give the sap heart in the bowl to the underworld lords, who are satisfied with it and burn it in a fire. The owls then take Lady Blood through a hole to the surface of the earth before returning to the underworld.

Lady Blood journeys across the surface of the earth to the house of One Hunahpu. She introduces herself to Xmucane and explains that she is pregnant with One Hunahpu's sons. Xmucane does not believe her because she knows that One Hunahpu and Seven Hunahpu have been sacrificed in the underworld. To test Lady Blood's claim, Xmucane sends Lady Blood to the milpa of the monkey twins to harvest a net bag full of corn. Xmucane knew there was only one ear of corn in the entire field. If Lady Blood could make the ear of corn turn into a full net bag, then it would demonstrate that she was carrying the sons of One Hunahpu. Lady Blood was able to do it:

> Then she went to the maizefield that belonged to One Batz and One Chouen, along the path that had been cleared by them. The maiden thus started out and arrived there at the maizefield. But there was only a single ear of maize [head] in the field. There was not even one or two or three more. Although there was maize there, it was but a single ear [head] that had been produced. Then the heart of the maiden sank: "See, I am a sinner! I am a debtor! Where shall I obtain the netful of food that is asked for?" she asked. Thus she called upon the guardians of the food: "Come, arise. Come, stand up Lady of the Day Toh, and Lady of the Day Canil, Lady Cacao and Lady of the Day Tzi, you the guardians of the food of One Batz and One Chouen," said the maiden. Then she took hold of the silk, the silk atop the ear of ripe maize [jal], and pulled it upward. She did not pick the ear of maize [jal], but it multiplied there in the net until the great net overflowed. (Christenson 2003a:136–38)

When Lady Blood returns to the household with the corn, Xmucane believes that Lady Blood must have stolen it, and she goes to the cornfield to see if the single ear of corn still remains. After finding the ear, she concludes that Lady Blood is, indeed, carrying her grandsons:

> The Grandmother thus rushed back to her home and said to the maiden: "This is but a sign that you are in truth my daughter-in-law. I will surely watch your deeds, for they that are to be my grandchildren are enchanted already," the maiden was told. (Christenson 2003a:139)

Soon after being accepted into One Hunahpu's household, Lady Blood goes to the mountains and gives birth to the hero twins, Hunahpu and Xbalanque. The text specifically states that she gave birth without the help of the midwife Xmucane

(Christenson 2003a:140). As will be discussed more fully in later chapters, these two brothers represent the sun and full moon, and their births are identified with the winter solstice.

After many adventures on the surface of the earth, including the defeat of a triad of dangerous earth-dwelling gods and the subordination of their own elder brothers, the hero twins clear a quadrilateral space on the earth's surface for corn cultivation. Because they are great sorcerers, the hero twins do not physically clear the milpa themselves, but have their tools magically perform these tasks. On the first day of clearing, they station a turtledove on a tree stump and tell it to sing out and warn them when their grandmother approached with their midday meal, for they do not want their grandmother to know that they are not doing the work themselves. In Yucatan, such birds as the white-winged dove, white-fronted dove, and red-billed pigeon are the birds of the deities who guard the cornfield (Redfield and Villa Rojas 1934:208). By instructing the turtledove, the hero twins establish the role of these birds in the milpa. When Xmucane delivers their lunch, she establishes the tradition of women bringing the midday meal to the milpa.

On the second day, the hero twins return to the milpa to resume their clearing and discover that the vegetation has been miraculously restored. They magically clear their milpa again and later that night return to see who is undoing their work. They discover that all the wild animals have gotten together and brought the vegetation back to life. They try to catch the animals but only succeed in apprehending a rat (ch'o). In pursuing the milpa animals, the hero twins set up a model for hunting in the milpa at night (Girard 1979:163).

After the hero twins capture the rat in a net, they punish him by burning his tail and making his eyes bulge (Christenson 2003a:150). The rat tells the boys not to kill him, and in exchange for their providing him with food, he informs them that their destiny is to be ball players and that the gaming equipment of their father and uncle is hidden in the house rafters (Christenson 2003a:150–51). As a reward, the hero twins tell the rat he may have any discarded maize, squash seeds, chile peppers, beans, pataxte (a type of cacao), and cacao from the house. When the hero twins go to retrieve the equipment, they place the rat in the corner of the house and he scurries up into the thatch where the ball is hidden.

After seeing the ball in the rafters of the house, the hero twins send their grandmother and mother to the river to fetch a jar of water, because they know the women do not want them to play ball. To delay the women, they send a mosquito to pierce a hole in the jar. The rat then gnaws through the lashings of the ball-game equipment, and it drops to the floor. With the ball-game equipment safely hidden on the road leading to the ballcourt, the hero twins go down to the river, patch the water jar, and returned to the house with the women. Then the hero twins journey to the Nim Xob' Karchaj ballcourt, sweep it out, and begin playing ball together.

Rats and mice are natural inhabitants of Maya thatched roofs because they are attracted to the household food, and they are a particular nuisance in houses that have attics for storing corn. These rodents are notorious for running along the longitudinal members of the roof frame, and these roof purlines are actually called "the road of the rat" in Yucatec Maya, K'iche', Kaqchikel, Tz'utujil, Mam, Jakalteko, Q'eqchi' and Poqomchi' sources (Wauchope 1938:49). The hero twins, in effect, transform the rat from a field rodent to a house rodent, and by doing so, they establish its role in the household. It is odd that the hero twins trap the rat in their field because this is not a common practice of the Maya. They do, however, trap gophers in this manner (Redfield 1945:57; Hunn 1977:206; Hostettler 1996:283). This fact suggests that the hero twins actually transformed a gopher, which has small eyes and a hairy tail, into a rat, which has bulging eyes and a hairless tail. The T757 glyph for *bah,* "gopher," and the T758 glyph for *ch'o,* "rat," also reflect the difference in the eyes of these two creatures: the T757 symbol has small eyes, while the T758 symbol has large eyes.

The transformation of these animals is also seen in the Kaqchikel town of San Antonio Palopó, where there is a belief that rats turn into gophers (Redfield 1945:57). The close association between gophers and rats is reflected in the word *taltuza* (*tlalli,* "earth," + *tozan,* "rat"), the Mexican name for a gopher. A gopher-rat is illustrated in Classic Period art. This supernatural rodent is named in the accompanying text as the *k'an bah chok,* "yellow gopher rat" (Grube and Nahm 1994:699). On the Tonina stucco facade, the yellow gopher rat carries a ball with One Ajaw's head on it. This association with the ball surely can not be a coincidence. Given the association of *k'an* with the center, it is likely that the *k'an* sign in the gopher-rat's name, *k'an bah chok,* refers not only to his yellowish color, but to his role as the rat of the center house. As noted in chapter 1, the Maya begin clearing their fields at the full moon, which suggests that the hero twins trapped their gopher-rat at this time. This is supported by the Q'eqchi' belief that gophers come out during a full moon to eat but hide at new moon (M. Wilson 1972:398). The close association between rats and twins is seen in a Tz'utujil belief that the rat is the caretaker of twins (Woods 1968:209).

The ball-playing noise and territorial intrusion of the hero twins again anger the lords of the underworld, who dispatch their owl messengers to bring the hero twins to Xibalba. The route that the messengers take from Xibalba is described as a great cleared pathway (*nima jok k'u*) that leads to the house of One Hunahpu (Christenson 2003a:155). If the messengers had exited the underworld at the Nim Xob' Karchaj ballcourt, they would have passed right by the hero twins playing ball there, but the text says that the owls went directly to the hero twins' house. This suggests that the messengers followed the same path they took when they escorted Lady Blood out of the underworld. Lady Blood was a waxing moon goddess, and this pathway represented the western ecliptic (see chapter 10). Only Xmucane is home when the birds arrive; she sends the louse messenger to inform the hero twins of the underworld challenge, and the message is eventually delivered by the laughing falcon, Wak.

The clearing of the milpa by the hero twins establishes a seasonal time frame for the events in this section of the *Popol Vuh,* for such an activity would have occurred just before the start of the rainy season. A late dry-season theme is found in the water jar that Xmucane and Lady Blood fill at the river. The first rains of the season were thought to be dispensed by rain gods who filled water jars and then emptied them as they flew across the sky. The filling of the water jar thus precedes the rains. Another late dry-season indicator is found in the nature of the messenger bird Wak, who is thought to be the announcer of the rains.

Several events in this section of the *Popol Vuh* reflect other agricultural practices and beliefs. There is a common understanding in the Maya area that a farmer can acquire land rights in a virgin forest simply by clearing it for corn cultivation (Holland 1961:144; R. Wilson 1990:48). Landa refers to this practice in the Postclassic as well (Tozzer 1941:97). This means that when the hero twins clear their field, they are also establishing their ownership of this quadrilateral space. The cornfield was one of the models for the quadrilateral world, and the corners and center of the quadrilateral world were defined by the sun. The quadrilateral world was the domain of the sun (Hunahpu), just as this cornfield was the domain of Hunahpu and his brother Xbalanque. A farmer seeks the aid of his kin and neighbors when performing labor-intensive activities such as clearing, planting, and harvesting, with the understanding that he will reciprocate when his kin and neighbors are in need. The Q'eqchi' refer to such exchanges of labor using the term for "pair" or "matrimony" (M. Wilson 1972:93). The hero twins' clearing of the field together is reminiscent of this practice.

The hero twins eventually defeat the death lords. After subjugating them, the hero twins learn that the remains of One Hunahpu and Seven Hunahpu are at Crushing Ballcourt, and they go there to adorn them. They speak with Hunahpu's skull in the tree and attempt to restore his face:

> Here now is the adornment of their father by them, along with the adornment of Seven Hunahpu. For they went to adorn them at Crushing Ballcourt. They merely wanted his face to be restored. Thus they asked him to name everything—his mouth, his nose, and his eyes. He was able to recover the first name, but then little more was said. He did not say the corresponding names for that which is above the mouth. Still, this had been said, and thus they honored him. Thus the heart of their father was left behind at Crushing Ballcourt. His sons then said to him: "Here you will be called upon. It shall be so." Thus his heart was comforted. "The child who is born in the light, and the son who is begotten in the light shall go out to you first. They shall worship you first. Your name shall not be forgotten." (Christenson 2003a:190–91)

The adornment of One Hunahpu and Seven Hunahpu is similar to a Postclassic Yucatec Maya funeral practice. After death, the head of the ruler was severed from his body (Tozzer 1941:131). While the body was burned and the ashes placed in an urn, the head was cooked and stripped of flesh. After the back of the skull was sawn off, they replaced the flesh with a bitumen-like substance and sculpted it to resemble the lord. These remains were placed in the temple, and offerings were made to the image during all of the subsequent festivals. The twins' adornment of One Hunahpu and Seven Hunahpu is also similar to the pan-Mesoamerican practice of dressing idols or deity impersonators in the clothing and accoutrements of the deity in order to bring the deity to life.

The hero twins' declaration that their father would not be forgotten and would be the first to be worshipped by humans instituted a practice that is still followed today in the highlands, in which *Hunahpu* (*Ajaw*) days in the 260-day calendar are the designated times to visit graves and make offerings to the ancestors (La Farge and Byers 1931:157–65, 173–75; Bunzel 1952:280; Schultze-Jena 1954:71; B. Tedlock 1982:124–25; D. Tedlock 1996:286n141, Christenson 2003a:191).

The adornment episode concludes with the hero twins rising as sun and moon:

> Then they arose as the central lights. They arose straight into the sky. One of them arose as the sun, and the other as the moon. Thus the womb of the sky was illuminated over the face of the earth, for they came to dwell in the sky. The Four Hundred Boys who had died at the hands of Zipacna also rose up to become their companions. They became a constellation of the sky. (Christenson 2003a:191)

Dennis Tedlock (1985:369, 1996:287) and Barbara Tedlock (1992:31) have provided evidence that the full moon was considered male, referred to as a sun, and paired with the sun as the hero twins were paired. The light from the full moon dims all of the other celestial bodies and is second in power only to the sun. This celestial role of the full moon echoes the senior–junior relationship between Hunahpu and Xbalanque.

The Classic Period counterpart of Hunahpu has been identified as One Ajaw (Mathews, cited in Coe 1978:58; Coe 1989). The *Popol Vuh* states that the Four Hundred Boys became the Pleiades constellation. Later it says that while the first humans were waiting for the rising of the sun (Hunahpu), they saw the morning star first. The tzolk'in date for this first heliacal rising of the morning star can be ascertained from the *Dresden Codex* Venus pages, which indicate that the first occurrence of Venus as morning star was thought to have occurred on the date *1 Ajaw*. As discussed in chapter 3, this cluster of celestial events is important in relation to corn planting because the Pleiades are one of the indicators used to mark the zenith passage, and the Maya plant the first corn at this time of year at dawn with the full moon and the morning star still in the sky. In fact, the Chuj still consider *Ajaw* days the best for planting (La Farge and Byers 1931:224). The Jakaltekos of Santa Eulalia say that *Ajaw* days are for ceremonies (La Farge 1947:124–25). In the Ch'orti' region, it is believed that the rising of the Pleiades establishes the day of planting and announces "the first annual passage of the sun across the zenith, a phenomenon said to be responsible for the fertilization of the seeds" (Aveni 1980:34). The association of the morning star with essential ceremonies is found in the Mam area, where all important rituals begin when the morning star rises over the sacred mountain (Wagley 1948:86, 91), and in the K'iche' area, where the ceremonial day begins with the rising of the morning star (B. Tedlock 1992:61).

When One Ajaw/Hunahpu rose as the sun for the first time, he rose as the zenith passage sun that heralded the burning of the fields and the planting of the corn. This is reflected in the statement that Hunahpu and Xbalanque rose into the sky as the *nik'aj saq,* "center lights." The term *nik'aj,* indicating something in the middle or center, exactly describes the zenith passage. It can be concluded that One Ajaw/Hunahpu was named for the calendar date on which he first rose as zenith passage sun. The *Popol Vuh* presents the basic ordering of the Maya universe in which the cycles of sun, moon, Venus, and the Pleiades were first synchronized for the planting of corn at the beginning of the rainy season.

## One Ixim and Seven Ahaw

One Ixim and his unmarried brother Seven Ahaw are the Classic Period equivalents of One Hunahpu and Seven Hunahpu. A number of Classic Period texts that refer to ball playing describe a ruler in the guise of Seven Ajaw, but there are no known portraits of him in the Classic Period (Zender 2004a). The limited references to Seven Ajaw restrict our understanding of this deity and his Classic Period roles, but one would expect him to be the ritual assistant for his brother One Ixim and, like him, to be a diviner and sorcerer. Because Seven Ajaw is specifically associated in several texts with different kinds of rubber balls, Zender proposes that Seven Ajaw might have been the patron deity of the ball game. The *Popol Vuh* states that the Nim Xob' Karchaj ballcourt belonged to One Hunahpu, and as assistant to One Hunahpu, Seven Hunahpu was likely in charge of maintaining their ball game paraphernalia. The close association of Seven Ajaw with specific types of balls suggests he may have also had such a role.

The *Popol Vuh* implies that One Hunahpu and Seven Hunahpu were twins, so we may surmise that Seven Ajaw looked something like One Ixim. Early Classic examples of One Ixim illustrate him with the buckteeth of a gopher (Coe 1973: 110; Stuart 2005a:135). As we have seen, the animal closely associated with the ball equipment of One Ixim/One Hunahpu in both the *Popol Vuh* and Classic Maya art is the *k'an bah chok,* "yellow gopher rat." It is possible that the rat that helped the hero twins with their ball equipment was a manifestation of their uncle, Seven Hunahpu.

One Ixim was a corn god who was first recognized in the codices by Schellhas (1904), who gave him the designation of God E. Other researchers have also recognized examples of corn deities in Classic Period art and have commented on their

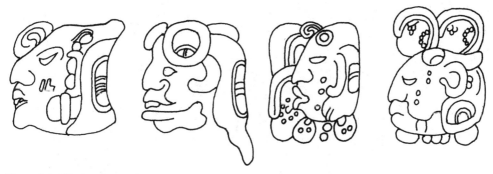

Figure 8.1. Corn god portraits

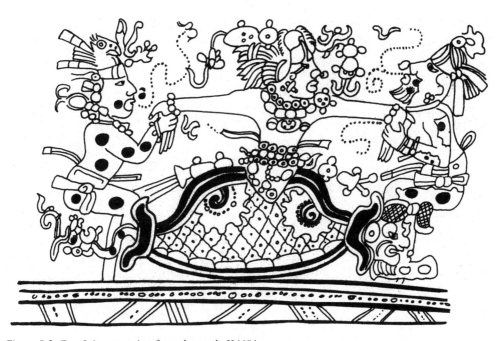

Figure 8.2. One Ixim emerging from the earth, K4681

feminine demeanor. Taube (1985) has separated the Classic corn gods into two classes that he called the Foliated Maize God (T1006) and the Tonsured Maize God. Taube interprets these two corn gods as aspects of the same deity; the Foliated Maize God representing the young, green corn plant, and the Tonsured Maize God (One Ixim) representing the mature corn plant (Houston, Stuart, and Taube 1992:499; Karl Taube, personal communication 1997).

The Foliated Maize God appears as the full-figure variant for the number eight and as the syllabic sign for *tzi* (fig. 8.1; Stuart 1987). In the context of the number eight, the foliage of the Foliated Maize God is bent back against his head, just as a maturing cornstalk is bent over. In my opinion, this corn god should, therefore, rep-

Figure 8.3. K1892

resent a yellowed plant with a mature ear of corn ready for harvest. In several Classic Period scenes, the Tonsured Maize God is seen sprouting from the earth, which suggests that he represents the young, green, male plant in these contexts (fig. 8.2).

One Ixim (the Tonsured Maize God) is frequently seen interacting with other deities in scenes on pots, several of which name him in caption texts (fig. 8.3). His nominal phrase is composed of the number one, a portrait glyph read as *ixim*, "corn" (T1000a), and a zoomorphic head that has been identified as a crocodile (Stuart 2003a; Taube 2005). The T1000a sign is a portrait of One Ixim (fig. 8.4). In the hieroglyphic writing system, the number one can be represented by either a dot or the T1000a sign. Consequently, One Ixim's name could conceivably be spelled with two T1000a signs, but this is never the case. In the context of his name, the dot is always used. The T1000a portrait of One Ixim is also used to represent the syllabic *na* sign in other contexts, which has created some confusion in the reading of his name (Freidel, Schele, and Parker 1993).

Figure 8.4. One Ixim portrait glyphs, T1000a

Taube has demonstrated that One Ixim was parallel to One Hunahpu of the *Popol Vuh*. Although the date *1 Hunahpu* is equivalent to *1 Ajaw*, it was One Ixim's son who carried the calendar name 1 Ajaw during the Classic Period. The reason that One Ixim was also referred to by this calendar name will be discussed in chapter 15.

A significant attribute of One Ixim is that the crown of his head is bald, with cropped hair at the base and top of his head (see fig. 8.3). Taube (1985) relates this tonsure to an ear of corn, but I think it more likely that the smooth head relates directly to a gourd. In Central Mexico, the young males who took care of the temples were called *elocuatecomame*. Their heads were shaved on top, leaving the hair around the face and neck. Durán's description of this hairstyle indicates that the crown was likened to a gourd:

> These youths who lived in seclusion were called *elocuatecomame*. When this name is explained in our language, it almost sounds nonsensical since it refers to the *tecomate* [gourd] which is smooth and was used in referring to their shaved heads. And to indicate that their heads were tonsured, the word *elotl* (ear of corn) was employed. People call this tonsure "a smooth head like a gourd with a round rim like that of an ear of corn," for that is what *elocuatecomame* means. (Durán 1971:82)

The Tzotzil term for a bald person is "gourd-head" (Laughlin 1975:398; personal communication 2001). In the Ch'ol region, it is a believed that a young girl who wears a gourd as a hat will bear bald-headed children (J. Beekman 1960:60).

The Maya use both vine gourds and tree gourds for a variety of purposes. Vine gourds (*Lagenaria siceraria*) often serve as water bottles. The narrow top of these gourds allows a cord to be tied around it to fasten it to a belt or a traveler's backpack. Whether on a trip to the milpa or to farther locations, travelers journeying to an area without a ready supply of fresh water could use the water in their vine gourds to mix their corn drinks.

Tree gourds (*Crescentia cujete*) are spheres that can be cut in half and used as cups for corn gruel and chocolate drinks or as corn strainers. The close association between the tree gourd and a skull is recorded in a Spanish document from A.D. 1620 that describes the Alta Verapaz practice of cutting off the head of an opponent as a sign of victory and using the skull as a drinking bowl in the principal feasts (Feldman 2000:39). The Maya carried tree-gourd containers on their heads when they traveled, as this excerpt from John L. Stephens's journal describes:

> Each Indian carried, besides his burden, a net bag containing his pro-visions for the road, *viz.*, a few tortillas, and large balls of mashed Indian corn wrapped in leaves. A drinking cup, being half a calabash, he carried sometimes on the crown of his head. At every stream he filled his cup with water, into which he stirred some of his corn, mak-ing a sort of cold porridge; and this throughout the country is the staff of life for the Indian on a journey. (Stephens 1841:264)

Mixtec women also wear such tree gourds on their heads (Cordry 1968:291; John Pohl, personal communication). Given these parallel uses of skull caps and tree gourds, it is apparent that the skull cap of One Ixim/One Hunahpu was specifically equated with a gourd container.

Like One Hunahpu, One Ixim was a diviner. The Tzotzil believe that a person who dreams of receiving a calabash will become a shaman (Breedlove and Laughlin 1993:151). One Ixim is shown in this occupation on K1185 and K5824, where he is illustrated creating a book. In most examples where One Ixim wears a headdress, it is a simple headband with a flower or jewel attached. He also wears the long, green tail feathers of the male quetzal bird. Quetzal tail feathers are very flexible, and Taube (2000) has demonstrated that these pliant tail feathers were used all over Meso-america as a symbol of corn foliage. Like Itzamnaaj's flower, One Ixim's flower has a bowl decorated with water beads, and a dew-covered stamen in the form of a serpent. It is possible that this flower represents the white tassel of the corn plant. The white pollen from the tassel falls onto the silks of the ear and fertilizes it. In many exam-ples, One Ixim has long flowing hair and wears a skirt that is a diagnostic trait of women. The reason for this will be discussed below.

Another costume element One Ixim often wears is a loincloth decorated with a *xook,* "shark," motif. This motif is composed of a supernatural shark with a *Spondylus* shell below its mouth. In Early Classic contexts, the xook monster has a large shark tooth protruding from its mouth (Hellmuth 1987:111–27). The shark tooth also appears as the central element in the bowl of GI's headdress in the Early Classic; a stingray spine bloodletter is found in the same context in the Late Classic. The stingray spine is also found perforating the septum of the Old Paddler God. In the examples where he does not wear this device, the Old Paddler God wears a headdress composed of the xook monster with the shark tooth. The parallel posi-tions of the shark tooth and stingray spine perforator point to the conclusion that the xook monster was a personified bloodletter. Given the bloodletting symbolism associated with the xook monster, it would seem that this loincloth motif of One Ixim was a reference to the fact that One Ixim made sacrificial offerings from his penis. Penis bloodletting is well documented in the Maya area, and the offering of blood is an important part of corn rituals.

### Ixik/Lady Bone Water, First Wife of One Ixim/One Hunahpu

The wife of One Ixim/One Hunahpu was, like her husband, identified with corn. Xbaquiyalo was the first wife of One Hunahpu and the mother of his firstborn sons, One Batz and One Chouen. The most likely etymology of her name is *x-* (lady), *baqi* (bone), *ya'* (water/river), *lo* (unknown value) (Christenson 2003a:113). The *Popol Vuh* gives very limited information about Lady Bone Water, but many of her attributes can be surmised, beginning with her name. Her husband has been identified as a corn god, yet most Maya consider corn ears and seed to be female, and modern myths often identify corn seed as the manifestation of a female deity. Given the importance of the male/female principle of complementary opposition, and given that a mature corn plant is incomplete without its female ear of corn, it seems quite reasonable to propose that One Ixim/One Hunahpu represented the "male" parts of the corn plant (stalk, foliage, and tassel), and that Lady Bone Water represented the ear and seed, which the Maya refer to as bone.

Dennis Tedlock (1996:250, 341) translates Xbaquiyalo's name as "Egret Woman" because *bak ha'* is a name for a white heron or egret (Barrera Vásquez 1980:27). Herons are also called just *bak,* "bone," or *sac bak,* "white bone," which suggests that the term *bak ha'* might be a compound noun meaning the bone of the water. Given that wives are often pictured flanking their husbands in Classic Period art, it is possible that the white water bird that sometimes flanks portraits of One Ixim is a manifestation of his wife.

As the epitome of a young married couple, One Hunahpu and Lady Bone Water were role models for human marriage. To be a successful wife, a woman had to bear children, and Lady Bone Water produced healthy twins that survived into adulthood. As a goddess who died young, she had eternal youth and was the quintessential young mother, in contrast to her mother-in-law, Xmucane, who was the ideal grandmother. A primary job of elite women was to produce finely woven and embroidered cloth for gift-giving and trade. Evidence that Lady Bone Water was the patronness of these female artisans is reflected in her sons' designation as the patrons of artisans. In this regard, Lady Bone Water shared characteristics with the Central Mexican goddess Xochiquetzal (Flower Quetzal), the young patronness of weavers and artisans.

Goddesses are not well represented in Maya art, but a Classic Period portrait of Lady Bone Water is found in the title *ixik,* "woman, lady" (T1002), that designates elite women (fig. 8.5a). This sign illustrates a beautiful young woman with an

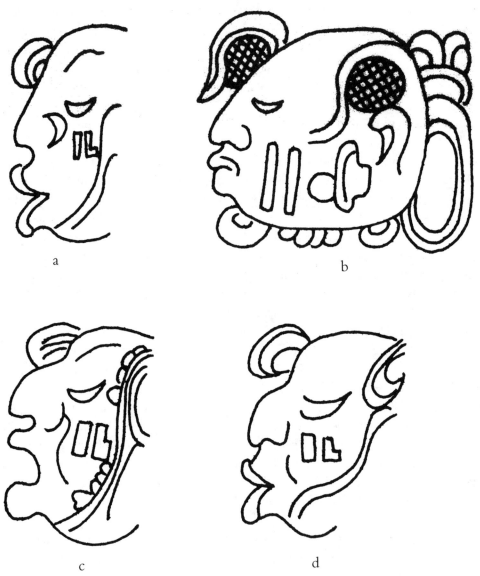

Figure 8.5. a. Ixik title, T1002; b. Ixik title; c. One Ixim portrait, T1000a; d. Ixik title

elongated head and long, flowing hair. The hair is sometimes replaced with black cross-hatching, used in Maya art to represent the color black (fig. 8.5b; Bassie-Sweet 1991:141). Her black hair is analogous to corn silk, which turns black when fertilized.

The long strand of hair is often seen in variations of the T1000a sign that is a portrait of One Ixim. This has caused some authors to equate T1000a with T1002 (Thompson 1950:131). However, David Stuart has pointed out that One Ixim has a jade flower headdress and that the full-figure forms of the T1000a sign illustrate One Ixim. A comparison of a T1000a sign and the T1002 *ixik* sign on the

Palenque Tablet of the Slaves demonstrates this difference (figs. 8.5c–d). The two signs are remarkably similar, but the T1000a sign has jade beads in the hair.

## THE DIAMOND-PATTERNED JADE SKIRT

Some scenes portray One Ixim wearing not only his jade headband, but a jade skirt with a diamond pattern. It can be demonstrated that it was the skirt of Ixik/Lady Bone Water and that it represented a cornfield. The main sign of the glyph that represents the word *pik,* "skirt," in the *Dresden Codex* has a diamond pattern (Fox and Justeson 1984:35). Humans also wear this diamond-patterned skirt on numerous Classic Period monuments, where the diamond pattern is formed by jade tubes and beads sewn onto cloth. As noted by Taube (1996, 2000, 2004, 2005), jade was often a metaphor for corn. Both Proskouriakoff (1961) and Joyce (1992:64) have observed that the females wearing the diamond-patterned skirt are frequently paired with an adjacent male ruler who wears a different costume. There are also examples where male rulers are illustrated alone wearing this skirt. Taube (1988a, 1992a:48) has suggested that these males were impersonating One Ixim. Following this interpretation, Andrea Stone (1991:201) has suggested that it was a male costume, and that "women wearing this costume are impersonating a male image of power, specifically a view of kingship that iconographically condenses the ruler's connection to the cyclical forces of nature." Because skirts are typically a female costume, Joyce (1992:68) has concluded that male rulers were impersonating a female and attempting "to subsume in themselves the totality of social differentiation."

The marriage of One Ixim/One Hunahpu and Ixik/Lady Bone Water represented the male/female principle of complementary opposition and united the two deities into one form, the male corn plant with its female ear of corn. The costume of One Ixim —a conflation of his own costume (the male tassel) and that of his wife (long hair and skirt)—represents the merging of the married couple's clothing. The Postclassic marriage ceremony involved symbolically knotting the clothing of the newly married couple together.

The diamond pattern was used by many Mesoamerican groups to symbolize the green surface of the earth (Joyce 1992:68, Quenon and Le Fort 1997:885). The diamond pattern is found on contemporary Tzotzil women's huipiles, where it represents the surface of the earth covered in cornfields (Morris 1987:106). In the Q'eqchi' planting ceremony, the farmer plants the first corn mound in the center of the field and then plants a mound in each of the four directions. A similar planting pattern is seen on BOD vessel 116, where the central image illustrates One Ixim sprouting from a water lily skull (fig. 8.6). In each corner of the scene is a shell, and adjacent to each shell on the rim of the plate are more water lily skulls.

The planting pattern is also evident on K4681 (see fig. 8.2). The turtle is decorated with two *Spondylus* shells in the corners. Assuming that the turtle shell is symmetrical, two more shells would appear on the other side. A flat diagram of this image would

Figure 8.6. One Ixim sprouting from a water lily skull, BOD 116 (after Robicsek and Hellmuth)

replicate the corner orientations of the BOD vessel 116 water lily skulls. The Maya plant their rows of corn mounds so that the mounds are offset. The first planting at the center of the field establishes this offset pattern. When joined together, the mounds of the cornfield form the diamond pattern. When the diamond pattern appears on the surface of the turtle shell, it indicates that the surface of this earth symbol is covered in cornfields.

On both K4681 and K1892, One Ixim is positioned at the center of such a carapace (see figs. 8.2 and 8.3). When One Ixim wears the diamond-patterned skirt, it symbolically places him at the center of the world, sprouting from the center corn hole. The association of a cornfield with the skirt of a goddess is seen in a story from Socotz, Belize, in which the daughter of a giant creates a milpa by spreading her skirt over the forest, causing the forest to be cut down, ready for burning (Thompson 1930:168).

## THE PLANTING OF CORN

In some modern Maya communities, the earth is thought to be female. The Q'e-qchi' believe that the male earth becomes female only when corn is planted in it. When the ancient Maya planted corn seeds, they were planting the bone remains of Ixik/Lady Bone Water, which may be why it is believed the earth turns into a female when corn is planted in it. Using a human metaphor, the center of the corn-field is called a heart or navel. If we apply this to the first planting at the center of the cornfield, the center mound represents the navel or heart of Ixik/Lady Bone Water. The four corn mounds oriented to the corners represent her hands and feet. In other words, each time the Maya planted corn at the center and four corners, the body of Ixik/Lady Bone Water was symbolically laid out spread-eagle on the surface of the earth. In this model, her hands and feet marked the corners of the quadrilateral world and her limbs formed the boundaries of the quadrants.

The intimate relationship between digits and corn kernels is reflected in the Jakalteko, Poqomam, and Chuj words for fingers and toes. They are called the corn seeds of the arm and the corn seeds of the leg (John Fought, personal communication). Another metaphor for digits is "the children of the arm" and "the children of the leg." The parentage term used in this expression in Mayan indicates that the arm and leg belong to a female.

The association between the surface of the quadrilateral world and the human body is found in the modern curing practice of San Pedro Columbia known as pulsing. This Q'eqchi' technique requires the ritual specialist to feel four pulse points on the patient's body. The blood communicates information to the ritual specialist that assists him in a diagnosis and cure. These pulse points are located at the wrists and ankles. They are called "the four sides of one's being" (*caxcutil acue*) and are thought to be analogous to the four sides or corners of the milpa, home, and world (James Boster, cited in B. Tedlock 1982:137).

The curing ceremony of Zinacantan known as "the great seeing" also has aspects that relate to Ixik/Lady Bone Water. This complex healing ceremony is divided into twenty different episodes over a two-week period (Vogt 1969:425–45, 1976:83). The perimeter of the Zinacantan valley is defined by sacred mountains and water holes that belong to the ancestors (Vogt 1969, 1976). The most senior mountain is located in the east and is called "Senior Large Mountain" (Bankilal Muk'ta Viz) as well as "Three Hearthstones." A low hill on the eastern outskirts of the town is called the navel of the world and is thought to represent the center of the world. In the healing ceremony, a bed is constructed for the patient. A gourd of water from each of the seven sacred water holes is placed under the bed, and a "corral" that prevents supernatural forces from harming the patient is constructed around it. The corral and water gourds create a safe space that replicates that of the community. A patient who lies on this bed is metaphorically positioned on the surface of the quadrilateral earth. The bed of the patient is oriented with the head aligned with the east.

The ritual materials used in the healing ceremony include four ears of corn, one of each color. The ritual specialist places thirteen kernels from each in a gourd filled with water. He gently shakes the gourd, and the resulting positions of the kernels communicate to him how many of the thirteen parts of the soul have been lost. In this ceremony, the kernels represent the soul of the patient (Vogt 1976:95). Like the corn goddess Ixik/Lady Bone Water, who had four color aspects, the soul of a Zinacantan patient is represented by four kinds of colored corn. And like the remains of Ixik/Lady Bone Water, these corn kernels are used as divination lots. At the end of the ceremonial portion of the healing rite, the patient eats the corn, literally assimilating the four colors of corn. After undergoing the healing ceremony for two weeks, the patient is still in a delicate state and needs to recover lost "heat" (the patient is spiritually, not physically, cold). Warming is achieved first at the hearth fire, then by undergoing a series of sweat baths at three-day intervals.

Corn seed is also ritually heated. Hot and cold categories are one of the paired opposites used by the Maya. When the soul of an ill person is diagnosed as being too hot or too cold, foods with the opposite heat level are ingested. The spiritual heat level of these foods may not be related to their physical state or to the physical reaction caused by eating them, but frequently it is. Richard Wilson (1995:120, 132) notes that a pregnant woman avoids eating too many cold foods because hotness is critical in the creation of her baby. He also notes that the prevalent state prior to planting is cold and that certain hot elements must be added so that the corn seed will become heated and sprout. During the night vigil, the corn seed is heated by placing it near a candle and by pouring blood (thought to be hot) over the seed (R. Wilson 1995: 95, 105, 141). The male planter changes from his cold state to a hot one by drinking liquor and smoking cigarettes. Furthermore, the action of splitting open the earth and dropping in the corn seed is viewed as a sexual act between the male planter and the female earth. This action heats the corn seed because sexual intercourse is considered to be heat-generating. The candle placed beside the first planting hole is also thought to heat the corn seed. The ancient Maya did not use candles; rather, they used torches. On K1892, the center corn hole has a skull juxtaposed beneath it. A burning torch appears above the skull. I suggest it appears in this scene because it has heated this corn seed/skull (see chapter 15). The identification of this k'an skull as a female will be reviewed in the next chapter.

An association between bloodletting and the turtle/earth is graphically displayed on four effigy figures found in a cache at Santa Rita Corozal, Structure 213 (Chase and Chase 1986, 1988, 1998:322; D. Chase 1991:95). The cache consisted of twenty-five ceramic figurines. Four identical male figures were located on the edges of the cache, one for each direction. Each male stands on the back of a turtle while drawing blood from his penis. The placement of the four males recalls the four plantings of corn for each quadrant of the world. The center of the cache was defined by a figure seated on a stool and blowing a conch shell. Beneath the center figure was a piece of jade and four small shells, which are evocative of the planting pattern.

Over twenty small stone turtle sculptures have been found at Mayapan (Taube 1988a). Four of the turtles had a hole carved in the center of the carapace (in the position of the center planting). On one of the sculptures, the hole was sealed with a stone disk. When the disk was removed, stingray spines and obsidian blades used in bloodletting were found. Taube suggests that the Maya performed genital bloodletting into these holes. I propose that this bloodletting was directly related to the heating of the corn seed.

## THE CENTER CORN PLANT

The corn plants in the field of the monkey twins contained only one stalk that had an ear of corn. The *Popol Vuh* does not describe where in the field this corn plant was located, but it seems a safe assumption that it was located in the center of the field and that it was a manifestation of One Hunahpu and his wife. I propose that the black corn silk that Lady Blood pulled from the ear of corn was the black hair of Lady Bone Water. I believe it is the same hair that is featured on the T1002 *ixik* "woman" sign and that occasionally appears on the *Ixim* portrait glyph.

The identification of Ixik/Lady Bone Water with the ear of corn and its seed provides insight into several Classic Period practices. The Maya frequently inlaid their teeth with jade disks. In fact, the syllabic *ko,* "tooth," sign is a pictograph of an open mouth, and in one example, the teeth are shown with jade inlays (Grube 1987, his fig. 8d). Considering that the Maya refer to corn kernels as teeth, it seems likely that these inlays were intended to represent green corn kernels. The Maya also flattened their foreheads to mimic the shape of an ear of corn. Although both males and females at Late Classic Tikal had flattened foreheads, the practice began with women in the Early Classic and remained a predominantly female custom (Haviland 1997). It is apparent that these cosmetic devices had important cosmological significance and that they were an attempt to imitate the form of Ixik/Lady Bone Water.

Furthermore, I suggest that the Maya were metaphorically counting out the fingers and toes of Ixik/Lady Bone Water each time they performed a divination. The Maya counted out the day names in units of twenty using corn seeds. They practiced a vigesimal system because they counted the digits on both their hands and feet. In the planting model discussed above, the four corner corn-mounds represented the hands and feet of Ixik/Lady Bone Water, and it is apparent that the five seeds of corn that were traditionally planted in each mound represented her fingers and toes.

## ONE IXIM AS THE WIND GOD

In Mesoamerican mythology, the morning star was a wind god who was thought to sweep the path for the sun, and as I will discuss in chapter 15, this star was a manifestation of One Ixim/One Hunahpu. The San Bartolo murals illustrate a Preclassic version of One Ixim/One Hunahpu: a god blowing wind from his mouth (Saturno,

Taube, and Stuart 2005). A wind god found in Classic Period art who appears as the day regent for *Ik'*, the Number 3 Deity, and the patron of the month *Mak* is designated as God H in the codices (Taube 1992a:56–64). His diagnostic trait is the T503 *ik'*, "wind, breath," sign. This wind god has been identified as the personification of the "breath soul." His close association with flowers, singing, and music has been noted, and he has been compared to the Central Mexican wind deity Ehecatl-Quetzalcoatl; the Mixtec hero Nine Wind; and Xochipilli, the Aztec "flower prince" of dancing, feasting, music, and game playing (Taube 1992a, 2001, 2004; Houston and Taube 2000; A. Stone, cited in Houston and Taube 2000).

In some examples, this Maya wind god wears a red flower headdress and plays a pair of gourd rattles marked with *ik'* "wind, breath" signs. His woven headband, also worn by the monkey twins, has been identified as a likely marker of courtly artisans (Taube 2004:74). In the *Popol Vuh*, it is said that One Hunahpu and his brother Seven Hunahpu were musicians, singers, writers, carvers, jewelers, and game players who taught their skills to One Hunahpu's sons One Batz and One Chouen. These monkey twins became the patron deities for these arts, while their mother, Lady Bone Water, embodied the female arts of weaving and decoration. The artisan traits of One Hunahpu and Lady Bone Water were similar to those of the Central Mexican pair called Xochipilli and his wife Xochiquetzal. These two were thought to embody the finest characteristics of the nobility, which was also the case with One Ixim/ One Hunahpu and his wife Ixik/Lady Bone Water. Given these many parallels, I think it is quite certain that the wind god was a manifestation of One Ixim.

## One Ixim as Bakab, Xib Chahk, and Pawahtun

As the personification of corn, One Ixim and his wife had four color aspects that represented the four colors of corn (white, yellow, red, and black) identified with the four directions. Landa records four directional deities (Hobnil, Can Tizic, Sak Cimi, and Hosan Ek), who were associated with the four yearbearers. Each of these deities was designated by the three names Bakab, Xib Chahk, and Pawahtun along with the appropriate color. Hobnil, for example, the god of the south, was appropriately called the yellow Bakab, yellow Xib Chahk, and yellow Pawahtun. The Yucatec Maya sources indicate that the world trees were identified with the gods known as the Bakabs, but there has been much debate about just who these gods were. Landa's statement that they held up the sky has led many researchers to equate them with the God N deities who are pictured at the corners of various quadrilateral objects holding up such things as the Milky Way crocodile and sky bands (see Taube 1992a:92–99 for an overview of these identifications). The God N deities were manifestations of the four directional mountains, so it is reasonable that they would be shown holding up the sky, but that does not automatically make them equivalent to the Bakab, Xib Chahk, and Pawahtun world trees.

In milpa metaphors, the center of the world is demarcated by the first corn mound, and the plant that grows from that mound was thought to be a manifestation of One Ixim. It is tempting to equate the many images of One Ixim emerging from the center of the world with the center world tree, as Taube (2003:461; 2005) and Martin (2006a) have proposed. Evidence that One Ixim/One Hunahpu was the center tree is found in the fact that gourd seeds and pods are placed in the ceiba tree during the Yucatec Maya tree festival to indicate that the center tree has flowered and produced fruit. The equivalence between a gourd and One Ixim/One Hunahpu's head has already been discussed.

If we follow this identification of One Ixim as the world tree to its logical conclusion, then the Bakabs, Xib Chahks, and Pawahtuns were also manifestations of One Ixim. The Xib Chahks, or "young thunderbolts," were four lightning bolt gods, and Xib Chahk gods appear in several Classic Period scenes and in the codices wielding lightning axes (Schele and Miller 1986). The four Pawahtuns are referred to as wind gods in colonial documents, and both the Bakabs and the Pawahtuns appear in the *Ritual of the Bacabs*, where they are closely identified with the winds that bring disease (Brinton 1883; Tozzer 1941:137; Roys 1965). Contemporary healing rituals in which the illnesses in the form of winds are swept up and sent back to the four directions recall this tradition. A glyph that represents the winds of the four directions has been identified by Houston (cited in Taube 2001:109). It is composed of four T503 *ik'*, "wind, breath" signs attached to a sky sign. As discussed above, One Ixim had a wind form, which suggests that Pawahtun wind gods were aspects of One Ixim.

The Spanish priest Francisco Hernández asked a Maya ruler what the term Bakab meant, and he replied, "the son of the great Father"—certainly an apt description of One Ixim/One Hunahpu, son of creator god Itzamnaaj/Xpiyacoc (Saville 1921:212). The literal translation of the term *bakab*, "first in the world," relates very well to One Ixim/One Hunahpu as the creator grandparents' firstborn son, whose corn plant manifestation was the first plant to emerge after the field was burned, and whose ceiba form was the first to regenerate after a storm.

A number of figures in Maya art represent the tree form of certain deities (Thompson 1970:337; Taube 2003, 2004). They usually appear as though standing on their hands with their heads positioned at the trunk, their hands forming roots, and their legs forming branches. Itzamnaaj, God A, Chahk, and One Ixim are shown in tree form on *Dresden Codex* 15, 23a, and 41. Many other *Dresden Codex* depictions of trees show a supernatural being at their base. The ancestors of K'inich Janab' Pakal are illustrated on the sides of his sarcophagus emerging from cave-like cracks in the earth. Behind each ancestor is a fruit tree. Each juxtaposed figure and tree represents the conflation of the ancestor with a specific fruit tree, and it has been suggested that together they represent a grove of fruit trees (Schele and Freidel 1990:221; Schele and Mathews 1998). The scene on the sarcophagus lid shows K'inich Janab' Pakal emerging in the guise of One Ixim from a centipede mouth (fig. 8.7). It has been proposed that K'inich Janab' Pakal was transformed into One

Figure 8.7. Palenque Temple of the Inscriptions sarcophagus lid (drawing courtesy Merle Greene Robertson)

Ixim in the afterlife or that K'inich Janab' Pakal was pictured undergoing the same apotheosis that One Ixim underwent after his own death (Schele 1992; Taube 1992a: 48–50; Freidel, Schele, and Parker 1993:276; Schele and Mathews 1998:115–17). Juxtaposed with One Ixim is a stylized ceiba tree that has been interpreted as the center world tree.

Martin (2005, 2006a) has argued that the fruit trees on the sarcophagus were meant to be seen as sprouting from and being fertilized by the decomposing body of K'inich Janab' Pakal/One Ixim. What I find interesting about these ancestral fruit trees is that K'inich Janab' Pakal's sarcophagus box is a model of the quadrilateral world, which in turn is viewed metaphorically as a cornfield in many contexts. When a slash-and-burn milpa has reached the end of its productive cycle, it is often replanted with fruit trees, which greatly assist in regenerating the soil. These fruit trees are planted amid the old cornstalks that remain after the last corn harvest. This practice fits well with Martin's concepts regarding the fertilizing power of One Ixim. The nourishing ability of One Ixim is also demonstrated by the fact that the ash from the burning of an established milpa comes primarily from old cornstalks left over from the previous year's harvest. In addition, the leaves annually shed by ceiba trees, which the Maya normally leave standing, contribute to reconditioning the soil.

## THE DANCE OF ONE IXIM

One Ixim is frequently shown dancing with a back rack on the exterior of Maya drinking vessels. He is shown multiple times on the same cup to indicate dancing in the four directions. He is often depicted in a dance on the interior surface of plates, such as vessels K1270, K5076, K5358, K5379, K5603, and K5875. The rims of many of these plates are decorated with motifs that demarcate the corners and midpoints of the world, an indication that One Ixim's dances climaxed with a dance at the center of the world. Processions and dances that demarcate the quadrilateral world are common, and One Ixim's dances are clearly related to these events. These pottery scenes do not include musicians and singers, but their participation can be assumed based on the role of music and song in Mesoamerican dance. Given the identification of One Ixim as the Bakab, it is apparent that his dance festival included the establishment of the directional world trees as well as the establishment of the year-bearer ceremonies. As evidence, One Ixim is shown dancing on the center of plate K5379 (Stuart 2004, his fig. 5). The twenty day names are painted on the rim in four groups of five each, one group for each direction. Stuart (2004) notes that the first glyph in each sequence of five day names on this vessel is the yearbearer. In other words, One Ixim's dances were directly related to directional yearbearers and the establishment of the quadrilateral world.

The three Cross Group temple/pyramids represent the three hearthstones at the center of the world. In the center of the Cross Group plaza is a small dance platform with four radial staircases that represent the four world roads. In terms of the world model, the center of the dance platform not only marks the place where the fire of the hearth was first created, but it also symbolically represents the location of the center corn mound and the center tree. I think it is likely that this dance platform was used by the lords of Palenque to reenact the dance of One Ixim.

## One Ixim and Cacao

Cacao (*Theobroma cacao*) was a prestige commodity in Mesoamerica. While it can be grown in limited amounts in a variety of environments including the cenotes of northern Yucatan, the production of large volumes of high-quality cacao is restricted to areas with abundant rainfall and humidity, warm temperatures, and lack of frost. Such environments are found along the slopes of the Pacific piedmont of southern Mexico and Guatemala. Cacao was the dominant crop in this area from Preclassic to late colonial times. It is on this strip of coastal land that some of the earliest complex communities emerged, and the raising of cacao for trade appears to have been central to this development.

Cacao was consumed most often as a drink, with the beans themselves used as currency well into the twentieth century (Standley 1920:805; McBryde 1947; Millon 1955; Coe and Coe 1996). According to mid-sixteenth century reports from Central Mexico, cacao was categorized into four varieties. In addition, a second type of cacao called *pataxte* from the Nahuatl word *pataxtli* (*T. bicolor*) was also grown. The beans of this tree are larger and less savory than *T. cacao*. They also contain less theobromine, the chemical stimulant naturally occurring in cacao. The ancient Maya name for *T. bicolor* is not known. In most Maya areas today, pataxte is called simply by its Nahuatl-derived name, but in Q'eqchi' it is also called *balamte,* "jaguar tree," and in K'iche' it is *peeq*. *Theobroma cacao* trees require shade, and the much taller pataxte trees were occasionally used in cacao plantations to provide this shade. The importance of pataxte is seen in the *Popol Vuh,* where Paxil Mountain is said to have contained both cacao and pataxte, and contemporary Tz'utujil prayers often pair cacao and pataxte.

An observation made by Simeon Habel (1878) indicates that gourd trees were found in proximity to both cacao and pataxte. At the start of the rainy season in A.D. 1863, Habel journeyed from highland Cobán to the lowland salt mines at Salinas de los Nueve Cerros on the Chixoy River and back again following an ancient footpath. He noticed en route that the mayor of a small village had a cacao tree growing beside his house.

> In the hamlet of Jaschkanal the Alcalde had a tree before his door, the fruit of which brought him five dollars every year. Really, there were three trees standing together, the interlacing branches forming apparently but one of the size of an ordinary pear-tree. One of

these was cacao, the fruit of which usually brought three dollars; another was a wild cacao tree with fruit of inferior quality [pataxte], and the third was a calabash tree. (Habin 1878:9)

While it is understandable that a pataxte tree would be grown with a cacao tree to provide shade, it is not clear why the calabash tree would have been planted with these two trees. It may have been that such triad plantings were common in the limited space of household gardens.

Several sources indicate that the preparation of cacao drinks took great skill, and that the women who made them well were held in high esteem. Different kinds of drinks were prepared using a mixture of cacao, pataxte, and corn. *Theobroma cacao* was toasted; ground into a fine powder; boiled with vanilla, flowers, spices, nuts, honey or chile; and then stirred or shaken into a frothy beverage. *Achiote* paste was also added to give a pleasing red color. Corn was mixed into these chocolate drinks, and conversely, cacao was added to corn-based drinks for flavor. Pataxte was mixed into corn-based drinks as well, and sometimes used as a substitute for cacao. Wisdom (1950:847) notes that pataxte was also used as a substitute for corn in some drinks based on *T. cacao*. Landa describes three kinds of drinks that included cacao (Tozzer 1941:90). Chocolate drinks were served in calabash gourds and special pottery cups.

We have only a limited understanding of how the Classic Maya categorized cacao types and what kinds of drinks were made from these beans, but there are terms found on the dedicatory texts of chocolate drinking-vessels that seem to qualify the particular drink. One such term is *ixim te'el kakaw,* "corn tree cacao" (Stuart 2005a:121). On a Dumbarton Oaks vessel, One Ixim is portrayed with cacao pods sprouting from his limbs, and his body is marked with elements that in other contexts denote trees and branches (Coe and Coe 1996:45; Taube 1996, 2003; Miller and Martin 2004; Martin 2006a). The text identifies this figure as a young lord called Ch'ok Chan, "young snake," who has taken on the guise of a deity called Ixim Te'.

Several species of trees are called *ixim te,* one of which is *Citharexylum schottii* (Roys 1931:249). Martin has argued that Ixim Te' was a manifestation of One Ixim as *Theobroma cacao,* and that One Ixim did not just represent the corn plant, the gourd tree, the center world tree, and the cacao tree, but that he represented all the plants of sustenance in the world. In his interpretation, the corn seeds and fruit found in Paxil Mountain were the remains of One Ixim. Martin views God L as the principal lord of the underworld, and he has proposed that God L was rich in cacao because he was in possession of One Ixim's body (the gourd tree at the Crushing Ballcourt). In my interpretation, God L was parallel to Gathered Blood (the father of Lady Blood), and he became the leading lord of the underworld after his grandsons (the hero twins, Hunahpu and Xbalanque) defeated One Death and Seven Death. I believe that God L/Gathered Blood became rich in cacao when One Ixim/One Hunahpu paid his bride price in this commodity. The bride payment symbolically compensates the bride's family for the economic loss of their daughter.

Given that cacao was used as currency, the payment of cacao could be viewed as solely a monetary compensation. If, however, the cacao actually represented the bride, then Ixik/Lady Bone Water was not only corn seed, but she was also cacao beans. A young goddess covered in cacao beans is illustrated on a censer lid and on a hollow figurine from the south coast of Guatemala (Schmidt, de la Garza, and Nalda 1998:169, 545, 562).

## One Ixim as Ek Chuah

Landa notes that the Yucatec Maya patron gods of the cacao plantations were named Ek Chuah, Chahk, and Hobnil (Tozzer 1941:165). As discussed above, Chahk was a manifestation of One Ixim, and Hobnil was the main Bakab god, another manifestation of One Ixim. Ek Chuah was a third manifestation of One Ixim. A ritual travelers performed in which they erected three stones and three altars to make offerings was in honor of Ek Chuah:

> And travelers even carried incense on their journey and a little dish to burn it in; so that at night, wherever they came they erected three little stones and placed on each several grains of the incense; and in front they placed three other flat stones, on which they threw incense, as they offered prayers to the God whom they called Ek Chuah, that he would bring them back home again in safety. And this they did every night until they returned to their own houses, where there was always some one to do the same thing for them and even more. (Tozzer 1941:107)

Francisco Hernández, the Spanish priest for the expeditions of Francisco de Montejo II, reported that Ek Chuah meant "merchant" (Saville 1921:212, Tozzer 1941: 207). Seler has identified Ek Chuah in the codices as the black God M (Taube 1992a:88). In many scenes, God M wears a tumpline cord around his head, the standard method used by the Maya to transport goods. The close relationship between merchants and cacao is obvious. The name glyph of God M is the eye of GIII, which is often used as the abbreviated sign for the GIII full portrait glyph, and God M is shown drilling fire, carrying a flint spear, or wielding an ax, all attributes of GIII. The fact that the Postclassic Maya created the three hearthstones in order to make offerings to Ek Chuah supports his identification with GIII, who was one of the hearthstones. The corn deity God E (a manifestation of One Ixim) is pictured as a merchant with a walking stick and backpack on *Madrid Codex* 108. It should be expected that as the patron of cacao, One Ixim would have a merchant manifestation.

## The Triad and the Catholic Trinity

The *Popol Vuh* indicates that the creator grandparents had numerous manifestations that performed separate, but interrelated, duties. We would also expect their sons to have multiple, complementary manifestations. As the principal son of the creator grandparents, One Ixim was a paramount god, who in his manifestations as the three principal thunderbolt gods, the four Bakabs, four Xib Chahks, and four Pawahtuns, embodied the elements necessary to ensure life. The Paxbolon-Maldonado papers in the Archives of the Indies, Seville, record a speech that the Spanish priest Diego de Béjar gave in his conversion of the Acalan Maya in A.D. 1550. He explained the Catholic doctrine of the Trinity, the concept that one god exists in three persons (the Father, the Son, and the Holy Ghost):

> Look, the first thing I have to say to you is that it is impossible to serve two lords or two fathers. Only one Father is to be loved. I come to tell you that (there is) only one god in three persons, God the Father, God the Son and God the Holy Ghost, who created heaven and earth and all there is to be seen today. (Scholes and Roys 1968:395)

During the same colonial period, the Spanish priest Francisco Hernández wrote to his superior, Las Casas, to inform him that the Maya knew about the doctrine of the Trinity. He said he had met a Maya ruler who told him:

> they knew and believed in God who was in heaven; that that God was the Father, the Son and the Holy Ghost. That the Father is called by them Icona and that he had created man and all things. The Son's name was Bakab who was born from a maiden who had ever remained a virgin, whose name was Chibirias, and who is in heaven with God. The Holy Ghost they called Echuac [Ek Chuah]. (Saville 1921:211)

The Spanish priests embraced this statement as proof that the Catholic faith was present in the New World before their arrival, and Las Casas even went so far as to directly identify Chibirias with the Virgin Mary (Saville 1921:214). I believe that the Maya ruler made this statement because Itzamnaaj was the supreme god and his son One Ixim (who was his *k'exel,* "replacement") had three manifestations (GI, GII, and GIII, as well as Bakab, Xib Chahk, and Pawahtun). The doctrine of the Trinity must have resonated with the Maya. The concept that One Ixim/One Hunahpu had three manifestations may clarify a statement made by the Spanish priest Jerónimo Román y Zamora that Itzamnaaj and Ix Chel had three sons (Brinton 1881:32).

# 9

# THE MARRIAGE OF ONE IXIM/ONE HUNAHPU AND IXIK/LADY BONE WATER

The most important organizing system in Mesoamerican culture was the male/female principle of complementary opposition. This chapter explores the first marriage of One Ixim/One Hunahpu and the complementary role this wife, Lady Bone Water, played in his life. While the *Popol Vuh* gives little information about her, numerous stories about courtship and marriage among the contemporary Maya help shed light on One Hunahpu's marriage to Lady Bone Water. Although these stories vary in their level of detail, they follow a consistent storyline related to inappropriate courting behavior and its punishment. In the highland Guatemalan stories, the transgression is that the couple elopes without the groom paying the bride price. The highland Chiapas stories that deal with the acquisition of a wife are concerned with punishing the husband for treating his wife badly. In both the Guatemala and Chiapas stories, the wife is the daughter of the mountain lord. This chapter explores these stories and attempts to flesh out the details of One Ixim/One Hunahpu's first marriage.

## MARRIAGE TRADITIONS AMONG THE MAYA

A general understanding of traditional marriage procedures can be gleaned from a variety of contemporary Yucatec Maya, Mam, K'iche', and Tzotzil sources (Redfield and Villa Rojas 1934; Laughlin 1962; 1977; Vogt 1969; Peck 1970; B. Tedlock 1982). A marriage petition begins with the groom's family conducting a divination to ascertain the suitability of the prospective bride and the viability of the union. If the divination is favorable, the groom's family hires a marriage negotiator. He may simply be the father of the groom, but usually he is the head of the groom's patrilineal group or another respected community elder. The groom refers to the marriage negotiator as his "father" or "grandfather." The marriage negotiator is frequently assisted by his wife or an older female who is given the respectful title of "grandmother."

Marriage petitions involve numerous visits to the girl's household by the negotiator and his entourage of assistants to obtain the family's consent. Each visit requires gifts from the groom's family, such as cacao, liquor, and fruit, as well as food and drink to be consumed during the petition. Acceptance of the first gift by the bride's family initiates the negotiation, while the refusal of a gift at any point terminates it. The bride's family takes careful note of all the gifts, because if they terminate the negotiation or the bride turns out to be sterile, all the gifts must be paid back. An effective marriage negotiator is an eloquent speaker who can convince the girl's family that the boy (and by extension his family) is worthy. His petitions may last for hours. After these numerous, lengthy, and costly visits that may stretch on for over a year, a final bride price is agreed on and is paid in cacao, labor, and other gifts. For poor families, the payment is reduced, but the nature of the goods paid is the same. A wedding feast at the girl's household is followed by the transporting of the bride to the house of her new husband and her ceremonial initiation into the new household. The mother of the groom usually provides a new set of clothing for both the groom and bride. At the climax of the Tzotzil wedding ceremony, the attendants dress the couple in new clothing that symbolizes their attainment of adulthood.

Even when a couple elopes, the groom frequently pays a bride price to make peace with the bride's family. Presumably, the marriage negotiator helps establish the amount of payment. The father of the groom encourages and even pressures his son to make a bride payment because the groom will likely have to borrow the money for this expense from his father. The son will then have to continue to work for his father after the marriage to pay off this debt (Robert Laughlin, personal communication).

Colonial-period accounts of pre-conquest marriages indicate a similar process (Tozzer 1941:100–101, 218; Miles 1955; Las Casas 1967:624–25). In the marriage ceremony as recorded by Las Casas, the couple was seated on a mat, and their clothing was knotted together to symbolize the marriage. Tozzer noted that the ruler performed the mat ceremony. A wedding scene similar to Las Casas's description is found in the *Codex Mendoza* and on *Codex Nuttall* 19 (Pohl 1994:4). These illustrations show the matchmaker carrying the bride by a tumpline to her new household. The newlyweds are next shown seated on a mat with the ends of their clothing knotted together. One of the key economic values that a woman brought to her new family was her ability to produce woven cloth for trade, gift-giving, and tribute. The bride was carried into the new family just as a trade commodity was transported, and, in fact, that is what she represented. The arrival of a Maya wedding party with multiple brides appears to be illustrated on K5847. In this scene, two women are being carried by tumpline, while a third woman stands in front of them.

## HIGHLAND CHIAPAS MARRIAGE TALES

In a Tzeltal marriage story, a man walking in the woods finds an injured snake (Hermitte 1964:41). It is later revealed that the snake is the son of the mountain lord. The snake asks the man to return him to his cave. The man calls out at the entrance and a huge toad (presumably the mountain lord's wife) appears. The man asks if the toad knows the snake, and the toad withdraws into the cave and returns with the mountain lord, who invites the man into the cave. The mountain lord calls his three daughters, who have the form of toads, to heal his snake son. They hop over their brother's body, which magically heals, and they transform him into human form. As a reward for returning his son, the mountain lord offers the man one of his daughters as a wife. The toads transform themselves into beautiful maidens, and the youngest daughter agrees to go with the man. Back at their household, the young woman asks her new husband if she may harvest some of the young, tender corn in their field. He gives her permission to gather two ears, but when she places them in the corner of her house, they multiply into many. The husband beats his wife because he believes she has harvested too much corn. She wipes her bloodied nose on a corn ear, creating red corn in the process. She and her two children die soon after.

A number of similar stories have been recorded in the Tzotzil area about X'ob, the spirit of corn, who is the daughter of the mountain lord (Guiteras Holmes 1961:40; 216, 218, 191–92, 268, 291; Gossen 1974:267; 1999:123–26; 2002:1064; Laughlin 1977:165–67, 238–46; Morris 1987). In one tale, a hunter sees beside the path a beautiful flower that he wants to pick. The mountain lord tells him the flower is really his daughter, who may also take the form of a snake. Picking the flower is a metaphor for accepting the mountain lord's daughter as his wife. If the man accepts, he is told that he must treat the girl with respect and put the flower into a water jar so that it will not wilt. When the man picks the flower, he sees a huge snake on the ground beside the plant, and the snake turns into the beautiful daughter of the mountain lord. Back at the man's house, the couple begins their married life. The man's mother lives with them and cares for their child. Although the wife only harvests small amounts of corn and beans, they multiply into vast amounts in her hands.

In another corn girl story, the man encounters an injured snake who is the son of the mountain lord. The snake asks the man to transport him to his cave, and as a reward for saving his son, the mountain lord gives the man one of his daughters, X'ob, who has the form of a toad. The mountain lord cautions the man that he must treat her with respect or he will strike him with a bolt of lightning. The man and his wife return to his home and begin their life together. At first, their marriage goes well, and X'ob gives birth to two children. She is able to produce huge amounts of corn from a single net bag of green corn. When the man sees the corn, he assumes that she has harvested his entire crop and strikes her in anger. X'ob returns to live with her father, but she leaves two clay drums that produce food for her sons. When the man breaks the drums, the sons are turned into squirrels who have to forage for themselves. Laughlin (1977:246) has pointed out the parallels between X'ob and Lady Blood, who also produced abundant corn. X'ob is also similar to Lady Bone Water, whose children were turned into wild animals.

## HIGHLAND GUATEMALA MARRIAGE STORIES

In highland Guatemala marriage stories, the mountain lord is specifically identified as Xucaneb and is thought to live on a mountain called Xucaneb in Alta Verapaz. At 2,648 meters, Xucaneb is the highest point in Alta Verapaz and has a cloud-forest environment suitable for quetzals. Along the southern base of the mountain are the river valleys of the upper Cahabon River and Polochic River. The towns of Tactic and Tucuru in these valleys were the leading producers of cotton in the eighteenth century (Solano 1977).

Xucaneb, considered to be the most powerful of the mountain gods, is the focus of contemporary Poqomchi' and Q'eqchi' worship (Sapper 1897; Burkitt 1902; Thompson 1930:58–59; Dieseldorff 1966; Mayers 1966:89; Carlson and Eachus 1977; Schackt 1984, 1986; R. Wilson 1990; Sieber 1999:85). Xucaneb's cave/house is located halfway up the mountain slope adjacent to a white cliff. The veneration of this god has an exceedingly long history. The sixteenth-century Morán dictionary of Alta Verapaz notes that Xucaneb was the most powerful *mam* (grandfather mountain-god), and that his mountain was the source of the earth rumblings often heard in the region (Feldman 2004:239). These earthquake noises were characterized as underground thunder. In one of the Guatemalan elopement stories, Xucaneb causes the first earthquake when he thrashes around after inhaling the chile pepper in his blowgun (Thompson 1971:365). A noise like thunder is commonly heard during earthquakes. Burkitt (1920:223) records the belief in Alta Verapaz that the *mam* is an earth-shaking animal living inside the mountain.

Versions of the Xucaneb courtship story have been recorded in the Q'eqchi, Poqomchi', K'iche', Mopan, Achi', and Kaqchikel areas, and by combining the information from the different versions, a core story-line can be fleshed out (Gordon 1915; Thompson 1930:126–32; 1971:363–67; Jessup and Simpson 1936; Redfield 1945; Mayers 1958; Cruz Torres 1965; Dieseldorff 1966; Shaw 1971; Quirín 1974; Maxwell 1980:60–66; Colby and Colby 1981:180–83; Búcaro Moraga 1991; R. Wilson 1995:327–28; Akkeren 2000:233–35). The tale begins in the distant past before the creation of humans. Xucaneb lives on his mountain with his young, beautiful daughter, Basket Grass, who sits on the patio of their house each day and weaves fine cotton cloth. One day, the hero of the story, named Thorn Broom, is out deer hunting on the mountain when he sees the girl and immediately falls in love. He decides to win her over by amazing her with his exceptional hunting skills. In order to give the illusion that he is able to kill a deer every day, he takes the skin of a deer and fills it with ashes and dried grass. Each morning he walks down the path past the girl's house to the forest and later returns with his false deer over his shoulder. Soon Basket Grass starts to admire him, but Xucaneb is not so easily deceived, and he instructs his daughter to take the nixtamal water from soaking corn and empty it onto the path in front of their house. The next time Thorn Broom passes with his deer, he slips and falls on the muddy path. The deerskin bursts open and scatters its stuffing on the ground. Basket Grass laughs at this sight, and the humiliated hero runs away. In the stuffing of the deer is tobacco seed, and with the fertilizing ashes from the stuffing and the moisture of the corn water, it soon germinates and grows into a flowering plant.

Like all persistent young men, Thorn Broom does not give up, but devises a new plan to gain access to the girl. Borrowing the skin of a hummingbird, he transforms himself into this beautiful bird and flies to the tobacco plant. He begins to sip the nectar in the yellow flowers while the girl sits weaving. When Basket Grass sees this exquisite bird, she decides to copy its pattern in her weaving. She asks her father to shoot the bird with his blowgun, and he accommodates her. The girl places the stunned bird in her calabash where she keeps her cotton for spinning, and continues to weave. In some stories, the bird is not stunned, but dead. Eventually she places the bird in her bosom and retires for the night.

This episode is loaded with sexual innuendo. Hummingbirds are related to sexual conquest and are used in love charms (Hunt 1977:69). For example, a Tzotzil man will carry a dead hummingbird on a green ribbon when he is visiting his lover, in order to warm her heart. The Petén Itzaj believe that the hummingbird is a sign of promiscuity (Atran 1999:173). The hummingbird hero sipping at the tobacco flower is a metaphor for sexual intercourse, as are spinning and weaving (Thompson 1939; Sullivan 1966:14; Morris 1987; Ciaramella 1994, 1999). In the privacy of her room, the hummingbird Thorn Broom is revived, transforms back into his human form, and has sexual intercourse with the girl. He proposes that they elope together, but Basket Grass is afraid her father will pursue them and punish them for their inappropriate behavior. In an attempt to thwart the father, Thorn Broom smears achiote on Xucaneb's divination mirror (in some versions it is a crystal) so he can not locate them, and he loads Xucaneb's blowgun with ground chile. The couple flees, presumably toward the territory of Thorn Broom. When Xucaneb discovers that his daughter is missing, he soon realizes that the hummingbird was his daughter's suitor and that the couple has eloped. Although his divination device is smudged, Xucaneb is able to look into a small area that is not completely covered. He sees the couple in a canoe on a body of water far away, and he picks up his blowgun to either suck them back or shoot them. Much to his distress, he sucks in the chile pepper and begins to cough violently.

Determined to punish the wayward couple, Xucaneb asks a thunderbolt god to strike them dead. In the Thompson version of the story, the thunderbolt god tries to convince Xucaneb to wait for his anger to pass, but Xucaneb insists. The thunderbolt god sets out in pursuit after dressing in black clothes (rain clouds) and picking up his drum (thunder) and ax (lightning). As the dark cloud of the thunderbolt approaches the couple, Thorn Broom borrows a shell from a turtle and dives under the water. In various versions, Basket Grass borrows either a crab shell or armadillo shell for her escape. While Thorn Broom is able to swim deep underwater, his wife is not so lucky, and the thunderbolt god succeeds in killing her. In one version, the lightning comes from a volcano (Shaw 1971:154). The association of a crab and armadillo with a goddess is not random. In an Achi' story, a yellow corn goddess turns her headdress ribbon into a crab (Shaw 1971:48). The mountain lord has an armadillo form, so it is logical that his daughter should also.

After Thorn Broom surfaces, he is dismayed to see the remains of his wife spread across the water and her blood turning it bright red. Little fish prey on her, but he has dragonflies gather her remains into thirteen water jars. He leaves the containers with an old woman who lives beside the water and returns to make amends with his father-in-law. Although the stories say nothing about their reconciliation, it must have involved Thorn Broom's paying the bride price, which was always paid in cacao after an elopement.

When Thorn Broom returns, he discovers that strange noises have been coming from the jars. He opens the first jar and discovers that the remains of his wife have turned into snakes. Various insects, worms, lizards, spiders, scorpions, caterpillars, and toads are in the other jars, but he finds his wife restored in the thirteenth jar. Although it is glossed over in most versions, one of the stories explains that Thorn Broom dumps the contents of the first twelve jars into a canoe filled with water and crushed tobacco leaves. Braakhuis (2005) notes that this tobacco is said to be the source of the venom now found in these animals. The word *may* is used for both tobacco and poison, especially venom (Burkitt 1902:449). These noxious animals then escape into the world.

The restored Basket Grass is, unfortunately, lacking sexual organs, so Thorn Broom has a deer walk on her crotch, and the hoofprint creates a vulva. He also has a rat urinate in his wife's vagina to lessen the attractiveness of sex for people. This act is in itself a strong indication that this woman was a role model for human females. Thorn Broom and his wife begin their new life together at his home. Life does not progress smoothly, because Thorn Broom begins to suspect that his brother and wife are having an affair. Thorn Broom becomes abusive toward Basket Grass while trying to confirm his suspicions about her alleged adultery. After a confrontation, the wife leaves and goes to live with a vulture god. Eventually Thorn Broom retrieves her.

In the final episode found in a Poqomchi' tale, Basket Grass becomes pregnant and they decide to notify her father (Shaw 1971:207–209). Thorn Broom leaves his wife in a cave on a cliff and goes on his own to inform his father-in-law of the impending birth. The wife turns into corn seed and remains there in the cave. Eventually, various small animals enter the cave and find the corn. A series of lightning bolt gods try but fail to break open the cliff to get at the corn. Finally, the smallest lightning bolt god has a woodpecker tap the stone to find its weakest point, and then he splits it open with a powerful bolt of lightning. The story ends with the statement, "It (the corn) was blessed, also, that it might not cease until the judgment, until the end of the age. Years have passed, and this body of our mother has never ceased (Shaw 1971:209).

In some of these elopement stories, Thorn Broom and his wife are named as Saq'e (sun) and Po (moon), and the story often ends with these two rising into the sky as these entities. In the earliest versions of the Q'eqchi' myths, the protagonist is named either Thorn Broom or Xbalamké. The latter name is a cognate of Xbalanque of the *Popol Vuh* (Thompson 1971:364). The actions and relationships of the Thorn Broom/Saq'e/Xbalamké character do not match the bachelor Hunahpu (the sun) or his bachelor brother Xbalanque (the full moon), but they do correspond to their father, One Hunahpu, his first wife, Lady Bone Water, and their uncle, Seven Hunahpu.

How can we explain this apparent shift in characters? I believe it is not a shift per se, but a post-conquest merging of two generations of deities into one deity. If we examine the manner in which Jesus Christ appears in many contemporary Mayan stories, it is apparent that he has the characteristics of both One Hunahpu (the first son of the creator god) and his bachelor son Hunahpu (the sun). For example, some myths explain that corn came from the body of Christ, and the sun is frequently identified as Christ. The conflation of two generations of Maya deities into one Catholic figure is also seen with the goddesses. In many stories, the Virgin Mary has the qualities of both the creator grandmother and her young daughters-in-law. In some tales, the moon/Virgin Mary is the mother of the sun/Christ, while in other cases she is the wife of the sun.

The *Popol Vuh* lays out the genealogy for most of its central characters, but no parentage information is given for Lady Bone Water. When the wife of a man dies, it is a common practice for the man to marry his wife's sister. Because of this practice, I have suggested that Lady Bone Water and Lady Blood were sisters, and that both of these goddesses were the daughters of Gathered Blood (Bassie-Sweet 2004; see also chapter 12). In the case of the elopement stories, I believe that two of Gathered Blood's daughters were merged into one figure.

If we look at the elopement stories from this perspective, the ancient core of the story is likely to be primarily based on the courtship of One Hunahpu and his first wife, Lady Bone Water. If I am correct, and we can apply the information in these stories to Lady Bone Water, then these stories are further confirmation that it was Ixik/Lady Bone Water's buried remains that were found inside Paxil Mountain and used to create the first humans.

### THE DEATH OF THE GODDESS

The story of Thorn Broom sheds light on the courtship and death of Lady Bone Water. In Mesoamerica, deer hunting was a metaphor for both bride acquisition and warfare (Braakhuis 2001). Although the elopement stories describe Thorn Broom as a lone deer hunter, the technique for hunting deer in highland Guatemala was to have several hundred men enclose a large tract of forest and drive the deer into the open (Feldman 2000:102). In Mesoamerican hunting and war festivals, hunters were portrayed as warriors and the deer were the warrior enemy. A further association between the theme of warfare and the elopement stories is the hummingbird who lends Thorn Broom its clothing or skin. Hummingbirds are extremely aggressive, despite their small size, and were identified in Mesoamerica with warriors (Hunt 1977:63). The concept of a hummingbird assisting a protagonist is also seen in the *Annals of the Cakchiquels,* where the leader Q'aq'awitz has a warrior assistant called Zakitzunun, "white hummingbird," when he captures the flint of the volcano (Brinton 1885:99; Akkeren 2000:158; see chapter 13). The characterization of the couple in the elopement story as a deer hunter/warrior and a weaver is found in both Mayan and Mesoamerican initiation rituals that babies and children undergo. During these ceremonies, hunting and warfare weapons are given to male children, and weaving implements are given to female children (Clark and Houston 1998:39–40).

Xucaneb's daughter dies twice in the elopement stories. The first time, Basket Grass is struck by the thunderbolt and dismembered while fleeing with her warrior husband. In other words, she is the first female victim of war. In the Poqomchi' version of the story, the second time Basket Grass dies she is pregnant, which suggests that she might have died in childbirth. This was the leading cause of death for women, and illness or death during childbirth was often viewed as one of the punishments for eloping. The first penalty Xucaneb's daughter receives is that parts of her remains are transformed into noxious animals.

The association of women who died in childbirth with vessels that unleash noxious animals is seen on *Codex Borgia* 47 and 48, which illustrate five Cihuateteo (goddesses who died in childbirth; Braakhuis 2005:179). Adjacent to the goddesses is a container from which emerge a goddess, a scorpion, five snakes, and four centipedes. Braakhuis (2005:176) has associated the blood-red water where Xucaneb's daughter died with the Aztec western region called Cihuatlalpan, where the women who died in childbirth lived. He notes that the Totonacs of the Gulf Coast characterize the west as a great lake full of blood stemming from those who died in childbirth. Hemorrhaging is a common problem during difficult labor. Given these parallels, I think it highly likely that the goddess Lady Bone Water died during childbirth.

Circumstantial evidence to support this conclusion is found in the names of Lady Bone Water's sons, One Batz and One Chouen. *Batz* and *Chouen* are the highland and lowland names for the eleventh tzolk'in day name, Monkey, and these twins were named for the day on which they were born (Thompson 1950:80). The association of the day name Monkey with the arts is well known, and in the Yucatec Maya list of day name auguries that is found in the Chilam Balam of Kaua, a person born on *Chuwen* will become a master of all arts. The description of the Aztec day name Monkey (*Ozomatli*) given by Sahagún indicates that a person born on *1 Monkey* would be a singer, dancer, scribe, or artisan, but this day was also the time when the Cihuateteo goddesses descended and stole children or caused them harm. The Cihuateteo were vengeful goddesses who required supplication. The fact that Lady Bone Water's children were born on *1 Monkey* implies that she was the first goddess to die in childbirth and that she was the role model for these types of goddesses.

## THE VALUE OF THE BRIDE

A marriage proposal begins with a prognostication to establish the suitability of the union, followed by petitions to the bride's family. Under ideal circumstances, Xpiyacoc would have acted as the marriage diviner and negotiator for his son One Hunahpu, and he would have approached Gathered Blood to petition for his daughter Lady Bone Water. The *Popol Vuh* story and the parallel ethnographic evidence indicate that One Hunahpu did not follow this traditional model for obtaining either of his wives. The elopement stories discussed in this chapter, however, provide a powerful message for young adults; the bride price must be paid or the woman will die. Bride payment is intended to symbolically compensate the bride's family for the loss of their daughter. The K'iche' still say that the cacao given to the bride's family is a replacement for her (Bunzel 1952:115). In my reconstruction of the central myth, One Hunahpu pays for his wife with cacao, but what services or commodities does he receive in return?

In addition to the obvious mundane advantages of having a wife to prepare food and tend to other household needs, a woman produces the offspring that become a primary source of labor and expanded production. Like corn, cacao production is labor-intensive at certain points in the cycle, and sons would be expected to take part in managing not only the corn production, but the cacao plantations. The monkey twins, sons of Ixik/Lady Bone Water, became artisans and craft specialists, had a cornfield, and were closely associated with cacao plantations (see chapter 11).

Numerous colonial period sources refer to the importance of the textile trade and the high regard that the Maya had for fine cotton weaving (see chapter 10). One of the economic values of a young girl rested on her ability to produce exceptional woven cloth for trade, tribute, and gift-giving. The exquisitely woven costumes of the elite women illustrated in the Yaxchilan lintels attest to the skill of Classic Period weavers. Xucaneb's daughter was weaving cotton when she first drew Thorn Broom's attention.

While these reasons for obtaining a wife are important, a wife from any area would have been sufficient for these purposes. The implication of the warfare/marriage metaphors is that Thorn Broom was not just deer/wife hunting in Xucaneb's territory, but that he was intent on capturing the wealth of the region, and Xucaneb's daughter symbolically represented those resources. The region of Alta Verapaz is located in northeastern Guatemala, which is demarcated on the west by the Chixoy River and on the south by the Sierra de las Minas and the Motagua River. Two of the most important trade resources found in this zone were jade and quetzal tail feathers. Quetzals require high cloud-forest with thickly wooded lower slopes, and the area between the Motagua River and Xucaneb Mountain contains prime quetzal habitat. Sixteenth-century accounts of Alta Verapaz indicate that quetzal-harvesting rights to a territory were inherited, and that traders came from as far away as Central Mexico to purchase the ten thousand feathers harvested annually from this zone (McBryde 1947:72; Feldman 2000:96). The quetzal merchants harvested their feathers during the mating season (March to June) when the birds descended from their mountaintop locations to nest on the lower slopes, and the tails of the male birds were still in prime form. The birds were trapped at watering holes or captured while they sat on their nests, their tail feathers were harvested, and they were released. Given the heavy forest and difficult terrain of the quetzal habitat, harvesting the feathers must have been a labor-intensive activity at a time when most men were busy clearing the fields and preparing for planting.

Taube (1996, 2000) has documented the pan-Mesoamerican convention of depicting corn as jade and quetzal feathers, and he has noted that One Ixim in his role as the corn god was identified with these materials. I have argued that One Ixim dressed in his jade skirt was a manifestation of both the corn god and his wife, the epitome of the male/female principle. I propose that the quetzal was specifically thought to be a manifestation of Ixik/Lady Bone Water and that One Ixim first obtained his quetzal-feather accoutrements when he took Ixik/Lady Bone Water as his wife. Las Casas states that elite married men who committed adultery had to compensate the family of the maiden by paying them sixty to one hundred quetzal feathers (Miles 1955:85). This suggests a close symbolic relationship between quetzal feathers and young maidens. An entry in Coto's dictionary indicates that parents referred to their unmarried daughters as *nuq'uq' nuraxon*, "my quetzal feathers, my blue feathers" (Akkeren 2000:424). In the dance called Rab'inal Achi', a young woman who is analogous to Xucaneb's daughter is referred to as *ri uchuch q'uq', uchuch raxon, yamani* and *xtekoqib'*, "mother of the quetzal, blue feathers, precious stones and gems." She is said to be from Tzam Q'am Karcha, and the place called Karcha was closely identified with Xucaneb Mountain.

## The Jade Skirt as a Wedding Costume

The jade skirt of Ixik/Lady Bone Water that is worn by One Ixim was most likely her wedding skirt. Some of the elopement stories associate a mountain called Raxon Mountain with Thorn Broom. In Fray Alonso de Escobar's description of Alta Verapaz, Raxon Mountain is explicitly called Quix Mez, "thorn broom" (Feldman 1988). Raxon Mountain is in the Sierra de las Minas range, which runs parallel to the Motagua River and forms the north side of the river valley. The only known jade deposits in Mesoamerica are found in this area, the highest concentrations of which are located along the tributaries of the Motagua running off the mountains into the river valley. The deposits of jade that skirt the base of Raxon Mountain, the highest peak in the area, contain even the blue jade preferred by the Olmec (Seitz,

Harlow, Sission, and Taube 2001). The name raxon, "blue/green," is appropriate for this source of jade. If I am correct in my interpretation that Thorn Broom was parallel to One Ixim/One Hunahpu and that Raxon Mountain was also one of One Ixim/One Hunahpu's manifestations, then jade was literally believed to be a manifestation of One Ixim/One Hunahpu.

It is customary in some Mesoamerican wedding traditions for the groom or his family to give the bride a new garment. In A.D. 1695, Spanish priests who visited the unconverted Ch'ol Maya of Chiapas reported that part of the Ch'ol wedding ceremony involved the husband giving new skirts to his bride (Tozzer 1912). This raises the possibility that Ixik/Lady Bone Water's jade skirt was a wedding gift from One Ixim/One Hunahpu. The prototype for Xucaneb was God L (see chapter 12), whose costume elements include a long string of large jade beads. It is quite possible that Ixik/Lady Bone Water's bride price included jade beads.

## THE THIRTEEN PARTS OF THE HUMAN SOUL

The elopement stories indicate that the bone remains of Basket Grass, Xucaneb's daughter, became the corn used to create humans. As Basket Grass and Thorn Broom were role models for humans, it is reasonable to think that her transformation into thirteen categories of noxious animals was the role model for the human soul with its thirteen parts or co-essences. As noted in the previous chapter, the Tzotzil identify these thirteen soul parts with corn kernels in their healing ritual. Paul Wirsing, who recorded the earliest version of the elopement story, noted that it was recited by Q'eqchi' shamans during healing rituals (cited in Thompson 1939: 143), and Braakhuis (2005:174) has argued that the principal concern of the elopement story is disease and curing. He has shown the widespread association between illness and the kinds of venomous animals created from the remains of Xucaneb's daughter. For example, "evil" Tzotzil shamans are thought to introduce thirteen items, including poisonous snakes, ants, wasps, and scorpions, into the body of the victim to cause illness (Guiteras Holmes 1961:135). In a Q'eqchi' curse recorded by Burkitt (1902:445), the list of animals that the shaman summons to inflict illness includes poisonous snakes, toads, and ants. A common method used in witchcraft is to insert a snake into a victim (Maynard 1963:98). Núñez de la Vega describes sixteenth-century Tzeltal sorcerers who introduced toads, frogs, snakes, and centipedes into a person's body to provoke illness (Brinton 1894:19). Illness is also thought to be induced by soul loss, the most frequent cause of which is fright. Shamans can send their co-essences or transform themselves into frightening beings that are thought to literally scare people to death. The thought of encountering any of the grotesque *way* creatures illustrated on Maya pottery would certainly be terrifying. The animals that cause the most fright for the Maya are snakes, and not surprisingly, these were the first animals that came out of the jars containing the remains of Xucaneb's daughter.

## BASKET GRASS AS THE *IC BOLAY*

The *ic bolay* was the first snake to emerge from the remains of Basket Grass. *Ic bolay* can be used to refer to poisonous animals in general, but it is a specific name for *Bothrops asper*, also known as the fer-de-lance, tommygoff, yellow jaw, or barba amarilla. *Bothrops asper* is one of the snakes most commonly encountered around human habitations and milpas, and the most feared because of its deadly venom and aggressive behavior (Burkitt 1902; Lee 2000:369).

The elopement stories refer to a variety of other poisonous snakes found in the jars that hold the remains of Basket Grass, including a *chac bolay*. A number of early Yucatec Maya sources refer to a *chac bolay, k'an bolay,* and *sak bolay* (red, yellow, and white *bolay*, respectively; Roys 1931:313; 1933:132). *Bolay* is a generic term for animals that kill, while *chac bolay* is defined as an evil spirit, serpent, jaguar, cougar, or spotted wildcat. In the Ch'ol region, the *ik'bolay* is a kind of jaguar (Juan Jesús Vásquez, personal communication). These definitions raise the possibility that Basket Grass had both a fer-de-lance and a feline guise. While there is no direct evidence linking Lady Bone Water to these creatures, Ic Bolay was also the indigenous name for the lower Chixoy river system, which today is named the Usumacinta, and the term is still used for a tributary of the Chixoy (Feldman 2000:25, 155, 240). The Chixoy River was closely associated with corn goddesses, as will be discussed in chapters 14 and 15.

## IXIK/LADY BONE WATER AS TOBACCO

In one of the elopement stories, the tobacco seed from Thorn Broom's deer stuffing grows into a plant, and the hummingbird hero sucking at the flower is a metaphor for sexual intercourse between Thorn Broom and Xucaneb's daughter. In this metaphor, Basket Grass is the tobacco flower. The notion of a female as a tobacco flower is parallel to the Central Mexican belief that their goddess of the Milky Way, called Citlalicue, "star skirt," had a tobacco plant manifestation (Torquemada 1975, vol. 2, 83). The placement of the remains of Xucaneb's daughter in a jar and in a canoe with tobacco leaves is similar to the practice of growing tobacco seedlings. To protect them from ants, tobacco seeds are first planted in jars or in old canoes (hollow logs) until they have sprouted and grown into young plants, at which time they are transplanted into the tobacco field (Wisdom 1940:51).

The sons of the first K'iche' lineage heads journeyed to a powerful city to receive the symbols of their lordship, which included a gourd of tobacco (Christenson 2003a:258). Tobacco was used in Mesoamerica as a remedy for illnesses, to protect, and to kill (Roys 1931:259; Thompson 1971:103–23; Berlin, Breedlove, and Raven 1974:445; Laughlin 1975:241; Robicsek 1978). For example, Sahagún (1959–63, book 11, 83) describes the practice of throwing small jars of tobacco powder at a rattlesnake to incapacitate it, and then filling its mouth with tobacco to kill it. One can overcome a snake or sorcerer by spraying or throwing tobacco, and ground tobacco is still carried in a gourd to protect against sorcery. Tobacco plasters are placed on venomous bites to draw out the poison. As a cure for various illnesses, the healer places tobacco powder in his mouth and sprays it on the face or body of the patient (Wisdom 1940:349). These uses of tobacco suggest that it was thought to be a kind of venom that could be used to counteract other sources of venom. In a curing recorded by Burkitt (1902:447), the healer refers to the bolay snakes causing the illness and mentions that the canoe of Xbalanke (Thorn Broom of the elopement stories) was the source of their venom (Braakuis 2005). In the elopement story, the *ic bolay* was the first snake manifestation of Xucaneb's daughter to emerge from the jar, and the source of its venom was the tobacco in the canoe (one of her plant manifestations).

The Maya believe that the breath of a snake is deadly (Fought 1972:85; R. Wilson 1972:71), so the act of the healer spraying tobacco juice on a patient would mimic the snake breathing or spitting venom. But how does this cure rather than harm the patient? It would seem that the healer directs his tobacco spray at the soul of the sorcerer causing the illness rather than at the soul of the patient. Núñez de la Vega describes sixteenth-century Tzeltal and Tzotzil healers who applied their medicine by blowing on their patients to cure them (Brinton 1894:19). One of the consequences of chewing tobacco is yellow staining of the mouth and teeth. A physical relationship between the *ic bolay* (fer-de-lance) and tobacco is that the fer-de-lance has a yellow throat (the female fer-de-lance is called *aj k'an k'ok'o*). The word *k'anti* is a general term for any venomous snake, but it literally means "yellow mouth." The Q'eqchi' name for a healer who cures snakebite is *aj k'anti*, literally, "he of the yellow mouth" (Braakhuis 2005:182).

## THE BREATH SOUL

Whether or not they understand the germination of the corn plant, all corn farmers know that the corn seeds grow after the white pollen is blown across the field. When environmental conditions reduce or prevent an adequate release of the pollen, the corn crop is greatly diminished, so corn growers have a clear understanding that the pollen release is directly connected to good seed development. I have identified One Ixim as the male tassel of the corn plant. The pollen blown across the field represents the semen (the engendering force) of One Ixim. It is analogous to the spittle/semen that One Hunahpu spits into Lady Blood's hand to transfer his essence to his sons. This suggests to me that the white pollen wind and white spittle of One Ixim/One Hunahpu are directly analogous to the white T533 wind soul of humans. This concept can also be extended to One Ixim's role as the center ceiba tree that disperses its white seeds across the milpa at the start of the planting season. In the Ch'orti' region, three male wind gods bring the rains that water the cornfield. It is believed that these wind gods also blow the first breath into a newborn child and take this breath away at death (Wisdom 1940:397). The pre-Columbian prototype for these wind gods is surely the triad manifestation of One Ixim.

In my reconstruction of the core myth, humans derived their characteristics from the primordial young couple, One Ixim/One Hunahpu and Ixik/Lady Bone Water. The flesh of humans was made from Ixik's corn-seed remains, the thirteen creatures she turned into were the model for the *way* souls, and One Ixim was the source of the breath soul. In chapter 15, I will present evidence that One Ixim was also intimately related to the engendering heat and the lightning in the blood of humans.

## HOBNIL AND THE BEE GODDESS

The *Popol Vuh* relates that, in addition to containing corn and fruit, Paxil Mountain also contained honey (Christenson 2003a:194). In the highlands, wild honeybees often make their nests in limestone cliffs such as those found on Paxil Mountain. One of the most important uses of honey, a primary trade commodity, was in the production of fermented ritual drinks. The *Madrid Codex* has numerous almanacs related to beekeeping, which is still a profitable enterprise (Ciaramella 2002). Although the more productive, imported *Apis mellifera* honeybees have replaced the indigenous domesticated bees (*Melipona beecheii*) in the majority of Yucatec Maya communities, the honey of the latter is still the most highly prized (Redfield and Villa Rojas 1934; Merrill-Sands 1984; de Jong 1999). The *M. beecheii* bees, called *ko'olel kab* or *xunan kab,* "lady bee," and *ix chuuahcab,* "lady wild bee," are thought to be female (de Jong 1999). Although the Maya only domesticate *M. beecheii,* they also collect the honey from three other species of wild bees called *xiik'* (*Frieseomellita nigra*), *e'hol* (*Trigona fulviventris*), and *kansak* (*Scaptotrigona pectoralis*), all three of which are considered to be male.

*Melipona beecheii, or xunan kab,* is a stingless bee that makes its nest in hollow tree branches and trunks in high forests. The beekeeper hollows out logs for hives and places them on an A-frame rack in an apiary. The apiary is a simple thatched-roof structure without walls, where as many as two hundred log hives can be housed. Abundant honey production depends on ample flowers near the apiary, and the honey is harvested four times a year (March, April, May, and November) following the major blooming periods of certain plants. The predominant flowers of the season impart distinct flavors to the honey. Rituals for the consecration of the apiary and protection of the bees are similar to house and cornfield ceremonies. It is thought that *xunan kab* bees produce honey of superior quality because they collect it from the supernatural place at the center of the sky called *u gloria*. Some Yucatec Maya believe a canoe (*xmaben)* filled with divine honey is at this location, while others describe *xmaben* as a celestial field of divine flowers owned by the chahks. In either case, only the *xunan kab* bees are allowed to collect this heavenly honey.

Landa notes that the Bakab deity called Hobnil, "beehive," was the patron god of the beekeepers (Tozzer 1941:157). As described in the previous chapter, this deity was a manifestation of One Ixim. The *Chilam Balam of Chumayel* refers to four Mucencab bee deities, each a different color, located in the four world trees, and to four groups of colored bees that feast on appropriately colored flowers at these locations (Roys 1933:64–66). The text also says that the wild bees swarm in the ceibas and gourd trees of the land. Given the association of the four Mucencab gods with the world trees, it seems reasonable to conclude that they were also four manifestations of One Ixim/Hobnil. Similar deities are found in contemporary beliefs. There is a guardian bee-deity named *Noh Yum Cab,* "great lord bee," and below him in the hierarchy are the *mulzencab* and the *bolon hobon,* "nine beehive" (Roys 1933:64; Redfield and Villa Rojas 1934:117).

The beekeeper has a husband-like relationship with the *xunan kab* (lady bee), much like the farmer has when he plants his corn seed (de Jong 1999), which suggests that *xunan kab* was thought to be a manifestation of Ixik/Lady Bone Water. In the Ixil and Kaqchikel elopement stories, some of the remains of Xucaneb's daughter are turned into bees rather than noxious animals (Redfield 1945:292–370; Colby and Colby 1981:182), and this also suggests that Ixik/Lady Bone Water had a bee manifestation. Like the remains of Xucaneb's daughter that were poured into a canoe, fermented honey drinks were mixed in hollowed-out logs and old canoes (Tozzer 1907:125).

A Yucatec Maya myth reminiscent of the Guatemalan courtship stories explains why *xunan kab* bees are found in the forest. Xunan Kab is courted by a prince who grows impatient with the process and violates her. She flies away to the forest (de Jong 1999:145). The close association between *xunan kab* bees and corn is reflected in the Yucatec Maya belief that there is a direct relationship between the productivity of the *xunan kab* bees and the success of the corn harvest. If the farmer's bees produce abundant honey, he will have a successful corn crop.

### The Fruit of Paxil Mountain

The description of Paxil Mountain, also known as Cayala, suggests that it was like a granary or a storage house full of tribute food. These are the same foods commonly consumed during festivals and marriage negotiations. This is reflected in a Zoque myth in which their corn cave is also filled with fruit, cacao, and beans (Cordry and Cordry 1941:64). The Zoque cultural hero called Chalucas obtains the fruit that is an essential part of marriage negotiations from this cave. The *Popol Vuh* states that Paxil/Cayala contains *zapote, anona, jocote, nance,* and *matasano* fruit (Christenson 2003a: 194–95). Like honey, these lowland fruits were used to create intoxicating beverages.

The association of women with fruit trees is seen in the Tzotzil area (Guiteras Holmes 1961:46). If a fruit tree does not produce, the owner will take a leather thong and attempt to beat it. The owner's wife will defend the tree, and the owner will then beat the wife. The tree is thought to be frightened by this, and the following season, it will produce abundant fruit. Fruit is also associated with women during the Easter celebrations of Santiago Atitlán. A wooden structure is erected in front of the center altarpiece of the church and decorated with scarlet bromeliad flowers and fruit brought from the coast (Christenson 2001:94). The same kind of fruit is hung from the rafters of the San Juan cofradía house. The fruit is equated with women with large breasts (Mendelson 1957:240), and the red bromeliad flower is one of the manifestations of the corn goddesses (see chapter 14). Similarly, in Momostenango, the Easter flowers and greenery brought from the coast are from *coyol* palms that are thought to turn into fer-de-lances if the participants of the ceremony do not maintain ritual purity (Cook 2000:168). As noted above, this snake was another manifestation of Xucaneb's daughter.

If my interpretation of One Ixim and Ixik/Lady Bone Water as a manifestation of the male/female principle is correct, then fruit trees were thought to be manifestations of One Ixim/One Hunahpu, while the fruit itself represented his wife Ixik/Lady Bone Water. This concurs with Martin's insight that One Ixim represents all the sustenance in the world, but adds another aspect to it that incorporates the vital role of women in Maya society.

# 10

# THE PATERNAL GRANDMOTHER
# AND HER DAUGHTERS-IN-LAW

The creator grandmother of the *Popul Vuh*, Xmucane, had two daughters-in-law, Lady Bone Water and Lady Blood. They were the wives of her firstborn son, One Hunahpu, and the mothers of the monkey twins and the hero twins. This chapter reviews the interrelated roles of Xmucane and her daughters-in-law, their Classic Period parallels, and their similarities with other Mesoamerican goddesses.

## MESOAMERICAN GODDESSES

The colonial accounts of Maya goddesses are relatively meager in comparison with the rich descriptions and illustrations of Central Mexican goddesses found in codices and in reports by Spanish priests such as Sahagún, Durán, and Ríos. Many traits of the Central Mexican goddesses overlapped, and occasionally the various sources contain what appears to be contradictory information. Nevertheless, a general outline of the functions and diagnostic features of the main Mesoamerican goddesses can be constructed, and a review of their characteristics increases our understanding of their Maya counterparts.

In the mythology of the Nahua people, the place of duality was inhabited by an elderly creator couple known variously as Ometecuhtli and Omecihuatl or Tonaca-tecuhtli and Tonacacihuatl (Nicholson 1971:410–11). This primordial pair embodied the principle of male/female complementary opposition. The goddesses Toci (grand-mother), Teteo Innan (mother of the gods), Tlalli Iyollo (heart of earth), and Temaz-calteci (grandmother of the sweat bath) were all manifestations of the female creator goddess. Toci was a healer and midwife who often wore cotton spindles and raw cotton as part of her costume.

Several sources describe some of the younger Nahua goddesses as manifestations of the same goddess, while others characterize them as sisters. Sahagún (1959–63, book 2, 22) mentions three closely associated goddesses: Chalchiuhtlicue (Jade Skirt), Chicomecoatl (Seven Snake), and Huixtocihuatl (Salt Woman). The first two represented corn as well as all food and drink. Illustrations of Chicomecoatl show her carrying twin ears of corn in each hand, and the quetzal feather adorning her headdress represented the corn tassel. Sahagún calls them sisters, but Durán (1971:221) states that Chalchiuhtlicue and Chicomecoatl were manifestations of the same goddess, also called Xilonen (tender ear of green corn). Meanwhile, the *Codex Ríos* gives Xochiquetzal (Flower Quetzal) as yet another name for Chicomecoatl.

Ruiz de Alarcón (Coe and Whittaker 1982:293) indicates that Xochiquetzal, Chalchiuhtlicue, and Citlalicue (Star Skirt) were sisters. In one of the festivals recorded by Sahagún (1959–63, book 2, 67), the impersonator of Tezcatlipoca was ritually married to four women who represented the goddesses Xochiquetzal, Xilonen, Huixtocihuatl, and Atlatonan, and he was allowed to live with them for the twenty days prior to his sacrifice in the festival. Sahagún indicates that the corn god Centeotl was the son of the creator grandmother Toci. While the *Histoyre du Mechique* names Xochiquetzal and her husband Piltzintecuhtli as Centeotl's parents, the *Codex Telleriano-Remensis* states that Xochiquetzal was Centeotl's wife. *Centli* refers to dried ears of corn ready for harvest, and Centeotl symbolizes this stage of corn, as demonstrated by a harvest ritual recorded by Sahagún (1959–63, book 2, 60). In this festival, ears of corn were bundled into groups of seven and carried to Chicomecoatl's temple. The ears of corn, thought to represent Centeotl, were ritually consecrated at the temple in order to become the heart of the stored corn and the seed corn for future planting. Centeotl was also the patron of ritual drinking and inebriation (Pohl 1999:190).

Xochiquetzal was a youthful goddess associated with beauty, sexuality, and pleasure, and the patroness of weavers, embroiderers, feather workers, jewelers, sculptors, artists, and craftspeople. In the *Codex Magliabechiano*, a bat is created from rock anointed with the semen of Quetzalcoatl, and the gods send the bat to bite off a piece of Xochiquetzal's vulva. They wash this flesh, and from the water that spills, the first flowers are created. Flowers were symbols for all the sensual pleasures, such as love, art, music, and the life-force.

Although no sources directly associate Xochiquetzal with bees and honey, her role as a flower goddess, and by extension, as a nectar goddess strongly points to that function. The *Historia de los mexicanos por sus pinturas* states that Xochiquetzal was the first woman to die during warfare, and by dying young, Xochiquetzal permanently retained her association with youthful sexuality and beauty.

A male deity closely associated with Xochiquetzal was Xochipilli (Flower Prince), who was also known as Seven Flower (Furst 1978; Pohl 1994). In some sources, he was equated with Centeotl, Piltzintecuhtli, and Tonacatecuhtli. Xochipilli/Seven Flower was the god of precious gifts including textiles and jewelry; the patron of dancing, feasting, and game playing; and a cacao trader. On the day name 7 *Flower*, scribes, artists, and artisans celebrated the feast of flowers in honor of Seven Flower and Xochiquetzal. People born on this day sign were said to become good artisans

(Sahagún 1959–63, book 4, 7). Another day name associated with these deities of artists and artisans was *1 Flower* (*1 Ajaw*; Sahagún 1959–63, book 4, 25). Males born on this day were said to be destined to become singers and artisans, while females would become good embroiderers.

The *Historia de los mexicanos por sus pinturas* and *Codex Telleriano-Remensis* indicate that Xochiquetzal and Seven Flower were the Aztec creator couple Tonacacihuatl and Tonacatecuhtli, which seems at odds with other descriptions of these dual deities. If, however, Centeotl/Seven Flower/Xochipilli and Chicomecoatl/Xochiquetzal were viewed as manifestations of the male/female principle, this identification would be most appropriate. In some instances, Centeotl was thought to have a female form, which would fit with such an interpretation. This complementary pairing of deities was also exemplified by Citlaltonac and Citlalinicue, who were identified with the Milky Way.

Chalchiuhtlicue, like Chicomecoatl, was thought to embody all human sustenance, and she was also specifically identified with fresh water. Her green jade skirt represented the springwater that flowed from the depths of the mountains, and the green trees on the mountain slopes. The waters of Chalchiuhtlicue were said to originate at Tlalocan, the mythical home of the rain gods.

Midwives invoked Chalchiuhtlicue while ritually washing newborn babies in a basin of water, spring, or stream. Durán (1971:267) also notes the custom of washing the dead in the waters of Chalchiuhtlicue before their interment or cremation. The washing ceremony was intended to remove the "filth" from the newborn and presumably the excrement of the newly deceased. Baths were also part of healing ceremonies. In a ritual recorded by Ruiz de Alarcón (Coe and Whittaker 1982:193), four manifestations of Chalchiuhtlicue were invoked to clean the patient of his illness. These goddesses of filth were named Quato, Caxoch, Tlahui, and Xapel. Another goddess of filth was Tlazolteotl, who also had four manifestations considered sisters: Tiacapan, Teicu, Tlacoyehua, and Xocoyotl (Sahagún 1959–63, book 1, pp. 23, 71). Washing in the waters of Chalchiuhtlicue was not restricted to humans; the first step in the preparation of corn was to boil the seeds in water and lime and then to wash off the outer shell before grinding.

The freshwater associations of Chalchiutlicue contrast with the saltwater associations of Huixtocihuatl, a salt goddess. Salt, an essential dietary element, was often manufactured from salt water using a variety of reduction techniques. Not all areas had salt sources, so the trading of this essential commodity was widespread.

Citlalicue and another closely related goddess, Cihuacoatl (Woman Serpent), were role models for pregnant women and midwives. Complications from pregnancy and childbirth were the leading cause of death for women. The stories and rituals involving these goddesses of procreation provided information to assure a successful birth. They also imparted lessons to the expectant mother about inappropriate behavior and practices that might result in her death or that of her child. The midwife and the woman in labor invoked the goddesses Citlalicue and Cihuacoatl during difficult births, and the woman was told to be like Cihuacoatl.

The group of patron goddesses for women who died in childbirth was collectively called Cihuateteo, "women deities." They belonged to a category of deities called the Tzitzimime, who were expelled from the heavenly paradise of Tamoanchan for destroying a sacred tree. Tzitzimime took the form of stars that were thought to descend from the heavens and attack humans during periods of crisis. The Cihuateteo illustrated in the *Codex Borgia* and *Codex Vaticanus B* are shown as five bare-breasted goddesses. Two of the goddesses have centipedes and snakes emerging from their mouths, and the *Codex Borgia* goddesses wear human crossbones on their skirts.

Women in labor were viewed as brave warriors who brought forth a child as a warrior captures an opponent for sacrifice (Sahagún 1959–63, book 6, 167). When a fetus dies during pregnancy or childbirth, it is naturally expelled from the body, but there are occasions when the fetus remains within the womb, and without its removal the woman will die as well (Cal Greene, personal communication). Sahagún describes the rather gruesome but necessary task of the midwife in such cases, which was to extract the fetus by inserting obsidian blades into the womb, slicing apart the fetus, and removing the pieces (Sullivan 1966:81, 87). In these instances, the child was not a captured warrior, but a soldier who died on the battlefield and was dismembered.

Death on the battlefield was considered to be a great honor, and women who died during childbirth were equally revered. They were given the title *mocihuaquetzqui,* "woman warrior," and were thought to join the Cihuateteo goddesses in the afterlife and continue their warrior role. The souls of male eagle-ocelot warriors who died in battle were thought to live in the east, and at dawn, they dressed in their war costumes and accompanied the sun across the sky to the zenith. The souls of women who died in childbirth lived in the west. After the sun began its ascent, they also dressed in their war costumes and journeyed to the zenith to take the place of the male warriors and accompany the sun until sunset.

## THE TRAITS OF XMUCANE

In her role as the quintessential first female and mother, the creator grandmother Xmucane made food and drink, hauled jars of water and bundles of firewood, maintained the hearth fire, tended the garden plot of the house, and gathered herbal remedies. The creator grandmother was also the first woman to spin and weave cotton, and she most likely did so while sitting on a mat in the patio of her home, just as Maya women do today. Xmucane shared many of the duties of her husband, and like him, she was a healer and diviner. Her most prominent role was as a midwife and goddess of the sweat bath.

## THE OLD GODDESS IX CHEL

The Classic Period parallel of Xmucane was the grandmother Ix Chel. She is often portrayed in the inscriptions with a wrinkled mouth, receding gums, and sagging

Figure 10.1. Chak Chel form of Ix Chel, *Dresden Codex* 39b (after Villacorta)

breasts indicative of old age. The images of Itzamnaaj's head superimposed on the body of his wife Ix Chel have already been discussed in chapter 8. There are two kinds of Ix Chel goddesses (Ciaramella 1994). Although both wear a *hix* jaguar ear, one is shown as a rather kindly-looking old woman with a human face, hands, and feet, while the other is a ferocious-looking woman with a square eye and jaguar paws for hands and feet. On vessel K5113, two old-woman Ix Chels and the jaguar Ix Chel are pictured together as midwives assisting a young goddess in labor (Taube 1994).

Madrid Codex 75 and 76 illustrate a model of the quadrilateral world that includes two portraits of Itzamnaaj and the old-woman version of Ix Chel sitting together back-to-back at the center and on the west side of the world. On *Madrid Codex* 10b and *Dresden Codex* 39b, the old-woman Ix Chel is shown pouring water from a jar.

She is named in the accompanying caption text as Chak (red) Chel (fig. 10.1; Kelley 1976:69; Ciaramella 1994). Her name is represented in the *Madrid Codex* by the syllabic signs T145:612, *che le,* while in the *Dresden Codex* example her name is spelled with simply T145, *che.* The jaguar version of Ix Chel is shown pouring water from a jar on *Dresden Codex* 67. The first part of her name is eroded, but enough remains of the second part to indicate it was also Chel. The fact that she is illustrated with a red body suggests her name is also Chak Chel.

## THE CREATOR GRANDMOTHER IX CHEL AND CLOTH PRODUCTION

The creator grandmother was the first weaver of cotton textiles, which played a central role in Maya economics. Cotton (*Gossypium* sp.) was grown in the milpas along with corn, and as with corn, women were in charge of transforming it into a useful product (McBryde 1945:143). On *Madrid Codex* 102b, the old-woman Ix Chel is shown weaving (Morris, cited in Ciaramella 1999:37). Her costume reflects her occupation; here, as elsewhere, she is pictured with cotton strips and spindles of cotton thread in her hair (see fig. 5.6; Taube 1992a, 1994; Ciaramella 1994, 1999). After being spun into thread, cotton is looped around the pegs of a board to create the warp. On *Madrid Codex* 102c, the creator grandmother is twice shown holding a cotton spindle as she creates the skein on a warping board (Ciaramella 1999). In several scenes, the Chak Chel goddesses wear a tied warp-skein as a headdress, and in some examples, the skein takes the form of a tied serpent (see fig. 10.1; Ciaramella 1994, 1999). The Itzamnaaj/Ix Chel deity wears the snake headdress along with a cotton spindle on *Dresden Codex* 9 and also on *Madrid Codex* 30, 32, and 79.

The word *chel* means both "rainbow" and "stretched out" in Yucatec Maya, and the T145 *che* sign used in Ix Chel's name is a pictograph of a warp skein (Thompson 1930:134; Ciaramella 1994:203). This is an appropriate logograph for "stretched out," because the warp threads are stretched out on the warping board. The warp-skein or tied-serpent headdress is also worn by young goddesses who are named in the accompanying caption texts as Ixik and Sak Ixik (*Dresden Codex* 15, 18, 20, 22, and 23).

## THE SNAKE HEADDRESS AS A CORAL SNAKE

The red, coiled headdress that married women wear in the Poqomchi' area and the winding headband used by the principal women of Santiago Atitlán have been identified with Ix Chel's serpent headdress (Ciaramella 1994; Christenson 2001:95, 120, 199–200). The latter headband is identified as a "rainbow serpent" and is thought to have been first worn by the grandmother Yaxper, goddess of weaving, childbirth, and midwives (Christenson 2001:95, 120, 199–200). A close association between rainbows and snakes is found in the Kaqchikel and Tz'utujil areas, where rainbows, which are used to predict rain, are thought to be the breath of a snake (Redfield 1945:134; Mendelson 1957:560). In Tzotzil-speaking Chenalhó, it is said that there is a snake under every rainbow, and great caution must be taken to avoid one (Guiteras Holmes 1961:203, 235). The Tzotzil refer to rainbows as *me'kinabal,* "mother of drizzle," and they believe that rainbows are the origin of the norte (a cold storm), and that they are a cold, female devil who steals the soul of corn and prevents rain from coming (Laughlin 1975:232; 1988:441).

The Poqomchi' specifically identify their red headdress with a coral snake, thought to be the companion spirit of married women. The Q'eqchi' women of Cobán wear a multicolor hair-ribbon that also represents a coral snake (M. Wilson 1972). In Kaqchikel, the coral snake is called *xaqab' xoqajaw,* "the queen's hairband" (Akkeren 2000:271), while the coral snake is called *xotochel* in Ch'ol (Aulie and Aulie 1978:138). Given these pervasive beliefs, it seems reasonable to conclude that the creator grandmother had both a coral snake and rainbow manifestation.

## THE GRANDMOTHER AS MIDWIFE AND HEALER

The *Popol Vuh* specifically refers to Xmucane as a midwife. According to Landa, her counterpart, Ix Chel, was likewise the goddess of childbirth (Tozzer 1941:129). Tz'utujil midwives are thought to transform into the grandmother Yaxper while performing their duties. It is likely that pre-Columbian midwives summoned the Ix Chel/Xmucane goddesses to help with the delivery and that midwives were symbolically transformed into these goddesses while practicing their arts.

The old-woman Ix Chel is pictured in a parturition scene on vessel K559 (Miller and Martin 2004:96). In this scene, a young goddess in a squatting position is giving birth to a rabbit. The blood from the birth rises from her loins into a stylized tree. A divination mirror is seen in front of the rabbit and goddess; such devices were closely associated with the prognostications carried out on the day people were born in order to determine their destiny. The blood tree is reminiscent of the croton tree Lady Blood tapped to make a faux heart (see chapter 8). In the adjacent scene, a young goddess kneels before Ix Chel, who holds a gopher on her lap. The breast of the young goddess is extended to the gopher, who appears ready to begin nursing. The pairing of a gopher and rabbit also occurs on a vase in the American Museum of Natural History (Stuart, in Stuart, Houston, and Robertson 1999, pt. 2, 23). I suspect that the K559 scene may represent the birth and first nursing of the hero twins in their animal manifestations.

The Ix Chel goddesses assist a young goddess in labor on vessel K5113 (Taube 1994). The woman giving birth clings to the birthing ropes while the jaguar form of Ix Chel supports her under the arms. The old-woman Ix Chel stands to the side holding a bowl. This is a scene of a difficult birth, and the participation of the jaguar Ix Chel implies that she played a dominant role in such trying times. The crossed bones on the dress of the old-woman Ix Chel may allude to the possibility that the young goddess giving birth in the scene died. On *Dresden Codex* 74, the jaguar form of Ix Chel wears such a skirt while she destroys the world with a flood.

## THE MEANING OF IX CHEL'S HEADDRESS

Ix Chel's headdress may refer to women who have given birth. On vessel K5113, the young goddess in labor stands stretched out, holding the birthing ropes. In Maya cosmology, an umbilical cord descended from the center of the sky to the earth (Freidel, Schele, and Parker 1993, Kappelman and Reilly 2001; Looper and Kappelman 2001), and Taube (1994:659) has noted that the birth rope suspended from the rafters of a house represents this umbilical cord. In Santiago Atitlán, the rainbow-snake headdress of the grandmother Yaxper is thought to represent an umbilical cord that ties a holy woman to the sky (Christenson 2001:95, 120–21, 199–200). In Tz'utujil weaving, the cord that ties the loom to the tree or post is also thought to represent a metaphorical umbilical cord (Prechtel and Carlsen 1988:126). On a Jaina figurine in the Museo Nacional de Antropología, Mexico City (Schmidt, de la Garza, and Nalda 1998, cat. 182), a woman is pictured weaving. The rope that ties her loom to the post is twisted like an umbilical cord. The image of the stretched-out goddess on K5113 holding the umbilical cord–birth rope evokes the warp threads stretched on a loom, ready for weaving. The Tz'utujil associate the movement the weaver makes during weaving with a woman having birth contractions (Prechtel and Carlsen 1988:124). As noted above, *chel* means both rainbow and stretched out, and I propose that it is also a reference to women who have given birth. One of Xmucane's names is Alom, She Who Has Borne Children (Christenson 2003a:60).

## THE YOUNG GODDESSES

Some of the young goddesses whose portraits appear frequently in the codices are named in the caption text as Ixik, who I have suggested was equivalent to Lady Bone Water of the *Popol Vuh*. Their long, flowing hair is usually parted in the middle in two long strands that sometimes curl at the ends (fig. 10.2). The portrait glyph for Ixik has one of these strands of hair cascading down in front of her face and another positioned over her eye. The strand of hair resembles the curl of the *kab'an* sign, although the strand of hair of the goddess curls to the left, and the *kab'an* always curls to the right. Because Landa's alphabet used a *kab'an*-like curl to represent the phonetic sound *u,* and *u* is a word for moon, Ixik has been identified as a moon goddess (Thompson 1950:86). In contrast, I have identified her as a honey goddess (Bassie-Sweet 1991) while Vail and Stone (2002) have identified her as an earth goddess (*kab* can refer to both honey and earth). In some examples, her portrait sign has the syllabic postfix *ki,* which strongly indicates that it is simply the Postclassic version of the T1000b/T1002 *ixik* sign, which also has the *ki* syllabic postfix. A comparison of a Classic Period *ixik* glyph from Tonina demonstrates this (see fig. 8.5d). The diagnostic trait of this head is a circle of hair on her forehead and long, flowing hair down her cheek. None of the illustrations of the Ixik and Sak Ixik goddesses in the codices include the T181/T683 moon sign on their bodies, so I conclude that they were not lunar goddesses.

Figure 10.2. Ixik, *Dresden Codex* 16 (after Villacorta)

The young goddess Ixik is also named Sak Ixik, "white woman," in both the Dresden and Madrid codices. The old-woman Ix Chel is also named as Sak Ixik on *Madrid Codex* 72a, 102c, 107b, and 108c. It has been suggested that the *sak* "white," sign in this context refers to *sakal*, "weaving" (Thompson 1939:132), but it may also refer to cotton, salt, or even white corn. In the contemporary stories, the corn goddesses are viewed as versions of the same goddess or as sisters. The Preclassic San Bartolo murals also illustrate multiple corn goddesses, as do many Classic Period pots. It is my contention that these goddesses were manifestations of Ixik/Lady Bone Water, but that these manifestations were also characterized as sisters, much as the chahks were seen as brothers.

## THE TOAD FORM OF IXIK/LADY BONE WATER

In addition to her role as a corn goddess, Ixik/Lady Bone Water had a toad form. On vessel K7451, the same shell motifs that on BOD vessel 116 represent the four directional planting holes (Robicsek 1981) appear on the back of a toad (Coe and Kerr 1998:189). In the Tzotzil and Tzeltal elopement stories, the daughter of the mountain lord has a toad form, as does Xucaneb's daughter in the Guatemalan versions. In one Tzotzil myth, a toad sings at the mouth of the mountain lord's cave while his daughters spin cotton to make rain clouds (Morris 1987:105). As noted in chapter 3, the Maya naturally associated the loud mating calls of toads with the arrival of the rainy season, and in many areas, it is believed that the toads actually call for rain.

Among the great number of toad species in the Maya area, the uoh toad (*Rhinophrynus dorsalis*) in particular has many characteristics that are suitable for a corn goddess. The emergence of these underground toads with the onset of the rainy season is reminiscent of corn that germinates and emerges from the earth at this time. The body of the uoh toad is a shapeless mass like a mound of corn dough, and when disturbed, the toad secretes copious amounts of sticky white material with the consistency of corn dough (Janzen 1983:420). Thompson (1970:258) notes that the Maya believe this toad is full of green corn gruel. In contrast to the poisonous *Bufo marinus*, the uoh is a delicacy and an important food source in the Petén, where "it is impaled on the center section of a palm frond and roasted over an open fire," as the Maya roast corn (Campbell 1998:47). Another method of cooking is to dunk the toad in boiling water to remove the surface secretions and then bake the toad in a tamal (Baer and Merrifield 1971:239).

## LADY BLOOD AS A MOON GODDESS

The second wife of One Hunahpu, Lady Blood, was a moon goddess. The Maya relate the monthly menstruation cycle to the synodic period of the moon. They use the phases of the moon to time sexual activity and to predict when a woman will give birth (Thompson 1939:134; Schultze Jena 1954; Neuenswander 1981; Earle and Snow 1985:242). The intimate relationship between the moon and blood is revealed in the K'iche' term for menstruation, *ri quic' rech ri ic'*, "the blood from the moon" (Schultze Jena 1954), or "the sign of the moon" (Earle and Snow 1985:242). It is also reflected in the Yucatec Maya word *u*, which refers to the moon, the lunar month, and menstruation (Barrera Vásquez 1980:897), and the Tzotzil term for menstruation, *'il 'u*, "to see the moon" (Laughlin 1975:71).

The swelling of Lady Blood's pregnant belly represents the waxing moon (D. Tedlock 1985:39; Bassie-Sweet 1991:191). Her exit from the underworld and her journey to the home of One Hunahpu at the center of the earth correspond to the appearance of the waxing moon in the west and its eastern progression each subsequent night. Her action of bleeding the croton tree for its sap just before she leaves the underworld also indicates her journey was identified with the waxing moon. As noted in chapter 4, the Maya believe that the sap from trees flows more freely during the new moon, so this is the optimum time to slash their incense trees. The journey of Lady Blood also establishes the ecliptic pathway, as the moon is always found within five degrees of the ecliptic.

## THE ECLIPSE CYCLE

The *Popol Vuh* specifically tells us that Lady Blood remained in the underworld for six months before her pregnancy was discovered, which means that her pregnancy is also a metaphor for larger lunar cycles. In the Classic Period Lunar Series, the Maya grouped synodic periods of the moon into sets of six and five. One reason they did this was that they were interested in calculating eclipse cycles (lunar eclipses occur at minimum intervals of six synodic lunar periods). The first six months of Lady Blood's pregnancy initiated the first six-month lunar semester, that is, the basic eclipse cycle.

Solar and lunar eclipses can only occur at new moon and full moon, respectively. As noted, the final destiny of the hero twins was to become the sun and full moon. The Classic Period counterparts of the hero twins are depicted as youthful males who are distinguishable by their facial and body markings. One Ajaw frequently has a large, black spot on his cheek and black spots on his body, sometimes outlined in red. Yax Bolon typically has patches of jaguar skin attached to his face and body. A common Maya belief is that a pregnant woman who sees an eclipsed sun or full moon will give birth to a baby with dark or red birthmarks (Saville 1921:186–87; Villa Rojas 1945:140). A Tzotzil man described his newborn son as having so many dark spots on his body that he looked like a jaguar (Guiteras Holmes 1961:251). It may be that the spots and jaguar patches found on the bodies of the hero twins refer to the capacity of these celestial beings to leave similar markings on human beings.

If a woman conceives at full moon, she will give birth approximately nine full moons later, and the K'iche' describe a human being as "one of nine moons, one of nine stars" (Schultze Jena 1954; Earle and Snow 1985:242). It is highly probable that Lady Blood's pregnancy was thought to establish the nine-lunation time frame for human gestation. It surely can not be a coincidence that her son Yax Bolon/Full Moon was the god of the number nine.

## THE FERTILITY OF THE WAXING MOON AND THE TWIN EARS OF CORN

There is a prominent Maya belief that the waxing phase of the moon promotes fertility and growth in both plants and humans. While this may have been the sole reason why Lady Blood was able to transform the silk of the corn plant into multiple ears of corn, additionally, she was a waxing moon because she was carrying the hero twins in her belly. Hunahpu and Xbalanque, the hero twins of the *Popol Vuh,* were specifically associated with twin ears of corn.

When the hero twins receive their message from the laughing falcon Wak, they return to their house to bid their grandmother and mother farewell (Christenson 2003a:160). In the center of their house, each hero twin plants a stalk of green corn, and they tell their grandmother and mother that the corn will act as an omen of their fate in the underworld. If the corn dries, it will mean they are dead, but if the corn sprouts, it will mean they are alive.

When the hero twins descend into the underworld, they take the same cave route as their father and uncle and are subjected to the same series of trials by the lords of death. In one confrontation, Hunahpu and Xbalanque decide to jump into a burning underground oven. The Maya use such ovens to bake ceremonial corn-breads and meat. Before entering the oven, the hero twins make arrangements for their burned bones to be finely ground up like corn and thrown into a river. After five days in the river, they appear in the water as fish. The next day they rematerialize as young men. When the hero twins are burned in the oven, Xmucane sees the effigy corn ears dry up, but then, much to her relief, they sprout again. Christenson (2001: 123) has noted that the burning of the hero twins is the likely prototype for the contemporary Tz'utujil planting ritual of burning twin ears of corn and placing the ashes in the center offering hole of the field.

After the green effigy corn indicates that the hero twins are still alive, Xmucane makes offerings to the corn (she burns incense), deifies them, and gives them ritual names (Christenson 2003a:189). Andrés Xiloj notes that the hero twins' effigy corn is similar to the guardian ears that the contemporary K'iche' cense with incense and place with the stored corn in the house rafters (D. Tedlock 1985:295). This is a prevalent practice across the Maya region. In the San Juan cofradía house at Santiago Atitlán, there is an image of the Virgin Mary carrying her two twin maize boys, and twin ears of corn hang from the ceiling of the house. As observed by Christenson (2001:124–25), a custom performed many years ago in this cofradía house was strikingly similar to the hero twins' effigy corn. At harvest, the Atitecos erected an effigy corn plant inside the house, and an old woman who represented the goddess Yaxper would tend to it. The effigy consisted of a forked wooden pole with two cornstalks tied to it and bunches of corn ears hung in its fork. It can be concluded from these striking parallels that the twin ears of corn placed in the granary to protect the female corn spirit were manifestations of the hero twins.

It is a common Maya practice to relate the life cycle of humans metaphorically to that of corn. The Tzotzil say that a fetus is like an ear of corn wrapped in its husk (Rosenblum 1993:77). When Lady Blood arrives at the single corn plant, she is carrying the hero twins in her womb. The hero twins are like twin ears of corn wrapped in a husk, and their presence causes the silk from the ear of corn to multiply in the same way as the guardian ears in the granary cause the stored corn to increase. This suggests

a        b

Figure 10.3. a. Moon goddess's name glyph (T1025 sign); b. T1025 used as syllabic *ja* sign

that the reproductive power of the waxing moon was directly related to the supernatural power of her sons in her womb. Xmucane recognized this power when she
said that her grandsons were already enchanted while in Lady Blood's womb.

### THE NAME OF THE YOUNG MOON GODDESS

A young goddess with a T181 moon sign attached to her body appears in several
scenes, such as vessels K504 and K5166. This goddess is a likely parallel to Lady
Blood, and I interpret her name as One Moon. The T683 sign is a symbol for the
moon, with the T181 sign being the reduced form of the moon glyph. A Postclassic
version of this same goddess is illustrated on page 49 of the *Dresden Codex* Venus pages.
She appears as the regent of the morning-star interval and is illustrated with the moon
sign emerging from under her arm. In the adjacent caption texts and in several Classic
Period scenes, the name of this young moon goddess is composed of a T1000a sign
(the portrait of One Ixim) and a T181 moon sign (fig. 10.3a). This compound sign
has its own designation of T1025 in the Thompson catalog. Both T181/T683 and
T1025 are used in other contexts to represent the syllabic sound *ja* (fig. 10.3b). How,
then, is the moon goddess's name to be read? Depending on the context, T1000a
represents the word *ixim,* "corn"; *hun,* "one"; or the syllabic *na* sound. Given the
common use of numbers at the beginning of deity names, it is most probable that
the T1000a sign in the moon goddess's name is to be read *hun* "one," and that the
entire name is simply One Moon.

My interpretation of One Moon's name explains several illustrations that show
One Ixim juxtaposed with the T683 moon sign. These images have been characterized as a conflation of One Ixim and the moon goddess (Taube 1992a:67; Saturno,
Taube, and Stuart 2005:37). I propose that these images of One Ixim with the moon
cartouche are simply full-figure forms of the name One Moon.

Figure 10.4. Glyph C

This interpretation of the name glyphs for One Moon has implications for Glyph C of the Lunar Series. Glyph C is composed of a variable number with an outstretched hand holding a head with an attached lunar sign (fig. 10.4). The variable number indicates which month it is in a series of five or six months. Three categories of heads appear in the outstretched hand: One Ixim's head (T1000a), GIII, or a skeletal deity. All three of these deities appear as head variants for numbers. The portrait of One Ixim is the head variant for the number one, GIII is the number seven, and the skeletal deity is the number ten. The Glyph C head can thus be read One Moon, Seven Moon, and Ten Moon, respectively, although what these names indicate is unclear. All three may simply be different names for the moon goddess.

## THE WANING MOON

The two dominant traits of contemporary Maya moon goddesses are that they are grandmothers and that they reside in lakes or other pools of water found in caves or cenotes. The slim crescent of the waning moon is seen in the east near dawn. An entry in the Motul dictionary characterizes the end of the waning moon cycles as *benel u tu ch'e'en,* "the departure of the moon to her cave." The K'iche' characterize the waning moon as a woman growing old and its disappearance in the east as her burial (B. Tedlock 1982, 1992). The diminishing moon is visually like a grandmother shrinking and becoming hunched over with age. Barbara Tedlock (1992:31) specifically associates the waning moon with Xmucane. This goddess is further associated with the waning moon in her role as a healer. Among the Q'eqchi', birth defects are thought to occur when the fetus is exposed to certain conditions, and the curing of these imperfections requires a ceremony that must be conducted during the last days of the waning moon.

Although none of the sources directly states that Ix Chel was a moon goddess, Thompson (1939:137, 1970:83, 244) has suggested that she was a waning moon goddess based on the strong relationship between the moon and Ix Chel's role in weaving, childbirth, and rain production. In the ideal planting model, corn is planted at full moon and the rains must begin immediately after sowing. The thirteen-day period of the waning moon that follows the planting is the critical time for the seed to germinate. In the codices, Ix Chel pours water from a jar to create rain, and the metaphors that relate the moon to a water jar have been discussed in chapter 4. The hero twins send both Xmucane and Lady Blood to fetch water in a jar when they want them out of the house so they can search for the hidden ball–game equipment of their father and uncle (Christenson 2003a:152–53).

## WOMEN WARRIORS

In Mesoamerican culture, midwife goddesses are often portrayed carrying a shield in one hand and a weaving batten as a weapon in the other (Sullivan 1966:18; McCafferty and McCafferty 1991). The Lacandon believe that the moon goddess carries her loom–sticks as a weapon when she crosses the sky to protect herself from the jaguars who threaten to eat her (Thompson 1970:246). Although she does not carry a batten, Ix Chel is illustrated as a warrior in a Jaina clay figurine, where she carries a rectangular shield and a stick (Miller and Martin 2004:117).

Evidence of women warriors in the art of the Classic Maya is seen on Yaxchilan Lintel 25 and Stela 32. Lintel 25 shows a woman kneeling before a double-headed centipede serpent (fig. 10.5). Such centipede serpents have been referred to as vision serpents and war serpents (Taube 1992c). The scenes that show figures emerging from serpents have been interpreted as the conjuring of a deity. From the mouth of the beast, a supernatural warrior emerges carrying a small, round shield and a stick with flint blades at either end. The warrior is dressed in a jade cape and a distinctive balloon-shaped headdress. The warrior also wears a Tlaloc mask with a round eye. The war serpent, balloon headdress, and mask have been identified as Teotihuacan motifs associated with warfare (A. Stone 1989; Taube 1992c; Freidel, Schele, and Parker 1993). Dos Pilas Stela 2 and Aguateca Stela 2 commemorate Ruler 3's victory over Seibal in A.D. 736, and on both of these monuments, Dos Pilas Ruler 3 is dressed in the same war costume as the Lintel 25 warrior, including the jade cape, balloon headdress, and mask (Martin and Grube 2000:61).

The Lintel 25 woman tilts her head to look up at the warrior. She is dressed in a richly decorated huipil with the same kind of jade cape worn by the warrior above her. In her right hand, she holds a skull. The earring of the skull is composed of a k'an sign and corn foliage. A centipede emerges from the top of the k'an skull. The woman wears a similar k'an skull with a centipede body as her headdress. The caption text behind the head of the upper centipede serpent begins with the *u b'aahil* phrase that refers to deity impersonation, which can be loosely translated as "it is the image of." As is customary in these phrases, the name of the deity appears next, and then the name of the human who is impersonating the deity (Stuart and Houston 1996). Following the *u b'aahil* phrase is the name of a goddess called Ixik Ohl, followed by the name of Lady K'ab'al Xook in the lower caption text. The caption text containing Lady K'ab'al Xook's name is framed by a scroll that curves

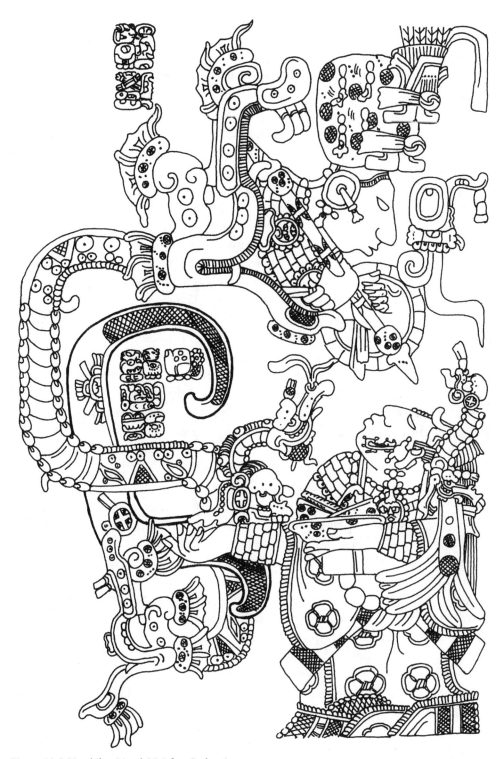

Figure 10.5. Yaxchilan Lintel 25 (after Graham)

down to the right hand of the kneeling woman and identifies her as Lady K'ab'al Xook, the wife of the ruler Itzamnaaj B'alam. It is apparent from the placement of the caption text and the k'an-skull headdress worn by Lady K'ab'al Xook that the k'an skull represents the goddess Ixik Ohl, and that Lady K'ab'al Xook is impersonating this goddess.

On Stela 34, another of Itzamnaaj B'alam's wives, Lady Ik' Skull, is also shown impersonating Ixik Ohl (Bassie-Sweet 1991, fig. 47). Lady Ik' Skull is standing rather than sitting, but she holds in her right hand the k'an skull of Ixik Ohl with the centipede emerging from the top. The war serpent appears behind her.

What is interesting about this scene is that Lady Ik' Skull not only wears the jade bead cape, but her headdress contains the same elements found decorating the balloon headdress of the Lintel 25 warrior. The k'an skull of Ixik Ohl that Lady Ik' Skull has in her headdress also wears these elements. In other words, both Lady K'ab'al Xook and Lady Ik' Skull are dressed as warriors, as is the skull. Furthermore, both Lady K'ab'al Xook and Lady Ik' Skull carry the *kaloomte'* title associated with warriors (Stuart 2000a). The centipede serpent of Ixik Ohl's skull is reminiscent of the centipedes found with the Cihuateteo warrior goddesses illustrated in the *Codex Borgia* and *Codex Vaticanus B*. It is possible then that Ixik Ohl was a goddess who died in childbirth.

The most common identification of the warrior emerging from the Lintel 25 centipede serpent is that it represents either the ruler Itzamnaaj B'alam or a male ancestral warrior. Marc Zender (personal communication) has suggested that the warrior might be Lady K'ab'al Xook in the guise of Ixik Ohl. I think it is more likely that the conjured warrior is Ixik Ohl, who has been manifested from her k'an skull.

## Summary

Like other Mesoamerican goddesses, the three Maya creator goddesses exemplified the role of females, whose duties were generally centered on the house and included the mundane activities of household chores, water hauling, food production, gardening, child care, and the production of textiles. As the wise grandmother, Ix Chel/Xmucane was also a healer and midwife, a function of elderly women in the community. The lives of the young goddesses also reflected the reality of women in Maya society. Lady Bone Water died an early death, likely as a result of childbirth—a common fate of young Maya women. Lady Blood was a widow who lived in the household of her in-laws and raised her children under the tutelage of her mother-in-law. Apparently marriage alone did not give Lady Blood automatic membership in One Hunahpu's family, because Xmucane did not accept Lady Blood into the household until it was certain that she was pregnant with Xmucane's grandchildren. Being able to produce children was an essential function of young Maya women. The following chapter discusses the twin sons of Lady Bone Water and Lady Blood.

# 11

# THE TWINS

Both of One Hunahpu's wives produced sets of twins: the monkey twins, One Batz and One Chouen, and the hero twins, Hunahpu and Xbalanque. This chapter is an overview of these paired brothers. It also includes a discussion of the companions of the hero twins, the Four Hundred Boys.

### The Monkey Gods

Michael Coe (1977) has identified monkey gods of the Classic Period whose traits are parallel to those of One Batz and One Chouen of the *Popol Vuh* (fig. 11.1). In several pottery scenes, these monkey gods are shown either reading or writing a codex or dancing with a divination mirror (K505). Although they are often referred to as monkey scribes, the fact that these monkey gods are shown creating and consulting divination almanacs indicates that they were not merely literate, they were diviners. One of the titles found in Maya inscriptions, which has been read as *itz'aat*, "artist, wise man," takes the form of the monkey god (Stuart, cited in Coe and Kerr 1998:90). Another feature of the monkey gods illustrated in Maya art is that they frequently appear in conjunction with cacao beans and pods (Grube and Nahm 1994:696; Miller and Martin 2005:87).

### The Monkey Twins of the Popol Vuh

As discussed in previous chapters, the monkey twins, One Batz and One Chouen, were musicians, singers, writers, carvers, jewelers, and ball players. When the pregnant Lady Blood comes to the surface of the earth and gives birth to the hero twins, One Batz and One Chouen immediately understand that their half-brothers are destined to surpass them. They know this because as the *k'exel*, "replacement," for

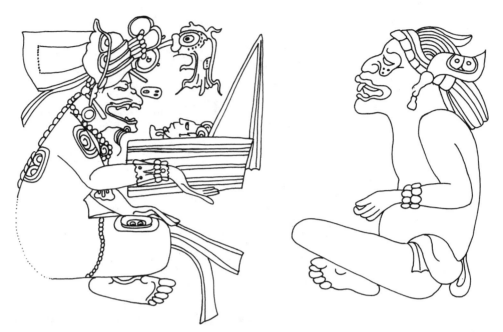

Figure 11.1. Monkey gods, K501, Palenque Palace Tablet

One Hunahpu, they are great diviners. Motivated by jealousy and anger, One Batz and One Chouen first try to kill the hero twins. After failing at that, they exclude Hunahpu and Xbalanque from the family by not allowing them into the house. While the monkey twins stay home playing their flutes and singing, the hero twins are sent out to hunt game birds. The monkey twins repetitively take away these birds for their own meals and deny the hero twins food. As the contemporary first-fruits ceremonies demonstrate, the sharing of food serves to strengthen kinship and community bonds. By denying them food and access to the house, the monkey twins are refusing to give the hero twins legitimate membership in the family. The hero twins complain that their brothers treat them like slaves, that is, as illegitimate sons of One Hunahpu (Christenson 2003a:142). The monkey twins' jealous behavior, which the Maya would have considered inappropriate, demonstrated that they were not worthy of being the *k'exel* of One Hunahpu.

To subordinate the monkey twins, Hunahpu and Xbalanque return one day without any game birds and tell their grandmother that all the birds they have shot remain in the branches of a *q'an te'*, "yellow tree" (*Gliricidia sepium*). They ask their brothers to help them get the birds down, so the next day at dawn the four brothers go to the tree, which is full of singing birds. Although the hero twins shoot some of the birds, none fall from the tree, so the monkey twins climb up to get them. After they climb to the top, the tree begins to grow and swell in size. In desperation and fear, the monkey twins beg their brothers for help, so the hero twins instruct them to untie the ends of their loincloths and let them hang down. These cloths immediately become tails, and One Batz and One Chouen are transformed into howling and chattering spider monkeys (Christenson 2003a:143).

After returning home, the hero twins inform their mother and grandmother that their brothers have turned into monkeys. Knowing that the hero twins are great sorcerers, their grandmother rightly suspects that they are the cause of their brothers' predicament. The hero twins give their grandmother the opportunity to restore the monkey twins, but they warn her that if she laughs when she sees them they will not transform back. The hero twins then begin singing and playing the Hunahpu spider monkey song. The monkey twins come dancing back to the house, but the grandmother can not contain her laughter, and they flee back to the forest. The hero twins tell their grandmother they will give her three more chances, but each time they entice the monkey twins back with their music, the grandmother laughs. On the fourth and final try, the monkey twins will not come back from the forest, and they remain there in their monkey form. Still, the hero twins honor their brothers by making them the patrons of flautists, singers, writers, and carvers.

The monkey twins are enticed back to the house to dance four times. I believe this is a subtle reference to the four New Year festivals and the quadripartite ordering of the world. The creation story of the *Popol Vuh* is about establishing the order of the world, as are the four New Year ceremonies depicted in the *Dresden Codex*. The *Popol Vuh* monkey episode alludes to this four-year festival cycle.

The *Popol Vuh* monkey episode has parallels with some contemporary myths about the ceiba tree that emphasize the divine nature of the ceiba and its association with planting festivals. In Q'anjob'al creation stories, Christ is treated badly by his elder brothers (La Farge 1947:50–57). While his brothers conduct a dance festival, he is forced to perform menial tasks. Christ then creates human beings to take part in his dance to form the world, and he creates the musical instruments and costumes for this purpose. He obtains his feathered dance costume from the crotch of a ceiba tree. His older brothers become jealous and want bird costumes as well. So Christ takes them to the ceiba, which is full of birds, and tells them to climb up to get these bird costumes. As the brothers climb higher, so do the birds. At the same time, Christ makes the tree grow higher, and he touches the ground to form a lake at the base of the tree. He leaves his brothers stranded in the tree and returns home. His mother (the Virgin Mary) demands that he take her to see her sons in the ceiba. The sons beg their mother to help them down, so she throws her hair wrap up into the tree. Still they could not climb down. Christ has repeatedly warned the Virgin not to laugh, but she can not contain herself when she sees them trying to climb down like monkeys. The brothers are then transformed into monkeys and can not return. The Virgin baptizes the tree and creates fruit for the monkeys to eat. The Virgin's hair wrap becomes the vines in the tree.

In a parallel story from the neighboring community of San Miguel Acatán, the widowed Virgin Mary/Moon gives birth to the Sun/Christ (Siegel 1941:66; 1943: 120). Her brothers are suspicious of him and treat him with disrespect. They take him to clear a field, and despite his ability to clear the trees miraculously with just two swings of his ax, they continue to abuse him. The next day, they tie him to a tree in the field and set the field on fire, hoping to kill him. Instead, the Sun/Christ has an agouti chew through the ropes, and he hides in the agouti's burrow until the fire is out. Next, the brothers don their dance masks and costumes and hold a festival (it can be assumed this was a planting festival, which follows the burning of the field). The Virgin/Moon hides her son under the cotton in her basket and takes him to see the fiesta. The Sun/Christ takes the bones from the fiesta food and buries them in a corral beside his house. Three days after the planting, the bones turn into all the animals in the world. Many of the animals escape after the brothers open the corral, so the Sun/Christ is left with only the domesticated animals. The Sun/Christ then arranges his own festival, which turns out much better than that of his brothers. The shamed brothers throw away their costumes and ask the Sun/Christ to get them costumes like his. The Sun/Christ takes them to a very great tree and has them climb it. The tree begins to grow, stranding the brothers in it and turning them into monkeys. The Sun/Christ then creates a lagoon at the base of the tree. His mother goes to the tree to see the brothers, but when they shake the tree, some refuse falls into her eye, and in anger, she commands that they stay there and eat the fruit of the tree. The Sun/Christ is pursued by the "kings of the Jews," who finally seize him and nail him to the cross. From there the Sun/Christ takes a ladder to heaven and the sun dawns.

These stories are reminiscent of a dance festival that was celebrated in northern Yucatan and Belize (Thompson 1930:111; Redfield 1936; Villa Rojas 1945:127). A procession that included a coati impersonator, musicians, and prayer singers went to the forest and cut down a ceiba. Although the coati impersonator was a man, he played the role of a female coati in the festival. Carrying a net bag over her shoulder, the coati impersonator climbed into the tree, and the men hoisted the tree on their shoulders. With much music, singing, and joking, the procession returned to a prepared bullring in the town. The tree was planted in the center with the coati still clinging to its branches. From the top of the tree, the coati scattered gourd seeds from her bag as a sign that the tree had flowered, and tied gourds and yams to the branches to show that the tree had produced fruit. While this was happening, the people began to dance. The coati had a monkey on a stick which she slid up and down to make the crowd laugh. This coati is obviously parallel to Xmucane, who was called Great White Coati, and who made the monkey twins retreat to the trees of the forest by laughing.

These various ceiba myths, as well as the monkey twins' playing of flutes and singing while the hero twins hunted for birds, suggests that their actions were a model for the preliminary preparations for a dance festival. A prominent component of these festivals is the ritual offering and consumption of birds, and the primary decorations on dance costumes are bird feathers. Thus, the hero twins were likely hunting the birds for both meat and feathers. An association between monkeys and dance costumes is found in the K'iche' town of Momostenango (Cook 1981:143;

2000). All of the festival dancers are thought to have first obtained their costumes from a deity living in a large rock called C'oy Abaj, "spider monkey stone," located northeast of the town. The Momostenango ritual specialists are said to be able to call all the animal spirits from C'oy Abaj so that they will enter the bodies of the dancers who are portraying them in the dance festival.

Participating as a dancer in a festival was a high-status accomplishment. By designating the monkey twins as the patrons of singers, musicians, and artisans, the hero twins were assigning them a secondary role as the producers of the ritual costumes and providers of the music, songs, and entertainment that accompanied the dance. The role of the monkey twins as scribes also fits into the festival theme. One of the important actions at the beginning of a festival is the counting and recording of the offerings and the ceremonial foods and drink. I believe that the monkey scribes were in charge of tallying and distributing this inventory. In terms of divinatory hierarchy, they became the patron deities for diviners in the lower echelons. The subordinate position of One Batz' and One Chouen is reflected in the modern K'iche' practice of initiating diviners on a day called *Batz* (B. Tedlock 1982:47). Novice diviners are not yet sages, and therefore, an association with the subordinate monkey twins is appropriate.

Cacao trees require shade to produce abundant fruit. *Gliricidia sepium* is called "the mother of cacao" because it provides shade to the cacao trees in plantations. *G. sepium* also fixes nitrogen in the soil and increases the productivity of the cacao tree. Spider monkeys live in the *G. sepium* trees and eat the cacao fruit. The belief that trees have spirits, and that these spirits can take an animal form, is widespread in the Maya area. The monkey twins episode in the *Popol Vuh* can be seen as establishing the role of the monkey twins as the spirit animals of *G. sepium*. As such, these two gods were the protectors of the cacao and probably oversaw the preparation and distribution of this indispensable drink during festivals. Such an interpretation would explain the many images of monkeys on chocolate vessels. The essential role of *G. sepium* in the core creation myth will be further investigated in chapter 15.

## The Hero Twins of the *Popol Vuh*

Some of the attributes of Hunahpu and Xbalanque, the hero twins of the *Popol Vuh*, and their destiny as the sun and full moon have been discussed in previous chapters. They were diviners, magicians, sages, and the true *k'exel* of One Hunahpu. Their skills were apparent even before they were born. After the pregnant Lady Blood produced the net bag full of corn, Xmucane declared that the twins were already *nawinaq*. While this word means "enchanted," it is also used to refer to magicians and diviners (Christenson 2003a:139).

In contemporary practice, magicians and healers undergo formal initiation rituals, and an episode in the *Popol Vuh* seems to refer to the initiation of the hero twins as healers. After Lady Blood gives birth to the hero twins, she returns to the house with them. Xmucane orders the monkey twins to take them away and abandon them because they do not sleep and they cry all the time. They are placed on an anthill, but are unharmed (Christenson 2003a:140).

There is a common belief that anthills contain a powerful supernatural snake, based on the fact that snakes often inhabit anthills (Brinton 1884:18–21; Tozzer 1907:96, 157; Thompson 1930:68–69, 109; Redfield 1945; Sahagún 1959–63, book 11, 91; M. Wilson 1972:439; Hunn 1977:259; Villa Rojas 1978:299; de Jong 1999: 142). Thompson records a Q'eqchi' initiation of a healer that involved an anthill and this snake. After the initiate was trained in the prayers and practices associated with illness, he was sent to a nest of leaf-cutter ants, where he encountered the Ochcan snake that resided in the nest. The snake would put its tongue in the initiate's mouth and communicate the final mysteries of sorcery to him (Thompson 1930:68–69). A similar initiation occurred at the village of Socotz, but in this case, the snake swallowed the person and then excreted him (Thompson 1930:109).

Núñez de la Vega describes the initiation of a healer by a master that is remarkably similar to those recorded by Thompson, although Núñez characterizes a healer as a sorcerer who makes a pact with the devil:

> He then conducts him to the wood, glen, cave or field where the pact with the Devil is concluded, which they call "the agreement" or "the word given." In some provinces the disciple is laid on an ant-hill, and the Master standing above him calls forth a snake, colored with black, white and red, which is known as "the ant mother." This comes accompanied by the ants and other small snakes of the same kind, which enter at the joints of the fingers, beginning with the left hand, and coming out at the joints of the right hand, and also by the ears and the nose; while the great snake enters the body with a leap and emerges at its posterior vent. Afterwards the disciple meets a dragon vomiting fire, which swallows him entire and ejects him posteriorly. Then the Master declares he may be admitted, and asks him to select the herbs with which he will conjure; the disciple names them, the Master gathers them and delivers them to him and then teaches him the sacred words. (Brinton 1894:19–20)

Núñez de la Vega is describing Tzeltal initiations, and his name for the anthill snake, *me' c'isim,* literally means "mother of the ants." This is the name for the false coral snake (*Lampropeltis triangulum*), which the Tzeltal and Petén Itzaj categorize as a coral snake, and which is found in anthills (Hunn 1977:241; Atran 1999:161). Coral snakes are also found in anthills, and the identification of the coral snake with the creator grandmother has been discussed in chapter 10. In light of these initiation practices, it seems likely that the placing of the hero twins on the anthill referred to their initiation as healers. One Ajaw was the Classic Period equivalent of Hunahpu, and there is a scene in which One Ajaw embraces a snake that is marked with black bands like a coral snake (Schele and Miller 1986, plate 121). One Ajaw is wearing a divination mirror on his waist, and this may be a scene of his initiation as a healer.

The role of the hero twins as healers is also seen in the *Popol Vuh* episode where they shoot Wak, the laughing falcon, in the eye with their blowguns. The wounded Wak informs them that he will not give them their message until they repair his eye. The twins take a piece of the rubber from their ball and place it in Wak's eye, and immediately he is cured (Christenson 2003a:158). The rubber of the hero twins remains on Wak, and this is why laughing falcons have a black circle around their eyes. The use of rubber as a healing agent is found in many parts of Mesoamerica (A. Stone 2002). Wak was a manifestation of the twins' paternal grandfather, who was the ultimate healer. It would seem that Wak was testing their ability to heal, and they passed his test.

## THE TRIALS OF THE UNDERWORLD

The hero twins must endure a number of trials in the underworld before defeating the lords of death. After receiving the message from Wak, the hero twins return home, plant their twin ears of corn, and bid goodbye to their mother and grandmother. Following the same path as their father and uncle, they descend along the road of the underworld and arrive at the council house of One Death and Seven Death. The hero twins are clever in their exchanges with the death lords and succeed in outwitting them. They must twice play ball against the lords of death. Between games, they are forced to spend their nights in houses filled with dangerous beings and phenomena. When Hunahpu and Xbalanque are sequestered for the night in the House of Bats, they escape from these creatures by crawling into their blowguns. Near dawn, Hunahpu pokes his head out and is promptly decapitated by one of the death bats. His head is placed at the top of the Crushing Ballcourt. Xbalanque quickly summons all the animals and has them bring food so he can choose something to transform into a replacement head for Hunahpu. The text specifically refers to the peccary and the coati (animal forms of the creator grandparents) and says that it was the squash food of the coati that was chosen to create the head. It also says that Heart of Sky and the opossum form of Xpiyacoc were present:

> Numerous sages came down from the sky. For Heart of Sky, he who is Huracan, appeared here. He arrived here in Bat House. But the face wasn't completed successfully in time. Only its beautiful covering had appeared. It only had the ability to speak by the time the horizon of the sky began to redden, for it was about to dawn. "Blacken it again with soot, old man," the possum was told. "Fine," replied the Grandfather. And he blackened the sky with soot until it was dark again. Four

> times the Grandfather blackened it with soot. Thus today people say,
> "The possum blackens it with soot." Finally the sky succeeded in
> turning red, and then blue when it began its existence. "Is it not
> good?" Hunahpu was asked. "Yes, it is good," he replied. For his head
> was well supported. It became just like a true head. Then they planned
> a deception; they took counsel together: "Don't play ball. Just look
> threatening. I will surely be the one to accomplish it," said Xbalanque
> to him. (Christenson 2003a:173–74)

After placing the squash head on the headless shoulders of Hunahpu, Xbalanque gives directions to a rabbit to hide at the end of the ballcourt in a tomato patch, and when the ball bounces near the rabbit he is to hop away. When Xbalanque and the squash-headed Hunahpu begin playing ball the next day with the Xibalbans, they have the underworld lords use the real head of Hunahpu as a ball. When the head is thrown into play, Xbalanque strikes it and sends it bouncing into the tomato patch beside the rabbit. Following his instructions, the rabbit jumps up and bounds away. Believing that the rabbit is the ball, the Xibalbans follow in hot pursuit. While they are gone, Xbalanque and Hunahpu quickly go to the tomato patch and trade the squash head for Hunahpu's real head. When the Xibalbans finally return and the squash ball is subsequently put into play, Xbalanque strikes it, which causes the squash to burst and spread its seeds over the ballcourt. The Xibalbans then realize they have been deceived.

Xbalanque's ability to direct the rabbit during the ball game strongly suggests that this animal was one of his manifestations. As noted, Xbalanque was identified with the full moon. In Mesoamerica, the dark pattern on the face of the full moon was interpreted to be a rabbit, and there are numerous examples of rabbits in association with moon symbols in Maya art (Aveni 1980:68; Schele and Miller 1983).

After the ball game, the underworld lords devise a game in which the hero twins are to jump over a burning pit-oven four times. The death lords plan on pushing the boys into the fire and killing them, but knowing the plan, the hero twins face each other and voluntarily jump into the pit together. They have left instructions with a pair of diviners that their bone remains should be ground up and thrown in the river. After six days in the river, the boys reemerge and disguise themselves as vagabond entertainers. They perform a number of impressive dances for the inhabitants of the underworld, and word of their delightful acts soon reaches the underworld lords, who invite them to perform for them. During one of their dance performances, the brothers sacrifice each other and then bring themselves back to life.

This life- and death-giving ability emulates the visual relationship between the sun and the full moon (Bassie-Sweet 1991:190). When the sun rises in the east, the full moon sets in the west, and when the full moon rises in the east, the sun sets in the west. The underworld lords are so impressed by and envious of this sacrifice and regeneration that they request that the trick be performed on them. The hero twins sacrifice them but do not bring them back to life, thus defeating them. The remaining population of Xibalba is told that they will no longer receive human sacrifices, but only the sap of the croton tree and other lowly offerings. The episode concludes with the adornment of One Hunahpu and Seven Hunahpu and the rising of Hunahpu and Xbalanque as the zenith passage sun and full moon—which marks the beginning of the rainy season and indicates that it is time to burn the fields and plant the corn.

## THE RUBBER BALL AND THE ZENITH PASSAGE SUN

The ball that the hero twins used in the underworld had originally belonged to their father, One Hunahpu, and uncle, Seven Hunahpu. The rat of the milpa tells the hero twins about this equipment and declares that their destiny is to be ball players, not milpa makers. Given that the final destiny of the hero twins was to become the sun and full moon, it is apparent that ball playing and celestial cycles were intimately related. The use of Hunahpu's head as the ball implies that the ball actually represented him. The notion that the ball corresponded to a specific participant is found in some Classic Period images where the portrait or name of the defeated player is shown on the ball itself. Given that Hunahpu became the sun, it seems reasonable to suggest that his rubber ball represented the sun, and that its movement up and down the alley of the ballcourt was intended to represent the apparent daily and annual movement of the sun.

The fact that Hunahpu's first rising was specifically at zenith passage provides some understanding of the placement of the ball in the rafters of his house. The world is metaphorically referred to as a house, and the sky is identified with the roof. In a Ch'ol story, the sun's passage across the sky is described as the sun god climbing up and over the roof of his house (Nicholas Hopkins and Kathryn Josserand, personal communication). When he reaches the ridgepole, the sun god is at his zenith position. If the ball symbolizes the sun, attaching it beneath the ridgepole would symbolically associate it with the zenith passage sun. A further association of Hunahpu with zenith passage is found in the timing of the hero twins' arrival at the house to retrieve the ball. The text specifically states that they arrived at *tik'il q'ij,* noon, that is, at the sun's daily apex.

The house of One Hunahpu was situated at the center of the world. When the hero twins first saw the ball game equipment in the rafters, they were eating their evening meal beside the three-stone hearth. In other words, they had taken possession of the house from their monkey twin brothers and assumed their rightful role at the center of the world.

## THE CLASSIC PERIOD HERO TWINS

The Classic Period versions of the hero twins, One Ajaw and Yax Bolon, were originally nicknamed the Headband Gods after the headbands they frequently wear (see

Figure 11.2. *Ajaw* glyphs

fig. 8.2; Coe 1973). I suspect that these headbands were the insignia of diviners. Like the hero twins of the *Popol Vuh*, both Headband Gods are shown in several pottery scenes shooting birds with blowguns. A portrait of One Ajaw is also often used to represent the word *ajaw* in the Ajaw title used by rulers and lords. The logographic signs that represent the word *ajaw* vary, but most frequently they are either the T533 sign or a portrait glyph of One Ajaw (fig. 11.2). In these latter examples, his headband may be plain or decorated with a black spot, the T533 sign, or the so-called Jester God (Fields 1990).

A portrait of One Ajaw also appears as the T1008 sign. In these contexts, he usually has the diagnostic spot on his cheek, but his head is shown without its usual headband. Instead, the top of his head appears to be slicked-back hair. Two slash marks often decorate this motif. Depending on the phonetic complement, the T1008 portrait is read as *winaak*, "man," *keleem*, "youth," or *xib'*, "male" (Zender 1999: 64), which implies that One Ajaw was considered the quintessential young man. The use of his portrait in the Ajaw title suggests that One Ajaw was a role model for young lords and male rulers. Several texts refer to elite youth entering into the state of being an Ajaw. It is possible that this refers to young men who have demonstrated the exemplary qualities of One Ajaw. They may not have been destined to become the ruler, but they emulated the characteristics of this admirable deity. The association of One Ajaw with elite humans is also found in Central Mexico. The equivalent Aztec day name is *1 Flower*, and the Codex Ríos says that he who is born on *1 Flower* will become a musician, physician, weaver, or principal person.

The role of One Ajaw/Hunahpu as the zenith passage sun appears to compete with the role of God G, who has long been identified as the sun, and who is found

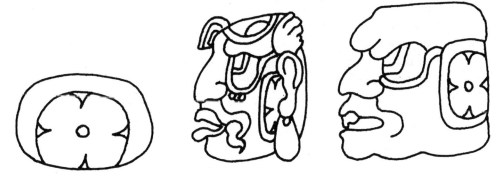

Figure 11.3. *Kin* signs and portrait glyphs of God G

in contexts where his portrait represents the word *k'in,* "sun, day" (fig. 11.3). The use of God G's portrait in the day position of the Long Count and in the month name *Yaxk'in* demonstrates that God G's portrait represents the word *k'in.* A portrait of God G as the rising sun is also used in the logograph that represents the word *pas,* "dawn," and he is depicted as the rising solstice sun on a Copan bench (Bassie-Sweet 1996:65). God G is also the Number 4 Deity. In these various contexts, God G is depicted as a square-eyed deity with T544 *k'in* signs on his cheek and forehead. God G's name occurs in conjunction with his portraits in the codices. It is composed of two glyphs that are read *k'inich ajaw,* and this compound name has been interpreted to mean "the sun-faced lord" or "the hot lord" (Wichmann 2000). Landa noted that the deity called K'inich Ajaw was one of the principal gods of the New Year ceremonies, and the *Dresden Codex* New Year pages show God G/K'inich Ajaw performing New Year functions (Tozzer 1941:144). The name K'inich Ajaw, however, also appears as a title for other deities, such as the god K'inich Ajaw Itzamnaaj. On *Dresden Codex* page 50, One Ajaw is illustrated as a Venus regent of the morning star period, while on page 48, God G is named as a Venus regent of superior conjunction.

Stuart (1995:194) notes a close visual association between God G and One Ajaw. For example, God G in his role as the Number 4 Deity on Yaxchilan Lintel 48 wears the headband of One Ajaw. He also exhibits the three small dots found under the eye of Early Classic forms of One Ajaw. These parallels lead me to conclude that the sun god was a manifestation of One Ajaw. It is not surprising that such an important celestial body would have more than one manifestation. It is likely that One Ajaw also had an eagle manifestation (see chapter 15).

The Classic Period hero twin who was equivalent to Xbalanque is portrayed as a young man with patches of cured jaguar skin on his face and body, and he sometimes has a jaguar ear (Mathews, cited in Coe 1978:58; Hellmuth 1987; Taube 1992a:60–63). On his forehead is a *yax* sign. His designation in the codices is God CH. He appears as the Number 9 Deity, where his portrait represents the word *bolon,* "nine." In other contexts, his portrait is employed to represent the syllabic *ba* sign, but in yet other contexts, it represents the word *yax*. While it is unclear how the Classic Maya pronounced the name of this deity, I use the designation Yax Bolon, as suggested to me by Marc Zender. On K1892, One Ixim is illustrated at the center of the world with One Ajaw and Yax Bolon flanking him (see fig. 8.3). The twins are positioned at the edges of the world (the horizon), just as the sun and full moon are when rising and setting.

## Twin Ears of Corn

The hero twins of the *Popol Vuh* were identified with twin ears of green corn. The corn plant with the twin ears illustrated on the Tablet of the Foliated Cross at Palenque also represents green corn. Like the *Popol Vuh* gods, the hero twins One Ajaw and Yax Bolon were strongly associated with the color *yax*, "blue/green," for they frequently have *yax* signs decorating their headbands or bodies. As noted above, the portrait of Yax Bolon is sometimes used to represent the word *yax*. The association of the Classic Period hero twins with corn imagery is found on vessel K1183, where One Ixim and his son One Ajaw are illustrated sitting together. Both wear the netted skirt associated with One Ixim, but One Ajaw also has a *yax* sign in his headdress.

As discussed in chapter 4, the *k'an* sign is used to represent the concept of the center, and in the Tablet of the Foliated Cross it appears to designate these twin ears of corn as a center plant in a manner similar to the names for the twin ears of corn found in the *Popol Vuh* (Center House and Center Ancestral Plot). The *k'an* sign may also indicate the specific color of the hero twins' unripe corn. The notion that these guardian corn ears were yellow fits with the commonly found associations of the color yellow with abundance. The use of yellow corn as a guardian is found in the Tzeltal area, where the soul of a Tzeltal child is thought to be very delicate, and if the parents must leave the child alone for some reason, they place a yellow ear of corn with the child to protect its soul (Blom and La Farge 1927:360).

In the Q'eqchi' planting ceremony, the farmer plants his first corn just before sunrise with the morning star in the east and the full moon setting in the west. One Ixim is juxtaposed with the planting hole at the center of the turtle/earth on vessel K1892 (see fig. 8.3). At the edges of this turtle/earth are One Ajaw and Yax Bolon, who stand in opposition to one another in the same way as the rising sun and setting full moon appear on the horizon on the first day of planting. The hero twins were more than the sun and the full moon of the zenith passage; they were the twin ears of corn that assured that the planted corn would be productive. As noted in chapter 3, the Maya also harvest at full moon. At this time, the hero twins would again be in the sky at dawn to ensure that the harvested corn would be abundant.

## The Four Hundred Boys

In a section of the *Popol Vuh* that can be placed chronologically during the era of the wooden people, Hunahpu and Xbalanque defeat a supernatural bird called Seven

Macaw and his two sons Zipacna and Cabracan. Zipacna, who has the form of a crocodile, spends his days hunting for fish and crabs in the Chixoy River and his nights moving mountains around on his back.

One day as Zipacna is bathing in the river, the Four Hundred Boys (*O' much' k'ajolab'*) appear dragging a great tree that they want to use as a doorway lintel in the construction of their hut. After the boys complain that they can not hoist their tree onto their shoulders to carry it properly, Zipacna offers to do it. Displaying his phenomenal strength, he transports the tree to the door of their hut by himself. The Four Hundred Boys fear the great strength of Zipacna and plot to kill him. They dig a posthole and ask Zipacna to climb down into the hole to finish digging it out. Given that their hut was almost complete, it is apparent that the posthole was for a ceremonial tree. As will be discussed below, this pole was the center world tree. Their plan is to drop the tree into the hole on top of Zipacna and crush him to death. Anticipating their plan, Zipacna digs a side chamber and hides there until the log is dropped in. Believing that Zipacna is dead, the Four Hundred Boys then brew an alcoholic drink to use in their house-dedication ceremony. After the boys become intoxicated during their celebration, Zipacna makes the hut collapse on them, killing them all.

Enraged by the deaths of the Four Hundred Boys, Heart of Sky sends Hunahpu and Xbalanque to defeat Zipacna. The hero twins construct a fake crab from a hollowed-out stone and a red *Bromelia* plant and place it just inside a cave near Meauan Mountain to entice Zipacna there. They find the hungry Zipacna desperately hunting for food in the river and tell him about the crab. Zipacna begs the twins to be his guide, so the trio follows the course of the river to the cave. The cave mouth is narrow, and when Zipacna enters on his stomach, he can not reach the crab. The hero twins convince him to go into the cave on his back, and once he is in this vulnerable position, the mountain collapses on his chest and turns him to stone. Only his body below the kneecaps remains outside the cave (Christenson 2003a:107).

The name *O' much' k'ajolab'*, "Four Hundred Boys," is composed of *O' much'*, "five sets of eighty," and *k'ajolab'*, "boys or youths." *K'ajolab'* is sometimes used to describe the hero twins, who also belonged to this category of unmarried men. In Postclassic Yucatan, Landa describes a house for unmarried men where youths played games and slept until they married (Tozzer 1941:124). Miles (1955:106) notes that the Poqom Maya had dormitories near the temples for men who were participating in rituals, novice priests, and young boys. The Aztecs also had houses for young men where they were educated in customs and ceremonies (Duran 1977:81–89, 112–14, 293). Another possible function for the hut of the Four Hundred Boys was as a feasting house.

Some functions of the Four Hundred Boys can be assumed based on their actions. They physically erected the world tree, and they were obviously house builders and makers of ritual drink. The ritual drink they prepared to celebrate the completion of their hut and the world tree was likely pulque, made from the fermented sap of the maguey plant. The Four Hundred Boys rose as the Pleiades when Hunahpu and Xbalanque rose as sun and full moon, and they became the *achb'ilay*, "companions," of the hero twins. In this role, they were like the souls of the dead warriors who accompanied the sun on its journey from rising until midday. Girard (1979:77) notes the Ch'orti' belief that the Pleiades are angels that lift up the Lord (the sun) on the day of zenith passage at the beginning of the planting season.

The K'iche' name for the Pleiades is *Motz*, derived from the word meaning "to gather together in large numbers" (Christenson 2003a:104). The Four Hundred Boys most likely assisted One Ixim/One Hunahpu during deer-hunting expeditions, which were closely associated with warfare. To hunt deer, large groups of men make their way through the forest to drive the deer toward hunters waiting in a cleared area. The contemporary K'iche' describe the Pleiades and the adjacent Hyades star group as two fistfuls of corn seeds and bean seeds, respectively (B. Tedlock 1985). When these star groups set in the west, they symbolize the sowing of seeds in each corn mound. Large numbers of young men who have no cornfield of their own are often employed to help with the planting and harvest. It is likely that the Four Hundred Boys also had these duties.

The roles of warrior and corn harvester were not mutually exclusive. The optimum time to conduct warfare was at the start of the dry season when the pathways were dry and the fields were full of corn ready for harvesting. When warriors were in the countryside for any length of time, they often had to rely on these fields for their food supply. In addition, many wars were fought over the unequal success of corn production. Landa's description of famine years indicates that the raiding of neighboring cornfields was probably common (Tozzer 1941:146).

A conflation of the base of a tree with a crocodile head is shown on Izapa Stela 25 and on a Classic Period pottery scene. These crocodile trees have been identified as cognates of Zipacna in his hole (Schele 1992; Freidel, Schele, and Parker 1993; Taube 1998). The pole of the Four Hundred Boys has long been associated with the Dance of the Voladores pole (Rodas, Rodas, and Hawkins 1940:80–82; Girard 1948; 1952:358; Termer 1957). For example, the Voladores ritual specialist climbs into the hole and digs an offering hole in the wall, just as Zipacna dug his burrow. As discussed in chapter 4, the Voladores pole represents the center tree, which implies that the hut of the Four Hundred Boys was located near the center of the world. Further evidence that Zipacna's tree was the center tree is found in Classic Period images of One Ixim and other rulers that illustrate them as the center corn plant or center tree. Taube (2005:25–27) notes that these personified trees rise above a crocodile mouth.

## Summary

This overview of the attributes and functions of the hero twins indicates that these brothers embodied the same male/female principle of complementary opposition as their parents and grandparents. Their roles as sun and full moon also create a day-and-night opposition, with male being associated with day and female with night. Complementary opposition is also found in the hero twins' relationship with their monkey twin brothers. Although older than their brothers, the monkey twins were subjugated by the hero twins and placed in the junior position. Their junior role as producers of festival commodities echoes that of women who produce the food and costumes used for these ceremonies. The next chapter explores the nature of the maternal grandfather of these two sets of twin brothers.

# 12

# THE MATERNAL GRANDFATHER
# AND HIS VIRGIN DAUGHTERS

It has been suggested in earlier chapters that Lady Bone Water and Lady Blood, first and second wives of One Hunahpu, were sisters and that both were the daughters of a secondary lord of the underworld named Gathered Blood. Gathered Blood shares many characteristics with Xucaneb of the contemporary highland elopement stories and with the Classic Period deity known as God L. It is my supposition that these three grandfather deities—Gathered Blood of the *Popol Vuh*, Xucaneb of the contemporary stories, and God L of the inscriptions—were analogous, and that they were the maternal grandfather of both the monkey twins and the hero twins.

## GATHERED BLOOD

The underworld rulers One Death and Seven Death resided at the center of Xibalba and governed the underworld. The *Popol Vuh* lists six pairs of secondary underworld lords under the authority of this primary pair of death gods. Gathered Blood (Kuchuma Kik') and his partner Flying Scab were one of these pairs. As stated in the *Popol Vuh*, Gathered Blood was the father of One Hunahpu's second wife, Lady Blood, and the maternal grandfather of the hero twins. When Gathered Blood first noticed that his daughter Lady Blood was pregnant, he went to meet with One Death and Seven Death to discuss what to do:

> Then the maiden was discovered by her father, for he saw that she was now with child. Thus all the lords, One Death and Seven Death along with Gathered Blood, gathered their thoughts: "This my daughter is with child, O lords. It is merely the result of her fornication," said Gathered Blood when he met with the lords. "Very well then. Question

her about this, and when she doesn't tell, she will be sacrificed. She will go far away to be sacrificed." "Very well, ye lords," he replied. He therefore questioned his daughter: "Who is responsible for the child that is in your womb, my daughter?" he asked. "I have no child, my father," she replied. "I have not known the face of any man." "Very well then. It is true that you are a fornicator." "Sacrifice her, you war councillors," the four owls were told. "Then bring back her heart inside a bowl so that the lords may examine it this day." (Christenson 2003a:131)

Every community has rules for proper conduct, and the message in this episode appears to be that premarital sex is punishable by death. This theme is also found in the story of Xucaneb's daughter, who was punished for illicit sex before marriage.

The four owl messengers that the secondary lord, Gathered Blood, sends to dispatch Lady Blood belonged to a third tier of underworld lords. They were named Arrow Owl, One Leg Owl, Macaw Owl, and Skull Owl. The text refers to them as *raj pop achij,* "he of the mat of warriors," which refers to an office held by warriors (Christenson 2003a:119). Owls are viewed across the Maya realm as omens of illness and death, and this is a suitable association for third-ranking warrior-lords whose primary job is to kill people and sacrifice captives. In other sections of the *Popol Vuh,* the underworld lords send the four owls to deliver their ball-game challenges to One Hunahpu, Seven Hunahpu, and the hero twins, who were playing ball at the Nim Xob' Karchaj ballcourt. The *Popol Vuh* makes it clear that the owl messengers had the form of birds and flew to deliver the challenges.

## THE LOCATION OF THE NIM XOB' KARCHAJ BALLCOURT

The route that One Hunahpu, Seven Hunahpu, and the hero twins took to the underworld court of One Death and Seven Death began near the Nim Xob' Karchaj ballcourt and descended into the earth through various canyons; rapids; rivers filled with scorpions, pus, and blood; and a crossroads. Considerable evidence exists that this ballcourt was specifically located adjacent to Xucaneb Mountain in Alta Verapaz. In the sixteenth century, Las Casas (1967) referred to the myth of a cultural-hero–god named Exbalamquen (Xbalanque) who journeyed from an Alta Verapaz cave to the underworld, and Christenson (2003a:154) has noted that there is still a widespread belief in highland Guatemala that the route to the underworld is located in Alta Verapaz. Recinos suggests that the Nim Xob' Karchaj ballcourt was a reference to the Postclassic Alta Verapaz communities of Nim Xor and Carchah, mentioned in the *Annals of the Cakchiquels* (Recinos 1950:113–14; Recinos and Goetz 1953:64). Carchah is near the present-day town of San Pedro Carchá. Christenson (2003a:119–20) has noted that One Hunahpu and Seven Hunahpu failed to honor the Xibalbans before playing ball, and this lack of *nim,* "honor," and *xob',* "respect," resulted in their ball-game challenge. The creator deities wanted to create humans who would honor and respect them; thus Christenson translates Nim Xob' Karchaj as "Honor and Respect at Carchah."

San Pedro Carchá is on the banks of the Río Cahabón, the major river system in Alta Verapaz. The other Q'eqchi' towns of the area are Cobán (six kilometers upstream to the west) and San Juan Chamelco (six kilometers to the southwest). To the north and south of these three communities are San Vicente Mountain (Little Xucaneb Mountain) and Xucaneb Mountain, respectively. Richard Wilson describes the relationship between these two mountains: "San Vicente and Xukaneb' are younger and older brothers, respectively, on opposite sides of the vast highland valley that is the cradle of the Q'eqchi's. The brothers speak to each other, thundering across the three main Q'eqchi' towns" (R. Wilson 1995:55). Although he recognizes that Xibalba was underground, Recinos (1950:114) proposes that the *Popol Vuh* description of the route to the underworld actually described a journey from San Pedro Carchá to the lowland region of the Itza' Maya. Dennis Tedlock (1996:255–56) follows Recinos's interpretation that the Xibalba route followed the Río Cahabón downstream toward the east, and that the canyons, rapids, and rivers of scorpions, pus, and blood were places along this waterway.

I propose a different direction for this journey. The extensive cave passageways in the Maya region are found in karst areas where ancient underground rivers have eroded the limestone. It is likely that the geological features along such subterranean rivers served as models for the underground route to the center of Xibalba. South of Cobán, San Pedro Carchá, and San Juan Chamelco lies Xucaneb Mountain. The area between these three towns and the mountain contains two river systems (Río Mestelá and Río Chió) whose headwaters are on Xucaneb Mountain. The Río Mestelá and Río Chió are tributaries of the Cahabón and join this river at Cobán and San Pedro Carchá, respectively. The two rivers flow through a karst region riddled with limestone sinkholes and streams that emerge from and disappear into the earth. These landscape features, along with the supreme ritual importance of Xucaneb Mountain, are strong evidence that the hero twins did not go down the Río Cahabón to the underworld; rather, they went toward Xucaneb Mountain and took a nearby cave passageway.

## THE ROLE OF GATHERED BLOOD AS A SECONDARY RULER

In the Late Classic Period, some of the major cities such as Yaxchilan had communities on their borders that were ruled by secondary lords under the authority of the central king (Martin and Grube 2000). Carmack (1995:40) notes that, likewise, the K'iche' established communities along their borders that were ruled by secondary lords. The political organization of the underworld in a three-tiered hierarchy implies that some of the twelve secondary lords of Xibalba might also have ruled communities or regions at the periphery of the underworld. Although located on the surface of the earth, the Nim Xob' Karchaj ballcourt was said to be on the road of the underworld, which indicates it was inside the domain of the underworld lords. If we view the palace of One Death and Seven Death as the center of the kingdom of Xibalba, then the Nim Xob' Karchaj ballcourt was at the periphery of this kingdom. I propose that Gathered Blood was the prototype for Xucaneb, and that he was the secondary ruler who governed the area around Nim Xob' Karchaj and Xucaneb Mountain.

In the *Popol Vuh*, Gathered Blood is paired with the deity Flying Scab. Because the other paired deities in this story were brothers, it is quite possible that Flying Scab was the younger brother of Gathered Blood. As noted above, Xucaneb Mountain also had a younger brother, San Vicente.

## THE BALLCOURT AS A CANYON

The Nim Xob' Karchaj ballcourt of One Hunahpu and Seven Hunahpu was located at one of the gateways to the underworld. The specific location of the Nim Xob' Karchaj ballcourt is a mystery, but given that the fact that Maya pyramids represent mountains, it is possible that ballcourts replicated another kind of geological feature: the river canyon.

Ballcourts in the Maya region were often formed by two long, parallel structures. The playing field was the narrow strip of land between the walls of the two structures, and the ball was knocked back and forth against these sloped walls. The entrances to the ballcourt were at the open ends of these alleys. In terms of the natural landscape, a ballcourt is like a canyon.

The Río Mestelá has carved a river canyon adjacent to Xucaneb Mountain. The river originates between the two peaks of Xucaneb Mountain (Cerro Xalijá and Cerro Rocjá) and flows west. When it finally turns north, it passes through a deep canyon formed by the end of Xucaneb Mountain and the adjacent Cerro Tzanour. Near the middle of this canyon, the river disappears underground. It then re-emerges five hundred meters away and continues northward to Cobán. I speculate that the Nim Xob' Karchaj ballcourt was modeled after such a canyon.

## SUPERNATURAL WARFARE

I have argued that one of the underlying themes of the hero twins' saga is the conquest of neighboring territories through marriage alliance. In my reconstruction of the core myth, One Hunahpu went to Alta Verapaz as a deer hunter and warrior and eloped with Gathered Blood's daughter Lady Bone Water. He later made amends to Gathered Blood by paying the bride price. After the birth of the monkey twins and the death of Lady Bone Water, One Hunahpu played ball together with his brother and the monkey twins at the Nim Xob' Karchaj ballcourt adjacent to Gathered Blood's house or palace (Xucaneb Mountain). The Popol Vuh states that this court belonged to One Hunahpu (Christenson 2003a:154). The ruling death lords must have looked upon the construction of a building in the territory of the underworld as an intrusion. In response, One Death and Seven Death sent a challenge to One Hunahpu and Seven Hunahpu to come and play ball at their Crushing Ballcourt. After the defeat and sacrifice of One Hunahpu and Seven Hunahpu at this location, One Hunahpu magically impregnated another of Gathered Blood's daughters. The pregnant Lady Blood fled her homeland, took up residence at the house of her in-laws, and gave birth to the hero twins. The hero twins established their dominance on the surface of the earth by subordinating their older half-brothers and conquering a number of supernatural beings. They then returned to the land of their mother and played ball at One Hunahpu's ballcourt. Again the lords of death were angered by this incursion, and they sent a challenge to the hero twins, but Hunahpu and Xbalanque succeeded in killing One Death and Seven Death.

The *Popol Vuh* says nothing directly about the fate of Gathered Blood after this defeat, but as the maternal grandfather of the hero twins, he was the obvious choice to become the new leading ruler of the underworld. The hero twins allude to this role when they address the secondary underworld lords after the demise of One Death and Seven Death and tell them they will no longer be allowed to have copal incense and the fresh blood of human sacrifice as offerings. In the future, these lords would only be allowed to have the sap of the croton tree and blood that was spilled on the ground. Gathered Blood's name is a reference to this very blood, and as Christenson (2003a:116) notes, K'iche' storytellers still describe Gathered Blood as a cruel underworld lord who gathers the blood that has spilled on the ground as a result of injury, illness, or violence and serves it to his fellow lords at a banquet.

As someone subordinate to the paternal line of creator deities, Gathered Blood would have been required to pay tribute to them. Despite his subservience to these deities, he would still have been wealthy in bride-price goods and services. The accumulation of even a small amount of capital allows a person to engage in trade, and as will be discussed below, this was an important occupation for the maternal grandfather of the hero twins.

## GOD L

God L appears in Classic Period art as an old, bald man who occasionally wears black body paint, a jaguar ear, a jaguar-skin cape, and a long string of jade beads (figs. 12.1, 12.2; see also 5.2). His diagnostic trait is a headdress with an owl and feathers. On *Dresden Codex* 14 and 46, God L's name glyph is composed of the *ha'al* "rain" sign and his portrait (Lacadena 2004). The only Classic Period illustration of God L that seems to include a caption text with a personal name glyph is found on K5359 (Miller and Martin 2004:281; Martin 2005). It is composed of the number thirteen, an unidentified sign, a syllabic *yu* sign, and a *chan* sign. Martin suggests the name glyph might be read 13 Bird Sky. The name glyph for God L's owl, *Oxlajuun Chan Kuy,* "Thirteen Sky Owl," often appears in God L's headdress along with the owl. Thirteen Sky Owl has been interpreted to be one of God L's bird manifestations (Grube

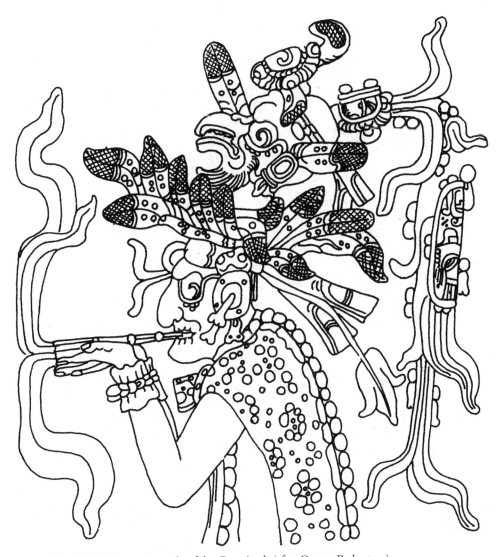

Figure 12.1. God L, Palenque Temple of the Cross jamb (after Greene Robertson)

and Schele 1994). Coe (1973:14, 91, 107; 1978:18), noting the death imagery associated with God L and his palace, identifies him as a primary god of the underworld.

In the *Dresden Codex* Venus pages, God L is pictured as the warrior deity associated with the first heliacal rising of Venus as morning star on the date *1 Ajaw* (Thompson 1972:67). An explanation of the thirteen-sky reference in the name of God L's owl may be found in the Venus tables. Venus as morning star makes five different configurations in the dawn sky (Aveni 1990). It takes five cycles of Venus for the first configuration to reappear in the sky, but this next occurrence will begin 2,920 days after *1 Ajaw* on the date *9 Ajaw*. It takes thirteen cycles of the greater Venus cycle of 2,920 days before the first configuration of the morning star appears

Figure 12.2. God L, *center*, K511 (after Kerr)

again on the date *1 Ajaw.* The Dresden Codex Venus tables calculate all thirteen cycles. As the patron of the Ajaw morning star intervals, God L was in the sky thirteen times performing his duties. There is a cryptic entry in the Motul dictionary that defines Thirteen Sky as *luna llena* (full moon), *oposición* (opposition). The full moon is in opposition when it is setting at dawn and the sun is rising. It was on this kind of day that the morning star first appeared in the *Popol Vuh.*

God L is depicted in the *Dresden Codex* Venus pages as an elderly, black god who has just thrown his atlatl spear. The atlatl is raised above his head in the throwing pose, and he clutches his shield in his right hand. On *Dresden Codex* 74, he wears his owl headdress while brandishing his atlatl and spears (see fig. 5.2). The role of the owl as a symbol for death and sacrifice throughout the Maya area suggests that God L was a god of sacrifice, and by extension, war. On the Palenque Tablet of the Sun, God L holds up the bone throne that supports the spears and shield of GIII, who was a god of warfare (see fig. 6.7). One of the symbols for war, famine, and pestilence was a jaguar skin spread in the marketplace (Roys 1931:331), and God L is pictured in this scene wearing his jaguar skin spread over his back. It is likely that God L was a deity of sorcery as well, for witches are thought to be able to transform into owls (Maynard 1963:98).

As independently observed by Justin Kerr and Allen Christenson (personal communication), God L also took an armadillo form. In several pottery scenes, an armadillo wears the feathered headdress of God L (K3332), and God L's cape often has the form of an armadillo shell (K1560, K2696, K4635, K4966, K7750; see also fig. 12.2). Xucaneb was also linked with an armadillo, for he had an armadillo shell for a throne (Thompson 1930:58). The Kaqchikel and Tzotzil mountain lord also uses an armadillo seat for a throne (Redfield 1945:54, Robert Laughlin, personal communication). The armadillo, as a nocturnal animal that spends a good deal of time in underground burrows or digging for its food, is an appropriate manifestation for an underworld lord. This animal can also walk underwater when it crosses rivers and can stay under for more than six minutes. The route to the underworld involved crossing a river.

Bruce (1975:289) records the Lacandon belief that the first two armadillos on earth served as benches for two fire deities who were the gods of war and sacrifice. On the Tablet of the Sun, God L is paired with the Jaguar Paddler God beneath the central icon, which represents a bone bench (see fig. 6.7). The Jaguar Paddler God was associated with sacrifice (he often wears a stingray spine in his nose), and in other scenes he wears a banded cape that is similar to God L's armadillo cape.

Many examples of God L show him carrying a merchant backpack and walking stick and smoking a cigar. He has been characterized as a god of tribute, tobacco, and cacao; and a patron god for merchants, especially long-distance traders (Taube 1992a:79–88). There is a close relationship between warriors and traders in Mesoamerica. God L's stick takes the form of a fire serpent in some scenes, and fire serpents are also associated with warfare. A merchant would use a walking stick to steady himself as he traveled over rough terrain, and when he lowered his backpack frame, he would thrust his stick into the ground and prop the pack frame against it so his goods did not touch the ground and become wet or soiled. The stick could be used as a weapon if the merchant was attacked.

A number of pottery scenes show God L in the process of losing and regaining his headdress, clothing, necklace, and walking stick (Taube 1992a:79–88; Miller and Martin 2004:63; Wald and Carrasco 2004). In collusion with One Ajaw, the rabbit manifestation of Yax Bolon confiscated these objects. Martin (2006a) believes that God L was parallel to One Death and Seven Death, but that unlike these two death lords, God L survived his encounter with the hero twins. He proposes that God L was then subordinated by the hero twins and forced to pay tribute to them. On K2796 and K7750, God L sits on his throne before a series of gods. The date in the adjacent caption texts refers to the 13.0.0.0.0 Period Ending, and it has long been recognized that God L played a role in this mythological event (Coe 1973:108). Martin (2006a) has suggested that, "perhaps this scene expresses not so much untrammelled infernal majesty and power, but the reconfiguration and restriction of God L's influence to his own domain in the Underworld." I would concur with Martin on this point, but the role of God L in these scenes is more suited to that of Gathered Blood after the defeat of One Death and Seven Death.

God L is addressed as a *mam,* "grandfather." On K1398, which features spoken words in its caption texts, the young sun god (a manifestation of One Ajaw) refers to the old God L as *nimam,* "my grandfather" (Stuart and Stuart 1993:170; Wald and Carrasco 2004). In another caption text, God L refers to the rabbit manifestation of Yax Bolon as *nimam.* As noted, grandsons are considered the replacement for their grandfathers, and a grandfather will use the term *nimam* to address his grandson. Given that he is an old man, God L's use of the term *nimam* is clearly referring to the rabbit as a grandson. Although it could be argued that these terms were simply titles of respect, the text on K1398 is strong proof that God L was the maternal grandfather of the hero twins. In addition, some of the characteristics of God L match those of both Gathered Blood and Xucaneb. God L was a god of tobacco, and in the elopement stories, a tobacco plant grew at the doorway of Xucaneb's house. Both Xucaneb and God L are old men who are associated with armadillos. God L's association with an owl and sacrifice is reminiscent of Gathered Blood, who sent the messenger owls to sacrifice his daughter, and of Xucaneb, who also sacrificed one of his daughters.

## THE VIRGIN DAUGHTERS OF GOD L

On vessel K511, God L sits on his throne surrounded by five goddesses who have been characterized by various researchers as his wives, daughters, concubines, or servants (see fig. 12.2). The goddess standing behind the throne has black hair tied into a bun, while the other four have bald heads with wisps of hair. The Maya flattened their foreheads to mimic the shape of an ear of corn, which suggests that these goddesses with their flattened foreheads are corn deities. The bald goddess on the far right pours a chocolate drink into a container at her feet, a method designed to create the desired foam of the beverage (Coe and Coe 1996:50). The grouping of four bald goddesses is reminiscent of the four corn goddesses petitioned by Lady Blood when she produced a net bag full of corn from a single ear. As noted in chapter 8, one of these was called Lady Cacao. The other three *Popol Vuh* goddesses are given K'iche' day names: Lady of the Day *Toh*, Lady of the Day *Canil,* and Lady of the Day *Tzi.* Together they are referred to as the guardians of the monkey twins' corn. The fact that these goddesses guard the corn is reflected in a contemporary ritual performed by K'iche' farmers when someone has robbed their cornfield. At midnight, the farmer goes to his field, takes an ear of corn, breaks it in half, and places a candle between the two pieces. He then petitions the days *7 Qanil (Canil), 8 T'oj (Toh)* and, *9 Ts'j'(Tzi)* to punish the thief (Bunzel 1952:283). While no epigraphic evidence definitively states that these two sets of corn goddesses were the daughters of God L/Gathered Blood, the circumstantial evidence that they were is overwhelming.

The bald heads of the Classic Period goddesses are reminiscent of the Aztec maidens of penitence. The Aztecs had two compounds adjacent to the temples of Huitzilopochtli and Xochiquetzal that housed virgin males (elocuatecomame, "ear of corn/gourd") and females (the maidens of penitence). These youths lived in their respective compounds for one year in chastity and seclusion. After their year of service, the elocuatecomame and the maidens of penitence left the compounds to marry, but if they broke their vows of chastity during their year of service, they were immediately put to death. These youths had complementary duties: the elocuatecomame decorated the temples, maintained the temple fires, and burned incense to the gods, while the maidens of penitence cleaned and watered the temples, prepared the foods for the gods and priests, and spun and wove the clothing for the idols and temple (Durán 1971:83–85). When a woman entered this service, her hair was cropped off. Another parallel between the God L goddesses and the maidens of penitence is that during the May rain rituals, the maidens were led by an old man who served as a steward of Tezcatlipoca. Like God L, this old man was associated with tobacco, for he wore a tobacco gourd decorated with flowers on his back. He is described as humble and contrite, with his head lowered (Durán 1977:106).

## The Wife of God L/Gathered Blood

The *Popol Vuh* does not mention Gathered Blood's wife or wives. In fact, no under-world goddesses other than Lady Blood are specifically mentioned. As discussed in earlier chapters, both the wife and daughter of the mountain lord in contemporary stories often have a toad form. It is highly likely that the wife of God L/Gathered Blood also had some kind of toad form. In Alta Verapaz, an important female mountain called Itzam is found ten kilometers west of Cahabon. Itzam is thought to be the wife of Xucaneb, and the pair are said to be the most powerful of the mountain lords in this region (Thompson 1930:58; Goubaud Carrera 1949; Carlson and Eachus 1977). I speculate that this mountain was a manifestation of God L/Gathered Blood's wife.

## The Complementary Roles of Itzamnaaj and God L

Peter Mathews and Michael Coe have insightfully suggested that God L was the underworld counterpart of Itzamnaaj (Coe 1978:18–21). Coe argues that this rela-tionship was similar to the vertical relationship between Ometeotl (god of the place of duality) and Mictlantecuhtli (god of the underworld) in the Central Mexican pantheon. In my reconstruction of the genealogy, Itzamnaaj was the paternal grand-father and God L was the maternal grandfather of the hero twins. The complementary male/female principle has a vertical aspect, with male being associated with up and female associated with down. If we compare the relationship of Itzamnaaj and God L in terms of the vertical order, there is a complementary opposition between these two gods, with Itzamnaaj representing the senior/male line and the maternal grand-father God L representing the junior/female line. There is also a life/death and day/night complementary opposition, with Itzamnaaj as the supreme god of the heavens, the day sky, and life, and God L/Gathered Blood as the god of the underworld, the night sky, and death.

This opposition is apparent in the animal manifestations of these gods. Itzamnaaj had the form of a laughing falcon, a bird that is active during the day, while God L's bird manifestation was an owl, the quintessential bird of the night. This contrast is also between life and death, for the call of the laughing falcon brings the life-renewing rains, while the call of the owl is an indication of death. There is also a day-and-night complementary opposition between Itzamnaaj's turtle shell and God L's armadillo shell. Turtles are animals of the daytime that enjoy basking in the sun, while armadillos are nocturnal. I suggest that the defeat of God L placed the maternal line in the subordinate position and established the patrilineal descent for rulership. It also provided a role for the relatives of the king's wife as secondary lords who ruled adjacent, subordinate communities. In addition, the occupations of the monkey twins as diviners, artisans, and musicians provided the role model for children of the king who were not in the direct line of descent.

## CROSS-COUSIN MARRIAGE

As noted in chapter 8, the marriage of One Ixim/Hunahpu and Ixik/Lady Bone Water was a manifestation of the male/female principle, and it represented an ideal marriage for humans to emulate. The Maya practiced cross-cousin marriage, a system in which a man is entitled to marry the daughters of his father's sisters or the daughters of his mother's brothers (Hopkins 1988). Conversely, a woman is entitled to marry the sons of her father's sisters or the sons of her mother's brothers. If the marriages between One Ixim/One Hunahpu and the daughters of God L/Gathered Lord were the role model for cross-cousin marriage, then Ix Chel/Xmucane and God L would have been siblings (see chart 1.1). If this was the case, Ix Chel/Xmucane, like her brother, God L, originated from the underworld. Certainly Ix Chel's jaguar characteristics, the crossed bones of her skirt, and her role as a fierce midwife and world destroyer point to such an identification.

In this scenario, the marriage of the creator grandparents would also have represented the complementary opposition of life and death forces. I would tentatively speculate that in the beginning, the marriage of Itzamnaaj/Xpiyacoc with Ix Chel/Xmucane may have been the union between a god from the sky and a goddess from the underworld in the waters that separated these two places, and that this marriage created the place of duality.

## THE BENEFITS OF MARRIAGE

Most studies of Maya economics have focused on long-distance trade networks, tribute, festivals, and markets. The importance of these institutions is well established, but the gift exchange during marriage negotiations and bride payment was another fundamental tradition of commodity exchange (Pohl 1994, 2003; Reents-Budet 2000). At every level of society, the basic building block for social relationships and allegiances was the family. No matter what political or economic system was in place, kinship affiliations played a significant role in establishing shared labor, commodity exchanges, and defensive strategies. Marriages created fundamental bonds between families and provided opportunities for families to expand their networks and resources. The power brokers in the marriage negotiation were the two fathers of the prospective couple. In my reconstruction of the genealogy, Itzamnaaj/Xpiya-coc and God L/Gathered Blood were the quintessential father of the groom and father of the bride.

A ruler had two role models to follow when negotiating marriages for his children. When he was arranging a marriage for his sons, he would be a negotiator like Itza-mnaaj, but when he was marrying off a daughter, he would be following the role of God L. In his discussion of Mixtec commerce, Pohl (1994, 2003) draws attention to a comment by Spanish historian Antonio de Herrera y Tordesillas that a Mixtec lord with many daughters considered himself to be rich because of all the presents he would be given for them in marriage. This comment likely explains the image of God L sitting in his palace surrounded by women whom I have identified as his daughters. He was a rich man indeed.

Contemporary accounts of marriage contracts indicate that the type of goods given as gifts remains similar despite the status of the family, but the volume and quality of the goods increases with the wealth of the family. Las Casas notes that all of the kinsmen and subjects of the ruler contributed to the cost of the marriage gifts, dowry, and feasts when a ruler was negotiating for a bride, so the volume of gifts at an elite marriage must have been impressive (Miles 1955, 1957). The various accounts of marriage negotiations indicate that the entourage of messengers sent to deliver the petition and gifts was extensive even in smaller communities. It has been argued that many of the Classic Period secondary lords were tribute collectors for the ruler, but it is equally possible that these messengers were also part of the mar-riage negotiating entourage. As noted in chapter 5, there is a scribe who wears a paper list under his arm. While this might refer to tribute lists, it is also possible that another of this scribe's duties was to record the bride gifts.

As the head of the lineage, the ruler likely received gifts for his role as a mar-riage negotiator. If the ruler had exclusive access to cacao, all males would need to come to him to obtain their cacao bride-gifts and final bride payment. Even the lowly farmer would have to pay him in some commodity, labor, or service. The gifts that the ruler received for his daughters would have significantly increased his wealth. Not only would he be able to trade these goods and diversify his wealth, but he could also give these commodities to kin and allies to build goodwill. If labor was part of the bride price for a ruler's daughter, a ruler would have been in an ideal position to receive labor from his new in-laws for building a temple, improving his palace, or expanding the plaza to accommodate even bigger wedding feasts and festivals. It is likely that secondary lords were eager to supply the ruler or his son with a wife in order to obtain not only the status of such a marriage, but the bride-gift commodi-ties controlled by the ruler. In other words, everyone wanted to buy into the system.

In addition to the political connections that a good marriage would provide, the ruler would also be interested in the skills of the women. Women were the producers of prestigious, finely woven textiles. Females with exceptional weaving skills would have been highly valued. It is not a coincidence that the highland elopement stories focus on the weaving ability of Xucaneb's daughter. The ability to bear children was also crucial. A barren woman would be returned to her father, and the bride price would have to be repaid.

John Pohl (personal communication) has suggested, and I concur, that the exchange of gifts and payment of a bride price played a significant role in the exchange networks of the ancient Maya. As the head of the ruling lineage group, it is likely that the ruler would have had the power to direct and arrange not only the marriages of his own children, but those of his lineage group and quite possibly those of his entire community. The ruler was also in a unique position to choose additional wives for himself. It is highly likely that all spouses were selected for optimum political, social, and economic advantage.

## Summary

An underlying theme of the *Popol Vuh* is the domination of the creator deities over the lords of the underworld and the establishment of the supernatural hierarchy. When One Hunahpu impregnated Lady Blood and forced her expulsion from the underworld, it was a form of bride capture, an act that was a key strategy in the later defeat of the Xibalbans. Ixik/Lady Bone Water and One Moon/Lady Blood gave birth to the two pairs of twin sons of One Ixim/One Hunahpu, and these children inherited the skills and talents of their parents and grandparents. The *Popol Vuh* indicates that the relationship between these two sets of twins was hierarchical, with the hero twins clearly being the superior brothers. It is the hero twins who are declared to be the replacement for One Hunahpu, and who take on the dominant role of warriors, while the junior monkey-twins take on the role of commercial activities such as jewelry making. In this regard, they are like the junior God L/Gathered Blood, whose concerns are trade and commerce.

The parallels between God L/Gathered Blood and Xucaneb are significant and suggest that they shared a common origin. The identification of God L/Gathered Blood as the ancient prototype of Xucaneb raises the question of where on the surface of the earth the house of the creator deities was located, and how this house was situated in relation to Xucaneb Mountain. The following chapter explores this subject.

# 13

# SACRED LANDSCAPE

An analysis of numerous indigenous place names and stories allows us to identify mythological locations in the *Popol Vuh* with specific places in the Guatemalan highlands. This chapter examines those places and explores how the quadrilateral world order was based on the landscape of central highland Guatemala. The center house of the creator grandparents with its three hearthstones was modeled after the topography surrounding Lake Atitlán. Mountains were considered manifestations of specific creator deities, and volcanoes were viewed as the source of sacred fire and lightning.

Very little has been written about the ritual importance of Guatemala's volcanoes, but ethnographic sources indicate that these pyramid-shaped mountains were places of worship. For example, Sapper (1897) describes a Mam ceremony at the crater of Volcán Tacaná that included turkey sacrifice and divination, and he found ritual offerings including censers at the top of both Volcán Tajumulco and Volcán Santa María. Colonial documents indicate that humans were sacrificed at the crater of Volcán Atitlán.

## THE FOUR RIVERS OF THE WORLD

In the *Popol Vuh*, the rivers of the world were created when the mountains arose from the waters of the place of duality. Four major rivers drain highland Guatemala: the Samalá, the Grijalva, the Motagua, and the Chixoy (Map 2). The headwaters of these four rivers are all in the same general vicinity just northwest of Lake Atitlán; in some cases, within a kilometer of one another. The four rivers flow away from this central area to the south, west, east, and north, respectively.

The ancient Maya believed that the surface of the earth was a quadrilateral space with its corners defined by the rising and setting points of the sun at the solstices (see fig. 4.1). They also believed that four roads radiated out from the center of the

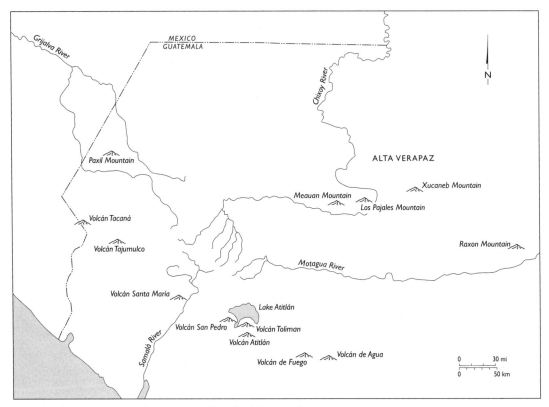

Map 2. Major rivers and mountains of highland Guatemala

world, one for each direction. Because the Maya characterize rivers as roads, it is apparent that these four rivers were the model for the four directional world roads.

Each of these four river systems has special features related to trade. The Samalá River flows south between Volcán Santa María and Volcán Santo Tomás and passes down the Pacific piedmont and across the coastal area with its rich cacao plantations before emptying into the Pacific.

The Grijalva Valley was well known for its cotton. This western route heads in the direction of Central Mexico and the rich trading partners of that zone. The Grijalva River flows northwest through Chiapas to the Tabasco coast and the Gulf of Mexico. The upper rivers of the Grijalva encompass Paxil Mountain, which was thought to be the source of the corn used to create humans.

The third river is the Motagua, whose headwaters are east of Santa Cruz del Quiché. This river flows east and terminates at the Gulf of Honduras. The valley of the Motagua River is the only known source of jade in Mesoamerica, and the Sierra de las Minas mountain range north of the river is a primary location for quetzals. Both of these commodities were among the most important of trade goods.

All the rivers along the north side of the Continental Divide that are found east of the Grijalva headwaters and west of Santa Cruz del Quiché flow into the northern

Chixoy River system. The headwaters of the Chixoy flow north until they hit the Cuchumatanes mountain range, where the river turns almost due east and passes the famous salt beds at Sacapulas. The Chixoy continues east past Chimiagua Mountain (the highest mountain in this area) and abruptly doubles back to the west as it loops around Los Pajales Mountain. Finally, it turns north again and begins a seventy-kilometer-long descent through a series of canyons and foothills into the lowlands and arrives at another important salt source at Montaña Nueve Cerros. This low range of hills is the last elevation that the river encounters before snaking further north through the lowlands. Below this point, the Chixoy is called the Salinas River because of these salt works. After joining with the Pasión and the Lacantún rivers further downstream, this system becomes the Usumacinta River, the major river system of the lowlands.

Two prominent land routes between the Guatemalan highlands and lowlands converged near the bend in the Chixoy River at Los Pajales Mountain. One route went from central Guatemala to Sacapulas, continued along the north side of Chimiagua Mountain, crossed the Chixoy River, and went on to the San Cristóbal Verapaz and Cobán area. The southeastern route from the lower Motagua River jade beds and the Sierra de las Minas quetzal range to the lowlands also came through the Cobán area by crossing over the Sierra de Chuacús into the Salamá Valley, down the valley to Los Pajales Mountain, and then on to San Cristóbal Verapaz and Cobán. From Cobán, traders could either proceed northwest to Nueve Cerros and continue down the Chixoy River to the central Petén or proceed northeast down into the lowlands to the headwaters of the Pasión River and follow that river system to the Petén.

## LAKE ATITLÁN AND ITS THREE VOLCANOES

Karl Taube (1992a, 1998, 2000) has written extensively on the pan-Mesoamerican concept of the place of duality in the sky. He has noted that the center of the world was thought to replicate this sacred location and that both places were marked by a fire surrounded by three hearthstones. The *Popol Vuh* provides important details about both the place of duality and the center of the world. It describes the place of duality before the creation of the earth as a pool of still water inhabited by the creator grandparents. After the earth rose from these waters, the creator grandparents lived in a house at the center of the world with their children. The *Popol Vuh* does not indicate when the creator grandparents left this center place and ascended to the heavens, but the narrative makes it clear that their center house with its three-hearthstone fire was thought to be located in highland Guatemala.

The most obvious place that replicates a pooled body of water and three hearthstones is Lake Atitlán and its three dominant volcanoes (Volcán Tolimán, Volcán San Pedro, and Volcán Atitlán), which are located just southeast of the headwaters of the four major rivers. The association of volcanoes with hearthstones is a natural one, given that volcanoes spew forth stones, fire, ash, and smoke. During the destruction

Figure 13.1. Lake Atitlán (photo courtesy of Leon Reinhart)

of the wooden people in the *Popol Vuh*, their hearthstones shot out at them and hit them in the head. Andrés Xiloj compares this episode to stones shooting out of a volcano (D. Tedlock 1995:236).

Lake Atitlán is the largest body of water in highland Guatemala, and with no visible outlet, the lake is truly a pooled body of water like the waters of the place of duality (fig. 13.1). The Tz'utujil believe that the lake is even older than the sea (Mendelson 1957:474). Christenson (2003:67) notes that "the Maya of the region consider Lake Atitlán to be the waters of creation from which all things emerged." He recorded the following Tz'utujil creation story: "Before the world was made, only Lake Atitlán existed at the center of everything. Everything was covered with water. Then the three volcanoes grew out of the lake and lifted up the sky to support it. Today, when our town is threatened with disaster or enemies try to attack us, these volcanoes come together and form a barrier that protects us from harm" (Christenson 2001: 74). Christenson (2001:76) suggests that the three Atitlán volcanoes are analogous to the three hearthstones mentioned in Classic Period texts. The Tz'utujil also believe that the old midwife Yaxper inhabits Lake Atitlán, and as discussed in chapter 9, this goddess has many traits that directly identify her with the creator grandmother Xmucane. Lake Atitlán is one of the sacred lakes that the K'iche of Momostenango believe is the source of the "lightning in the blood" that brings them divination knowledge (B. Tedlock 1982:54, 139, 157). As will become apparent in the following discussion, the concepts associated with the place of duality were modeled after this central body of water.

## Lake Atitlán as the Primordial Place of Reeds

Marriage was the definitive manifestation of the duality principle, and as a replication of the place of duality, the center was the ultimate place of marriage. In ancient Mesoamerica, the final act of the marriage ceremony occurred when the couple kneeled on a mat beside the hearthstone fire and had their garments tied together by the groom's parents. A mat was a symbol of marriage for the ancient Maya and other Mesoamerican groups.

As noted in chapter 3, mythical places of origin were often referred to as the Place of Reeds. Lake Atitlán is famous for the reed beds located along its shores where reeds are still harvested and used to weave mats (McBryde 1947:68). One of the Lake Atitlán goddesses is known as María Tul, and she is thought to have the form of a water reed (Tarn and Prechtel 1986:176).

The name of Volcán Tolimán, which dominates the southern edge of the lake, is a Nahuatl word meaning "place of reeds" (Jonathan Amith, personal communication). Other places of origin in Mesoamerica are also suggestive of Lake Atitlán. For example, the Mexica migration began at the mythological Aztlán (place of herons) that was characterized as an island on a lake. Herons are frequent inhabitants of Lake Atitlán. During the Preclassic Period, the water levels of Lake Atitlán were more than fifty meters lower than they are now, and a large island was located just off the south shore at the base of Volcán Tolimán. An underwater archaeological survey is currently being undertaken to explore the Preclassic site on this island.

In a Q'eqchi' creation myth, the water of the world was first contained in a lake inside a mountain (Thompson 1930:142). The mountain was smashed open and the water poured out in four directions, which is suggestive of the four directional rivers of highland Guatemala. There is a prevalent belief across the Maya area that underground passageways connect sacred locations or radiate from the center of Maya towns to the perimeters of the community. Atitecos believe that a series of cave passageways radiate out from under the floor in the church of Santiago Atitlán, and they relate these passageways to water and rain (Christenson 2001:78). If we view this in the context of the creation stories, it is reasonable to conclude that the Maya thought Lake Atitlán fed the four major river systems through underground passages.

## A Comparison of the Lake Atitlán Volcanoes and the Palenque Cross Group

The Tz'utujil names for Volcán San Pedro are Nimajuyú, "great mountain," and Chuchuk (etymology uncertain; Allen Christenson, personal communication). The names for Volcán Atitlán and Volcán Tolimán are Huncat (*1 Kan*, a day name) and Ox Ic'ajol, "the three sons of a male," respectively (Orellana 1984:5). Each of the Palenque Cross Group temples is a manifestation of its respective thunderbolt god and represents both a mountain and one of the three hearthstones. In various Palenque

Figure 13.2. Palenque Cross Group (*left to right*): Temple of the Cross, Temple of the Foliated Cross, and Temple of the Sun (Temple XIV in foreground)

texts, the three thunderbolt gods are named as the offspring or creations of the deity Muwaan Mat, a relationship comparable to the Volcán Tolimán name of Ox Ic'ajol.

A comparison of the physical layout of the three Palenque buildings (fig. 13.2) with the volcanoes of Lake Atitlán produces some interesting parallels. The Temple of the Cross and the Temple of the Foliated Cross are aligned on a north-south axis, as are Volcán Tolimán and Volcán Atitlán. The two buildings are joined together at the northeast corner and share a terrace, while Volcán Atitlán and Volcán Tolimán are joined by a saddleback ridge. The Temple of the Sun is a freestanding building physically separated from the other two, just as Volcán San Pedro is separated from its two brother volcanoes by the Bay of Santiago. When the Cross Group plaza was flooded by rainy-season downpours, the Temple of the Sun would also have been separated from the Temple of the Cross and Temple of the Foliated Cross by a body of water.

A number of ritual locations associated with Volcán Atitlán can be correlated with the Temple of the Foliated Cross. The three wooden altarpieces in the church of Santiago Atitlán contain niches that house statues of Christ, the Virgin Mary, and various saints (Christenson 2001). Originally dating from the early colonial period, these fragile altarpieces were heavily damaged by earthquakes in 1960 and 1976 but were repaired and modified by two Tz'utujil sculptors from Santiago Atitlán named Diego Chávez Petzey and Nicolás Chávez Sojuels. During his study of the three altarpieces, Christenson (2001:74) was told by Nicolás Chávez that they represented the three Atitlán volcanoes. Volcán Atitlán is the largest of the three volcanoes and the center volcano when viewed from Santiago Atitlán. This suggests that the large center altarpiece replicates Volcán Atitlán. Chávez also indicated that the niches on the center altarpiece represented the sacred cave Paq'alib'al, which is located on a ridge to the west of Volcán Atitlán.

The cofradía house of San Juan (located in Santiago Atitlán) also replicates this cave, and Christenson writes (2001:168) that the ceiling decorations in this cofradía house are arranged to give the illusion of standing in the mouth of a volcanic crater. Sixteenth-century writers indicate that Volcán Atitlán was a focus of worship for the Tz'utujil Maya (Orellana 1984:102). The crater is still used by the Tz'utujil for ceremonies related to obtaining wealth and for protection against locusts (Mendelson 1957:454, 491). As noted above, Volcán Atitlán and the Temple of the Foliated Cross are physically similar in orientation. The San Juan cofradía house that replicates both Paq'alib'al and Volcán Atitlán was the location of the effigy corn tree discussed in chapter 10. The ceremonial planting of this effigy corn in the center of the cofradía house corresponded to the center-house corn the hero twins planted and the creator grandmother worshipped (Christenson 2001:125). The *k'an nahb' ixiimte,* "the precious pool, maize tree," illustrated as the central icon on the Tablet of the Foliated Cross, represents a corn plant with twin ears of corn and is analogous to the center corn-plants of the hero twins. These striking parallels between the Tablet of the Foliated Cross imagery and the San Juan cofradía house support the idea that the Temple of the Foliated Cross replicated Volcán Atitlán.

Each of the pib'naah sanctuaries of the three Cross Group buildings has a specific name. The pib'naah names of the Palenque Cross Group buildings may refer directly to the mythological houses of the three thunderbolt gods who were thought to be located on the three Atitlán volcanoes. While none of these names has been completely deciphered, Stuart (1987:38, 2006) and Houston (1996) note that the elements found in these names correspond to the decorative elements on the exterior of the sanctuaries. One of the elements used to name the pib'naah of the Temple of the Foliated Cross is a square-nosed serpent, which Stuart compares to Xiuhcoatl, the Central Mexican fire serpent associated with the fire god Xiuhtecuhtli. Volcán Atitlán is the only one of the three volcanoes with a history of eruptions, and one of the indigenous names for Volcán Atitlán is the day name *Huncat,* which is associated with burning (B. Tedlock 1982:110).

## Volcán Tolimán and the Temple of the Cross

Many commonalities link Volcán Tolimán with the Temple of the Cross. The pib'-naah of the Temple of the Cross is called the Six Sky place of GI (see chapter 6). The Tablet of the Cross text refers to the 13.0.0.0.0 Period Ending at the three stones place where the three hearthstones were dedicated, and goes on to describe a house dedication ceremony a year and a half later. On this date, GI is said to have descended from the sky and inaugurated his Six Sky place, also called his northern house (Zender 2005). Volcán Tolimán is the northernmost of the three Lake Atitlán volcanoes. I deduce from the text that when GI dedicated his house at the Six Sky place, he was, in fact, dedicating his house on Volcán Tolimán. GI was a god of wind and storms. The Tz'utujil see a rainbow on Volcán Tolimán as a sign of wind, and clouds over the volcano as a sign that a norte (northern storm) is approaching. By default, the western Temple of the Sun should replicate the western Volcán San Pedro.

## LAKE ATITLÁN AND THE PLACE CALLED MATWIIL

The region where the Palenque triad of lightning-bolt gods was born was called Matwiil. Stuart has argued (2000b, 2005b, 2006) that the bird used in the sign for the word Matwiil is based on a cormorant, and he notes that the rulers Akhal Mo' Nahb and Upakal K'inich are dressed in a costume representing this bird on the Palenque Temple XIX piers. He has characterized Matwiil as the Place of the Cormorant. I propose that Matwiil was one of the names for the place of duality, and by extension, for the Lake Atitlán area.

Lake Atitlán is a major migratory stopover for birds; large flocks descend on the lake semi-annually. In 1958, the lake was stocked with black bass in an ill-fated attempt to transform it into a sport-fishing destination for tourists. The bass destroyed the native fish population as well as the birds that relied on those fish. Shoreline development of tourist facilities and other factors have greatly reduced the reed beds and also caused a significant decrease in the number of water birds. Nevertheless, cormorants, herons, and egrets are still found along the shores of the lake (Land 1970). The cormorant makes an excellent symbol for the dark waters of the place of duality, for it has iridescent black feathers and it dives underwater for its prey.

GI and GIII are both associated with other water birds as well. Although the species is uncertain, GI has a water-bird manifestation that eats fish, and he is illustrated wearing this water bird as a headdress on the Palenque Creation Stone (see fig. 6.2d). The bird's feathers form GI's hair. On an incense burner featuring GI that is displayed in the Palenque museum, GI's mouth even has the form of this bird's bill. The south side of the Temple XIX platform illustrates the ruler Akhal Mo' Nahb wearing the costume of GI, and the water bird with a fish in its mouth is the focal point of his headdress (Stuart 2000b, 2005b). The deity GIII is also associated with water birds, for his costume includes heron feathers (Taube 2000:270).

## INCENSE BURNERS AND VOLCANOES

During the Late Classic Period, approximately one hundred elaborate incense burners, or *incensarios*, were cached on the terraces of the Cross Group buildings (Rands, Bishop, and Harbottle 1978; Cuevas García 2004:250–52; Carrasco 2005). It has been argued that these vessels were first used in the Cross Group temples during Period Ending ceremonies and ritually buried after they had served their purpose. The incensarios are composed of tall clay cylinders with portraits of the Palenque triad applied on the front. An old fire god is also illustrated on some of these incensarios. He is probably analogous to Itzamnaaj/Xpiyacoc. The incense offering was burned in a bowl set on top of the cylinder.

The Lacandon have deity houses that contain "god pots," perhaps reflecting pre-Columbian temples and incensarios (Tozzer 1907:105–47; Houston and Stuart 1996: 304; Taube 1998). These god pots are small clay bowls decorated with the deity's likeness on the outside. The bowl is thought to be the house of the deity, and inside each bowl is a little stone representing the seat of the god. Throughout the year, small amounts of meat and liquor are placed on the mouth of the deity, and incense and rubber figures are burned in the bowl as offerings. The incense is considered to be the god's tortillas (McGee 1990:44). The concept that incense is food for the gods is widespread in Mesoamerica. When the god pots become full of carbon residue, new pots are made and the old pots are deposited in ritual caves.

Fire played a central role in temple rituals (Stuart 1998), and Taube (1998:449) has noted that censers were "the concentrated embodiment of the temple" and served as the house and seat of the deity. I would expand his interpretation and say that the Cross Group temples and incensarios were manifestations of the three Palenque mountain gods, and when incense was ignited in the censer bowl, the incensario became the manifestation of a smoking mountain—a volcano. Whether the incensario was placed in the temple or on its staircase, the incense billowing out of the burner visually turned the temple into a burning mountain. In my interpretation, the small incense bowls placed on top of the incensario cylinders are like a volcanic crater.

During the Postclassic, young girls were thrown into the burning crater of Volcán Atitlán to feed the volcano, just as incense was thrown into the Palenque bowls, and just as incense and rubber figures are thrown into the Lacandon pots: "When the volcano thundered and cast forth fire and smoke, [the Indians] were persuaded that it was hungry and asking for food and that its favorite food was Indian girls whom they had also sacrificed in their gentility. They threw them into the burning mouth of that pyre" (Orellana 1984:102). The narrative on the Temple of the Inscriptions tablets names the Quadripartite Badge Monster as the headdress of GI, and numerous examples of GI show him wearing this headdress. The central element of the Quadripartite Badge Monster is a censer bowl (Houston, cited in Taube 2004:275). When wearing the headdress, GI symbolically became a burning volcano.

## Volcán Santa María and the Creator Grandparents

The creator grandparents were identified with the sweat bath, and the heating of the newborn child after its birth occurred in a sweat bath that replicated the sweat bath of the creator grandparents. The implication is that the creator grandparents were the source of the heat that animated the human soul and gave it life. The act of lighting the fire in the sweat bath is parallel to the act of placing fire in a new building and bringing it to life.

Anyone who has witnessed the smoke and steam pouring from volcanic vents and steam fissures can see how a sweat bath could be equated with a volcano. In several Mexican manuscripts, the firebox of the sweat bath even has the shape of a volcano (Geoffrey McCafferty, personal communication; see for example *Codex Bodley*, pp. 11, 13, 33; *Codex Vindobonensis*, pp. 15, 22, 30, 31; *Codex Nuttall*, pp. 16, 81; Groark 1997, fig. 2). The Kaqchikel refer to their sweat baths, which are conical, as "little volcanoes," (Fischer 1999:482). Goddesses and midwives were associated with the west in Mesoamerican culture (Nicholson 1971:422), which suggests that a volcano (and metaphoric sweat bath) located west of Lake Atitlán might be associated with the creator grandparents. A likely candidate is the prominent Volcán Santa María about thirty kilometers northwest of Lake Atitlán. The indigenous names for Volcán Santa María are Xcanul, "volcano"; Q'aq'xanul, "fire volcano"; and Yaxcanul (Bode 1961:231). The Mam and K'iche' of the region believe that Volcán Santa María is the most powerful of all mountains, and given its long history of eruptions, this is not unwarranted (Wagley 1949; Bunzel 1952:428; Saler 1960:111, 182; Watanabe 1992). *Ya* is a feminine prefix in Tz'utujil and Kaqchikel, so Yaxcanul could be translated as Lady Volcano (Allen Christenson, personal communication). The name Santa María also suggests that the volcano was considered female. A similar situation occurred in Alta Verapaz, where the female mountain called Itzam was renamed Santa María by the local Catholic priest (R. Wilson 1995:74).

Despite this female association, the Mam and K'iche' believe that an old supernatural called Juan Noq lives inside Volcán Santa María. Juan Noq will provide wealth to those who conduct themselves in an appropriate manner, but he sends illness and death to those who do not. In the Dance of the Conquest, the costumes for the principal indigenous leaders are thought to come from the mouth of Santa María volcano, and they are symbolically returned to this location after the festival (Bode 1961:234). In the contemporary stories, Volcán Santa María is thought to have been first located at a place called Kab'yo'k, Xecabyuc, or Xeococ, "leg of turtle," which is suggestive of the *kok* turtle form of the creator grandfather. The crater of Volcán Santa Mariá is called "the wizard" and "the priest," which are both appropriate names for the creator grandfather.

## THE FLINT OF THE VOLCANO

Volcán Santa María during the Postclassic Period was believed to be a powerful mountain and a source of sacred fire. In the *Annals of the Cakchiquels*, the warriors of the seven tribes gather at the base of the erupting Volcán Santa María to capture its fire and put out the eruption (Brinton 1885:99; Akkeren 2000:158). Only the Kaqchikel leader Q'aq'awitz and his assistant Zakitzunun are brave enough to enter the crater. While Q'aq'awitz goes into the inferno, Zakitzunun pours water on it to extinguish its blaze. The resulting smoke spreads great distances and causes everyone at the foot of the mountain to flee in terror. Although some sparks fall from the volcano, the tribes are not able to obtain the fire. The crater of Volcán Santa María contains thirteen colored stones, and from these Q'aq'awitz takes the *saqchoq*, "white flint stone," and descends from the mountain with it. The *saqchoq* represents the fire of the volcano, and it is said to be the heart of the mountain (*ruk'ux juyu*). The text also names this white flint as a *k'olok'ik q'aq' chi ab'aj*, "round fire stone," and Q'aq'awitz called it his captive.

The *Annals of the Cakchiquels* indicates that a centipede was located in the crater of Volcán Santa María (Akkeren 2000:159). The association of flint with centipedes is found in Classic Period depictions of flint spears, where the flint blade emerges from the mouth of a centipede (fig. 13.3a). Another name for a centipede is *q'uq'kumatz* (feathered serpent; Coto 1983:128), one of the names of the creator grandparents. The association of a serpent with the crater of a volcano is found in the current belief that volcanoes contain a serpent, and when the serpent is angry, it opens his mouth and out comes fire and smoke (Glittenberg 1994:155).

Centipedes appear in a variety of contexts in Maya art (Grube and Nahm 1994; Boot 1999; Carrasco and Hull 2002; Taube 2003; Hull and Carrasco 2004; Kettunen and Davis 2004), and these supernatural beings are often the conflation of a centipede and a snake (see fig. 10.5). The open mouth of these centipede-snakes has long been associated with a cave mouth, and the maws have been characterized as an entrance into the earth or the underworld (Freidel, Schele, and Parker 1993; Stuart and Houston 1994:71–72, 77; Taube 2003). I propose that centipede mouths were also specifically identified with volcano craters and their fire. The association is a natural one, for centipedes have poisonous glands and can inflict painful bites. Stepping on a centipede or stepping into the crater of an active volcano creates a burning sensation on the feet.

The *Annals of the Cakchiquels* states that the centipede at the heart of Volcán Santa María was the origin of the wild Dance of the Centipede (Akkeren 2000:159). Although other colonial sources only briefly describe this festival dance, the hero twins also performed the dance after their immolation in the pit oven and being cast into a river (Akkeren 2000:162; Christenson 2003a:180). After their emergence from the river, they performed a variety of dances to impress the underworld lords, including the Dance of the Centipede. This act of immolation by the hero twins has been associated with the Central Mexican myth of the creation of the sun and moon recorded by Sahagún (1959–63, book 7, 2–7; Edmonson 1971:130–31; D. Tedlock 1995:279; Akkeren 2000:162). In this story, the Central Mexican gods called Nanahuatzin and Tecuciztecatl jump into a hearth at Teotihuacan and are transformed into the sun and moon. I think it likely that these immolation hearths were modeled after the fire in a volcanic crater.

The *saqchoq*, "white flint," and *k'olok'ik q'aq' chi ab'aj*, "round fire stone" of Q'aq'awitz, the Kaqchikel leader, also appears in the *Popol Vuh*, where it is called by the

K'iche' name *Saq Toq'*, "white flint." The *Saq Toq'* was a sacrificial knife found in the rubber ball of the underworld lords, and when the ball was put into play, the knife emerged and threatened to sacrifice the hero twins (Christenson 2003a:164–65). Like the *saqchoq*, the knife is also referred to as *kolok'ik cha*, "round blade." The *Saq Toq'* was also the sacrificial knife that the underworld owls took to remove the heart of Lady Blood, although she convinced them not to perform the deed. In Maya directional colors, white is associated with the north, and a flint knife cutting open the chest of a sacrificial victim is illustrated on the north side of the quadrilateral world model found on *Madrid Codex* 76. In this scene, the victim, blood pouring from his chest, is draped over a sacrificial stone shaped like a volcano. God A and God E sit flanking the stone, but the knife appears to act on its own like the white flint in the *Popol Vuh*.

A white flint is also found in an episode of the Central Mexican *Leyenda de los soles* (Bierhorst 1992:152). In this story, the goddess Itzpapalotl is defeated, and her burned body produces five colored flints (presumably one for each direction and one for the center). Mixcoatl (cloud serpent), a god of the north, chooses the white flint, and it becomes his spirit power. Q'aq'awitz's capture of the white flint stone from Volcán Santa María has been compared to the Itzpapalotl and Mixcoatl episode (Akkeren 2000:160, 165). Akkeren points out a direct relationship between Q'aq'awitz and Mixcoatl. He notes that in a later episode of the *Annals of the Cakchiquels*, Q'aq'awitz enters the waters of Lake Atitlán and is transformed into Sutz'ukumatz, which translates as "cloud serpent" in Kaqchikel. Itzpapalotl means "obsidian butterfly," and the knife-tipped wings on her costume have been identified as representing the *Rothschildia orizaba* moth (John Pohl, personal communication). This moth is only found on the Pico de Orizaba, which suggests an association of flint with volcanoes. Itzpapalotl's primary identification with obsidian—found only in association with volcanoes—again connects this goddess with a volcano.

Colored flints appear in the description of the four world trees of the *Chilam Balam of Chumayel* (Roys 1933:64). Each tree had a red, white, black, or yellow flint appropriate for its direction. Colored flints are also evident in the 819 Day Count (Berlin and Kelley 1961). In this calendar cycle, a red, yellow, black, or white GII/God K was placed in the appropriate quadrant associated with his color and direction every 819 days. As discussed in chapter 5, GII was the manifestation of the lightning-bolt ax, which was composed of a flint head. While the white flint knife was used for heart sacrifice, the flint ax was used to decapitate sacrificial victims. Many graphic examples are seen in Classic Period pottery images, including a *way* character who decapitates himself with a flint ax (Grube and Nahm 1994:708). It can be assumed that each of the Heart of Sky deities possessed a flint ax by virtue of being lightning-bolt gods. GI/Huracan was identified with the north, which suggests that his flint ax was white. As noted above, GI/Huracan and Mixcoatl also had many parallels.

White flint was also associated with the heart of Volcán de Fuego, a volcano in Guatemala. During their migration, according to the *Annals of the Cakchiquels*, the ancestors of the Kaqchikel travel through the region between Volcán de Agua and Volcán de Fuego southeast of Lake Atitlán. At the center of Volcán de Fuego, Q'aq'awitz encounters a supernatural boy called Zaqui Coxol, "white *coxol*" (Brinton 1885:87; Recinos and Goetz 1953:61). He is said to be the heart of Volcán de Fuego and the guardian of the road they have just taken. After they give him red-colored clothes, he descends from the mouth of the volcano to its base. Dennis Tedlock (1995) translates the term *coxol* as "he who strikes fire from flint," but the term also means to be lively or active (Christenson 2003a:229). Colonial-period sources indicate that Zaqui Coxol was a young dwarf who was the messenger of the earth lord and guardian of animals (B. Tedlock 1982: 149–50, 1986; Christenson 2003a: 229–30). In contemporary stories, he uses his lightning-bolt ax to strike knowledge (the lightning in the blood) into the ancestors of the K'iche'. Although he has been compared to GII/God K, whose titles indicate that he was a young dwarf who was shown as a personified flint ax (Houston 1992; Freidel, Schele, and Parker 1993, Martin 2002), Zaqui Coxol also shares attributes with the dwarf assistants who wield lightning-bolt axes in many Classic Period scenes.

One of the most dramatic events of volcanic eruptions is the vibrant display of lightning bolts that discharge from the volcano (Shaw 1971:155). In Zaragoza, some ten kilometers from Volcán de Fuego, Jody Glittenberg (1994:154) watched in amazement as lightning bolts from the fire-spewing volcano zigzagged through the streets during the 1975 eruptions. It seems logical to conclude that the fire of the volcano was thought to reside in these lightning bolts, given that the lightning bolts appear to originate from the fire of the volcano and given that they create fire when they strike the ground. As discussed in previous chapters, the earth was thought to be a manifestation of the creator grandfather, and the primordial fire at the center of the earth was his heart. I propose that the fire that erupted from volcanoes was also thought to be a manifestation of this supreme fire and earth god. The implication is that the lightning-bolt gods received their flints (their lightning bolts) from the cache of fire flints belonging to this omnipotent grandfather. When Q'aq'awitz and Mixcoatl took the white fire-flint, they were acquiring not only the fire, but the power embedded in that stone.

### THE VOLCANOES OF THE HERO TWINS

Volcán Santa María and the Atitlán volcanoes are not the only mountains associated with *Popol Vuh* deities and flints. A volcano called Hunahpu appears in the list of mountains that Zipacna moves (Christenson 2003a:96). As noted in the *Annals of the Cakchiquels*, Hunahpu is the indigenous name for Volcán de Agua, located southeast of Lake Atitlán (Brinton 1885:190). Because Hunahpu was the sun and the sun rises in the east, this eastern volcano seems a logical choice for a manifestation of Hunahpu. The *Popol Vuh* passage related to the birth of the hero twins hints at the possibility that they had mountain forms: Lady Blood did not give birth to them at the household of One Hunahpu, which was located at the center of the world, nor did she give birth in the presence of Xmucane:

> This, therefore, is the account of their birth that we shall tell. When the day arrived, the maiden Lady Blood gave birth. The Grandmother did not see it when they were born, for these two arose suddenly. Hunahpu and Xbalanque were their names. They arose in the mountains. (Christenson 2003a:140)

The slopes of Volcán de Agua were lush agricultural lands that produced many important commodities. The Spanish first established their capital city at the base of this volcano because of the abundant resources in this area. The resource-rich Lake Amatitlán is situated just east of the volcano. In Mesoamerica, there was a concept of a flowery mountain paradise associated with the rising sun (Taube 2004). Volcán de Agua may have been the model for this eastern paradise (see chapter 13).

East is an especially important direction, not only because of the rising sun, but because the prevailing east wind of the lowlands brings the all-important first rains of the planting season. As the Ch'orti' say, east "is the source of all life and good in the world" (Wisdom 1940:427). The association of the east as a place of abundance is also found in lowland agricultural practices. As noted in chapter 1, a garden of useful and edible plants is situated on the east side of the milpa so that the prevailing winds will not disperse the corn pollen on it (Atran 1993:679).

In Classic Period inscriptions, the solar cartouche that substitutes for the sun god's portrait is composed of a *kin*, "sun," sign infixed on a flint with centipede heads decorating the corners (fig. 13.3b). Several illustrations of the sun god also show a centipede as a headdress element (Taube 2004:411), and on a structure at Copan, the sun god emerges from the flint/centipede cartouche (fig. 13.3c). As noted above, a centipede and colored flints marked the heart of Volcán Santa María in the *Annals of the Cakchiquels*, and a flint-ax deity was associated with the heart of Volcán de Fuego. I suggest that the flint and centipede of the sun disk are references to the heart of Volcán de Agua, and specifically to its crater fire.

The indigenous name for Volcán de Fuego is Chigag, "mouth of fire," and it is another of the volcanoes in the Zipacna list. As discussed above, the young dwarf called Zaqui Coxol was said to be the heart of this volcano. In the contemporary stories that parallel the Zipacna episode, Volcán de Fuego is consistently paired with Volcán de Agua, which suggests that Volcán de Fuego might have been the manifestation of Hunahpu's twin brother Xbalanque. Its position adjacent to Volcán de Agua/Hunahpu also supports this identification.

An image of Volcán de Agua and Volcán de Fuego may appear in Maya art. On vessel K1398, the rabbit manifestation of Yax Bolon/Xbalanque stands on a mountain symbol with a snake emerging from the mountain's mouth. In the opposite scene, the sun god manifestation of One Ajaw/Hunahpu sits on a similar mountain

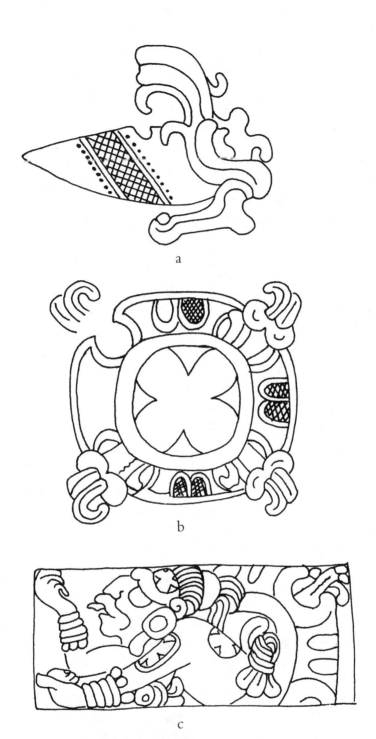

a

b

c

Figure 13.3. a. Naranjo Stela 8 flint; b. Copan flint cartouche; c. sun god emerging from flint cartouche, Copan Structure 8N-66C

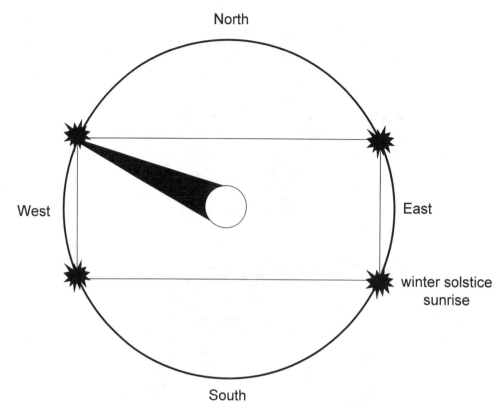

Figure 13.4. Diagram of volcano shadow at winter solstice sunrise

symbol, but the snout of this mountain has the form of the head of a male deer with a rattlesnake draped around its neck. The pairing of these two brothers on two different mountains is reminiscent of the paired nature of Volcán de Agua and Volcán de Fuego.

## VOLCANOES, SHADOWS, AND THE QUADRILATERAL WORLD

The *Popol Vuh* and the *Annals of the Cakchiquels* indicate that after the first tribes settled in their communities, they went to the tops of their respective sacred mountains and waited for the first sunrise (Recinos and Goetz 1953:80; Christenson 2003a:225). At the climax of the creation and ordering story in the *Popol Vuh*, the first rising of Hunahpu as the sun and Xbalanque as the full moon occurred on the first zenith passage date in late April. The birth of the hero twins was, however, associated with the winter solstice, which begins the annual journey of the sun. It is well established that the Maya created building complexes that were oriented to mark the locations of the sunrise at equinox, summer solstice, and winter solstice. For example, when a person is positioned on the center building of the Uaxactun Group E complex, the winter-solstice sun rises over the southeast corner of Temple E-II (Aveni 1980:279).

If we assume that Lake Atitlán marked the center of the Maya world, a person sitting on top of any of the three Atitlán volcanoes watching the sunrise would see the winter-solstice sun rising out of the slope of Volcán de Fuego. The doorway to the Temple of the Sun at Palenque, which I have identified with Volcán San Pedro, is oriented to face the rising winter-solstice sun (Aveni and Hartung 1979).

The rising sun creates an interesting volcanic shadow phenomenon that is related to the quadrilateral ordering of the world. At sunrise and again at sunset, a pyramid-shaped shadow of the volcano is visible, and if witnessed from the top of the volcano, the shadow extends to the horizon. If a person were to watch the winter-solstice sunrise and sunset from the top of a volcano, the pyramid-shaped shadow would demarcate the corners of the quadrilateral world. At sunrise, the shadow on the west side of the volcano would point directly to the western horizon where the summer-solstice sun would set (fig. 13.4). Conversely, as the sun sets on winter solstice, the pyramid-shaped shadow on the east side of the volcano would point to the rising point of the summer-solstice sun (fig. 13.5). The rising and setting of the winter-solstice sun literally lays out the corners of the quadrilateral world.

If a full moon occurs on winter solstice, it also demarcates the north corners of the quadrilateral world. While the winter-solstice sun is setting at the southwest corner of the quadrilateral world, a full moon at this time will rise on the northeast corner. The next morning, as the sun rises at the southeast corner of the quadrilateral world, the full moon will set in the northwest corner.

## The Northern Route

Previous chapters have discussed Xucaneb Mountain in Alta Verapaz and presented evidence that the mountain represented God L/Gathered Blood. The *Popol Vuh* does not explain why One Hunahpu and Seven Hunahpu initially went from the Lake Atitlán area to the Alta Verapaz territory of Gathered Blood, nor does it discuss One Hunahpu's courtship with Lady Bone Water. The contemporary stories concerning the elopement of Xucaneb's daughter indicate that Thorn Broom (the equivalent of One Hunahpu) was hunting deer on Xucaneb Mountain when he saw Xucaneb's daughter beside her house and fell in love with her. Braakhuis (2001) has presented evidence that deer hunting was a metaphor for the acquisition of a wife and for warfare. In the elopement stories, Thorn Broom courts the girl, has sexual intercourse with her, and convinces her to elope with him. The newly joined couple is pursued by Xucaneb, who kills his daughter for this illicit behavior. After Thorn Broom makes amends with Xucaneb, she is restored and the couple begins their married life. Later in this epic story, she dies and her remains are turned to corn seed.

The stories tell that the fleeing couple was crossing a body of water far away from Xucaneb Mountain when the thunderbolt struck and killed Xucaneb's daughter. Some translators of these stories have characterized the body of water as the sea, but the earliest recording of this tale (circa A.D. 1909) calls it a lake (Dieseldorff 1966).

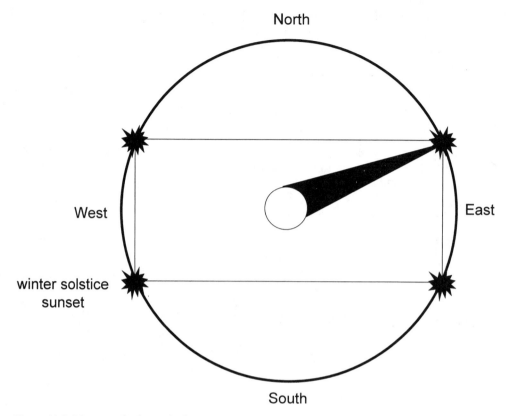

Figure 13.5. Diagram of volcano shadow at winter solstice sunset

In one story, the couple crosses the water and arrives on the opposite shore, which indicates it was a lake rather than the sea. The elopement stories do not specify the destination of the fleeing couple, but it seems likely that Thorn Broom was taking his new wife back to his home. There is no body of water between Xucaneb Mountain and Raxon Mountain, so it would seem that Raxon was not their destination. In the *Popol Vuh*, One Hunahpu lived with his first wife at the center house of his parents, and I have argued that this house was located at Lake Atitlán. If I am correct in my analysis that Thorn Broom and One Ixim/One Hunahpu were parallel, then the couple may have been fleeing to Lake Atitlán, and this lake may have been where Xucaneb's daughter was struck by lightning. As discussed in chapter 8, there was a turtle at the edge of this lake, which brings to mind the turtle form of the creator grandfather, who lived at this location.

## MEAUAN MOUNTAIN AND THE CORN GODDESSES

Another mountain associated with the northern route to Alta Verapaz is Meauan Mountain, which was the location where Zipacna was defeated in the *Popol Vuh*.

Zipacna spent his days hunting for fish and crabs in the Chixoy River and his nights moving mountains. When he first encounters the Four Hundred Boys dragging a great tree, he is bathing in the river. The hero twins place a fake crab inside a cave in a canyon near Meauan Mountain and take Zipacna there. To defeat Zipacna, they convince him to crawl into the cave on his back, and the mountain settles on his chest so that he can no longer move. Brasseur de Bourbourg (1861:128) recognized that Meauan Mountain was Chimiagua Mountain on the Chixoy River.

When the hero twins tell Zipacna about the crab, they describe the cave as being in a canyon at the base of the mountain. Zipacna does not want to go there alone, but the hero twins assure him: "There is no way that you will get lost if you just follow the course of the river until you reach the base of the great mountain. There it will be, situated below the canyon. Just go along over there" (Christenson 2003a:105–106). The exact location of the cave and canyon is not indicated, but contemporary stories parallel to the *Popol Vuh* episode indicate the general vicinity. In these tales, the protagonist is called Sipac, Sipaknay, or Yegua Achi' (Shaw 1971: 48–51; Valey and Valey 1979; Cook 1981; 2000; Akkeren 2000:254–61). The term Yegua Achi' is a corruption of the term *oyew achi'*, a K'iche' title for war captains (Cook 2000:197). The cave is described as being beside the Calá River above Pueblo Viejo (the pre-Columbian site of Kawinal) at a hill called Cerro Sipac (Shaw 1971:48–51). The Calá River is a tributary of the Chixoy, and it flows through the canyon that separates the east side of Chimiagua Mountain from Los Pajales Mountain. Pueblo Viejo is located on the Calá River just two kilometers upstream from the confluence of the two rivers, although it is currently flooded by the waters of the Chixoy Reservoir.

While the *Popol Vuh* only lists the volcanoes that Zipacna moved, modern accounts tell where some of these volcanoes were thought to have originated. In the Achi' stories from Cubulco, Sipac removes Volcán de Agua, Volcán de Fuego, and Volcán Santa María from the communities of Xinacati, Chicocox, and Xeococ, respectively (Shaw 1971:48–49). These towns are all adjacent to the Río Sajcap, another tributary of the Chixoy. The Río Sajcap valley is on the south side of the Chixoy, and the confluence of these two rivers is just five hundred meters upstream from the confluence of the Chixoy and the Calá.

Rabinal is located at the head of the Río Sajcap valley, and the stories from this town indicate that the hills known as Saqacho and Chuwa Kotz'ij on the western border of the community are the remains of Volcán de Agua and Volcán de Fuego (Akkeren 2000:256). Adjacent to these two hills is a long ridge called Sipac. When viewed from Rabinal, the outline of the ridge and hills could easily be interpreted as a crocodile carrying two mountains on its tail.

It seems odd that the stories from Cubulco and Rabinal would indicate different origin places for Volcán de Agua and Volcán de Fuego, but it is likely that the Rabinal features were thought to be the imprint that Sipac left on the landscape when he traveled through this area with the volcanoes on his back. This would be similar to a K'iche' story about Yegua Achi', who traveled to a mountain shrine near Huehuetenango and left the imprint of his knee and testicles on a stone there (Cook 1981:643–44).

In the K'iche' stories from Momostenango, Yegua Achi's motivation for moving the mountains stems from his desire to punish Santiago, the patron saint of the town, for not supplying him with a wife (Cook 1981, 2000). He attempts to move various volcanoes to the center of the community to cover up Santiago's shrine. He carries Volcán Cerro Quemada from a location near Antigua, but en route, Santiago makes him slip, and Yegua Achi' drops the volcano where it is now located. Next, Yegua Achi' attempts to move Volcán Santa María to Momostenango. Although this story does not say where he obtains Volcán Santa María, it describes how he carries the volcano along the coast but becomes hungry and sets it down. After his meal, he can not budge the volcano and is compelled to leave in its current location next to Volcán Cerro Quemada. In anger, he kicks a hill near Salcajá on the Samalá River (north of Santa María and Cerro Quemada). This hill slides up the Samalá Valley all the way to San Francisco El Alto, where it remains today.

In another episode, Yegua Achi' constructs a road from Momostenango to Totonicapán (east of San Francisco El Alto) and down to Lake Atitlán. On this road is a mountain pass called Chuwi Pur (Place of the Burro). This pass is in the mountain range between the southern Samalá River and the northern Chixoy River. K'iche' pilgrims took the Chuwi Pur route when they made pilgrimages to Lake Atitlán. Although the *Popol Vuh* does not elaborate on Zipacna's deeds, the contemporary stories indicate that he played a role in the layout of the landscape, and in particular, the routes along the Samalá and Chixoy rivers.

The contemporary stories about Sipac, Sipaknay, or Yegua Achi' are also concerned with how he obtains a wife. As noted above, Yegua Achi' tried to move the mountains to Momostenango because Santiago denied his request for a wife. In another story, Yegua Achi' agrees to build a bridge in order to obtain a virgin, but fails to complete the task in time. He goes from place to place trying to obtain one of the Virgin María saints for his wife.

In one of the Rabinal stories, Sipac makes a deal with the German plantation owners to move the mountains in exchange for a bun. He said he had a craving for bread. One of the main reasons a man needs a wife is to have someone to prepare his food. While the Maya diet is based on corn, foreigners and Germans usually eat wheat bread. Sipac's bun craving was a metaphor for a foreign woman. The marriage themes in the Sipac stories and the elopement stories indicate that the northern trade route through Alta Verapaz was intimately connected to bride negotiations and acquisition.

An Achi' story that recounts the defeat of Sipac also involves the moving of Belejuj, "nine," the indigenous name for Los Pajales Mountain (Shaw 1971:48). Los Pajales is composed of a large peak called Cerro Cauinal (Kawinal) and a twenty-kilometer-long ridge that runs on an east–west axis on the north side of the mountain.

Los Pajales was called Belejuj because it has nine peaks (Shaw 1971:50). The valleys between the peaks of Los Pajales Mountain are thought to have been created by the rope that Sipac used to carry the mountain. Although the story does not state where Sipac obtained Los Pajales Mountain, it indicates that he was carrying it when he saw three young goddesses bathing in a river. They are described as colored corn goddesses and caretakers of the earth. When women wash the family clothing, they go to a water source with flat rocks beside it and use these surfaces as a washing board. When they finish their washing and lay the wet clothing out to dry, the women often take the opportunity to wash themselves in the river. As will be discussed in chapter 14, it is highly likely that these corn goddesses had just finished their washing and were bathing themselves when they were approached by Sipac.

According to the story, the goddesses were bathing in the Río Calá near Pueblo Viejo, which separates Chimiagua Mountain from Los Pajales Mountain. The close association between Chimiagua Mountain (Meauan) and these goddesses is reflected in the etymology of these place names. Akkeren (2000:60, 66, 298) has analyzed Meauan (spelled Meajaw in the *Annals of the Cakchiquels*) as a contracted form of *me'al ajaw*, "the daughter of a lord." The daughters of the lord God L/Gathered Blood were the corn goddesses.

Sipac is smitten with the corn goddesses and immediately puts Los Pajales Mountain down and proposes to them. To entice the girls to marry him, Sipac offers to use the money he will be paid for the mountain to buy them new clothes. The girls counter by promising to marry him if he can catch a crab for them to eat. Land crabs are found near rivers and springs and are hunted during the dry season (M. Wilson 1972:424). While Sipac searches for crabs, the yellow corn goddess creates a crab from her hair ribbon and places it in a nearby cave. She instructs Sipac to enter the cave on his back to get the crab. When he is all the way in, the other goddesses stand on top of the rock and push down to close the cave, trapping Sipac. Thus he is defeated. The hill where the cave was located was then named Sipac Hill.

Females are not explicitly mentioned in the defeat of Zipacna as told in the *Popol Vuh*, but when Tedlock's informant Andrés Xiloj was translating this episode, he realized that the crab that the hero twins created from a hollowed-out stone and a *Bromelia* was a humorous metaphor for a woman (D. Tedlock 1995:248). A comparison of the *Popol Vuh* version and the contemporary stories makes it apparent that the hero twins created an effigy of the crab form of the yellow corn goddess to entrap Zipacna, and that Meauan Mountain was also her mountain manifestation. The association of the crab with the corn goddess is also seen in the elopement stories where Xucaneb's daughter tries to escape from her father by hiding in a crab shell.

## Montaña Nueve Cerros

The three corn goddesses of Meauan Mountain are reminiscent of the three goddesses Sahagún describes (1959–63, book 2, 22): Chalchiuhtlicue (Jade Skirt),

Chicomecoatl (Seven Snake), and Huixtocihuatl (Salt Woman), who were considered to be either sisters or aspects of the same goddess. The first two were thought to represent corn, while the last was specifically associated with salt. Although the Achi' story does not indicate from which place Sipac moved Los Pajales Mountain, there is an extremely important salt location downstream from Meauan Mountain called Montaña Nueve Cerros, "mountain of nine hills," that was likely the source. Montaña Nueve Cerros is adjacent to the Chixoy River and approximately seventy kilometers due north of Los Pajales. It is a limestone ridge fourteen kilometers long, composed of nine peaks that rise four hundred meters above the surrounding lowlands. Immediately below the ridge is a large salt dome (Cerro de Tortugas) that has been exploited by the Maya since Preclassic times (Dillon 1977). The names for both Los Pajales Mountain (Belejuj) and Montaña Nueve Cerros refer to nine peaks, and ridges are reminiscent of the body of a crocodile. In several of the Sipac stories, he left behind a remnant of the mountain he moved, and he also left his own imprint as he traveled across the landscape. I propose that Montaña Nueve Cerros was thought to be the remnant of the Los Pajales Mountain ridge. Given Sipac's role in creating the valley of the Samalá River between Salcajá and San Francisco El Alto, it is likely that he was thought to have created the Chixoy River valley between Montaña Nueve Cerros and Los Pajales Mountain when he moved Los Pajales.

## The Mountain of Cabracan's Defeat

After the hero twins defeat Seven Macaw and his son Zipacna, they set their sights on his second son, Cabracan. The word *cabracan* literally means "two his legs," but it is also a common word for an earthquake (Christenson 2003a:96). Cabracan lived on the surface of the earth during the era of the wooden people, and he spent his time destroying mountains by stamping his foot on the ground. As his name implies, his actions caused earthquakes and landslides. To defeat him, the hero twins tell Cabracan about a great eastern mountain and challenge him to destroy it:

> There is one great mountain that we saw that keeps growing until truly high it ascends. It simply rises up, far above the peaks of all the mountains. We could not catch even one or two birds before its face. (Christenson 2003a:109)

On their journey to this mountain, they feed Cabracan a bird coated in earth, which takes away his power. By the time they reach the eastern mountain, Cabracan is helplessly weak, and they are able to tie him up and bury him at the base of the mountain.

Seven Macaw and his sons were active during the era of the wooden people, which ended when the creator deities flooded the world with a black rain. Presumably, the defeat of Seven Macaw and his two sons was part of the end of this era. The *Popol Vuh* does not describe the physical nature of Cabracan, but given that his

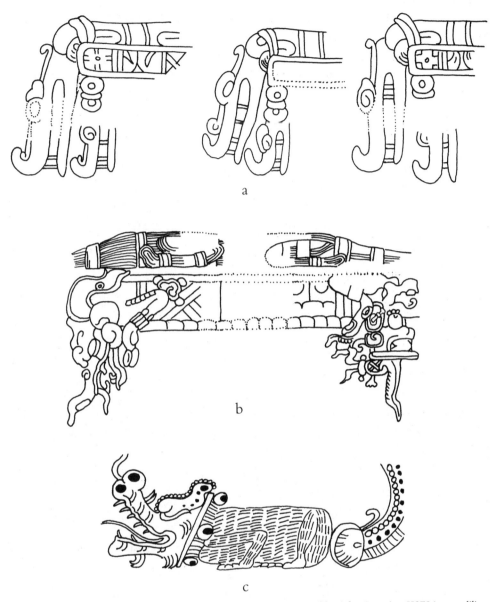

Figure 13.6. a. *Paris Codex* crocodiles; b. Piedras Negras Stela 11 crocodiles (after Stuart); c. K2796 crocodilian

brother Zipacna was a crocodile, there is a strong possibility that Cabracan also took the shape of a crocodile. In addition to the Milky Way crocodile, there is another type of crocodile illustrated in Maya art. K'atun ceremonies are illustrated on Piedras Negras Stela 11 and in the *Paris Codex*. In these scenes, a bound crocodile is juxtaposed with the Milky Way crocodile. Although the manuscript is eroded, there are clearly two crocodiles in the *Paris Codex* scenes: the body of the upper one has its limbs bound to its body, while the body of the lower one is represented by a sky band (fig. 13.6a). On Piedras Negras Stela 11, the lower crocodile is the Milky Way crocodile with the Quadripartite Badge Monster on its tail (fig. 13.6b). A sky band forms the body of this crocodile. The upper crocodile is headless, but like the *Paris Codex* crocodile, his limbs are bound to his body. It is quite likely that the bound crocodile in these scenes is a Classic Period image of Cabracan.

The *Popol Vuh* gives little information about the specific location of the great eastern mountain where the earthquake-causing Cabracan was buried, but Xucaneb Mountain is a good candidate. As noted in chapter 8, Xucaneb Mountain is thought to be a source of earthquakes, it is located east of Meauan Mountain, and it is the highest peak in Alta Verapaz. On two vessels (K2796 and K7750), the house of God L, which I have identified with Xucaneb Mountain, has a crocodilian animal perched on its roof (fig. 13.6c). If Xucaneb Mountain was the great eastern mountain and Cabracan also had the crocodilian form of his brother Zipacna, then this beast might be one of his manifestations.

## PAXIL MOUNTAIN

On the opposite side of the Guatemalan highlands from Chimiagua Mountain and Xucaneb Mountain is another limestone mountain called Peña Blanca, "white rock." Located about 115 kilometers northwest of Lake Atitlán, this mountain rises 3,518 meters between the two upper tributaries of the Grijalva River system. The Mam believe that the first corn obtained by humans came from Peña Blanca, also called by the indigenous names of Tui Xián, K'man Xián, Paxa, Xepaxa, and Paxil (Wagley 1941:20; Oakes 1951:244, 74; Valladares 1957:196–200; Miles 1960). In some of the Mam stories, humans gather the wild corn growing on the mountainside or obtain corn seed from one of its caves. Oakes (1951:244) notes the similarity between this mountain and Paxil of the *Popol Vuh*, and Miles (1960) suggests these corn mountains were one and the same. In the stories concerning the discovery of corn, the gods split Paxil open with a thunderbolt. The cave that the Mam identify with corn is located on a white cliff that has a large, vertical fissure splitting it in two (fig. 13.7). They refer to this cliff as Paxita. In the *Popol Vuh*, the second name for Paxil is Cayala (*k'ayala'*, "bitter or stagnant water"), a term that refers to the lime water used in corn processing (Akkeren, cited in Christenson 2003a:193). The Paxita cave is adjacent to a spring where rain ceremonies and divinations related to the success of the corn cycle are performed (Miles 1960:433–34).

## SUMMARY

I have identified nine mountains with specific *Popol Vuh* deities and their Classic Period counterparts. At the center of this cosmological model is Lake Atitlán with its three hearthstone volcanoes: Tolimán, San Pedro, and Atitlán. This location was identified with the home of the creator grandparents, which also housed One Hunahpu

Figure 13.7. Paxil Mountain

and his immediate family. To the east of the lake are Volcán de Agua and Volcán de Fuego, which were identified with the hero twins and with the rising sun and its paradise. The twins were the quintessential young, unmarried men, and their conquest of the underworld lords indicates their skill as warriors and leaders. In the far northeast is Xucaneb Mountain, the home of the god of long-distance trade, God L/Gathered Blood, whose daughters became the wives of One Ixim/One Hunahpu.

To the west of Lake Atitlán is the female volcano Santa María, which I believe was thought to be the sweat bath of the creator grandparents. Northwest of this volcano are the two highest volcanoes of Guatemala, Tacaná and Tajumulco, which are also considered to be female in ethnographic stories (Wagley 1949:59; Watanabe 1992:67). In the far northwest is Paxil Mountain, which contained the remains of Ixik/Lady Bone Water, who likely died during childbirth. Finally, on the west side of the northern Chixoy River is the female Meauan Mountain, associated with God L/Gathered Blood's daughters.

The people of Central Mexico envisioned the sun as being accompanied by two categories of supernatural warriors during its journey across the sky. The first were the souls of male warriors who had died in battle. These warriors, who lived in the east, escorted the sun from dawn until noon. At the sun's zenith, these male warriors turned their duties over to a group of female warriors, who escorted the sun until it set. The Cihuateteo, "women gods" who had died in childbirth, lived in the west. There is some evidence for this east/male and west/female dichotomy in the landscape of highland Guatemala, where the mountain manifestations of the principal male creator deities are situated in the east while the female mountains are in the west.

The Popol Vuh and other indigenous documents indicate that the highland Maya believed that their creation events happened at specific places in their landscape. There is ample evidence that the lowland Maya believed in the same creation story, but did they also identify those events with the same specific highland locations, and did they revere those sites? In one case, the triad of buildings that represented the three hearthstone mountains is an ancient architectural configuration that appears in the Preclassic era in its most dramatic form at El Mirador (Hansen 1990, 1992). Did Kan B'ahlam of Palenque merely replicate this ancient form and its associated mythology, or did he understand that his Cross Group buildings represented the Atitlán volcanoes? Although either scenario is possible, I am inclined to believe that the lowland Maya were well aware of the landscape across Mesoamerica, given that they engaged in long-distance trade. The importance of highland jade and quetzal feathers as symbols of power and prestige for the Classic Period Maya, and the fact that the lowland Maya identified their most sacred structures as mountains, suggests that they never lost their knowledge of these sacred places.

If the lowland Maya were aware of these sacred locations, does it follow that they would have made pilgrimages to the highlands in order to venerate the creator deities at these specific sites? While I do not discount the possibility of long-distance pilgrimage, I am not convinced that this was the case. From an economic perspective, the ruling elite had more to gain from creating sacred locations within their own territories and directing ritual actions to those places. Only limited archaeological investigations have been conducted on any of the volcanic peaks, and no scientific examinations of Paxil, Meauan, Xucaneb, or Raxon have been undertaken. Perhaps future archaeological research will shed more light on the history of these sacred locations.

# 14

# THE LANDSCAPE OF THE NIGHT SKY

The Maya envisioned the night sky as a reflection of their highland landscape. They considered the pathways formed by the Milky Way and the ecliptic as celestial rivers, which intersect twice, once near Gemini and once in Sagittarius. When the Three Hearthstones constellation in Orion is at its apex, it lies south of the center of the sky, and the Gemini/Milky Way crossroads lies north of center (fig. 14.1). At this time, the paths of the ecliptic and the Milky Way radiate out from this central crossroads to the four directions. This configuration echoes the four world roads leading out from the center of the world, and the four major rivers of central Guatemala. In my proposed model, the Gemini/Milky Way crossroads corresponds to the headwaters of the four rivers that originate just northwest of Lake Atitlán.

The Maya names for the stars along the river of the Milky Way are evidence that the northern section of the Milky Way was seen as a celestial counterpart to the northern Chixoy River. The southern Milky Way was identified with the southern Samalá River, while the eastern and western sections of the ecliptic were identified with the eastern Motagua River and western Grijalva River, respectively.

## THE MILKY WAY CROCODILE

The Milky Way was envisioned as a misty river with a crocodile floating in it. The "black rift" visible in the Milky Way was seen as the crocodile's mouth. When the crocodile of the Milky Way emerges from the eastern horizon, it comes out head-first like a crocodile lunging at its prey. When it sets, however, the crocodile's head is inverted, and it enters the western horizon on its back in the same way as the crocodile Zipacna entered the Meauan cave. Each time the black rift/crocodile mouth rises in the east, swims across the sky, and sets in the west, it visually represents Zipacna swimming along the Chixoy River to Meauan Mountain and inserting his

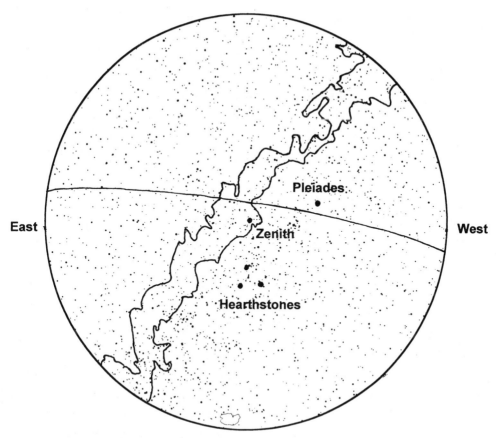

Figure 14.1. Sky chart of hearthstones constellation and Gemini crossroads

head and torso in the mountain. The defeat of Zipacna permanently established the position of this crocodile in the Milky Way river. The association of Zipacna (known as Sipac in this case) with the Milky Way is reflected in an Achi' version of the story, which indicates he did not stay under the Meauan cave, but went up to the sky (Shaw 1971:27). The text says he "went to where the sky meets the earth and entered under its edge" (the horizon).

In many images of the Milky Way crocodile, it has the ears and hoofs of a deer. No plausible explanation for these features has been proposed, but in light of the deer-hunting metaphors related to warfare and bride negotiation, it is conceivable that Zipacna was viewed as a deer warrior. This would explain why the contemporary version of Zipacna was also called *Yegua Achi'* (war captain).

The K'iche' refer to the area in the open mouth of the Milky Way crocodile as the road of the underworld (D. Tedlock 1985:358; 1996:354). Zipacna's mouth was specifically associated with Meauan Mountain. When the mouth of the Milky Way crocodile first rises in the east, its mouth extends from due east to northeast. When viewed from Lake Atitlán (the center of the world), the mouth indicates that the route to the underworld is northeast, precisely where Meauan Mountain and Alta Verapaz are in relation to Lake Atitlán.

The *Popol Vuh* states that when the hero twins rose as sun and moon, the Four Hundred Boys rose up as the Pleiades (Christenson 2003a:191). The Pleiades are found adjacent to the Milky Way, next to the Gemini crossroads (see fig. 14.1). The hut of the Four Hundred Boys has not been identified with any specific feature of the landscape, but it would have been located upstream from Meauan Mountain near the headwaters of the four major rivers. If one continues along the Milky Way a short distance south past the Pleiades, one encounters the stars of Alnitak, Saiph, and Rigel in Orion that are called the Three Hearthstones (D. Tedlock 1985:261; 1995: 119–20). These three stars are the celestial counterparts of the three Lake Atitlán volcanoes (Bruchez 1997).

The Four Hundred Boys first bury Zipacna in the center tree hole, and when he escapes, the hero twins arrange for Meauan Mountain to bury him. In both cases, he goes headfirst into his burial hole. Zipacna, then, has two aspects, which are reflected in Classic Period imagery: the Milky Way crocodile is either pictured at the base of the world tree (near the hut of the Four Hundred Boys) or swimming in the Milky Way river in the celestial scenes. The narrative on the Palenque Temple XIX plat-form mentions that GI performed two "decapitations" of the Milky Way crocodile, and Stuart (2005b) has suggested that these might be two aspects of one creature. I suspect the two decapitations refer to the two burials that were carried out in the process of Zipacna's defeat. The name of the first crocodile in the Temple XIX text includes the centipede jaws that indicate a hole in the earth, and in this context they likely refer to the world tree posthole.

## THE STARS OF ORION

The *Madrid Codex* illustrates the Three Hearthstones constellation of Orion clustered over a turtle; similarly, a celestial cartouche in Bonampak Room 2 shows a turtle with the three stars of Orion's belt on its back (Lounsbury 1982). Although the precise identifications are still debated, many of the stars in or around Orion have been identified with a turtle or a peccary (Milbrath 1999:268), and both creatures were manifestations of the creator grandfather. The Q'eqchi' refer to Orion as *aj q'inb'*, "the spinner," and *q'inleb' chahim*, "spindle star" (B. Tedlock 1992:38). The creator grandmother was the first deity to spin cotton, and one assumes that this took place at her house at the center of the world.

A Mesoamerican link between Orion and fire is reflected in the Aztec constel-lation called the fire-drill that is also located in Orion (Coe 1975). The connection between fire and Orion is also seen in the Orionid meteor showers, which appear to originate from the area between Orion and the Gemini/Milky Way crossroads. And, of course, the Orion Nebula resembles a smoking fire.

Between the Pleiades and Orion is Taurus with its dominant star Aldebaran. The Kaqchikel say that the cluster of stars around Aldebaran is a wedding party consisting of the newly wedded couple, godparents, and priest (Remington 1977:83). As noted in chapter 9, the bride and groom kneel on a mat beside the hearth and are knotted together during the marriage ceremony. The identification of these Taurus stars with the wedding party is consistent with the identification of the Orion stars as the three hearthstones and the center place.

The K'iche' refer to the three stars of Orion's belt as the three Marías (Remington 1977:83), as do the Ch'orti, Tzotzil, and Yucatec Maya (Sosa 1985:431; Vogt 1997; Milbrath 1999:39). As mentioned above, the Bonampak murals illustrate this constellation. One of the common traits of ancient and contemporary Mesoamerican cultures is the washing of the clothing of gods and saints before important ceremonies. In Santiago Atitlán, three flat washing-stones are kept in one of the community's cofradía houses (Mendelson 1957:246; 1959:58; O'Brien 1975:188; Christenson 2001:182, 189; personal communication). On the night of Holy Monday of Easter, the stones are put on the cofradía table and blessed with candles, incense, and prayer. At midnight, the stones are carried down to a cove on the shores of Lake Atitlán called the *r'muxux ruwachuliw,* "the navel of the earth," and placed in an east–west line in the water. Three male cofradía members wade into the water, bend over the rocks, and wash the clothing of the divinity Maximón. The wet clothing is put out to dry, and later the idol of Maximón is dressed in this clothing and taken to perform in the Easter ceremonies. The three washing stones are thought to be manifestations of the three female saints known as the three Marías (María Castellano, María Chiana, and María Luciana; Pieper 2002:91). The association of these goddesses with the center place ("the navel of the earth") again indicates that the stars of Orion were considered to be the center of the sky, that is, the place of duality in the heavens.

The narrative on the Palenque Temple of the Inscriptions tablets indicates that idols were dressed in the costumes of GI, GII, and GIII to represent these thunder-bolt deities during various Period Ending ceremonies (Carrasco 2005:72–73). Given the long tradition of washing the clothing of deities before dressing them, the custom of using three washing stones for Maximón's clothing likely derived from the washing stones used to launder the clothing of the three Heart of Sky thunder-bolt gods, who were also the three hearthstone gods.

## THE SOUTHERN CROSS AND THE QUADRIPARTITE BADGE MONSTER

While it is easy to see the mouth of the Milky Way crocodile because the black rift looks like the open mouth of a crocodile, the tip of the crocodile's tail is not so readily apparent. In many scenes, the Milky Way crocodile is seen arching over a ruler who is performing a ritual. If one assumes that this is the same view that can be seen in the night sky, then the crocodile mouth of the black rift would have to be setting

Figure 14.2. K1609 interior showing a chahk and the Milky Way crocodile (after Kerr}

on the western horizon, the body would be the section of the Milky Way that arches over the northern sky, and the tip of the tail would be the section that is emerging from the eastern horizon at the Gemini/Milky Way crossroads. Such an interpretation for the tip of the tail and the Quadripartite Badge Monster has been proposed (Schele 1992; Freidel, Schele, and Parker 1993), and in the episode of the Four Hundred Boys, the base of Zipacna's tail was identified with this crossroads location. As logical as this proposal may seem, I would like to suggest a different identification based on the rotation of the Milky Way: the Quadripartite Badge Monster was a symbol for the Southern Cross.

The Late Classic tripod vessel K1609 has a scene on its interior surface that illustrates a chahk standing in water (fig. 14.2). The head and foreleg of the Milky Way crocodile are seen emerging on the right side of the vessel, while the tip of the tail, marked by the Quadripartite Badge Monster, is seen on the left. In the area between the head and tail where the body would be expected are two star signs and a supernatural bird, but the body of the crocodile is not pictured.

The head of the Milky Way crocodile appears to be emerging from the horizon, not setting. So, what section of the Milky Way would the tail be in if this scene actually illustrates the rising of the crocodile's head on the eastern horizon? At this time, the crocodile's head ascends along the northeastern horizon, and the section of the Milky Way that represents the body of the crocodile is below the horizon. If we could follow the Milky Way below the horizon and keep following it under the earth until it emerged again above the horizon, we would come out on the southern horizon on the section of the Milky Way that is marked by the prominent constellation called the Southern Cross.

If, as I propose, the tip of the Milky Way crocodile was identified with the Southern Cross, then the entire head, body, and tail of the crocodile never appear in the night sky at the same time. The center of the crocodile, however, would be identified with the Gemini/Milky Way crossroads and the center of the world. A ruler standing under the body of a Milky Way crocodile is symbolically situated under the Gemini/Milky Way crossroads at the center of the world, and as discussed in previous chapters, the settings for rituals were often designed to replicate the center place.

Such an interpretation also works with the images of the world tree that have the head of Zipacna at their base. As noted, these ceremonial trees refer to the episode when Zipacna crawled into the posthole of the Four Hundred Boys, which was located adjacent to the Pleiades at the Gemini/Milky Way crossroads. In these images, the tip of Zipacna's tail is identified with the top of the tree. When Zipacna was in the posthole, the pole/tail would still have been visible above the ground. Similarly, when Zipacna entered the Meauan cave, his tail was still sticking out. When the part of the Milky Way that represents the head and body of the crocodile sets in the west, the tail of the crocodile should still be seen above the horizon. Similarly, when the Pleiades and crossroads set in the west, the part of the Milky Way that remains above the horizon should be the tail of Zipacna. At this time, the Milky Way is seen skirting the western horizon as it extends from the northwest down to the south horizon, where it is marked by the Southern Cross. Just past the Southern Cross is a small rift in the Milky Way that looks like a tail sticking up from the Milky Way river (fig. 14.3).

If the Quadripartite Badge Monster does represent the Southern Cross constellation, its appearance at the base of the tree on the Temple of the Inscriptions sarcophagus lid and Tablet of the Cross needs to be explained. Schele (1992; Freidel, Schele, and Parker 1993) has proposed that the Palenque sarcophagus lid was an image of the night sky. K'inich Janab' Pakal is seen on the sarcophagus lid emerging from the jaws of a centipede with the Quadripartite Badge Monster below (see fig. 8.7). In the sky behind K'inich Janab' Pakal is a stylized tree in the form of a cross with a double-headed serpent draped over the horizontal bar. When the Southern Cross is just above the horizon before it sets, the cleft in the Milky Way that I have identified

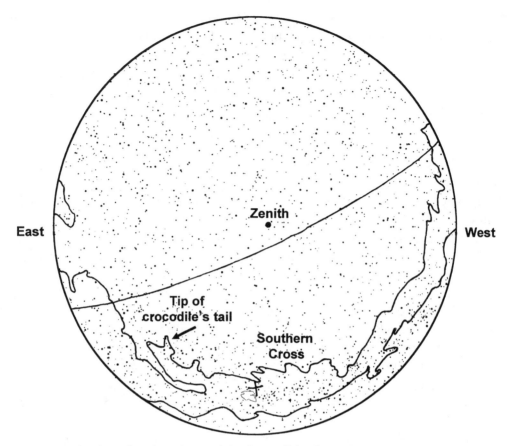

Figure 14.3. Sky chart of Southern Cross and tip of crocodile's tail

as the tail of the Milky Way crocodile is also just above the horizon (fig. 14.4). By the time the Southern Cross is setting, the cleft is in an upright position above the southern horizon and takes on the configuration of the centipede jaws.

Immediately above this cleft is the Sagittarius/Milky Way crossroads. A nearby constellation is identified as a cross by the K'iche'. It is called the Thieves' Cross and is formed by the Sagittarius stars Sigma, Phi, Delta, Gamma, Lambda, Epsilon, and Eta (Remington 1977:85; B. Tedlock 1985:83). The K'iche' identify the next constellation along the Milky Way, the constellation Aquila (Eagle), as Xik, "Hawk." At the start of the dry season in November, the Thieves' Cross is seen setting in the southwest in the early hours of the evening, and the Hawk constellation begins to set due west about half an hour later. The K'iche' say that the Hawk drops the Thieves' Cross into the sea at this time and this stops the rain. This belief implies that the Hawk is grasping the Thieves' Cross in its talons. Sitting on top of the Palenque tree is a bird of prey. It seems unlikely that these parallel concepts are a mere coincidence. I have proposed that the Palenque bird was equivalent to Wok, the collared forest falcon that was the messenger bird for Heart of Sky.

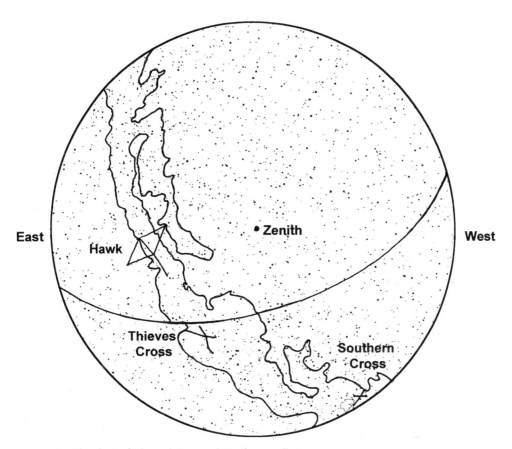

Figure 14.4. Sky chart of Thieves' Cross and Hawk constellations

The area of the night sky demarcated by the Three Hearthstones constellation, the Gemini/Milky Way crossroads, and the Pleiades was clearly associated with the center of the world and the place of duality. This area, however, was not the center or heart of the Milky Way. Pivot points are considered to be hearts in Maya thought (Christenson, personal communication), and the pivot point of the Milky Way is the Southern Cross. When the Southern Cross is positioned at its apex, the Milky Way rims the horizon from the summer-solstice sunrise point to the summer-solstice sunset point (see fig. 14.3). The descent of the Southern Cross coincides with the rising of the crocodile mouth of the Milky Way (see fig. 14.4). The K'iche' believe that the rising of the Southern Cross brings the rains (B. Tedlock 1985:81), and it is the mouth of the Milky Way crocodile that pours forth rain in many scenes.

## SIX SKY AND THE MILKY WAY

The inscriptions of Palenque state that the Quadripartite Badge Monster was the headdress of GI, who is described as the lord of the Six Sky place (see chapter 6).

The pib'naah sanctuary of the Temple of the Cross is called the Six Sky place, and the central icon on the sanctuary tablet is the cross tree and Quadripartite Badge Monster. Schele (1992; Freidel, Schele, and Parker 1993:76) argues that Six Sky was the name of this central icon, and that the Six Sky place was the Milky Way, but Stuart (2006) has recently noted that Six Sky does not directly name the central icon, and he doubts that Six Sky refers to the Milky Way. I am inclined to think that Six Sky does refer to the Milky Way in some way, considering that the northern Chixoy River was the model for the Milky Way river and that GI was said to be a god of the north. The Tablet of the Cross text refers to the making round or turning of the Six Sky. The verb *pet* is based on a numerical classifier used to describe round things, milpas, and plazas (Schele 1992:150). The Ch'olan word for spindle is *peteht,* and the verb *pet* appears to be a spindle whorl (MacLeod, in Schele 1992: 254). I speculate that the turning of the Six Sky may refer to setting the Milky Way in motion.

In the Central Mexican *Historia de los mexicanos por sus pinturas*, the sixth layer of the sky was a place of winds and storms (Coe 1975:8). In the mythology of the early twentieth century, Tozzer (1907:93, 155) recorded a Yucatec Maya belief that the sky was composed of seven layers and that in the sixth layer lived the Nukut-syumtsakob, "Great Father Lightning Bolts," or Yumtsakob, "Father Lightning Bolts." Tozzer also noted that the name Nukutsyumtsakob is similar to the Lacandon deity Nohotsakyum. As discussed in chapter 6, Nohotsakyum was associated with winds and hurricanes, and the Milky Way was his pathway. It is quite possible, then, that Six Sky is a reference to the Milky Way as being in the sixth layer of the sky.

An interesting phenomenon occurs in Lake Atitlán during volcanic eruptions and even small earthquakes. The movement of the earth creates a wave action across the lake, and as these waves encounter a large underwater landform in the waters off the southern shore, they form a whirlpool (Margaret Bruchez, personal communication). This whirlpool is depicted on the map in the *Relación Geográfica* of Atitlán (A.D. 1585; Orellana 1984, fig. 10). Bruchez (1997:52, 146) has insightfully equated the Lake Atitlán whirlpool with the transformation of Q'aq'awitz that is described in the *Annals of the Cakchiquels.* The leader Q'aq'awitz, "fire mountain," enters Lake Atitlán and changes himself into Sutz'ukumatz, "cloud serpent." "And when this Q'aq'awitz went it was truly frightening when he entered the water, he transformed into Cloud Serpent and the surface of the lake became suddenly black, suddenly a storm rose up, a howling whirlwind on the surface of the lake" (Akkeren 2000:165).

The turbulent water illustrated on the Relación Geográfica map has the same turbulent water curl found in the eyes of GI, god of storms and lightning. It seems likely, given the proximity of the whirlpool to the southern shore, that Sutz'ukumatz, "cloud serpent," was an aspect of this storm god, and that the Lake Atitlán whirl-pool was a manifestation of him. The description of Q'aq'awitz as a cloud serpent and the turning of the water suggests the pivoting of the Southern Cross around the southern pole that visually brings the Milky Way river into the sky. In Central

Mexican mythology, Mixcoatl is identified with the Milky Way, and his name literally means cloud serpent.

As discussed in previous chapters, the characteristics of One Ixim/One Hunahpu and his brother Seven Ajaw/Seven Hunahpu are also highly reminiscent of the Mexican god Quetzalcoatl and his brother Tezcatlipoca, who were also closely identified with Mixcoatl. Some sources indicate that these two brothers were the sons of the creator grandparents; they battled each other in many episodes, much like One Hunahpu and Seven Hunahpu competed against each other in the ballgame; and they were instrumental in creating the world and the Milky Way. In my reconstruction of the sacred landscape found in the *Popol Vuh*, the brothers One Hunahpu and Seven Hunahpu traveled from Lake Atitlán to the Nim Xob' Karchaj ballcourt in Alta Verapaz. A logical route for this journey would have been to follow the Chixoy River/Milky Way river north to this region. This journey may be analogous to the belief expressed in the *Historia de los mexicanos por sus pinturas* that the brothers Quetzalcoatl and Tezcatlipoca walked across the sky and created the Milky Way. I am not suggesting that the two sets of brothers were directly parallel, but rather that they evolved out of the same ancient core beliefs.

## The Dry and Wet Season Trees

I propose that the center world tree had two forms: one associated with the dry season and the Gemini/Milky Way crossroads, and the other identified with the wet season and the Sagittarius/Milky Way crossroads. The Gemini/Milky Way crossroads rises at the summer-solstice sunrise position, arcs across the northern sky, reaches its apex just north of the center of the sky, and then sets at the summer-solstice sunset position. When the Gemini/Milky Way crossroads is seen rising at the northeast corner of the quadrilateral world, the Sagittarius/Milky Way crossroads is positioned at the southwest corner with the setting sun. At midnight, when the Gemini/Milky Way crossroads is at its apex, the Three Hearthstones constellation is just to the south. At dawn, when the Gemini/Milky Way crossroads is setting at the northwest corner of the world, the Sagittarius/Milky Way crossroads is rising at the southeast corner with the sun. On such a night, these two celestial crossroads demarcate the five points of the quadrilateral world just as the world trees do.

During the Preclassic Period, the rising at sunset of the Gemini/Milky Way crossroads occurred in mid-November, but, due to precession, by the Classic Period it occurred around the end of November. Therefore, from Preclassic to Classic times, the sunset rising of the Gemini/Milky Way crossroads marked the approximate beginning of the dry season.

Six months later, at the beginning of the wet season, the rising and setting times of the Gemini/Milky Way crossroads and Sagittarius/Milky Way crossroads are reversed. In a general sense, the rising of the Sagittarius/Milky Way crossroads at sunset marks the beginning of the intense downpours of the rainy season. When the Sagittarius/Milky crossroads is at its apex position at midnight, the tip of the black rift/crocodile mouth of the Milky Way is near the zenith position. The Milky Way crocodile is most often illustrated with torrents of rain falling from its mouth. The Milky Way crocodile visually brings the rain at this time of year.

Taube (2005) has identified several examples of One Ixim as a tree with a crocodile mouth at its base. He also notes that many examples of One Ixim's name are followed by the word *ayiin,* "crocodile." He is so named on vessel K1892, which illustrates One Ixim at the center of the world. These examples demonstrate that the tree pole that was placed in Zipacna's burial hole, as described in the *Popol Vuh,* was a manifestation of One Ixim. When the Gemini/Milky Way crossroads was at its apex position near the center of the sky, it replicated the place where the center world tree was erected. As discussed above, the Palenque sarcophagus lid also illustrates the Sagittarius/Milky Way tree cross as a manifestation of One Ixim.

In the Yucatec Maya tree festivals described in chapter 11, the center tree is transformed into a flowering and then fruiting ceiba. I suggest that this represents the change of the center tree of the dry season into the center tree of the wet season, and that this dry season ceremony brought forth the rain for the coming season. The celestial counterpart of this event was seen in the night sky when the tree of the Gemini/Milky Way crossroads of the dry season is replaced with the tree of the Sagittarius/Milky Way crossroads of the wet season.

## The Transformation of the Corner Tree into the Center Tree

In the tree ceremonies practiced in highland Guatemala and northern Yucatan, the tree is brought from the wild into the center of the community. The tree of the Dance of the Voladores ceremony has been identified with the tree of Zipacna and the tree manifestation of One Ixim. In the various accounts of this ceremony, the tree was brought from a sacred mountain, stripped of its foliage, and erected at the center of the world. Monkey imitators played a prominent role in its procurement and preparation. The choice of tree used in the ceremony today is usually limited to pine because of highland deforestation. The participation of the monkey imitators, however, suggests that the tree was originally the *Q'an Te',* "yellow tree" (*Gliricidia sepium,* also known as "madre de cacao") of the monkey twins. Oviedo describes the uses of *G. sepium* in Nicaragua:

> they plant between the [cacao] trees other trees which the Indians call yaguaguyt and the Christians madera negra, which grow almost twice as high as the cacao trees and protect them from the sun, and they prune the branches to make them grow straight. These trees are of such a nature they live much longer than the cacao trees and never decay; it is one of the strongest woods known. The madera negra has very beautiful flowers, pink and white, in bunches, and they have a

> good odor . . . they never shed their leaves and are trees that the Indians value for making hedges about their lands, and for wood for their houses or huts, they say that it never decays. (Standley 1923:483)

Oviedo goes on to describe how he tore down a sacrificial temple and removed the *G. sepium* corner posts to make himself a horse stable. He notes that despite being over a hundred years old, the wood of the temple was still as green and fresh as if it had just been cut, and that the indigenous people believed it was imperishable. The Maya also employed this tree as corner posts in their buildings and as a shade tree for cacao; hence its common indigenous name, mother of cacao (Steggerda 1941:206).

Several aspects of *G. sepium* make it suitable as a world tree. Its wood is so dense that it frequently breaks axes, and it does not shed its leaves all at once, so it has the appearance of eternal strength and life. The world trees defined the borders of the quadrilateral world and divided supernatural space from human space. The branches of *G. sepium* were planted as fences, that is, boundary markers. These planted branches rooted and grew into new trees. *G. sepium* is used for corner posts in Maya houses because of its strength and longevity. There are many metaphors where the world is described as a house and the sky as its roof. According to Landa, the Yucatec Maya believed that the Bakabs held up the sky—which is reminiscent of the corner posts of the house that hold up its roof. In Ch'ol, the name for *G. sepium* is *chante'*—literally "sky tree" (Aulie and Aulie 1978:47).

How do we reconcile the use of *G. sepium* as a center tree with the many sources that indicate that the center tree was a ceiba? I believe the solution to this dilemma lies in the transformational aspect of the tree ceremony. When the *G. sepium* corner tree was brought from the wild into the center of town, stripped of its branches and bark, and re-erected, it ceased to be a *G. sepium* corner tree and became a center tree, that is, a ceiba.

In the same manner, the Gemini/Milky Way crossroads marked the northeast corner of the quadrilateral world when it rose on the horizon, but it then moved to the apex, where it marked the center of the sky. The association of the northeast with the tree of the monkey twins is seen in the Momostenango dance-costume stories where the costumes are first procured from a deity living in a large rock, *C'oy Abaj, or* "spider monkey stone," northeast of the town (Cook 1981:143; 2000). The *Popol Vuh* seems to allude to the transformation of *G. sepium* into a ceiba when it states that the tree began to grow and swell when the monkey twins reached the top. As noted in chapter 4, the ceiba is known for its rapid growth and swollen trunk. The hero twins tell One Batz and One Chouen that if they want to get down from the tree, they should undo their loincloths and let the long ends hang down. Had the monkey twins been clever, they could have lowered themselves down from the tree by their loincloths as the Voladores lower themselves down the rope.

## The Ecliptic River of One Moon/Lady Blood

The journey of the waxing-moon goddess Lady Blood from the underworld across the surface of the earth to the household of One Hunahpu represented the path of the western ecliptic (see chapter 10). In my model of the night sky, the western ecliptic was envisioned to be parallel to the Grijalva River. If this interpretation is correct, then Lady Blood must have exited the underworld somewhere along the Grijalva River and followed it along the continental divide and down to Lake Atitlán. Because Paxil Mountain is located on the Grijalva River system, I suspect that Lady Blood emerged from the underworld near this mountain. Another possibility would be the female Volcán Tajumulco. The waters on the northeast slopes of this mountain also flow into the Grijalva system.

## Seven Macaw and the Canícula

The defeat of Seven Macaw by the hero twins appears to be related to the phenomenon of the canícula. A brief overview of this episode is in order. During the era of the wooden people, Seven Macaw (Wuqub' Kaqix) declares himself to be both the sun and moon:

> "I am great. I dwell above the heads of the people who have been framed and shaped. I am their sun. I am also their light. And I am also their moon. Then be it so. Great is my brightness. By the brilliance of my silver and gold I light the walkways and pathways of the people. My eyes sparkle with glittering blue/green jewels. My teeth as well are jade stones, as brilliant as the face of the sky. This, my beak, shines brightly far into the distance like the moon. My throne is gold and silver. When I go forth from my throne, I brighten the face of the earth. Thus I am the sun. I am the moon as well for those who are born in the light, those who are begotten in the light. Then be it so. My vision reaches far," said Seven Macaw. Now Seven Macaw was not truly the sun, but he puffed himself up in this way because of his plumage and his gold and his silver. His vision did not reach beyond where he sat. It did not really reach everywhere beneath the sky. (Christenson 2003a:92–93)

Seven Macaw's declaration that he is both sun and moon is a direct challenge to the authority of the hero twins, for these roles belong to them. Heart of Sky sends the hero twins to defeat Seven Macaw. Their first plan is to go to the nance tree where Seven Macaw lands each day to eat fruit, and to shoot him with their blowguns. From their hiding place in the foliage of the tree, the hero twins wait for Seven Macaw. When he lands in the top of the tree, Hunahpu shoots him in the mouth, and Seven Macaw falls to the ground with a broken jaw. Still, Seven Macaw is not defeated, for when Hunahpu tries to grab him, Seven Macaw rips Hunahpu's arm from its socket. With the arm in his claws, he flies away to his home and deposits the arm over his fire. Seven Macaw sits on his throne moaning in pain from his broken jaw and damaged teeth.

After this setback, the hero twins devise a new plan involving the animal manifestations of their grandparents, Great White Peccary and Great White Coati. These two supernatural animals are healers who specialize in setting bones and curing toothaches and eye ailments. Knowing that Seven Macaw will require someone to cure the pain in his jaw and teeth, the hero twins have their grandparents go to Seven Macaw and offer to treat him. Although he is reluctant to surrender his finery, they convince Seven Macaw that he has to have the green jewels in his teeth removed to stop the pain. As a substitute, they replace them with white grains of maize. Then they treat his eyes by removing the precious metal:

> Thus the basis for his pride was completely taken away according to the plans of Hunahpu and Xbalanque. When at length Seven Macaw died, Hunahpu retrieved his arm. Then also Chimalmat died, the wife of Seven Macaw. Thus the wealth of Seven Macaw was lost, for the healers took it away—the jewels, the precious stones, and all that which had made him proud here upon the face of the earth. It was truly the enchanted Grandmother and the enchanted Grandfather that did it. Then the boys retrieved their arm and implanted it back into its socket, making it whole again. They had desired the death of Seven Macaw, and they were able to do it. For they saw pride as evil and went to do these things according to the word of Heart of Sky. (Christenson 2003a:100)

The term *kaqix* in Seven Macaw's name refers specifically to a scarlet macaw (*Ara macao*), which has a white beak, a distinctive patch of white feathers around its eye, and dramatic red feathers on its head, breast, shoulders, and tail. The glyph that represents the more common name for the macaw, *mo'*, is a macaw with its distinctive hooked beak in profile. The eye is highlighted by a circle of jade beads that is highly reminiscent of Seven Macaw's eyes that sparkled with glittering blue/green jewels.

Although Seven Macaw was neither the sun nor the moon, he did have a celestial identification. As noted by Dennis Tedlock (1985:360), *wukub cakix* is listed in the *Léxico médico quiché-español* as a name for the seven bright stars of Ursa Major (the Big Dipper). Tedlock (1985:330) identifies Seven Macaw's wife Chimalmat with Ursa Minor (the Little Dipper), which is called *chimal ek,* "shield stars" (Lamb 1981:243). Both these constellations have long "tails" like a flying macaw.

The *Popol Vuh* says that Seven Macaw puffed himself up in the days and months preceding the first rising of the sun. The Big Dipper rises after sunset in the northeast during the months preceding the April–May zenith passage date. The *Popol Vuh* also says that despite Seven Macaw's claim that he was both the sun and the moon, the vision of Seven Macaw did not reach beyond where he sat on his throne, and the Big Dipper rises and sets in a semicircle around the celestial north pole. The two brightest stars of the Little Dipper briefly set, but the majority of the constellation rotates around the north pole and is visible on any given night. As the house is the domain of women, it seems safe to assume that Chimalmat/Little Dipper marked the location of Seven Macaw's house and throne. It also seems safe to assume that their house was specifically the area around Polaris, as this star marks the end of Chimalmat's tail. In other words, she never flies farther than the yard of her house.

The relationship between the Seven Macaw and Chimalmat constellations is significant. When the Seven Macaw constellation rises, the body of the bird ascends first, like a bird flying up into the sky. As Seven Macaw flies across the sky, the Chimalmat bird follows. Macaws are monogamous birds that mate for life and that are most frequently seen flying in pairs. The paths of these two constellations are like two macaws flying together. The Lacandon identify the Little Dipper as a crocodile (Bruce, Robles, and Ramos 1971:15). While this seems to contradict the macaw identification, Chimalmat's son, Zipacna, had a crocodile form. A simple explanation is that Chimalmat was like the other supernatural beings who had more than one animal manifestation.

The *Popol Vuh* indicates that Seven Macaw acted according to his own desires before the face of Heart of Sky, and that this was an evil thing (Christenson 2003a: 95, 100). I have argued that the Quadripartite Badge Monster—the headdress of GI/Heart of Sky—was identified with the Southern Cross. The K'iche' refer to the stars Acrux of the Southern Cross and Polaris of Ursa Minor as corner stars that stand in opposition to each other (B. Tedlock 1985:86; 1992:29). When Acrux is at its apex and the Southern Cross stands erect in the southern sky, the "body" of Seven Macaw (Ursa Major) is just past its apex in the northern sky. In other words, the Southern Cross and Ursa Major stand in opposition to one another on a north–south axis. At this moment, Seven Macaw is before the face of Heart of Sky.

There is a relationship between macaws and droughts that may explain Seven Macaw's identification with the Big Dipper. Like quetzal feathers, the red plumes of the macaw were held in high regard and were extensively traded and given in tribute. To meet this high demand, macaws were domesticated and their feathers harvested by the Maya and other Mesoamerican groups. The red feathers of the macaw were associated with the sun in Central Mexico (Pohl 1994). A personal name found in Classic Period inscriptions is *tajal mo'*, "torch-like macaw" (Houston, Robertson, and Stuart 2001:35), and in the *Popol Vuh*, macaw feathers are identified with the fire of a torch. In the first test One Death and Seven Death give the hero twins, the twins are told that they must burn their torch all night in the House of Darkness and in the morning return it unused. To fool the underworld lords into thinking that the torch is burning, they place the red tail feathers of a macaw on the end of it. Such feather torches are also illustrated on *Dresden Codex* 45c. A macaw carrying burning torches is shown on *Dresden Codex* 40b, where it has long been associated with the concept of drought (Kelley 1976:171). This is not inconsistent with the macaw's identification with the fire of the sun, for the typical characteristics of a drought are a burning sun in a cloudless sky.

At sunset in late July during the Classic Period, Seven Macaw was seen plunging headfirst toward the northwest horizon, and he did not completely reappear in the night sky until mid-September, when he rose in the predawn sky. The disappearance of Seven Macaw from the night sky generally paralleled the period of the canícula, which lasts from the end of July to mid-September. I believe that the defeat of Seven Macaw took away his power to cause a prolonged drought during the canícula.

## XULU AND PAQAM AND THE PADDLER GODS

An old pair of diviners in the *Popol Vuh* are named Xulu (Descended) and Paqam (Ascended). They are given the title *eta'manel,* "sages," which is also used to describe the creator grandparents and other diviners. Christenson (2003a:177) adds that colonial sources also describe *xulu* as "[spirit] familiars appearing alongside rivers" and *ah xulu* as a diviner. When the hero twins realize that the lords of death are planning to kill them by pushing them into the pit oven, they devise a plan so that they may be resurrected later. They have to make sure that the death lords dispose of their bones in a manner that would allow for resurrection. Knowing that the death lords will consult Xulu and Paqam about the best means of getting rid of their remains, the hero twins summon the two diviners and tell them to have their bones ground like corn into a fine powder and then sprinkled on the river that "winds among the small and great mountains" (Christenson 2003a:177–78). It is unclear in which river the bones of the hero twins were scattered, but the description implies that it was on the surface of the earth; and of the four major rivers, the Chixoy winds back and forth the most.

In Classic Period art, a pair of old male deities is also associated with a river. They were initially nicknamed the Paddler Gods because they are seen paddling a canoe on a series of bone carvings from Tikal Burial 116 (Freidel, Schele, and Parker 1993:90). They are frequently pictured together, and they are named as a pair in hieroglyphic texts. The first old deity has the attributes of GIII, including his jaguar characteristics and the fire cord over his nose. The other has a stingray spine through his nose, and he often wears a headdress in the form of a *xook,* "shark." The close association of this latter Paddler God with stingray spines can be seen in an effigy stingray spine in the Peabody Museum collection. The caption text on this stingray spine identifies it as belonging to him (Stuart, Houston, and Robertson 1999, vol. 2, 46).

The celestial nature of the paddlers is indicated by their appearance in the sky on a number of monuments where they cling to S-shaped scrolls used to designate clouds and mist. They are consistently identified as lords of a place called Na Ho Chan, which has been translated as First Five Sky. On Jimbal Stela 1, they are called chahks, "thunderbolts"; on Sacul Stela 1, they carry a title of office represented by a supernatural bird wearing a plain headband (Stuart 2006). This headband bird also represents the day name *Men.* In the highland calendars, *Men* is called *Tz'ikin,* which is a general word for bird in most Mayan languages. No satisfactory decipherment of the headband-bird sign has been established, but the office was also held by secondary lords who were dressed in the accoutrements of Maya priests (Stuart 2005b; Zender 2005).

A clue to the function of the headband-bird office may be found on a wooden box from the Tortuguero region (Coe 1974; Stuart 2005b). This box was used to hold stingray spines, and the text carved on it refers to a priest-diviner of Tortuguero who acquired the headband-bird office in A.D. 680. One of the duties of a Maya priest was to draw blood from various parts of his body as an offering to the gods, and the primary tools used to perforate the skin were stingray spines. In light of the stingray-spine attribute of one of the paddlers, we may deduce that one of the duties of the headband-bird office was related to blood sacrifice using stingray spines (Stuart 2005b).

Like many of the gods, the paddlers' names are often represented by their portraits, but these portraits can be replaced with two paddle cartouches with infixed *k'in* and *ak'bal* signs. The pairing of day and night signs has been interpreted to mean that they represent the opposition of day and night, that they are a metaphor for a day and a night, or that they represent twilight (MacLeod, in Schele 1992:257–58; Schele and Mathews 1998:414; Wichmann 2004). In the context of the Distance Number Introductory Glyph, day and night signs are paired to convey the concept of complementary opposition (Stuart 2003b), and it may be that the *k'in* and *ak'bal* signs in the paddle cartouches have a similar function. What is interesting about the paddle cartouches is that they indicate the close association that these two deities had with their canoe, and by extension, the river. Because both pairs of diviner priests—Xulu and Paqam and the Paddler Gods—were closely associated with rivers, I suggest that they were parallel deities.

## The River of the Paddler Gods

On one of the bones (MT 38A) from Tikal Burial 116, the Paddler Gods are positioned at the bow and stern of a dugout canoe paddling along a river. One Ixim and four supernatural animals are their passengers. One Ixim and the monkey behind him hold their hands to their foreheads in a gesture directly associated on vessel K6547 with mourning (Schele and Mathews 1998:123; Taube 2004:81). On bones MT 38C and MT 38D, the bow of the canoe is shown sinking below the water as though going through rapids. The Old Stingray God has moved to the center of the canoe, and the order of the passengers has changed.

Schele (1992; Freidel, Schele, and Parker 1993:89–91) argues that the canoe was a manifestation of the Milky Way, and she equates it with the section of the Milky Way from the black rift/crocodile mouth to the Gemini/Milky Way crossroads. Although I find the reasons for this specific identification questionable, there is some evidence to place the canoe of the paddlers in the vicinity of the constellation Cassiopeia. The prominent stars of Cassiopeia form a distinctive zigzag line along the Milky Way, midway between the head of the crocodile and the Gemini/Milky Way crossroads. When the head of the crocodile is entering the western horizon, Cassiopeia is at its apex position in the northern sky. The constellation Perseus is immediately to the east on the Milky Way. As noted, the Old Jaguar Paddler wears the attributes of GIII, who was a meteor god, and like GIII, he was also thought to be a thunderbolt. The caption text on the Tikal bones refers to a "star over earth" sign that Stuart has suggested represents a meteor shower. Single meteors can happen at any time of the day or night, and meteor showers occur on a regular basis throughout the year. The most dramatic meteor showers, which occur in mid-August, are called the Perseids because they appear to be generated from the tip of the Perseus constellation closest to Cassiopeia. Given the association of the Old Jaguar Paddler with meteors, I speculate that the canoe of the paddlers was located near Cassiopeia on the Milky Way river. The canoe of the Paddler Gods brings to mind the Xmaben, "canoe," location in the center of the sky where the bees fly to obtain their honey. I further speculate that the scenes showing the Paddler Gods transporting One Ixim represent a journey One Ixim took on the Chixoy River. The following chapter examines this voyage.

# 15

# THE CORE MYTH

A series of mythological events formed the core creation story of the ancient Maya. The central figures of this mythology were One Ixim/One Hunahpu and his wife Ixik/Lady Bone Water in their roles as the ultimate providers of maize. The details of the core myth narrated in the *Popol Vuh* are fleshed out in this chapter by drawing on relevant Classic Period sources and ethnographic stories.

## TIME FRAME OF THE CORE MYTH

The *Popol Vuh* does not present all its mythological events in chronological order. The story begins with the various stages of creation, starting with the formation of the earth, the creation of the plants and animals, and the creation and destruction of the mud people and wooden people. The narrative then goes back in time to discuss the hero twins' defeat of Seven Macaw and his sons during the era of the wooden people. At the end of this episode, the narrative regresses to an even earlier time before the era of the wooden people and discusses the early life of One Hunahpu and his brother Seven Hunahpu at their household at the center of the world. It continues with their journey to the underworld, their death, the impregnation of Lady Blood, her escape from the underworld and journey to One Hunahpu's household, and the birth of her sons, the hero twins.

The focus then shifts to the exploits of the hero twins: their subordination of their older brothers, the making of their cornfield, their ball playing, the planting of the twin ears of corn in their house, their journey to the underworld, their ordeals and trials leading to their victory over One Death and Seven Death, and their subjugation of the secondary lords, vassals, and servants of these two underworld lords. The story then explains that the twin ears of corn that the hero twins planted in their house withered when they were burned in the oven, but that this corn came to life again when the hero twins defeated the underworld lords. This long series of events concludes with the adornment of One Hunahpu, the statement that his heart was left at the Crushing Ballcourt, the rising of the hero twins as the sun and full moon, and the rising of the Four Hundred Boys as the Pleiades.

The narrative again regresses and describes the creation of humans from corn, which occurred before Hunahpu and Xbalanque rose up as the sun and full moon:

> This, then, is the beginning of the conception of humanity, when that which would become the flesh of mankind was sought. Then spoke they who are called She Who Has Borne Children and He Who Has Begotten Sons, the Framer and the Shaper, Sovereign and Quetzal Serpent: "The dawn approaches, and our work is not successfully completed. A provider and a sustainer have yet to appear—a child of light, a son of light. Humanity has yet to appear to populate the face of the earth," they said. Thus they gathered together and joined their thoughts in the darkness, in the night. They searched and they sifted. Here they thought and they pondered. Their thoughts came forth bright and clear. They discovered and established that which would become the flesh of humanity. This took place just a little before the appearance of the sun, moon, and stars above the heads of the Framer and the Shaper. (Christenson 2003a:192)

The *Popol Vuh* indicates that after the first men and their wives were created from the corn of Paxil Mountain, they began to multiply and form ethnic groups. Some of the groups decided to search for a guardian deity, and after hearing of the city of Tulan, they journeyed there and acquired their patron gods. From Tulan, they embarked on long voyages to find a place to establish their own communities. These initial events occurred in darkness, for the sun had yet to rise. As they prepared for dawn, they watched the east for the rising of the morning star that would herald this event:

> Then they fasted and cried out in prayer. They fixed their eyes firmly on their dawn, looking there to the East. They watched closely for the Morning Star, the Great Star that gives its light at the birth of the sun. . . . Yet they fixed their eyes on the dawn, looking steadfastly for the coming forth of the sun. They occupied themselves in looking for the Great Star, called Icoquih, which appears first before the birth of the sun. The face of this Green Morning Star always appears at the coming forth of the sun. . . . It was there that they came to await the dawn. They would look for the first appearance of the star that precedes the face of the sun when it is born. (Christenson 2003a:207–21)

Finally, after the various tribes had established their towns and placed their patron gods in the landscape, they went to the tops of their respective sacred mountains to await the rising of the sun:

This therefore is the dawn, the appearance of the sun, moon, and stars. Greatly they rejoiced, Balam Quitze, Balam Acab, Mahucutah, and Iqui Balam, when they saw the Morning Star. It came forth glittering before the face of the sun. . . . The bloodletters and sacrificers were kneeling. They greatly rejoiced along with the bloodletters and sacrificers of the Tamub and the Ilocab, along with the Rabinals and the Cakchiquels, the Ah Tziquinahas and the Tuhalhas, the Uchabahas and the Quibahas, the Ah Batenas and the Yaqui Tepeus. However many nations there are today, innumerable people, they all had but one dawn. (Christenson 2003a:228–29)

In summary, the adventures of One Hunahpu and his hero-twin sons begin before the era of the wooden people, continue through that era, and end after the creation of the corn people.

Many Classic Period scenes show that One Ixim and his hero-twin sons performed various actions together that must have occurred after his dressing scene but before the hero twins became the sun and moon. These include a trip in a canoe and actions at the center of the world. Researchers have made numerous attempts to piece together a cohesive story from these scenes to explain the post-adornment actions of One Ixim (Robicsek and Hales 1981:149; Taube 1985, 2004; Coe 1989; Schele 1992; Freidel, Schele, and Parker 1993; Quenon and Le Fort 1997; Schele and Mathews 1998:122–23; Bassie-Sweet 2002; Miller and Martin 2004:52; Saturno, Taube, and Stuart 2005). Quenon and Le Fort (1997) propose that the One Ixim scenes follow a chronological sequence of four events: the rebirth of One Ixim from a serpent or water environment, the dressing of One Ixim in his costume, a canoe journey, and his resurrection at the center of the turtle shell.

Schele and others (1992; Freidel, Schele, and Parker 1993:92; Schele and Mathews 1998:116) have proposed that the scenes of One Ixim emerging from the turtle shell were celestial events that occurred at the Three Hearthstones constellation, and that the canoe scenes show One Ixim being taken from the underworld along the Milky Way so that he could be reborn from the turtle shell and create the new universe. Taube (1985, 1986, 2003, 2005; Saturno, Taube, and Stuart 2005) also characterizes these scenes as the resurrection of One Ixim, but he argues that One Ixim's ascent was associated with the passage of the sun across the sky. He proposes that One Ixim left his burial place in the underworld through a cave passageway that emerged on the surface of the earth on a "Flower Mountain." Taube argues that this mountain served both as an abode for gods and ancestors and as a means of ascending along the path of the sun into the sky. He situates Flower Mountain in the east but also calls it the "pivotal world axis," which suggests that he also identifies it with the world center. He compares "Flower Mountain" to Paxil Mountain of the *Popol Vuh*, Sustenance Mountain of Central Mexican mythology, and the Tz'utujil cave of Paq'alib'al.

This chapter is a review of the One Ixim scenes in light of the sacred landscape discussed in chapters 13 and 14. I present evidence that One Ixim/One Hunahpu's adornment occurred at Meauan Mountain, and that this adornment included a bathing ritual with the goddesses of the mountain. I propose that following this event, One Ixim/One Hunahpu obtained water from Meauan Mountain and corn seeds from Paxil Mountain, and delivered them to the center of the world at Lake Atitlán. He gave some of these seeds and water to his mother, who was in her house at the center of the world, to make the flesh and blood of the first humans. After these humans had populated the world, he planted the remaining seeds at the center corn mound to create the first cornfield of the new era.

The field that One Ixim/One Hunahpu planted was the cornfield his sons the hero twins created before their departure to the underworld; and after it was planted, the hero twins rose as the sun and full moon to begin the celestial cycles of the new era. I also propose that the morning star the first humans saw before the rising of the sun and full moon was a manifestation of the resurrected One Ixim/One Hunahpu.

## The Emergence of One Ixim

One Ixim is seen emerging from the mouth of a serpent on vessel K3033 in the reclining pose associated with newborn babies (Stuart, Houston, and Robertson 1999; Houston and Taube 2000:281). One Ixim is also illustrated in this reclining manner on K2723 and a vessel from Calakmul (Schmidt, de la Garza, and Nalda 1998:294–95, 448). On these latter vessels, One Ixim is positioned above a cleft skull with a T533 sign in its forehead. T533 is believed to refer to some kind of seed or egg, or perhaps a place name (Martin 2004:6). On vessel K1892, One Ixim is juxtaposed with a skull, and on BOD vessel 116, he sprouts from a skull (see figs. 8.2, 8.6). On the Palenque sarcophagus lid, K'inich Janab' Pakal in the guise of One Ixim emerges from the centipede jaws in the birth pose (see fig. 8.7). Where and when these various events occurred has been the subject of debate. A review of these scenes will demonstrate that they do not all represent the same moment in time.

## The Adornment of One Ixim

In the first scene on K1004, Yax Bolon is shown crouching with a huge pottery bowl over his head (fig. 15.1). As Coe (1989) convincingly argues, the bowl contains the head of One Ixim and his jade jewelry, and the action is thematically related to the adornment of One Hunahpu by the hero twins. To the left of the head of One Ixim is a bundle shape similar to the bundles used to contain idols such as those depicted on K1081, K1382, K1645, K1813, K3716, K6754, and K7838. These god figures, which have been described as "mummy bundles," are placed on thrones inside a temple. They are like the skulls of important Postclassic lords that were covered in

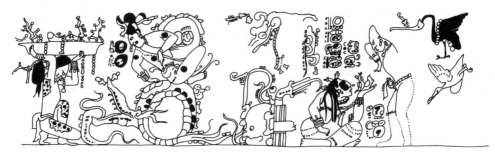

Figure 15.1. Yax Bolon (*left*) carrying dish with the remains of his father, One Ixim, K1004 (after Kerr and Schele)

Figure 15.2. One Ixim (*left*) carrying water gourd and corn seed bag, K731 (after Kerr)

resin, sculpted to look like the living lord, and then placed in the temple and venerated. The mummy bundles are in a seated position, while the One Ixim bundle is in a reclining position.

An assortment of white cotton bundles or bark-cloth bundles appears in other mythological and historical scenes (Taube 1985:178). Relic bundles containing symbols of power or the remains and paraphernalia of deities and cultural heroes are common in Mesoamerica (Pohl and Byland 1996; Christenson 2001:169–77; 2003a:234–35, 253–55; 2005; Ringle 2004).

On K1004, One Ajaw sits on a swirling serpent and has a sack slung over his right shoulder (fig. 15.1). He also carries this sack in several other scenes, while One Ixim carries it on K731 and K3033 (figs. 15.2, 15.3). On K731, the sack is shown in a cutaway fashion to reveal that it contains corn seeds (Taube 1985:177). The Maya usually carry idols and loads on their backs, but the sack is carried over the shoulder in these scenes, as a corn-seed bag is carried while planting.

In addition to the corn-seed bag, the hero twins and One Ixim are often shown carrying the type of gourd the Maya use to carry water (Saturno, Taube, and Stuart 2005). One Ixim carries the gourd along with the corn sack on K731, as does One Ajaw on K6979 (figs. 15.2, 15.4).

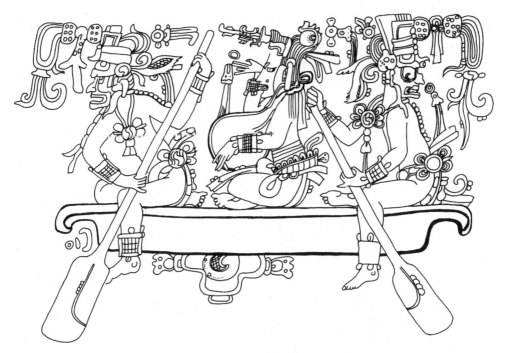

Figure 15.3. One Ixim (*center*) carrying corn seed bag, K3033 (after Kerr)

On another vessel, K512, One Ixim and the hero twins are seated in front of a water-related god and goddess. The gourd is positioned at the feet of One Ajaw, while the corn sack is held by Yax Bolon. The caption text between One Ixim and the water god has been deciphered as *yax tzuk tu kab' tu ch'een k'uh,* "it is the first gourd in the earth, in the cave of the gods" (Saturno, Taube, and Stuart 2005:33). The term *tzuk* refers to water bottles made from vine gourds. The relevance of the corn sack and water gourd will be discussed below.

### ENTERING THE WATER, ENTERING THE ROAD

In the second scene on K1004 (see fig. 15.1), the caption text states that on *13 Ok 8 Sip,* One Ixim entered the water (*och ha'*; Stuart 1998). This block of text ends with a glyph that means "it happened at," but the area to the right where the place glyph would have been is heavily eroded. Still visible is an image of One Ixim standing over a seated goddess who holds up what appears to be One Ixim's shell and xook-monster belt ornament. Two water birds that are suggestive of a water location are pictured behind One Ixim.

How One Ixim was revived from a bundled effigy figure and pile of jewelry into a functioning being is not entirely clear, but the dressing of a deity image is thought to bring the deity to life, and numerous other pottery scenes illustrate One Ixim in the process of donning his jade and quetzal-feather accoutrements with the

Figure 15.4. One Ixim "entering the water," K6979 (after Kerr)

assistance of various goddesses. In the dressing scene on K626, One Ixim is flanked on the left by his spider-monkey son (fig. 15.5). The monkey twins were in charge of the dance costumes, and dancing is another method of bringing life to the dead (McArthur 1977; Christenson 2001). One Ixim and the goddesses are frequently pictured dancing, standing, and sitting in water or near water motifs. The caption text on K6979 (see fig. 15.4) states that One Ixim "entered the water" on *7 Ajaw 8 Sak*, and the scene illustrates One Ixim, who has already put on his headdress and necklace. He is flanked by one goddess on the left and two goddesses on the right. The first goddess on the right has a painted face and death signs on her body, while the second holds up a piece of One Ixim's jewelry. Behind her are the hero twins. One Ajaw carries the corn sack over his right shoulder as well as the gourd. Behind the hero twins is another painted goddess with death signs on her cheek.

A similar dressing scene with the same date is also found on K1202 (fig. 15.6). On this vessel, the caption text states that One Ixim "entered the road" on *7 Ajaw 8 Sak* and that this event occurred at a place called Seven Water (Stuart 1998:388). One Ixim is flanked by five goddesses, two on the left and three on the right. Two of these goddesses carry his jewelry. Behind the goddesses on the right is One Ajaw carrying the corn sack, and a sixth goddess who holds another piece of One Ixim's jewelry. She is framed by five glyphs that give her name. Although she is not marked with death signs like the goddess on K6979, her name glyph is a portrait head marked with death signs.

Figure 15.5. One Ixim (*center*) dressed by two goddesses, K626 (after Kerr)

Figure 15.6. One Ixim (*top*) flanked by six goddesses and his son One Ajaw, K1202 (after Kerr)

While most researchers have assumed that these dressing events occurred at the Crushing Ballcourt, no overt ballcourt or gourd-tree imagery appears in these scenes, making this identification unlikely. On several vessels, the Seven Water place is shown as a solid black rectangle with a water band wrapped around it. One Ixim is shown in K7268 standing in front of the rectangle. He is flanked on either side by naked goddesses. The bundle appears behind him. A zoomorphic head with three stalks of corn is found at the left corner of the rectangle. On the right side of the rectangle, the hero twins stand before the open mouth of a mountain cave. On K626 (see fig. 15.5) and K4479, One Ixim sits on top of the rectangle, flanked by two naked goddesses. The head of a supernatural being that appears to be a bird with water lily foliage growing from its head is positioned in front of the rectangle. On the right corner of the rectangle is a zoomorphic skull with two stalks of corn growing out of it.

On K4479, One Ajaw steps off the rectangle away from his father and the naked goddesses. He holds the bundle on his chest and a stick in his hand. In some dressing scenes, such as K4358, One Ixim boards a canoe. On K3033 (see fig. 15.3), the narrative begins with two naked goddesses helping One Ixim dress, and this event is followed by the two Paddler Gods propelling One Ixim along a river in a canoe. He carries the sack bundle over his shoulder and rests the contents in his lap.

The obvious place where a watery mountain adjacent to a river/road that is associated with multiple naked goddesses, corn, and the underworld is Meauan Mountain. In the contemporary stories that were mentioned in chapter 13, the Meauan corn goddesses bathed at the base of their mountain and used their cave to defeat Sipac, as did the hero twins in the *Popol Vuh* when they defeated Zipacna. While it can be argued that all caves provide access to and from the underworld, it can be concluded that the Zipacna cave was specifically on the road of the underworld. The K'iche' call the black rift of the Milky Way that represents Zipacna's open mouth "the road of the underworld," and Zipacna stuck his open mouth into the Meauan cave. The rectangle likely represents a washing stone.

## The Bathing of One Ixim

The main reasons that Maya women go into the water of a river are to wash clothing and to bathe. The water location, the nakedness of the goddesses, and their unbound hair all suggest that the scenes of One Ixim's dressing involved the washing of this god and his costume elements. The concept of a specific river location where a god was bathed is found in the section of the *Popol Vuh* concerning the first three K'iche' lineage heads. These gods, Tohil, Auilix, and Hacavitz, were said to be the substitutes and remembrances of the creator gods. When the sun first rose, the three gods were turned into stone idols, but their spirit essences walked around in the form of three boys. The three gods would bathe at a place called the Bath of Tohil (Christenson 2003a:239–41). The K'iche' lords captured and sacrificed non-K'iche' people from neighboring regions to pay homage to their three lineage gods, and these neighbors decided to band together and defeat Tohil, Auilix, and Hacavitz. They devised a plan to send two beautiful virgin girls to the Bath of Tohil to seduce the gods. Lady Lust (Xtaj) and Lady Weeping (Xpuch') were told to pretend to wash clothes in the river, and when the gods arrived, to say they were daughters of lords and to sexually offer themselves.

A similar bathing story is told in the *Título de Totonicapán*, but this time there are three women (Puch, Tax, and Q'uibatzunaj), and it is three K'iche' lords whom they approach rather than the gods. Rulers and gods are often merged in Mesoamerican stories. Three women (Xur, Xpuch, and Xtax) are also mentioned in the *Título C'oyoi*, but in the Juan Torres Macario manuscript, four women are named (Xur, Xibt, Xpuch, and Xtas; Carmack 1973:311). The *Título de Totonicapán* explicitly states that sending the women to the river was a marriage proposition. However, the lords were not presenting their virgin daughters in a traditional manner; they were offering them to the gods as concubines.

In both versions of the Tohil bath story, the maidens do not succeed in tempting the rulers or gods, but they receive three beautiful cloaks painted with the gods' spirit companions to take back to their lords as gifts. The cloaks are supposed to be a sign that the "marriage" had been consummated. This appears to be parallel to a Postclassic Alta Verapaz tradition in which an adulterous woman could only denounce her lover by producing his mantle or loincloth as proof of their liaison (Miles 1955: 89). Although the gods chose not to do so, the Bath of Tohil story clearly indicates that if the gods had bathed with the women, it would have constituted a marriage. When the maidens give the cloaks to their lords, the lords put on the robes and display them. The spirit companions on the cloth spring to life, attack, and defeat them.

The fact that the women at the Bath of Tohil were washing clothes helps to clarify the role of the goddesses in the One Ixim dressing scenes. The washing of a god and his clothing is an integral part of contemporary ceremonies, and the clothing and accoutrements of saints are regularly washed before the saint is taken on a pilgrimage. In the Tzotzil town of Zinacantan, the mountain gods are thought to bathe in the seven sacred water holes in the surrounding countryside (Vogt 1969:387). The water is used to wash the saints' clothing and to bathe patients during the curing ceremony discussed in chapter 11. The seven Zinacantan water holes are evocative of the Seven Water place name. In other communities, the water used to wash saints is also obtained from a sacred or blessed source. Ruiz de Alarcón (Coe and Whittaker 1982:70) notes that a governor in Central Mexico was first bathed in a river at dawn before he assumed his office.

While the washing of One Ixim may simply have been the cleaning of his body and his costume, a Kaqchikel bathing ritual for curing soul loss may shed light on the nature of One Ixim's bath. The Kaqchikel believe that illness is the result of soul loss, and an ill person is bathed in river water and washed with aromatic leaves to return the soul to the body (Fischer 1999:482). The river water is thought to help return the soul to the body, and some kind of process to return his soul would have been necessary for One Ixim's resurrection. In the *Popol Vuh*, the bones of the hero twins are also deposited in a river as part of their transformation into new beings.

Another washing ritual related to transformation was characterized as "baptism" by the Spanish priests. Sahagún (1959–63, book 6, 175–77) records the Aztec rite in which newborn babies were washed with water representing the water goddess Chalchiuhtlicue. In Yucatan, Landa notes that the Yucatec Maya had a form of baptism for children that was called *sihil,* "to be born," and *caput sihil,* "to be born anew" (Tozzer 1941:102–106). Children underwent this ritual of transformation in order to become young adults. The Yucatec Motul dictionary and the Vienna dictionary define the phrase *och ha',* "enter water," as baptism. One Ixim's emergence from the T533 skull is called *sihil,* "to be born," and he is said to "enter water" in several dressing scenes. The Yucatec "baptism" rite for children recorded by Landa involved anointing them with virgin water from the rattlesnake aspergillum of Itzamnaaj and with a bone dipped in virgin water that had been mixed with flowers and ground cacao. The association of baptism with the verbs used to describe the bath of One Ixim indicates that his bathing was much more than simple cleaning, and that it was likely related to the return of his soul and life force to his body.

It is highly probable that bathing was an integral part of Classic rites of passage, such as when a young lord acquired a new office or became the ruler. For example, before Q'aq'awitz entered the crater of Volcán Santa María, he dressed in a cape of reeds (Akkeren 2000:158). When Q'aq'awitz descended into the fire of the crater, his assistant Zakitzunun poured water on the fire, and Q'aq'awtiz emerged from this immolation/transformation carrying the flint of the volcano. Later in the story, Q'aq'awitz entered the waters of Lake Atitlán and turned into Cloud Serpent.

On K1440, a young lord dressed in a cape of leaves is shown being anointed with an aspergillum-like device that appears to be made of leaves and perhaps strips of bark cloth (Robicsek 1981, fig. 23b). The verb in the text used to describe this scene is "birth." The device is similar to the branches of leaves that are used to slap the skin during the sweat bath to increase sweating and promote healing. On the Palenque Temple XXI panel, the young brothers Akhal Mo' Nahb and U K'inich Pakal are illustrated in the presence of their grandfather K'inich Janab' Pakal participating in a pre-accession event (Miller and Martin 2004, plate 129). They, too, wear capes made of leaves, and they are flanked by two priests who hold out a similar aspergillum-like device. The young Kan B'ahlam is illustrated in the Cross Group tablets wearing the aspergillum-like object as a headdress while he undergoes a pre-accession event to become the *Ba Ch'ok*.

## THE CREATION OF HUMANS

When describing the creation of the first humans, the *Popol Vuh* relates that they immediately had great vision: "Their knowledge of everything that they saw was complete—the four corners and the four sides, that which is within the sky and that which is within the earth" (Christenson 2003a:199). We can infer from this statement that the first humans stood at the center of the world and beheld the quadrilateral world laid out before them.

Numerous scenes on Classic Period pottery show One Ixim taking a journey in a canoe or standing adjacent to the split turtle shell that marks the center of the world. In several of these scenes, he carries the corn-seed bundle and water gourd. It appears that One Ixim made a journey along the Chixoy River from Meauan Mountain to Lake Atitlán in order to bring the corn sack and gourd to the center of the world. As the episode concerning the twin ears of corn indicates, the creator grandmother was at the center house at the time. I propose that when One Ixim arrived at the center of the world, he gave some of his corn seed and water to his mother to create the flesh and blood of the first humans.

It is reasonable to conclude that she processed this corn seed on the grinding stone in her house. Corn is usually ground three to five times, but the creator grandmother ground the corn nine times until it was transformed into a very fine paste. The ancient Maya used tripod metates, some in the shape of a turtle. The tripod was evocative of the three hearthstones, while the turtle was a symbol for the surface of the earth. A metate in the Kislak Collection actually has a turtle carved on its bottom (Dunkelman 2007:9). Each time a Maya woman ground her corn dough on the center of the tripod or turtle metate, she was symbolically grinding her corn at the center of the world just like the creator grandmother. Atitecos believe that the basalt cave of Paq'alib'al represents the center of the world. Basalt, a volcanic rock, was the preferred stone for making metates (grinding stones) and manos (hand stones), and it is highly appropriate that the region where the creator grandmother ground the corn to make the first humans contained this material.

## THE FIRST PLANTING OF CORN IN THE NEW ERA

The *Popol Vuh* indicates that the hero twins cleared a new cornfield before they departed to the underworld, although it does not indicate when the field was planted or who did the planting. It does refer to the planting in an early episode. After the first failed attempts at making humans, the creator gods state that they need to try again to make humans before the first sowing and dawning: "Let us try again before the first sowing, before the dawn approaches. Let us make a provider, a sustainer for us" (Christenson 2003a:78). The first dawn occurs just before Hunahpu and Xbalanque rise as sun and full moon at zenith passage. We can conclude that the first sowing also occurred on zenith passage, because the Maya plant at full moon following this date.

As the following discussion will demonstrate, several Classic Period scenes appear to feature this first planting at zenith passage. Robicsek and Hales (1991, vessel 117 and figs. 57–59) illustrate five scenes that show One Ixim emerging from or standing adjacent to the crack in the turtle carapace. The crack represents the corn mound at the center of the world. On two vessels, the hero twins appear opposite one another on the edge of the turtle shell, just as they appear in opposition to one another on the horizon in their roles as the sun and full moon (see figs. 8.2, 8.3). A center corn mound is split open twice: once when a farmer thrusts his planting stick into the ground and plants the seed and again when the germinated corn seed pushes through the soil and creates a plant. It is reasonable to interpret the scenes on K4681 (fig. 8.2) and BOD figures 57 and 58b as One Ixim emerging from the center corn mound as the young corn plant. The scene on K731 (see fig. 15.2) is, however, significantly different from the other turtle-shell scenes in that One Ixim stands with one leg in the hole and one leg behind the turtle shell. He cradles both the gourd and sack bundle in his right arm. Three chahk deities follow him in canoes.

It has been suggested by Taube (1985; 2004) that the K731 scene represents One Ixim emerging from the turtle crack with the corn that will be used to create humans, and that it is thematically parallel to the Central Mexican myths of Quetzalcoatl emerging from the underworld with the bones used to create humans, or Quetzalcoatl emerging from Sustenance Mountain with the corn used to feed the first humans. It has also been suggested that the gourd in this scene contained water taken from the underworld to the surface of the earth for drinking during One Ixim's journey, and for the welfare of the crops (Saturno, Taube, and Stuart 2005:31–34).

I propose a different interpretation. On K731, One Ixim holds his left hand in the scattering gesture farmers use when they drop their corn seed into the hole. Rather than representing the underworld exit location of One Ixim, I think this split turtle shell simply functions to indicate that One Ixim is standing at the planting hole at the center of the world. On K1892, One Ixim again stands adjacent to the split in the turtle shell, but juxtaposed with the base of the split is a k'an skull with a burning torch in its head (see fig. 8.2). Given that the Maya characterize corn seed as a skull, this skull likely represents the corn seed planted at the center corn mound. The torch is similar to candles that are placed adjacent to the corn mound in contemporary planting rituals to heat the corn seed and aid in its regeneration.

The k'an skull on Yaxchilan Lintel 25 was a goddess named Ixik Ohl, "lady heart," who was likely a manifestation of Ixik/Lady Bone Water (see fig. 10.5). I believe that the corn seeds brought to the center of the world were the remains of Ixik/Lady Bone Water, and I suggest that the k'an skull represents her remains. One Ixim/One Hunahpu was again manifested as the center corn plant when this corn seed sprouted into a young plant, matured, and produced an ear of corn. This center plant embodied the male/female principle that defined the place of duality. Each time the farmer planted his first mound of corn in the center of the field, he was reenacting the role of One Ixim planting the first corn at the center of the world.

I agree with the assessment that the vine gourd carried by One Ixim also contained water for the welfare of the crops (Saturno, Taube, and Stuart 2005), but I would stipulate that it was specifically for the germination of the corn seed. The middle chahk on K731 carries a gourd as well as a turtle-shell drum in his left hand (see fig. 15.2). In his right hand he holds up a deer antler, which he will use to beat the shell drum. Such musical instruments were reported during the colonial period (Ruppert, Proskouriakoff, and Thompson 1955), and turtle shell drums are still used in Tzeltal, Tzotzil, and other highland Guatemala ceremonies (Starr 1908:377, Laughlin 1975:67). In the Zinacantan *posada* ceremony, turtle-shell drums are beaten with two ears of corn to ensure an abundant harvest (Vogt 1977:144).

A central act in the Aztec *Leyenda de los soles* creation myth was the bloodletting by the gods to bring to life the bones used to create humans. This kind of regeneration is also seen in contemporary Maya corn rituals where blood and other "hot" substances are poured on the corn seed to heat it and bring about germination. One Ixim usually wears the xook monster and *Spondylus* shell motifs, associated with penis perforation, on his loincloth. Many of the *Spondylus* shells in caches contain jade beads—symbols of corn seeds—and blood residue and are found in association with bloodletters. The *Spondylus* shell's bright-red inner surface has been equated with a vagina and a womb (Miller 1992; Taylor 1992). Landa notes that young girls always wore a shell over their groin area that represented their virginity (Tozzer 1941: 102–104). Before they could marry and reproduce, the shell had to be removed during a ritual called *sihil,* "to be born." Given the bloodletting symbolism associated with the xook monster, it would seem that One Ixim's loincloth motif was a reference to his bleeding onto the bones of his wife to generate heat and life; like a farmer planting corn, his action had sexual overtones.

*Spondylus* shells are found on the turtle carapace on K4681 in the position of corner plantings (see fig. 8.4). One Ixim emerges from a skull on BOD vessel 116, and a *Spondylus* shell is positioned in each corner of the scene (see fig. 8.6). On the rim of the plate above each shell is another skull. This configuration is the planting pattern, which suggests that One Ixim planted not only the center corn mound, but the four directional mounds as well.

One Ixim's sowing of corn is reminiscent of a Q'eqchi' creation story that features a messenger from God and the Christian biblical figure of Adam (Thompson 1930:145). In the Q'eqchi' tale, Adam wants a cornfield, so the messenger of God cuts down each of the trees located in the four corners of Adam's field, which magically fells all the trees. After Adam burns the field, the messenger of God plants one mound in the center and one in each corner. By the end of the week, the field has produced maize, beans, squash, and all the fruit in the world.

In my reconstruction of the core myth, the center corn mound represented the heart of Ixik/Lady Bone Water, while the other four corn mounds represented her hands and feet. The body of Ixik/Lady Bone Water was symbolically laid out spread-eagle on the surface of the earth each time the Maya planted corn at the center and four corners. In the Maya calendar system, four different day names can begin a new year, and these day names are called the yearbearers. The yearbearer days are separated from each other by five days. This means that if you count out the day names using your fingers and toes, there is only one yearbearer for each limb. The yearbearers are each associated with a particular color and direction. The Maya always separate and plant corn according to color. I propose that each of the four corner mounds planted by One Ixim represented a different color of corn, and that the planting of the corner mounds not only laid out Ixik/Lady Bone Water's remains on the surface of the earth, but that the planting established the color and directional associations of the quadrants and yearbearers.

My proposal that One Ixim performed the first corn planting of the new era provides new meaning to the Santa Rita Corozal Structure 213 cache that was discussed in chapter 8. The sides of this cache are demarcated by four figures who are practicing penis bloodletting while standing on the back of a turtle. The center is defined by a piece of jade and four small shells. Seated at the center is a figure blowing a conch trumpet. It has been cogently argued that the Santa Rita cache is related to the wayeb' rituals that reenact the establishment of the Bakabs and the world trees in the four directions (Chase and Chase 1986; 1988; 1998:322; D. Chase 1991:95). I suggest that this ordering of the world was also intimately related to the first planting of corn at the beginning of the new era and the subsequent dance of One Ixim. The close association between the dance of One Ixim and corn planting is seen on K5356. In most scenes of One Ixim's dance, the ground is defined by a simple line, but on K5356, the scene is bordered by the diamond pattern that represents the surface of the earth covered in cornfields.

In my reconstruction of the core myth, One Ixim's final destiny and roles were multifaceted. When he planted the seed remains of his wife at the center of the world, he was creating the first cornfield of the new era and replacing the cornfield of the monkey twins that existed in the previous era of the wooden men. His corn seed sprouted into the center corn plant that symbolizes the male/female principle at the center of the world. In his role as the four Bakab deities and world trees, One Ixim danced to the four directions and physically defined the boundaries of the quadrilateral world. The guardian aspect of the Bakabs echoes One Ixim's role as the planter and owner of the field, for farmers remain behind after planting to protect their fields from marauding animals. The association of the cornfield with the world trees is seen in a field-making ritual the Q'eqchi'performed during the nineteenth century. In this ritual, the farmer demarcated his new cornfield by placing a small tree on each of the four sides (Sapper 1897:285).

## THE FEMALE EARTH

The Maya believe that a cornfield does not exist until corn seed is planted in it, and it ceases to exist when the corn is harvested. What brings a being to life is the presence of a soul. By planting the remains of Ixik/Lady Bone Water (the female spirit of corn) in the field, One Ixim not only brought the quadrilateral human world into existence, but transformed the male earth into a female. In other words, Ixik/Lady Bone Water became the earth goddess of human space. This is consistent with the planting metaphors in which the male planter is thought to be impregnating the female earth with his planting stick.

This kind of interrelationship is also seen in divination practices: the diviner is thought to have a spousal relationship with his tools and divination lots that meta-phorically represent corn seed. In the Mam region, the identification of divination lots as female extends to the divination table, which is also thought to be female. The table, referred to as María, represents the quadrilateral surface of the earth (Scotchmer 1986:201). When the diviner counts out his lots in units of twenty (the days of the tzolk'in) on the table, he is metaphorically counting out the twenty digits of Ixik/Lady Bone Water. When the farmer reaches into his seed bag and grabs his five corn seeds for planting, he is also counting out her digits.

## THE MORNING STAR

The words "sowing" and "dawning" occur together many times in the *Popol Vuh*. While these words are employed metaphorically to refer to the creation of humans

(Christenson 2003a:60), they may also refer to One Hunahpu's corn sowing and the dawn of Hunahpu as the sun. It seems odd that the *Popol Vuh* does not directly refer to One Hunahpu's corn sowing on *1 Ajaw*, but one event on this day is repetitively mentioned: the heliacal rising of the morning star, Venus, just before Hunahpu rose as the sun. Las Casas and other colonial sources commented on the primary importance of the morning star to Mesoamerican people and its identification with the god Quetzalcoatl, who was thought to be transformed into the morning star when he died (Christenson 2003a:218). In Central Mexican mythology, the souls of young warriors who died in battle were thought to accompany the sun on its journey from sunrise to noon. In terms of the planting metaphor, these young warriors would be like the planting party that goes to the field with the rising sun to sow the corn. The *Popol Vuh* parallel to these warriors was the Four Hundred Boys, who in their Pleiades form followed the sun into the sky.

An essential feature of planting is that the farmer journeys to his cornfield before the rising of the sun, in the same way as the morning star rises into the sky before the sun. One Ixim/One Hunahpu was the role model for the farmer. The close relationship between the action of the farmer and the rising of the morning star suggests that the morning star was a manifestation of One Ixim/One Hunahpu. The parallel aspects of One Ixim/One Hunahpu and Quetzalcoatl have already been discussed.

The *Popol Vuh* refers to the morning star as Ik'oq'ij, which literally means to pass before the sun (Christenson 2003a:218). The morning star, which precedes the dawning sun across the sky, is always located within five degrees of the sun's pathway. The sweeping of ceremonial routes and spaces was an important aspect of Mesoamerican rituals. For example, during the New Year ceremony, the world road that the lords, priests, and men from the center of the town took to the directional wayeb' statue was first cleaned and adorned with greenery. The morning star was thought to sweep the path of the sun (Sahagún 1959–63, book 7, 8; Vogt 1969:316–17). In several versions of the elopement myth, the hero who is parallel to One Ixim/One Hunahpu is specifically called K'ix Mes, "thorn broom" (Burkitt 1920:200; R. Wilson 1995:98). As a verb, *mes* means "to sweep," and as a noun it means "broom" in most Mayan languages. *Mes te'* refers to *Baccharis vaccinioides* (coyote brush), a type of shrub, the branches of which are tied together in a bunch and used for sweeping (Berlin, Breedlove, and Raven 1974:132; Laughlin 1975:235; Breedlove and Laughlin 2000:158). The cognate word for *mes* in Yucatec Maya is *mis*, which refers to brooms, sweeping, and the renewal of roads (Barrera Vásquez 1980:523). In the *Popol Vuh*, a name for the morning star is Raxa Ik'oq'ij, "green passes before the sun," and the alternative name for Thorn Broom is similarly Raxon. These morning-star names and attributes give credence to the idea that Thorn Broom is the morning star.

After One Ixim/One Hunahpu goes to the cornfield in the predawn hours and plants his corn seed, One Ajaw/Hunahpu rises as the zenith passage sun and follows him to this center position. The identification of One Ixim/One Hunahpu as the morning star explains why both One Ixim/One Hunahpu and his son One Ajaw/ Hunahpu use the *1 Ajaw* (*1 Hunahpu*) tzolk'in date as a personal name. One Ajaw/ Hunahpu was named for this day because this was the day on which he first rose as zenith passage sun. One Ixim/One Hunahpu was also named for this day because he first rose as the morning star on this date.

The mountain manifestation of Thorn Broom was Raxon Mountain. Burkitt's informant referred to Raxon as being between the sun and the wind (Burkitt 1920: 199). Although the informant had no explanation for the phrase, this is evocative of the morning-star manifestation of One Ixim/One Hunahpu. Raxon's location in the extreme eastern zone is also suggestive of the morning star. When viewed from the top of Volcán Atitlán, a morning star that rises on the April zenith passage appears just before the rising sun on the northeast horizon in the general direction of Raxon Mountain.

The ritual planting of the first corn was probably the template for other cere-monies. In the K'iche' area, ritual specialists are taught to rise in the predawn hours when the morning star is in the sky and to go directly to the particular shrine where they will be making offerings so that they can be there when the sun rises (B. Tedlock 1982:61). In Momostenango, there are three agricultural shrines, and the ritual cleaning of these shrines is called *mesebal,* "broom" ritual. If it is planting season, the ritual specialist symbolically plants and prays for good crops, while during the harvest season, he symbolically cuts corn and gives thanks for the harvest (B. Tedlock 1982:113).

## THE WIND OF ONE IXIM/ONE HUNAHPU

Quetzalcoatl/Ehecatl was called the guide and the sweeper of roads for the rain gods, and his wind brought the rains at the onset of the rainy season (Nicholson 1971:416). A similar role for One Ixim/One Hunahpu may be implied on K731, where the arrival of three chahks in their canoes follows One Ixim's planting of corn (see fig. 15.2).

The Popol Vuh states that when the sun rose, its heat was intense (Christenson 2003a:229). While the Popol Vuh does not indicate how the sun's heat is abated, the three patron deities Tohil, Auilix, and Hacavitz and the images of the puma, jaguar, rattlesnake, and pit viper are turned to stone at the rising of the sun. Deities turning to stone or dying with the first rising of the sun is a common theme in Mesoamerica. In the Aztec sun and moon myth recorded by Sahagún (1959–63, book 7, 8), the sun and moon emerge at the same time in the east but do not travel across the sky. After consulting with each other, the creator deities decide that by sacrificing them-selves, they will enable the sun and moon to move. They appoint Ehecatl (the wind god manifestation of Quetzalcoatl) from their midst to carry out the sacrifice, but even this does not move the sun and moon. Finally, Ehecatl blows on these celestial bodies to animate them and initiate their movement across the sky. Quetzalcoatl/ Ehecatl's conch shell was the symbol of his wind and breath. A Preclassic corn god who was parallel to One Ixim/One Hunahpu has been identified in the San Bartolo murals (Saturno, Taube, and Stuart 2005). This corn god is pictured with wind in the form of a conch shell emanating from his mouth. The conch-blowing figure at the center of the cache from Santa Rita Corozal also likely represents the wind god mani-festation of One Ixim/One Hunahpu.

After One Ixim/One Hunahpu rose for the first time as the morning star and the wind of the dawn, he planted his corn seed at the center of the world and in the four corners. The dance of One Ixim to the four directions represents this planting, and One Ixim is illustrated in these scenes wearing the long tail feathers of the quetzal that represent his corn foliage. He was then followed by One Ajaw/Hunahpu in his first rising as the sun. As discussed in chapter 4, the bird men of the Voladores festival represent the sun, and as such, they should represent One Ajaw/Hunahpu. Their flight condenses into a single performance the four-year cycle that is repeated thirteen times in the *Dresden Codex* New Year pages. The four directional dances of One Ixim/One Hunahpu are thematically equivalent to this New Year ordering event. In others words, the quetzal dance of One Ixim and the flight of the bird men are sequential episodes of the creation story.

## THE ORIGIN OF THE VINE GOURD AND ITS WATER

While the *Popol Vuh* says that the first corn seed came from Paxil Mountain, it does not name the source of the water used to create human blood. The following review will show that the mountain cave illustrated on the north wall of the San Bartolo murals was the source of this water, and that this cave was on Meauan Mountain.

The various dressing and adornment scenes indicate that One Ixim and the hero twins were in possession of both the corn-seed bundle and vine gourd when they were at Meauan Mountain. How the Paxil corn seeds were brought to Meauan Mountain is not readily apparent from these scenes, but the *Popol Vuh* indicates that the fox, coyote, parakeet, and raven were involved in procuring the corn.

The San Bartolo murals are painted on the inner walls of a small building (Saturno, Taube, and Stuart 2005). The order in which they should be read is unclear, but the north wall includes two scenes. The left scene shows a small deity with crab-like hands emerging from a vine gourd (*Lagenaria siceraria*) that has been split open. Vine gourds are planted in the cornfield with the corn and are har-vested at the same time (Breedlove and Laughlin 1993:135). Four other deities in the corners of the scene are illustrated in reclining poses associated with babies. To the right of these baby deities is an adult god in an elaborate costume. While the meaning of the San Bartolo scene is ambiguous, the babies are positioned in the planting pattern.

Figure 15.7. Left section of cave mural, San Bartolo north wall (after Heather Hurst)

The second scene takes place at the mouth of a mountain cave with the body of a serpent extending out from it (figs. 15.7, 15.8). The serpent's body forms the path leading out of the cave, and eight figures appear on this long cave passageway. The focus of the scene is the Preclassic corn god, who stands looking over his left shoulder to the characters behind him (fig. 15.7). These figures include two young goddesses kneeling just behind him as well as a young goddess and two gods striding toward him (fig. 15.8).

In front of the corn god is a black-faced god who is kneeling on one knee as though he is about to rise. On his head, he balances a very large bottle gourd which the corn god appears to be trying to grasp or steady. The black-faced god balances the gourd on his head in the same way as women carry water jars. Behind the black-faced god, another young goddess kneels inside the cave mouth beneath a hanging stalactite, and she holds up a vessel containing three balls of corn dough. The facial markings of the three kneeling goddesses are similar to those of the goddesses in the Classic Period dressing scenes of One Ixim.

Above the mouth of the cave is a pouch-shaped bird nest with three yellow birds busily weaving it. A serpent on the back side of the cave is in the process of eating a fourth bird. Although the size of the nest is indicative of an oropendola (blackbird), the the birds' yellow color suggests orioles. The extraordinary weaving skills of female orioles were naturally associated with the weaving skills of women, and the oriole is said to have woven the intricate feather designs into the wedding dress of a hummingbird in a Yucatec Maya myth (Bowles 1964:27). The San Bartolo nest-building scene is unusual because orioles do not help each other construct their nests. This triad arrangement does, however, suggest that these weaver birds are

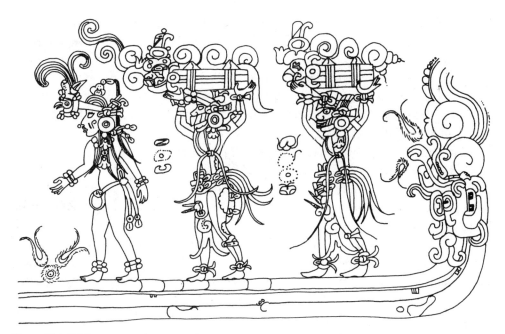

Figure 15.8. Right section of cave mural, San Bartolo north wall (after Heather Hurst)

manifestations of the three kneeling goddesses of the cave. As noted in previous chapters, quetzal feathers were closely identified with Ixik/Lady Bone Water, and two incantations in the *Ritual of the Bacabs* pair the tail feathers of the quetzal with the tail feathers of the oriole (Roys 1933:32, 34). Both quetzal feathers and oriole feathers were given as tribute payments (Christenson 2003a:291).

Saturno, Taube, and Stuart (2005) have equated the cave shown in the San Bartolo mural with the location of the dressing scene of One Ixim. They propose that this location is parallel to the Mesoamerican cave of emergence, which they characterize as a flower mountain. They have also suggested that the four males and four females may represent eight ancestral couples: "For the North Wall mural, the eight people atop the plumed serpent are probably ancestral couples, the maize god with his mate, and three pairs of young men and women. In fact, since the *Popol Vuh* and the *Annals of the Cakchiquels* both describe the making of people from maize, the arrival of the Maya maize god on the surface of the earth is a form of the emergence myth" (Saturno, Taube, and Stuart 2005:50). While I do not think that these figures are ancestral couples, I agree that the San Bartolo event is directly related to the dressing of One Ixim. As I have demonstrated, this event occurred at Meauan Mountain, and the three kneeling goddesses at San Bartolo are evocative of the three goddesses of Meauan Mountain. Ximénez described the Meauan cave as being over three kilometers in length (Akkeren 2000:299), and the San Bartolo cave is illustrated with a very long serpent pathway.

In discussing the nature of the bottle gourd, Saturno, Taube, and Stuart have said that it was likely related to the gourds the thunderbolt gods used to dispense rain. I agree with their assessment, but I add the caveat that the San Bartolo water gourd was used to dispense the first rain of the season, and that the Meauan cave was the source of the water. In Alta Verapaz, it is still believed that the female mountains have large caves and that they send the rain (R. Wilson 1995:54). As discussed in the previous chapter, the Chixoy River was equated with the Milky Way river, and the mouth of the Milky Way crocodile was identified with the mouth of the Meauan cave (the cave of Zipacna's defeat). The close association between the water of the Meauan cave and the rain of the planting season is seen in the role of the Milky Way crocodile, which pours forth rain from its mouth in numerous scenes. Taube (2001) has noted that many depictions of crocodiles in Olmec and Maya art show them blowing clouds and swirling wind from their mouths. On Copan Zoomorph P, the wind and cloud volutes of the crocodile contain chahks carrying water jars. If my reconstruction of the corn myth is correct, the scene on K731 that illustrates One Ixim carrying the water gourd and the corn seeds to the center of the world is an indication that the Chixoy/Milky Way water of Meauan Mountain was also the source of the water used to create the blood of the first humans.

The proximity of the water gourd and the stalactite in the San Bartolo mural suggests that the water in the gourd may have specifically come from the stalactites of the Meauan cave. The mouth of the San Bartolo cave encloses the young, kneeling corn goddess, and the stalactite hanging from the roof almost touches her head as though she were identified with the stalactite and its water. If this witz monster/cave is a manifestation of the corn goddess, then we should expect this association.

## Ixik/Lady Bone Water as a Water Goddess

Lady Bone Water's name suggests an obvious connection with water. Water is often represented in Maya art by a water lily; a logogram of a water lily represents the words for water, lake, and sea. A water lily in full bloom is brilliant white and often stands above the water on a long stem. In addition to the name *nahb*, the water lily is called *nicte ha'*, "the flower of the water," and *ixim ha'*, "the corn of the water" (Venture, cited in Schele n.d.). This latter name suggests that the water lily was one of the plant manifestations of Ixik/Lady Bone Water. In many examples of water lilies found in Maya art, there is a diamond pattern on the leaf that bears no relation to a natural water lily pad. It is, however, the same pattern found on the skirt occasionally worn by One Ixim, which I have argued is the skirt of his wife Ixik/Lady Bone Water.

The elopement stories support the notion that Ixik/Lady Bone Water had a water lily form and that she was a water goddess. These stories describe the bloody remains of Xucaneb's daughter spreading across the surface of the water with fish nibbling at them. This image evokes water lilies. In most illustrations of water lilies, fish nibble at the plant, and many of the white water-lily flowers found on polychrome pottery are tinged with red (see K717). In some examples of water lilies, the fish are replaced by a hummingbird sucking the nectar of the flower. The water lily illustrated on an Early Classic Tzakol lid has both fish and hummingbirds feasting on it (Hellmuth 1987, fig. 61). This is unusual for a hummingbird, because these birds primarily feed at yellow and red tubular flowers, not white water lilies. The hummingbird in these scenes evokes the hummingbird form of Thorn Broom sucking the nectar of the tobacco flower that represented Xucaneb's daughter.

There is evidence that Ixik/Lady Bone Water was specifically associated with the waters of the Milky Way and the Chixoy River. In one of the Xucaneb stories recorded by Mary Owens, a school of silvery fish collect the remains of Xucaneb's daughter, and these fish later become the river of the Milky Way (Gordon 1915). The elopement stories say that the first animal created from the bloody remains of Xucaneb's daughter was the *ic bolay* snake; the indigenous name for the lower Chixoy River was Ic Bolay. I propose that the water of the Chixoy River, and by extension, the water coming out of the mouth of the Milky Way crocodile were specifically identified with the blood of Xucaneb's daughter, who was parallel to Ixik/Lady Bone Water.

The identification of Ixik/Lady Bone Water as a water goddess follows the pan-Maya association of women and goddesses with water. This connection is not limited to the Maya area. In Central Mexican mythology, water that flows from mountains is thought to be an aspect of the goddess Chalchiuhtlicue, who, like Ixik, wears a diamond-patterned jade skirt. Furthermore, the skirt of the closely related corn goddess Xilonen was decorated with water lilies (Sahagún 1959–63, book 2, 103).

## Ixik/Lady Bone Water as a Salt Goddess

There is evidence that Ixik/Lady Bone Water was also considered a goddess of salt. The three Aztec goddesses of corn, water, and salt—Chicomecoatl (Seven Snake), Chalchiuhtlicue (Jade Skirt), and Huixtocihuatl (Salt Woman)—had overlapping aspects. The association of salt with a triad of goddesses is also found at Tzotzil Zinacantan (Vogt 1969:169–71, 319–26, 563–65; Laughlin 1977:196–200). At the time of the conquest, Zinacantecos controlled the Chiapas salt wells at Ixtapa and Salinas and greatly prospered from trading this commodity. At the hamlet of Salinas, which still produces the salt used in Zinacantan ceremonies, there is a chapel dedicated to the Virgin of the Rosary. She is said to be the youngest of the three Marías. The other two are the Virgin of the Rosary in Zinacantan center and the Virgin of Ascension in Ixtapa. The Virgin of Ascension and the Virgin of the Rosary are said to have taught men how to produce and care for salt.

The story concerning the founding of the Salinas chapel describes how a young Zinacantan farmer was examining some land to make a milpa when the Virgin of the Rosary appeared before him under an avocado tree. She asked him to build a chapel for her at this location, and in return, she would create a salt sluice. After the chapel had been built, the cliff behind the chapel split open and out sprang a stream to provide the community with salt. In other myths related to these Virgins, they mysteriously appeared from caves, and the Virgin of Ascension has the ability to fill water jars.

If I am correct that Ixik/Lady Bone Water was specifically associated with the water of the Chixoy/Milky Way river, then it is likely that she was also a salt goddess, given that the Chixoy has two prominent salt sources on its banks: Sacapulas and Montaña Nueve Cerros. Contemporary stories indicate that the salt beds at Sacapulas were thought to have had a female guardian, but after a flood she moved further down the Chixoy River (Reina and Monaghan 1981:17).

In Maya world view, the color white is identified with the north. The consistent association of Ixik/Lady Bone Water with the color white (white bone, white salt, white water-bird, white water-lily) fits with the northern orientation of Meauan Mountain.

## The Procurement of Corn at Paxil Mountain

Neither the *Popol Vuh* nor the *Annals of the Cakchiquels* describe how Paxil Mountain was broken open by a thunderbolt, but the contemporary stories often credit the youngest thunderbolt. In my reconstruction of the core myth, this would have been One Ixim in his GII/Youngest Thunderbolt form. In some stories, a series of lightning-bolt gods tries to smash open the rock, but finally an old, sick thunderbolt succeeds (Burkitt 1920; Thompson 1971:349). In Burkitt's version of this myth, a trio of bachelor thunderbolt gods tries but fails to break open the cliff containing the corn seed. An old thunderbolt god then borrows the fire stone of a god called *Xam Pek,* "fire stone or flint," and has him beat his drum to make thunder. Together they are able to smash open the mountain.

Numerous Classic Period scenes of lightning reconcile these two seemingly different versions. GII represents the flash of lightning, and Itzamnaaj/God N represents the noise of thunder as he emerges from the lightning bolt. In other words, it took the combined thunderbolt of One Ixim/GII and his father, Itzamnaaj/God N, to break open Paxil Mountain.

As soon as the first humans were created, they immediately had great divination skills and eyesight that set them apart from the previous creations made from mud and wood. This skill is characterized as "lightning in the blood." Modern Momostecan stories concerning the skills of the first fathers indicate that a red dwarf had to use his stone ax to strike lightning into their blood (B. Tedlock 1982:148). In my reconstruction of the core myth, the blood of humans was created from the water/blood of Ixik/Lady Bone Water. This blood was charged with lightning when she was struck down by a lightning bolt. Her bone remains that were used to create the flesh of humans were also charged with lightning when the thunderbolt gods pounded the rock covering her remains. As was discussed in chapter 13, the fire in the bolt of lightning was a manifestation of the creator grandfather, who was the first and greatest diviner. If we extend this identification to the lightning bolt that is thought to germinate the corn seed in the milpa, then the thunderbolt of One Ixim/One Hunahpu and his father, Itzamnaaj/Xpiyacoc, heated the corn seeds and regenerated life.

Many contemporary stories relate that ants first brought corn seed out of a mountain through a tiny crack in the rock, and that the other animals ate the corn and revealed its existence to the creator gods. The role of the ants in the corn mountain stories is similar to the myth recorded in the *Leyenda de los soles,* where Quetzalcoatl is transformed into an ant to obtain the corn hidden in Sustenance Mountain (Bierhorst 1992:146–47). As noted in previous chapters, One Ixim and Quetzalcoatl shared many characteristics, which suggests that One Ixim might have had an ant form and might have been directly involved not only in the breaking open of Paxil Mountain, but in the initial discovery of corn.

## Human Funerary Rites

The phrases "entering the road" and "entering the water" are metaphors related to the death of a lord (Stuart 1998:388). For example, the narrative on the west tablet of the Palenque Temple of the Inscriptions first notes the death of K'inich Janab' Pakal's wife using the death phrase that refers to the departure of the breath soul from her body and then restates her death in the next passage using the "enter the road" verb. Evidence that entering the water or the road specifically refers to something that happened on the day that the lord died, and not on the day that he was buried, is found on Quirigua Zoomorph B. The text notes the death of the ruler K'ak Tiliw on 9.17.14.13.2 *11 Ik' 5 Yax* (31 July A.D. 785) using the "enter road" verb, and then gives his burial date ten days later (Schele and Looper 1996:150; Marc Zender, personal communication). Many researchers have proposed that the death and afterlife of a ruler were thought to replicate the death and afterlife of One Ixim (Taube 1985, 1986, 2003, 2005; Coe 1988; Schele 1992; Freidel, Schele, and Parker 1993:92; Quenon and Le Fort 1997; Schele and Mathews 1998:116; Miller and Martin 2004:52; Saturno, Taube, and Stuart 2005). For example, the narrative on K'inich Janab' Pakal's sarcophagus states that he "entered the road" on a date that is recorded on the Palace Tablet as his death date. It has been suggested that the emergence of K'inich Janab' Pakal, in the guise of One Ixim, from the centipede jaws, illustrated on his sarcophagus, represents K'inich Janab' Pakal entering the road of the Milky Way after his death and journey to the Three Hearthstones constellation (Schele 1992; Freidel, Schele, and Parker 1993:92; Schele and Looper 1996).

Let us try to approach this death phrase and the burial practices of the Classic Period elite from a different perspective. In addition to K'inich Janab' Pakal's death, the "enter the road" verb is used in his sarcophagus narrative to describe the deaths of his ancestors who are illustrated on the sides of the sarcophagus. While the narrative names nine previous rulers including K'inich Janab' Pakal's grandmother Lady Yol Ik'nal, it also lists his parents and Lady Yol Ik'nal's husband, none of whom were rulers (Bassie-Sweet 1996:216–17). Consequently, "entering the road" was not restricted to rulers. In the context of One Ixim, the "enter the road" or "enter the water" phrases refer neither to One Ixim's death nor to the burial of his body at the Crushing

Ballcourt, but to his washing and dressing at the river. If we apply this information to the death of K'inich Janab' Pakal and his ancestors, their "entering the road" events refer specifically to the ritual cleansing of their bodies after death.

In discussing Aztec burial practices, Durán (1971:267) noted that all people were stripped naked and bathed after their deaths and then dressed for burial. Coe (1988: 223) describes a highland Maya Postclassic burial custom in which the deceased lord was bathed and purified with a decoction of herbs and flowers, dressed in his finery, and placed on a platform. For two days, the lords and principal men of the community conducted a vigil over the body. The body was then taken in a great procession to the burial location with the sons of the lord carrying the rich funerary offerings. Finally, the priests placed the body and offerings in the tomb.

An Early Classic vessel (K6547) indicates that the "enter the road" event was directly related to the preparation of the body. In the first scene on this vessel, the body of a deceased lord is shown laid out on a stone platform in the costume of One Ixim (fig. 15.9a; Schele and Mathews 1998:122–23; Eberl 2001:312; Taube 2004; Martin 2006a). Nine lengths of cloth are tied around the lord's body and knotted on top. On the right leg of the platform that supports the bundled body of the lord is the phrase "enter the road." Behind the deceased ruler is a double-headed zoomorphic mountain decorated with two symmetrical ears of corn. A monkey sits on the left head while a jaguar crouches on the right one. The cartouche that appears between the ears of corn contains phonetic signs that are thought to refer to the k'a'ay, "diminished," verb that is used in the expression for the departure of the soul at death (Martin 2006a). Above this is a motif composed of a flint cartouche, a lunar sign, and the head of a deity. On each side of the monkey/jaguar mountain are three females standing in water. They exhibit the mourning gestures of the goddesses who dressed One Ixim, and they wear the simple shell ornaments over their groins that Landa describes as a sign of virgins (Tozzer 1941). They are also evocative of Lady Weeping from the Bath of Tohil story.

The next scene illustrates a five-tiered pyramid (figs. 15.9b, 15.10). The bottom tier of the pyramid is shown in cross-section to reveal the decomposing, skeletal corpse of the lord inside his tomb. Above the corpse, the ruler rises as a fruiting *ixim te* tree, and his name glyph appears in his headdress (Martin 2006a). On either side of the central tree are portraits of the ruler's parents as fruit trees. The burial pyramid is conflated with a witz monster. Although the majority of the witz monster is obscured by the details of the trees, the outline can be seen through the foliage. Various researchers have suggested that the burial pyramid is a second representation of the monkey/jaguar mountain, and they have equated both of these locations with "Flower Mountain," Sustenance Mountain, and Paxil Mountain (Schele and Mathews 1998:122–23; Eberl 2000:312; Taube 2004; Saturno, Taube, and Stuart 2005; Martin 2006a). In their interpretation, the stone platform in front of the monkey/jaguar mountain is located inside the lord's tomb. I suggest, instead, that the monkey/jaguar mountain and burial pyramid are two separate locations, as indicated by their different

Figure 15.9. a. Mourning scene of a lord, K6547; b. burial pyramid of a lord, K6547 (after Houston and Martin; drawing simplified to show pyramid)

attributes. The scene in front of the monkey/jaguar mountain is probably the public display of the washed and dressed body of the lord.

If the women in this scene are imitating the goddesses who washed and dressed One Ixim, then the monkey/jaguar mountain would represent Meauan Mountain. The monkey on this mountain is evocative of the monkey twin who appears in the dressing scene of One Ixim on K626 (see fig. 15.5). A logical sequence of events would be that the six women washed the lord's body and prepared it for public display at a location in the community that replicated Meauan Mountain, and then the body was transported to the tomb for burial. The position of the tree immediately over the tomb implies that the burial pyramid was conceptually at the center of the world. I propose that the route of the funeral procession symbolically represented One Ixim's journey from Meauan Mountain along the Chixoy River to Lake Atitlán. The water that encompasses both mountains on K6547 suggests such a journey. The burying of the bundled lord in this funeral pyramid would be like the ceremonial planting of the first corn seed at the center of the cornfield.

Taube (2005:25) has noted that when K'inich Janab' Pakal's body at Palenque was positioned in his sarcophagus, pieces of jade were placed at the deceased's groin, hands, and feet, and he described these pieces as being oriented to the center and four quarters. I suggest that this jade arrangement replicates the ritual planting of corn,

Figure 15.10. Burial pyramid of a lord, K6547 (after Houston and Martin)

in which the farmer first plants a mound of corn in the center of the field and four adjacent mounds aligned with the corners of the field. I would further speculate that the tomb preparation and offerings paralleled the planting ceremony. As discussed in chapter 3, this involved heating the corn seed so that it could be regenerated. Perhaps the common practice of coating the interiors of Maya tombs with red cinnabar and red paint is related to this heating ceremony.

On the edges of the sarcophagus lid and on the legs of the box are portraits of three secondary lords who were closely associated with K'inich Janab' Pakal. On the Temple XIX platform, the ruler K'inich Akhal Mo' Nahb is flanked by a similar trio of secondary lords who participate in his accession rituals. Secondary lords had a variety of functions, but Zender (2004) has noted that the costumes these individuals are wearing are those that lords wear when performing priestly duties. I suspect that the secondary lords on the sarcophagus were the priests that placed K'inich Janab' Pakal in his box, positioned his grave goods, and officiated over the ceremony. I further speculate that these individuals were responsible for the ongoing veneration of K'inich Janab' Pakal.

The Mesoamerican practice of placing ground corn or a piece of jade in the mouth of a deceased person is well documented (Tozzer 1941:129–30). While some sources indicate that the corn and jade were thought to be food and money for the afterlife, Coe (1988:225) cites a remark by Las Casas that jade beads were placed in the mouths of Poqom Maya lords just after they expired in order to capture their breath souls. In certain contexts, jade beads represent corn seed. It would seem that the breath of the ruler was symbolically transferred onto the jade bead so that the ruler could be regenerated in the afterlife, just as the corn seed regenerates into the corn plant.

The layout of the site of Palenque suggests that the funeral rites of Maya lords were intended to replicate One Ixim's journey from Meauan Mountain to the center of the world. The river that runs through the central area of Palenque is the Otulum, and its headwaters are located at a pair of springs in the ravine just behind Temple

XIX and the Cross Group (French 2004). The river flows generally north down the ravine along the west sides of Temple XIX and the Cross Group terraces. When the river reaches the flat area around the Palace, it continues northward along its east side. The Maya walled this section of the river and created an aqueduct that is still partially intact. At the north end of the Palace, the walled river exits the end of the vaulted aqueduct, and about 27 meters from the aqueduct exit is a large crocodile sculpture (3.44 meters long) embedded in the east wall of the river. When the river is flowing at its high mark, this crocodile appears to be swimming down the river. The ballcourt is located another 70 meters past the crocodile. The positioning of the three hearthstone mountains (the Cross Group), the crocodile, and the ballcourt along a northern flowing river suggests that the Maya of Palenque were replicating locations associated with the north world road. In terms of the funeral of K'inich Janab' Pakal, a likely location for the washing of his body would have been in the river at the crocodile sculpture.

## THE AFTERLIFE PARADISE

Tozzer (1907:154) records the belief among the Yucatec Maya that a ceiba tree at the center of the world provided access to the heavens. The center tree on vessel K6547 is positioned in front of the burial pyramid where one would expect to find a staircase leading up the pyramid to a temple. The burial pyramid is a mountain reaching up to the place of duality in the heavens. Tozzer also noted the Lacandon belief that valiant people went to a paradise in the highest level of the sky. Many Classic Period scenes show the deceased parents of the ruler in the sky above the ruler's head. A statement Landa made indicates that virtuous people were thought to journey to a ceiba tree after their death, where they would rest and have abundant food and drink for eternity (Tozzer 1941:131). As discussed by Taube, the center of the world replicates the place of duality. As such, we should expect that a ceiba also marked the place of duality and that the honored dead rested under this tree. Landa does not mention where the afterlife ceiba was located, except to say that it was someplace higher than the underworld. Landa's vague description may have been based on his reluctance to equate this location with the Christian heaven.

The center tree was a manifestation of One Ixim in his role as a Bakab. "Bakab" was the most common title of Classic Period rulers, and the juxtaposition of K'inich Janab' Pakal with the center tree on the Palenque sarcophagus lid indicates that the people of Palenque expected him to continue this role in the afterlife.

The other deceased rulers and relatives of K'inich Janab' Pakal are juxtaposed with various fruit trees on the sides of the sarcophagus. This is consistent with Martin's interpretation that fruit trees are also manifestations of One Ixim, but it also implies that the place of duality was a garden paradise full of fruit trees. This is reminiscent of the contemporary Yucatec Maya stories of the heavenly paradise in the center of the sky where honeybees get their nectar. I propose that K'inich Janab' Pakal's ancestors are being illustrated as the various fruit trees that populated the place of duality.

This is not to say that these ancestors remained permanently at this location. A number of monuments indicate that the ancestors were thought to play a very dynamic role in human events. For example, on Tikal Stela 31, the deceased father of the ruler Siyaj Chan K'awiil has descended from the sky and hovers over his son's head (Martin and Grube 1999:34–35). Many contemporary highland Maya believe that the ancestors dwell with the deities in the surrounding mountains and protect the community from harm. K'inich Janab' Pakal's sarcophagus was a model of the quadrilateral world, and the portraits of his ancestors that are found on its sides likely relate to this. Guarding the edges of the community was also a function of the four directional Bakabs.

## Martín and the Dance of One Ixim

Some of the contemporary rituals performed in the San Juan cofradía house of Santiago Atitlán are parallel to the ceremonies associated with One Ixim/One Hunahpu. Christenson has brilliantly documented these similarities in a series of publications and lectures.

The San Juan cofradía house contains two sacred bundles. The first represents the deity called Martín, who is considered to be the highest authority among the Atiteco saints and who even supersedes Christ. Martín, the supreme patron of the maize harvest, is petitioned in the blessing of the seed corn before it is planted (Christenson 2001:157). One of Martín's titles is "first of three brothers," which is reminiscent of the indigenous name of "three sons" for Volcán Tolimán and also reminiscent of GI, the first of the thunderbolt triad brothers. Martín rules over the spirits that control the rain, and he is invoked when there is a drought (O'Brien 1975:95). Martín's bundle is called the "heart of food, heart of water," and its presence in the community marks Santiago Atitlán as the "navel of the rain, navel of the earth." The bundle "embodies the power of the deity to bring rain and provide abundant harvests," and it is never opened until the doors and windows of the house are closed, because it is believed that otherwise the power of Saint Martín would be unleashed into the world and cause a great windstorm (Mendelson 1957:211–13; Christenson 2001:25).

During most of the year, Martín's bundle is kept in its wooden chest, but the *nab'eysil*, the most powerful of the ritual specialists, brings the bundle out during the dance of Martín, dons the clothing in the bundle, and "transforms" into this deity in order to ensure abundant rain (O'Brien 1975:95; Christenson 2001:24, 161–64). In his prayers, the *nab'eysil* invokes Martín using titles that include Heart of Sky, Heart of Earth, and Lord of Maize. He also lists the ancestral *nab'eysils* who performed this same dance in the past. These ancestors, thought to be present during the ceremony, are called the lightning men, the mist men, the rain men, and the earthquake men in the traditional Atitlán songs (O'Brien 1975:43). As he slowly dances around the perimeter of the cofradía house three times, the *nab'eysil* as Martín dances to the four cardinal directions to demarcate the limits of the world. At the end of the dance, he stands at the center of the house with his arms outstretched as all those present kiss his navel area.

After the first costume is returned, a second Martín costume is extracted from the bundle and another circuit dance is performed. A row of twin corn ears is hung above the altar of the house as a sign that maize is born there; the Martín bundle is considered to be the father of these corn ears. Fruit is also hung from the rafters. The second sacred bundle, the *ruk'u'x alaniem,* "heart of the placenta," belongs to Yaxper, the creator grandmother (Christenson 2001:122). As noted in chapter 2, this cloth bundle, which represents a womb, has two bags of dried corn dough attached to it that symbolize the seeds of the human race. The dough is described as being "made out of our mother maize" (Mendelson 1957:217). The faces of the three corn goddesses are painted on the cloth. The cloth is kept in a box that is hung from the house rafters by ropes that represent umbilical cords.

The parallels between Martín and One Ixim/One Hunahpu are striking. Like One Ixim, Martín dances to renew and reorder the world, and he is the father of the twin ears of corn. The pose of the *nab'eysil* at the center of the house is like the world tree and center corn plant that represent One Ixim/One Hunahpu. The box that contains Martín's bundled costumes is reminiscent of the platter carried by Yax Bolon on vessel K1004, which contains the bundled One Ixim and his costume. The Yaxper bundle that represents the first humans is parallel to the corn-seed sack One Ixim carried. It is surprising that the tradition of these relic bundles has survived until contemporary times, but when we consider that it represents a core belief about the renewal and regeneration of the world that was performed annually, its survival is more readily understood.

The Maya had a great need for various ceremonies to ensure a successful agricultural cycle. Strategies for managing a crisis—whether an agricultural disaster or an individual illness—entailed practical, effective methods that could be implemented immediately. However, these solutions were always embedded in ritual action and structured according to the community's world view. While the Maya world view has no doubt undergone significant changes from ancient times to the present, it is the consistencies that are most fascinating.

# 16

# SUMMARY AND CONCLUSIONS

Marriage and its resulting kinship groups formed the basic building blocks of Maya society. The marriages of the creator deities as well as their actions to order the world and create supernatural hierarchies provided models for the Maya elite. Rulers emulated the social, political, and economic strategies of the creators to consolidate their own power and expand their influence in their own communities as well as in those of their neighbors and competitors.

The primary ordering principle in Maya world view was complementary opposition, an ideology manifested in the relationships between the principal creator deities. The marriage of the creator grandparents and of their son One Ixim/One Hunahpu—first to Ixik/Lady Bone Water and second to One Moon/Lady Blood—exemplified male/female complementary opposition. The implied hierarchy in this pairing associated male/senior with "up" and the celestial domain, and female/junior with "down" and the underworld. In terms of the landscape, male/senior was identified with the east and the rising sun, while female/junior was identified with the west and the setting sun.

The various roads across the surface of the earth on which One Hunahpu, Seven Hunahpu, the hero twins, Lady Blood, and the owl messengers traveled to and from the house of the creator grandparents were world roads that radiated out from the center to the horizon. The land surrounding their home included the household's forests, milpas, orchards, and cacao plantations. The hut of the Four Hundred Boys and its adjacent plaza and tree were also clearly part of the creator grandparents' realm, given the role of the Four Hundred Boys as the companions of the hero twins and the use of their tree to mark the center of the world.

The house of the creator grandparents is characterized in the *Popol Vuh* as being similar to the dwelling of a common farmer. The stories describing the deeds of the creator deities, however, imply that the couple and their offspring were the source of knowledge, wisdom, and skill. Their house was the focus of specialized activities associated with sages, such as writing, sculpting, music making, jade- and metal-working, and ball playing. By emulating the creator deities, the courts of the ruling elite replicated the place of duality. Some cities were clearly more successful than others at establishing this association. The creation of locations within a community for the purpose of worshipping deities held great economic advantages for the ruling elite, because such sites attracted both local and regional pilgrims during the various religious festivals.

The acquisition of a unique patron deity allowed a lineage or group to claim superiority and to justify control over other groups and communities. An interesting aspect of these patron deities is that they were not a separate group of supernatural beings with exclusive attributes and skills. The *Popol Vuh* indicates that they were thought of as substitutes for the creator deities whom they emulated (Christenson 2003a:214). For example, the dominant K'iche' lineage had the deity called Tohil as its patron, whose fire and thunder attributes were primary qualities of the creator grandfather. Like the creator deities, the patron deities were thought to be manifestations of specific mountains.

In the *Popol Vuh*, the ruler of Tulan Zuyva provides the first K'iche' lords with their patron gods and symbols of rulership. The location of Tulan Zuyva is debated, but there were many such prestigious cities in Mesoamerica, including Teotihuacan, Tula, Cholula, Chichén Itzá, and Mayapán. Stuart (2000a) has presented epigraphic evidence that Teotihuacan played this role for the Maya during the Classic Period. Validation by a foreign state was a common phenomenon in Mesoamerica (A. Stone 1989).

A major theme in the *Popol Vuh* and in many of the Preclassic and Classic Period scenes is the ordering of the world for the production for corn. One Ixim/One Hunahpu and his sons One Ajaw/Hunahpu and Yax Bolon/Xbalanque initiated the first rising of the morning star, the sun, and the full moon at zenith passage at the start of the rainy season. This dawning began the regular cycle of celestial phenomena. One Ixim/One Hunahpu's planting of corn on this day established the core agricultural ceremony that some Maya corn farmers still follow. Although we know very little about how the Maya elite controlled labor, resources, and surpluses, the role of One Ixim/One Hunahpu and his sons in creating the first cornfield implies that Maya rulers, who emulated these deities, likely had a highly visible role in agricultural rituals and production.

As in all agricultural endeavors, the success of the corn harvest depended on many factors beyond human control. The creator gods were thought to be in command of these forces, and the ruling elite mediated between the deities and the people. In the *Popol Vuh*, the first fathers (the heads of the lineages) had this ability, and they passed their skills on to their immediate descendants. This does not mean that ordinary individuals did not also make personal petitions and offerings. Ethnographic studies show the pervasive nature of these rituals at all levels of a community, but the leaders and ritual specialists had the extraordinary expertise to communicate with the gods and interpret the signs of their acceptance or displeasure. These skills were particularly important in times of crisis.

The Maya replicated the quadrilateral world order, or parts of it, whenever they made a cornfield, built a house or town, or constructed a ritual space. While the Maya could transpose the quadrilateral model onto any landscape, I have provided substantial evidence to indicate that the original model was based on the landscape of highland Guatemala. The place of duality and the center of the world were modeled after Lake Atitlán and its surrounding area. I have identified six volcanoes and four other mountains as manifestations of specific gods and goddesses. Perhaps the most compelling evidence that the world model originated from highland Guatemala is the fact that jade, the leading high-status commodity from the earliest of times, and one intimately associated with One Ixim/One Hunahpu, is only found adjacent to the Motagua River. Furthermore, I have proposed that the four world roads represented the four directional rivers that flow from the center of highland Guatemala. This is the only place in Mesoamerica where four rivers flow from a central place to the four directions.

Many communities in highland Guatemala have four local mountains that they identify with the directional yearbearers, and they perform rituals directed to these deities on the mountain summits. In 1947, Maud Oakes climbed the southern yearbearer mountain (T'ui Bach) belonging to the community of Todos Santos in the Cuchumatán mountain range of western Guatemala. She described the altar at the top of this mountain as four slabs of rock arranged like a little house that opened at the front. Three of the slabs formed walls while the fourth formed the roof. Inside this cave-like house she found an idol that likely represented the yearbearer. This is her account of the view from the T'ui Bach altar:

> To the east, south, and west the earth was spread out beneath us. We could see five volcanoes clearly, as well as the cerro of Xepaxá [Paxil Mountain], legendary birthplace of corn, where the Indians go to pray for rain. My thoughts were of the rezadores and chimanes [ritual specialists] who make this climb in all kinds of weather, of the fires they build when they reach their destination, of the sacrifice of the turkeys. To the dueño [god] of this mountain, named also T'ui Bach, the rezador prays first, and then to the other dueños. He knows that other rezadores are doing at the other cerros just what he is doing here. He swings his pichacha [incense burner] as he prays. The smoke of the burning blood and the copal winds up into the sky as dawn lights the world below. No wonder the rezador has faith; he is apart from the world, he is at one with this God. At that moment, he is the Mountain. (Oakes 1951:74)

The most visually impressive natural feature in highland Guatemala is its long chain of high volcanoes that extends from Volcán Tacaná to Volcán de Agua. The thirteen dominant peaks in descending order of height are Tajumulco, Tacaná, Acatenango, Santa María, Fuego, Agua, Zunil, Atitlán, Santo Tomás, Siete Orejas, Quemado, Tolimán, and San Pedro. When the ritual specialists address the mountain gods in their prayers, they often list as many mountains as possible. Some petitions refer to thirteen specific deities and mountains. These mountains are usually regional and the list often varies. The petitioning in units of thirteen, however, suggests that there was originally a petition to the thirteen most sacred mountains.

The number thirteen appears in the cycle of thirteen k'atun periods. In his discussion of the calendar, Landa illustrates the thirteen-k'atun cycle as a circle with the thirteen *Ajaw* dates drawn around the outer edge (Tozzer 1941:167). Similar k'atun wheels appear in several colonial-period documents, such as the Chilam Balam of Chumayel and Chilam Balam of Kaua. In these illustrations, the circle is divided into four quadrants and labeled with the directions. Taube convincingly argues that the circle represents the surface of the earth, and he quotes as support Fray Andrés de Avendaño's account of the k'atun cycle: "These ages are thirteen in number: each has its separate idol and its priest, with a separate prophecy of its events. These thirteen ages are divided into thirteen parts which divide this kingdom of Yucathan and each age, with its idol, priest and prophecy, rules in one of these thirteen parts of the land, according as they have divided it" (Taube 1988b:198).

Taube also notes that thirteen Ajaw signs representing the k'atun cycle were inscribed on the edge of a turtle-shell sculpture from Mayapán, an image he compares to the k'atun wheel Landa illustrates. At the center of the turtle shell is a rimmed opening that would correspond to Lake Atitlán in my reconstruction of Maya world view. The placement of the k'atun signs around this opening suggests that they might represent thirteen mountains surrounding Lake Atitlán. Given that the four New Year ceremonies were each associated with a particular mountain and god, it would not be surprising if each of the k'atuns were also associated with a mountain and god.

It is also possible that each of the thirteen numbers was identified with a particular mountain. In hieroglyphic writing, the thirteen numbers were each manifested as a particular god in head-variant and full-figure form (Thompson 1952). While the identities of some of these number regents are unclear, One Ixim, One Ajaw in his sun god manifestation, Itzamnaaj/God N, GIII, and Yax Bolon are number regents, and I have identified specific mountains with each of them. The association of numbers with particular places is found in contemporary K'iche' divination, where the numbers one, six, eight, and nine in a day name indicate a particular shrine to be visited on that day (B. Tedlock 1982:71). In Momostenango, the "six place" is the shrine Paclom, located on a hill in the town center. It is considered to be the heart of the community and to be connected to the four inner hills of the four directions. This six place is reminiscent of the Six Sky place that I have identified with the center of the world and specifically with Volcán Tolimán, the mountain manifestation of GI. Fittingly, the Number 6 Deity is a portrait of GI with a lightning-bolt ax infixed on his eye.

The notion that the thirteen number deities were identified with specific mountains in highland Guatemala implies that the 260-day calendar might have been developed in this region. The headwaters of the four major rivers are located at approximately latitude 15° north. At this latitude, it is 105 days from the first zenith passage in April to the second zenith passage in August, and 260 days from the August zenith passage to the next April zenith passage. The importance of zenith passage in the agricultural cycle, and the division of the year into a 105-day period and a 260-day period suggests to several researchers that the 260-day calendar originated at this latitude (Nuttall 1928; Merrill 1945; Malmstrom 1973; Aveni 2000).

The journeys of One Hunahpu and his sons between Lake Atitlán and Alta Verapaz as well as the activities of Zipacna that took place between the hut of the Four Hundred Boys and Meauan Mountain on the Chixoy River indicate the importance of this northern route. The conflicts and negotiations between the creator deities and the lords of the underworld established the methods for bride acquisition and warfare. The marriages of One Ixim/One Hunahpu with goddesses from Alta Verapaz provided the template for both alliance-building and conquest through foreign marriage. Ashmore (1989, 1992) has documented a number of lowland sites that have buildings aligned on a north–south axis. It is quite possible that the preference for a north–south axis was based on this mythology.

Although the origin of Mesoamerican culture as a whole is beyond the scope of this book, it is worth pointing out that two of the most important mythological locations in Aztec cosmology, Tamoanchan and Tlalocan, have much in common with Lake Atitlán and Meauan Mountain, respectively. Tamoanchan was characterized as the abode of the creator deities and the birthplace of Centeotl, the corn god. Some sources indicate that the creator deities ground the bones to create humans there. While Tamoanchan was thought to be situated in the heavens, it was also seen as a terrestrial location. Although there has been a long debate over the etymology of this place name, Tamoanchan in Mayan would mean "at hawk sky." As I have argued in chapter 6, the muwaan falcon was a manifestation of GI/Huracan.

Another important Aztec location was Tlalocan, the home of Tlaloc and the water goddess Chalchiuhtlicue (Jade Skirt). The souls of people who died by drowning or lightning were thought to dwell there. Some colonial accounts indicate that Tlalocan was a watery mountain and the source of rain. I have argued that Meauan Mountain was the source of rain and the mountain manifestation of Ixik/Lady Bone Water, whose first death was the result of being struck by lightning while crossing a body of water (after her restoration, her second death occurred during childbirth).

The landscape of highland Guatemala also appears to have been incorporated into the urban plan of Teotihuacan. Teotihuacan-style architecture and artifacts are well documented across the Maya area, and Maya influences in the art of Teotihuacan are also known (Taube 2003). Theories and speculation on the nature and consequences of Teotihuacan's relationship with the Maya region vary. The Postclassic Aztec viewed the great metropolis of Teotihuacan as a sacred location where the gods actually performed acts of creation. The center of Teotihuacan is defined by a large compound, which, as Taube (2000) has convincingly shown, represented the center hearth. The east, south, and west roads that radiate out from this complex are modest compared with the north road, which is between forty and ninety-five meters wide. In Aztec belief, the entrance to the underworld was north, and consequently, they referred to the north road of Teotihuacan as the Avenue of the Dead. The road extends almost two kilometers from the center before terminating at the Pyramid of the Moon, which replicates Cerro Gordo, the hill on the horizon behind the pyramid (Tobriner 1972). Cerro Gordo, a primary source of water for Teotihuacan, was called Tenan, "our mother," by the Aztecs. Two large, monolithic sculptures of a water goddess were found near the Pyramid of the Moon, and one of them wears the diamond-patterned jade skirt.

The association of a northern road with the underworld and a water-goddess mountain is highly reminiscent of the northern world road of highland Guatemala that leads to Meauan Mountain and the underworld. Another example of Teotihuacan's association with the highlands of Guatemala is found in the east–west alignment of the site (Aveni 2000). The sun sets along this axis on April 29 and August 12. These are not the zenith passage dates for Teotihuacan, which are May 18 and July 21, but they are the zenith passage dates for locations near latitude 15° north.

The Maya may not have been the originators of Mesoamerican culture, for the ebb and flow of ideas in Mesoamerica was complex. However, the Motagua River was the only source of jade, a precious commodity that played a central role in Mesoamerican exchange and symbolism since the earliest of times. The landscape of highland Guatemala was a preeminent factor that shaped how the early Mesoamerican people envisioned their world.

# REFERENCES

Akkeren, Ruud van
2000        *Place of the Lord's Daughter: Rab'inal, Its History, Its Dance-Drama.* Leiden: Research
            School CNWS, School of Asian, African, and Amerindian Studies.

Álvarez del Toro, Miguel
1960        *Reptiles de Chiapas.* Tuxtla Gutiérrez, Mexico: Instituto Zoológico del Estado.

Ashmore, Wendy
1989        Construction and Cosmology: Politics and Ideology in Lowland Maya Settle-
            ment Patterns. In *Word and Image in Maya Culture*, ed. William Hanks and Don
            Rice. Salt Lake City: University of Utah Press.
1992        Deciphering Maya Site Plans. In *New Theories on the Ancient Maya*, ed. Elin C.
            Danien and Robert J. Sharer. Philadelphia: University Museum, University of
            Pennsylvania.

Atran, Scott
1993        Itza Maya Tropical Agro-forestry. *Current Anthropology* 34(5): 633–700.
1999        Itzaj Maya Folk-biological Taxonomy. In *Folkbiology*, ed. Douglas L. Medin and
            Scott Atran. Cambridge, Mass.: MIT Press.

Attinasi, John
1973        Lak T'an: A Grammar of the Chol (Mayan) Word. PhD diss., University of Chicago.

Aulie, H. Wilbur
1979        The Christian Movement among the Chols of Mexico, with Special Reference
            to Problems of Second Generation Christianity. D. Mis. thesis. Fuller Theological
            Seminary.

Aulie, H. Wilbur, and Evelyn W. de Aulie
1978        *Diccionario ch'ol-español, español-ch'ol.* Mexico City: Instituto Lingüístico de Verano.

Avendaño y Loyola, Andrés
1987        *Relation of Two Trips to Peten.* Culver City: Labyrinthos.

Aveni, Anthony F.
1980        *Skywatchers of Ancient Mexico.* Austin: University of Texas Press.
1990        The Real Venus-Kukulcan in the Maya Inscriptions and Alignments. In *Sixth Palenque Round Table, 1986,* vol. 8, ed. Merle Greene Robertson and Virginia Fields, 309–21. Norman: University of Oklahoma Press.
2000        Out of Teotihuacan: Origins of the Celestial Canon in Mesoamerica. In *Mesoamerica's Classic Heritage: From Teotihuacan to the Aztecs*, ed. David Carrasco, Lindsay Jones, and Scott Sessions. Boulder: University Press of Colorado.

Aveni, Anthony F., and Horst Hartung
1979        Some Suggestions about the Arrangement of Buildings at Palenque. In *Tercera Mesa Redonda de Palenque*, vol. 4, ed. Merle Greene Robertson and Donnan Call Jeffers, 173–77. Palenque, Mexico: Pre-Columbian Art Research Center.

Baer, Philip
1952        Materials of Lacandon Culture of the Pelhá Region. Microfilm Collection of Manuscripts on Cultural Anthropology, no. 34. Chicago: University of Chicago Library.

Baer, Phillip, and William Merrifield
1971        *Two Studies on the Lacandones of Mexico.* Norman: Summer Institute of Linguistics.

Bardawil, Lawrence
1976        The Principal Bird Deity in Maya Art: An Iconographic Study of Form and Meaning. In *The Art, Iconography, and Dynastic History of Palenque, pt. 3*, ed. Merle Greene Robertson, 181–94. Pebble Beach, Calif.: Pre-Columbian Art Research, Robertson Louis Stevenson School.

Barrera Vásquez, Alfredo
1980        *Diccionario Maya Cordemex.* Merida: Ediciones Cordemex.

Bassie-Sweet, Karen
1987        Illustrated Stories: The Relationship Between Text and Image. Paper presented at the 86th annual meeting of the American Anthropological Association, Chicago.
1991        *From the Mouth of the Dark Cave: Commemorative Sculpture of the Late Classic Maya.* Norman: University of Oklahoma Press.
1996        *At the Edge of the World.* Norman: University of Oklahoma Press.
2002        Corn Deities and the Complementary Male/Female Principle. In *Memoria de la Tercera Mesa Redonda de Palenque*, vol. 2, ed. Vera Tiesler Blos, Rafael Cobos, and Merle Greene Robertson. Mexico City: Instituto Nacional de Antropología e Historia.
2003        Maya Rain Predictions. Paper presented at the annual Chac Mool Conference, University of Calgary.
2004        Three Maya Goddesses. Paper presented at the annual Chac Mool Conference, University of Calgary.

Beekman, Christopher
2003        Agricultural Pole Rituals and Rulership in Late Formative Central Jalisco. *Ancient Mesoamerica* 14:299–318. Cambridge: Cambridge University Press.

Beekman, John
1960        Cultural Extensions of the Chol Church. *Practical Anthropology* 7:54–60.

Berlin, Brent, Dennis Breedlove, and Peter Raven
1974        *Principles of Tzeltal Plant Classification.* New York: Academic Press.

Berlin, Heinrich, and David Kelley
1961        *The 819 Day Count and Color-Direction Symbolism among the Classic Maya.* Middle
            American Research Institute, pub. 26, 9–20. New Orleans: Tulane University.

Berlo, Janet
1980        Teotihuacán Art Abroad: A Study of Metropolitan Style and Provincial Trans-
            formation in Incensario Workshops. PhD diss., Yale University.

Beyer, Herman
1928        El origen del jeroglífico maya akbal. *Revista Mexicana de Estudios Históricos* 2:5–9.

Bierhorst, John
1992        *History and Mythology of the Aztecs: The Codex Chimalpopoca.* Tucson: University
            of Arizona Press.

Blaffer, Sarah
1972        *Black-man of Zinacantan.* Austin: University of Texas Press.

Blom, Frans
1936        *Conquest of Yucatan.* Boston: Houghton-Mifflin.

Blom, Frans, and Oliver La Farge
1927        *Tribes and Temples.* New Orleans: Tulane University.

Bode, Barbara
1961        The Dance of the Conquest. In *The Native Theatre in Middle America.* Middle
            American Research Institute, pub. 27. New Orleans: Tulane University.

Bonar, Juan L.
1989        *Las cuevas mayas: Simbolismo y ritual.* Madrid: Universidad Complutense de Madrid.

Boot, Eric
1999        Of Serpents and Centipedes: The Epithet *Wuk Chapaht Chan K'inich Ahaw.*
            *Notes on Maya Hieroglyphic Writing* (Rijswijk, Netherlands) 25.
2004        Kerr No. 4546 and a Reference to an Avian Manifestation of the Creator God
            Itzamnaj. *www.mayavase.com/Kerr4546.pdf.*

Boremanse, Didier
1982        A Comparative Study in Lacandon Maya Mythology. *Journal de la Société des
            Américanistes* 68:71–98.

Bowen, Sharon, and Lloyd Anderson
1994        The Palenque Emblem Bird Mat and Matawil. *U Mut Maya* (Arcata, Calif.) 5.

Bowes, Anne
1964        *Birds of the Mayas.* Westport, N.Y.: West of the Wind Publications.

Braakhuis, Edwin
2001        The Way of All Flesh. *Anthropos* 96:391–409.
2005        Xbalanque's Canoe. *Anthropos* 100:173–91.

Brasseur de Bourbourg, Charles Étienne
1861        *Popol Vuh: Le livre sacré et les mythes de l'antiquité américaine.* Paris: A. Bertrand.

Breedlove, Dennis, and Robert Laughlin

1993    *The Flowering of Man: The Tzotzil Botany of Zinacantan.* Smithsonian Contributions to Anthropology 35. Washington, D.C.: Smithsonian Institution Press.

Brinton, Daniel G.

1881    *Names of Gods in the Kiche Myths, Central America.* Philadelphia: McCalla & Stavely, Printers.

1883    The Folk-Lore of Yucatan. *Folk-Lore Journal* 1:244–56.

1885    *Annals of the Cakchiquels.* Philadelphia: n.p.

1894    *Nagualism.* Philadelphia: American Philosophical Society.

Brody, Jill

1987    Creation That Endured: Three Tojolabal Texts on Origin. *Latin American Indian Literatures Journal* 3(1): 39–58.

Bruce, Robert

1975    *Textos y dibujos lacandones de Najá.* Departamento de Lingüística 45. Mexico: Colección Científica Lingüística.

1977    The Popol Vuh and the Book of Chan K'in. *Estudios de cultura maya* 10:173–208.

1979    *Lacandon Dream Symbolism.* Mexico: Ediciones Euroamericanas Klaus Thiele.

Bruce, Robert, C. Robles, and María E. Ramos C.

1971    *Los lacandones 2: Cosmovisión maya.* Mexico City: Instituto Nacional de Antropología e Historia.

Bruchez, Margaret

1997    Archaeological Investigations, Department of Sololá, Southern Maya Highlands: Premaya to Postclassic Settlement, Northern Terrestrial Rim and Subsurface Shore Lake Atitlán, Guatemala. PhD diss., Texas A&M University.

Búcaro Moraga, Jaime

1991    Leyendas de pueblos indígenas. Leyendas, cuentos, mitos y fábulas indígenas. *Tradiciones de Guatemala* 35/36:55–127.

Bunzel, Ruth

1952    *Chichicastenago: A Guatemalan Village.* Seattle: University of Washington Press.

Burkitt, Robert

1902    Notes on the Kekchí Language. *American Anthropologist* 4:441–63.

1920    *The Hills and the Corn.* Philadelphia: University of Pennsylvania Anthropological Publications.

Butler, James, and Dean Arnold

1977    Tzutujil Maize Classification in San Pedro La Laguna. In *Cognitive Studies of Southern Mesoamerica,* ed. Helen Neuenswander and Dean Arnold. Dallas: Summer Institute of Linguistics Museum of Anthropology.

Byland, Bruce, and John M. D. Pohl

1994    *In the Realm of 8 Deer: The Archaeology of the Mixtec Codices.* Norman: University of Oklahoma Press.

Calnek, Edward

1988    *Highland Chiapas before the Conquest*. Papers of the New World Archaeological Foundation 55. Provo: Brigham Young University.

Campbell, Jonathan

1998    *Amphibians and Reptiles of Northern Guatemala, the Yucatan and Belize*. Norman: University of Oklahoma Press.

Carlsen, Robert, and Martin Prechtel

1991    The Flowering of the Dead: An Interpretation of Highland Maya Culture. *Man* 26:23–42.

Carlson, Ruth, and Francis Eachus

1977    The Kekchi Spirit World. In *Cognitive Studies of Southern Mesoamerica*, ed. Helen Neuenswander and Dean Arnold. Dallas: Summer Institute of Linguistics Museum of Anthropology.

Carmack, Robert

1973    *Quichean Civilization: The Ethnohistoric, Ethnographic, and Archaeological Sources*. Berkeley: University of California Press.

1981    Quiché Mayas of Utatlán. Norman: University of Oklahoma Press.

1995    *Rebels of Highland Guatemala: The Quiché Mayas of Momostenango*. Norman: University of Oklahoma Press.

Carrasco, Michael

2005    The Incensario Stands of Palenque. PhD diss., University of Texas at Austin.

Carrasco, Michael, and Kerry Hull

2002    The Cosmogonic Symbolism of the Corbeled Vault in Maya Architecture. *Mexicon* 24(2): 26–32.

Carter, William E.

1969    *New Lands and Old Traditions: Kekchi Cultivators in the Guatemalan Lowlands*. Gainesville: University of Florida Press.

Chase, Diane

1991    Lifeline to the Gods: Ritual Bloodletting at Santa Rita Corozal. In *Sixth Palenque Round Table, 1986*, vol. 8, ed. Merle Greene Robertson and Virginia Fields, 89–96. Norman: University of Oklahoma Press.

Chase, Diane, and Arlen Chase

1986    *Offerings to the Gods: Maya Archaeology at Santa Rita Corozal*. Orlando: University of Central Florida.

1988    *A Postclassic Perspective: Excavations at the Maya Site of Santa Rita Corozal*. Pre-Columbian Art Research Institute Monograph 4. San Francisco: Pre-Columbian Art Research Institute.

1998    Architectural Context of Caches, Burials, and Other Ritual Activities for the Classic Period Maya (As Reflected at Caracol, Belize). In *Function and Meaning in Classic Maya Architecture*, ed. S. D. Houston, 299–332. Washington, D.C.: Dumbarton Oaks.

Child, Mark

2006    The Symbolic Space of the Ancient Maya Sweatbath. In *Space and Spatial Analysis in Archaeology*, ed. Elizabeth C. Robertson, Jeffrey D. Seibert, Deepika C. Fernandez, and Mark U. Zender. Calgary: University of Calgary Press.

Christenson, Allen

2001    *Art and Society in a Highland Maya Community: The Altarpiece of Santiago Atitlán.* Austin: University of Texas Press.

2003a   *Popol Vuh: The Sacred Book of the Maya.* New York: O Books.

2003b   Manipulating the Cosmos: Shamanic Tables among the Highland Maya. In *Mesas and Cosmologies in Mesoamerica*, ed. Douglas Sharon, 93–104. San Diego: San Diego Museum of Man.

Ciaramella, Mary

1994    The Lady with the Snake Headdress. In *Seventh Palenque Round Table, 1989,* ed. Virginia Fields. San Francisco: Pre-Columbian Art Research Institute.

1999    *The Weavers in the Codices.* Research Reports on Ancient Maya Writing, 44. Washington, D.C.: Center for Maya Research.

2002    *The Bee-Keepers in the Madrid Codex.* Research Reports on Ancient Maya Writing, 52. Washington, D.C.: Center for Maya Research.

Clarke, John, and Stephen Houston

1998    Craft Specialization, Gender and Personhood among the Post-conquest Maya of Yucatan, Mexico. In *Craft and Social Identity*, ed. Cathy Lynne Costin and Rita Wright. Arlington, Va.: American Anthropological Association.

Cline, Howard

1944    Lore and Deities of the Lacandon Indians, Chiapas, Mexico. *Journal of American Folklore* 57:107–15.

Coe, Michael

1973    *The Maya Scribe and His World.* New York: Grolier Club.

1975    Native Astronomy in Mesoamerica. In *Archaeoastronomy in Pre-Columbian America*, ed. Anthony F. Aveni. Austin: University of Texas Press.

1977    Supernatural Patrons of Maya Scribes and Artists. In *Social Process in Maya Prehistory*, ed. Norman Hammond, 327–47. London: Academic Press.

1978    *Lords of the Underworld.* Princeton: Princeton University Press.

1988    Ideology of the Maya Tomb. In *Maya Iconography*, ed. Elizabeth Benson and Gillett Griffin. Princeton: Princeton University Press.

1989    The Hero Twins: Myth and Image. In *The Maya Vase Book*, vol. 1, ed. Justin Kerr, 161–84. New York: Kerr Associates.

Coe, Michael, and Sophie Coe

1996    *The True History of Chocolate.* New York: Thames and Hudson.

Coe, Michael, and Justin Kerr

1998    *The Art of the Maya Scribe.* New York: Harry Abrams.

Coe, Michael, and Gordon Whittaker

1982    *Aztec Sorcerers in Seventeenth Century Mexico.* Albany: Institute for Mesoamerican Studies, State University of New York at Albany.

Coggins, Clemency
1980        Shape of Time: Some Political Implications of a Four-Part Figure. *American Antiquity* 45(4): 727–39.

Colby, Benjamin, and Lore Colby
1981        *The Daykeeper: The Life and Discourse of an Ixil Diviner.* Cambridge, Mass.: Harvard University Press.

Colby, Benjamin, and Pierre van den Berghe
1969        *Ixil Country: A Pluralistic Society in Highland Guatemala.* Berkeley: University of California Press.

Cook, Garrett
1981        Supernaturalism, Cosmos, and Cosmogony in Quichean Expressive Culture. PhD diss., State University of New York at Albany.
1986        Quichean Folk Theology and Southern Maya Supernaturalism. In *Symbol and Meaning Beyond the Closed Community*, ed. Gary Gossen. Albany: Institute for Mesoamerican Studies, State University of New York at Albany.
2000        *Renewing the Maya World: Expressive Culture in a Highland Town.* Austin: University of Texas Press.

Cordry, Donald
1968        *Mexican Indian Costumes.* Austin: University of Texas Press.

Cordry, Donald, and Dorothy Cordry
1941        *Costumes and Weaving of the Zoque Indians of Chiapas, Mexico.* Los Angeles: Southwest Museum.

Cortez, Constance
1986        The Principal Bird Deity in Preclassic and Early Classic Maya Art. Master's thesis, University of Texas at Austin.

Coto, Fray Thomás de
1983        *Thesaurus verborum: Vocabulario de la lengua cakchiquel u guatemalteca, nuevamente hecho y recopilado con summo estudio, travajo y erudición*, ed. René Acuña. Mexico City: Universidad Autónoma de Mexico.

Craine, Eugene, and Reginald Reindorp
1979        *The Codex Pérez and the Book of Chilam Balam of Maní.* Norman: University of Oklahoma Press.

Cruz Torres, Mario Enrique de la
1965        *Rubelpec: Cuentos y leyendas de Senahú.* Guatemala: Pineda Ibarra.

Cuevas García, Martha
2004        The Cult of Patron and Ancestor Gods in Censers at Palenque. In *Courtly Art of the Ancient Maya*, ed. Mary Miller and Simon Martin. New York: Thames and Hudson.

Davis, Virginia
1978        Ritual of the Northern Lacandon Maya. PhD diss., Tulane University.

de Jong, Harriet

1999    The Land of Corn and Honey: The Keeping of Stingless Bees (Meliponiculture) in the Ethno-Ecological Environment of Yucatan (Mexico) and El Salvador. PhD thesis, Utrecht University, Netherlands.

Devereaux, Leslie

1987    Gender Difference and Relations of Inequality in Zinacantan. In *Dealing with Inequality: Analysing Gender Relations in Melanesia and Beyond,* ed. Marilyn Strathern. Cambridge: Cambridge University Press.

Dickey, Donald, and A. J. Van Rossem

1938    *The Birds of El Salvador.* Zoological Series, vol. 23, pub. 406. Chicago: Field Museum of Natural History.

Dieseldorff, Herbert

1966    Historia de Balam Que y Po, la luna. *Folklore de Guatemala* 2:175–86.

Dillon, Brian

1977    *Salinas de los Nueve Cerros, Guatemala: Preliminary Archaeological Investigations.* Socorro, N.Mex.: Ballena Press.

Douglas, Bill Gray

1969    Illness and Curing in Santiago Atitlán. PhD diss., Stanford University.

Duby, Gertrude, and Frans Blom

1969    The Lacandon. In *Handbook of Middle American Indians,* vol. 7, *Ethnology.* Austin: University of Texas Press.

Dunkelman, Arthur

2007    *The Jay I. Kislak Collection at the Library of Congress.* Washington, D.C.: Library of Congress.

Durán, Diego

1971    *Book of the Gods and Rites and the Ancient Calendar.* Norman: University of Oklahoma Press.

Earle, Duncan, and Dean Snow

1985    The Origin of the 260-day Calendar. In *Fifth Palenque Round Table, 1983,* vol. 7, ed. Merle Greene Robertson and Virginia Fields, 171–81. San Francisco: Pre-Columbian Art Research Institute.

Eberl, Markus

2001    Death and Conceptions of the Soul. In *Maya: Divine Kings of the Rain Forest,* ed. Nikolai Grube. Cologne: Könemann.

Edmonson, Munro

1965    *Quiche-English Dictionary.* Middle American Research Institute, pub. 30. New Orleans: Tulane University.

1971    *The Book of Counsel: The Popol Vuh of the Quiche Maya of Guatemala.* New Orleans: Middle American Research Institute.

Escobar, Fray Alonso de

1841    Accounts of the Province of Vera Paz, in Guatemala, and of the Indian Settlements or Pueblos Established Therein. In *Journal of the Royal Geographical Society of London* 2:89–97.

Faust, Betty
1998    *Mexican Rural Development and the Plumed Serpent: Technology and Maya Cosmology in the Tropical Forest of Campeche, Mexico.* Westport, Conn.: Greenwood Press.

Feldman, Lawrence H.
1988    *History of the Foundation of the Town of Chamiquin by Francisco Aguilar.* Culver City, Calif.: Labyrinthos.
2000    *Lost Shores and Forgotten People.* Durham: Duke University Press.
2004    *A Dictionary of Poqom Maya in the Colonial Era.* Lancaster, Calif.: Labyrinthos.

Fields, Virginia
1990    The Iconographic Heritage of the Maya Jester God. In *Sixth Palenque Round Table, 1986,* vol. 8, ed. Merle Greene Robertson and Virginia Fields, 167–74. Norman: University of Oklahoma Press.

Fields, Virginia, and Dorie Reents-Budet
2005    *Lords of Creation.* Los Angeles: Los Angeles Museum of Art.

Fischer, Edward
1999    Cultural Logic and Maya Identity: Rethinking Constructivism and Essentialism. *Current Anthropology* 40(4): 473–99.

Florescano, Enrique
1999    *The Myth of Queztalcoatl.* Washington, D.C.: Johns Hopkins University Press.

Fought, John
1972    *Chorti (Mayan) Texts.* Philadelphia: University of Pennsylvania Press.

Fox, James, and John Justeson
1984    Polyvalence in Mayan Hieroglyphic Writing. In *Phoneticism in Mayan Hieroglyphic Writing,* ed. John Justeson and Lyle Campbell, 17–76. Institute for Mesoamerican Studies, pub. 9. Albany: State University of New York at Albany.

Freidel, David, Linda Schele, and Joy Parker
1993    *Maya Cosmos.* New York: William Morrow.

French, Kirk
2004    Creating Space through Water Management at the Classic Maya Site of Palenque, Chiapas, Mexico. Master's thesis, University of Cincinnati.

Furst, Jill
1978    *Codex Vindobonensis Mexicanus 1: A Commentary.* Albany: Institute for Mesoamerican Studies, State University of New York at Albany.
1995    *Natural History of the Soul.* New Haven: Yale University Press.

Gann, Thomas
1918    The Maya Indians of Southern Yucatan and Northern British Honduras. *Bureau of American Ethnology,* bull. 64. Washington, D.C.: Government Printing Office.

Garza, Mercedes de la, Ana Luisa Izquierdo, María del Carmen León, and Tolita Figueroa
1983    *Relaciones histórico-geográficas de la gobernación de Yucatán.* 2 vols. Mexico City: Universidad Nacional Autónoma de México.

Girard, Rafael
1948    *Esoterismo del Popol-Vuh.* Mexico: Stylo.

1952    *El Popul-Vuh, fuente histórica*. Guatemala: Ministerio de Educación Pública.

1962    *Los mayas eternos*. Mexico City: Antigua Librería Robredo de José Porrúa e Hijos.

1979    *Esotericism of the Popol Vuh*. Pasadena: Theosophical University Press.

Glittenberg, Jody

1994    *To the Mountain and Back: the Mysteries of Guatemalan Highland Family Life*. Long
        Grove, Ill.: Waveland Press.

Goetz, Delia, and Sylvanus Morley

1950    *Popol Vuh*. Norman: University of Oklahoma Press.

Gordon, G. B.

1915    Guatemala Myths. *The Museum Journal* 6(3): 103–44.

Gossen, Gary

1974    *Chamulas in the World of the Sun*. Cambridge, Mass.: Harvard University Press.

1999    *Telling Maya Tales: Tzotzil Identities in Modern Mexico*. New York: Routledge.

2002    *Four Creations: An Epic Story of the Chiapas Mayas*. Norman: University of Okla-
        homa Press.

Goubaud Carrera, Antonio

1949    Notes on San Juan Chamelco, Alta Verapaz. Microfilm Collection of Manuscripts
        on Cultural Anthropology, no. 23. Chicago: University of Chicago Library.

Groark, Kevin

1997    To Warm the Blood, to Warm the Flesh: The Role of the Steambath in Highland
        Maya (Tzeltal-Tzotzil) Ethnomedicine. *Journal of Latin American Lore* 20(1): 3–96.

Grube, Nikolai

1987    *Observations on the T110 as the Syllable* Ko. Research Reports on Ancient Maya
        Writing, 8. Washington, D.C.: Center for Maya Research.

Grube, Nikolai, and Werner Nahm

1994    A Census of Xibalba: A Complete Inventory of *Way* Characters on Maya Ceramics.
        In *The Maya Vase Book*, vol. 4, ed. Justin Kerr, 686–715. New York: Kerr Associates.

Grube, Nikolai, and Linda Schele

1994    Kuy, the Owl of Omen and War. *Mexicon* 16(1): 10–17.

Guest, Gregory

1995    A Tree for All Reasons: The Maya and the "Sacred" Ceiba. Master's thesis, Uni-
        versity of Calgary.

Guiteras Holmes, Calixta

1961    *Perils of the Soul*. Glencoe, N.Y.: Free Press.

Habel, Simeon

1878    *The Sculptures of Santa Lucia Cosumalwhuapa in Guatemala, with an Account of Trav-
        els in Central America and on the Western Coast of South America*. Washington, D.C.:
        Smithsonian Institution.

Hanks, William

1991    *Referential Practice: Language and Lived Space among the Maya*. Chicago: University
        of Chicago Press.

Hansen, Richard

1990    *Excavations in the Tigre Complex El Mirador, Petén, Guatemala.* Papers of the New World Archaeological Foundation. Provo: Brigham Young University.

1992    Archaeology of Ideology: A Study of Maya Preclassic Architectural Sculpture at Nakbe, Peten, Guatemala. PhD diss., University of California, Los Angeles.

Haviland, William

1997    The Rise and Fall of Sexual Inequality: Death and Gender at Tikal, Guatemala. *Ancient Mesoamerica* 8: 1–12.

Hellmuth, Nicholas

1987    The Surface of the Underwaterworld. PhD diss., Karl-Franzens-Universitaet. Culver City, Calif.: Foundation for Latin American Anthropological Research.

Hermitte, Ester

1964    *Supernatural Power and Social Control in a Modern Maya Village.* PhD diss., University of Chicago.

Hester, Joseph

1954    Natural and Cultural Bases of Ancient Maya Subsistence Economy. PhD diss. University of California at Los Angeles.

Hill, Robert M.

1992    *Colonial Cakchiquels: Highland Maya Adaptations to Spanish Rule, 1600–1700.* Fort Worth: Harcourt Brace Jovanovich.

Hill, Robert M., and Edward Fischer

1999    States of the Heart: An Ethnohistorical Approach to Kaqchikel Maya Ethnopsychology. *Ancient Mesoamerica* 10(2): 317–33.

Hofling, Charles, and Félix Tesucún

1997    *Itzaj Maya–Spanish-English Dictionary.* Salt Lake City: University of Utah Press.

Holland, William R.

1961    Highland Maya Folk Medicine. PhD diss., University of Arizona.

Hopkins, Nicholas

1988    Classic Mayan Kinship Systems: Epigraphic and Ethnographic Evidence for Patrilineality. *Estudios de cultura maya* 17:87–121.

1996    Metonym and Metaphor in Chol (Mayan) Ritual Language. Paper presented at the annual meeting of the American Anthropological Association, San Francisco.

Hostettler, Ueli

1996    Milpa Agriculture and Economic Diversification: Socioeconomic Change in a Maya Peasant Village of Central Quintana Roo, 1900–1990's. PhD diss., Universitaet Bern, Switzerland.

Houston, Stephen

1983    A Reading for the "Flint-Shield" Glyph. In *Contributions to Maya Hieroglyphic Decipherment* 1, ed. Stephen Houston. New Haven: HRAFlex Books.

1992    A Name Glyph for Classic Maya Dwarfs. In *The Maya Vase Book*, vol. 3, ed. Justin Kerr. New York: Kerr Associates.

1996    Symbolic Sweatbaths of the Maya: Architectural Meaning in the Cross Group at Palenque, Mexico. *Latin American Antiquity* 7(2): 132–51.

2000    Into the Minds of Ancients: Advances in Maya Glyph Studies. *Journal of World Prehistory*, 14(2): 121–201.

2001    Words on Wings: Messages and Embassies among the Classic Maya. Paper presented at the Maya Weekend, University of Pennsylvania Museum.

Houston, Stephen, John Robertson, and David Stuart

2001    *Quality and Quantity in Glyphic Nouns and Adjectives.* Research Reports on Ancient Maya Writing, 47. Washington, D.C.: Center for Maya Research.

Houston, Stephen, and David Stuart

1989    *The Way Glyph: Evidence for Co-essences among the Classic Maya.* Research Reports on Ancient Maya Writing, 30. Washington, D.C.: Center for Maya Research.

1996    Of Gods, Glyphs and Kings: Divinity and Rulership among the Classic Maya. *Antiquity* 70:289–312.

1998    The Ancient Maya Self: Personhood and Portraiture in the Classic Period. *Res: Anthropology and Aesthetics* 33:73–101.

Houston, Stephen, David Stuart, and Karl Taube

1992    Image and Text on the Jauncy Vase. In *The Maya Vase Book*, vol. 3, ed. Justin Kerr, 498–513. New York: Kerr Associates.

2006    *Memory of Bones.* Austin: University of Texas Press.

Houston, Stephen, and Karl Taube

2000    An Archaeology of the Senses: Perception and Cultural Expression in Ancient Mesoamerica. *Cambridge Archaeological Journal* (Cambridge, UK) 10(2): 261–94.

Hull, Kerry

2000    *Cosmological and Ritual Language in Ch'orti'.* FAMSI Research Report. www.famsi.org/reports/99036/index.html

Hull, Kerry, and Michael Carrasco

2004    Mak "Portal" Rituals Uncovered: An Approach to Interpreting Symbolic Architecture and the Creation of Sacred Space among the Maya. *In Continuity and Change: Maya Religious Practices in Temporal Perspective*, ed. Daniel Graña Behrens et al., 131–42. Markt Schwaben, Germany: A. Saurwein.

Hunn, Eugene

1977    *Tzeltal Folk Zoology.* New York: Academic Press.

Hunt, Eva

1977    *The Transformation of the Hummingbird.* Ithaca and London: Cornell University Press.

Jackson, Sarah, and David Stuart

2001    The Aj K'uhun Title. *Ancient Mesoamerica* 12:217–28.

Janzen, Daniel

1983    *Costa Rican Natural History.* Chicago: University of Chicago Press.

Jessup, Marie, and Lesley Simpson

1936    *Indian Tales from Guatemala.* New York: Charles Scribner's Sons.

Johannessen, Carl
1982        Domestication Process of Maize Continues in Guatemala. *Economic Botany* 36:84–99.

Jonghe, Edouard de
1905        Histoyre du mechique. *Journal de la Société des Américanistes de Paris* 2:1–41.

Josserand, J. Kathryn
2006        Languages of the Preclassic Period along the Pacific Coastal Plains of Southeastern Mesoamerica. Paper presented at the annual meeting of the American Anthropological Association, San Jose, California.

Joyce, Rosemary
1992        Images of Gender and Labor Organization in Classic Maya Society. In *Exploring Gender through Archaeology*, ed. C. Claessen. Madison: Prehistory Press.
1993        Woman's Work: Images of Production and Reproduction in Pre-Hispanic Southern Central America. *Current Anthropology* 34(3): 255–74.

Kappelman, Julia, and Kent Reilly
2001        Paths to Heaven, Ropes to Earth: Birds, Jaguars, and Cosmic Cords in Formative Period Mesoamerica. *Ancient America*, no. 3. Washington, D.C.: Center for Ancient American Studies.

Kaufman, Terrence
1976        Archaeological and Linguistic Correlations in Mayaland and Associated Areas of Mesoamerica. *World Archaeology* 8:101–18.

Kaufman, Terrence, and William Norman
1984        An Outline of Proto-Cholan Phonology, Morphology and Vocabulary. In *Phoneticism in Mayan Hieroglyphic Writing*, ed. John Justeson and Lyle Campbell, 77–166. Institute for Mesoamerican Studies, pub. 9: Albany: State University of New York at Albany.

Kelley, David
1965        The Birth of the Gods at Palenque. *Estudios de cultura maya* 5:93–134.
1976        *Deciphering the Maya Script.* Austin: University of Texas Press.

Kelsey, Vera, and Lilly de Jongh Osborne
1961        *Four Keys to Guatemala.* New York: Funk and Wagnalls.

Kettunen, Harri, and Bon V. Davis
2004        Snakes, Centipedes, Snakepedes and Centiserpents. *Wayeb Notes* 9. www.wayeb.org.

Konrad, Herman
1985        Fallout of the Wars of the Chacs: The Impact of Hurricanes and Implications for Prehispanic Quintana Roo Maya Processes. *In Status, Structure and Stratification: Current Archaeological Reconstructions,* ed. M. Thompson, M. T. Garcia, and F. J. Kense. Calgary: University of Calgary, Archaeological Association.

Lacadena, Alfonso
2004        On the Reading of Two Glyphic Appellatives of the Rain God. *In Continuity and Change: Maya Religious Practices in Temporal Perspective*, ed. Daniel Graña Behrens et al. Markt Schwaben, Germany: A. Saurwein.

La Farge, Oliver
1947        *Santa Eulalia.* Chicago: University of Chicago Press.

La Farge, Oliver, and Douglas Byers
1931        *The Year Bearer's People.* Middle American Research Series, pub. 3. New Orleans: Tulane University.

Lamb, Weldon
1981        Star Lore in the Yucatec Maya Dictionaries. In *Archaeoastronomy in Pre-Columbian America.* Austin: University of Texas Press.

Land, Hugh
1970        *Birds of Guatemala.* Wynnewood, Pa.: Livingston Publishing.

Las Casas, Fray Bartolomé de
1967        *Apologética historia de las Indias.* 2 vols. Mexico City: Universidad Nacional Autónoma de México.

Laughlin, Robert M.
1962        Through the Looking Glass: Reflections in Zinacantán Courtship and Marriage. PhD diss., Harvard University.

1975        *The Great Tzotzil Dictionary of San Lorenzo Zinacantan.* Smithsonian Contributions to Anthropology, vol. 19. Washington, D.C.: Smithsonian Institution Press.

1977        *Of Cabbages and Kings.* Smithsonian Contributions to Anthropology, vol. 23. Washington, D.C.: Smithsonian Institution Press.

1988        *The Great Tzotzil Dictionary of Santo Domingo Zinacantán.* Smithsonian Contributions to Anthropology, vol. 31. Washington, D.C.: Smithsonian Institution Press.

2004        *Mayan Hearts.* San Cristobal, Mexico: Taller Leñateros.

Laughlin, Robert M., and Carol Karasik
1988        *The People of the Bat: Mayan Tales and Dreams from Zinacantan.* Washington, D.C.: Smithsonian Institution Press.

Lee, Julian
1996        *The Amphibians and Reptiles of the Yucatan Peninsula.* Ithaca, N.Y.: Cornell University Press.

2000        *Field Guide to the Amphibians and Reptiles of the Maya World.* Ithaca, N.Y.: Cornell University Press.

León Portilla, Miguel
1988        *Time and Reality in the Thought of the Maya.* Norman: University of Oklahoma Press.

Le Plongeon, Alice
1889        *Here and There in Yucatan.* New York: J. W. Lovell.

Lincoln, Steward
1942        Maya Calendar of the Ixil of Guatemala. *Contributions to American Anthropology and History* 7(38): 97–128. Washington, D.C.: Carnegie Institution of Washington.

Looper, Matthew, and Julia Kappelman
2001        The Cosmic Umbilicus in Mesoamerica: A Floral Metaphor for the Source of Life. *Journal of Latin American Lore* 21(1): 3–54.

López Austin, Alfredo

1988    *Human Body and Ideology: Concepts of the Ancient Nahuas.* Salt Lake City: University of Utah Press.

1993    *Myths of the Opossum: Pathways to Mesoamerican Mythology.* Albuquerque: University of New Mexico Press.

Lounsbury, Floyd

1978    Maya Numeration, Commutation and Calendrical Astronomy. *Dictionary of Scientific Biography* 15, suppl. 1, ed. C. C. Gillispie, 759–818. New York: Scribner's.

1982    Astronomical Knowledge and Its Uses at Bonampak, Mexico. In *Archaeoastronomy in the New World*, ed. Anthony F. Aveni, 143–68. New York: Cambridge University Press.

1989    A Palenque King and the Planet Jupiter. In *World Archaeoastronomy: Selected Papers from the Second Oxford International Conference on Archaeoastronomy*, ed. Anthony F. Aveni. Cambridge: Cambridge University Press.

Love, Bruce

1994    *The Paris Codex.* Austin: University of Austin Press.

Love, Bruce, and Eduardo Peraza Castillo

1994    Wahil Kol, a Yucatec Maya Agricultural Ceremony. *Estudios de cultura maya* 15: 251–300.

Lowery, George, and Walter Dalquest

1951    *Birds from the State of Veracruz, Mexico.* Lawrence: University of Kansas.

Mace, Carroll

1970    *Two Spanish-Quiché Dance-Dramas of Rabinal.* New Orleans: Tulane University.

Makemson, Maud

1951    *The Book of the Jaguar Priest: A Translation of the Book of Chilam Balam of Tizimin.* New York: Henry Schuman.

Maler, Teobert

1880    *Explorations of the Upper Usumatsintla and Adjacent Region, Altar de Sacrificios; Seiba; Itsimté-Sácluk; Cankuen.* Cambridge, Mass.: Peabody Museum.

Malmstrom, Vincent

1973    Origin of the Mesoamerican 260 Day Cycle. *Science* 181:759–60.

Martin, Simon

2001    Unmasking "Double Bird," Ruler of Tikal. *PARI* [Precolumbian Art Research Institute] *Journal* 2(1): 7–12.

2002    The Baby Jaguar: An Explanation of Its Identity and Origins in Maya Art and Writing. In *Memoria de la Tercera Mesa Redonda de Palenque*, vol. 1, ed. Vera Tiesler Blos, Rafael Cobos, and Merle Greene Robertson. Mexico City: Instituto Nacional de Antropología e Historia.

2004    A Broken Sky: The Ancient Name of Yaxchilan as Pa'Chan. *PARI Journal* 5(1):1–7.

2005    Metamorphosis in the Underworld: The Maize God and the Mythology of Cacao. In *The Sourcebook for the 29th Maya Hieroglyphic Forum*. Austin: Department of Art and Art History, University of Texas at Austin.

2006a    The Great Sustainer: God N in Ancient Maya Religion. Paper presented at the Maya Weekend, University of Pennsylvania Museum.

2006b    Cacao in Ancient Maya Religion: First Fruits of the Maize Tree and Other Tales from the Underworld. In *Theobroma Cacao in Pre-Columbian and Modern Mesoamerican Communities*, ed. Cameron McNeil. Gainesville: University of Florida Press.

Martin, Simon, and Nikolai Grube

2000    *Chronicle of the Maya Kings and Queens*. London: Thames and Hudson.

Maxwell, Judith M.

1980    Yarns Spun by Ixils. In *Mayan Texts* 3, ed. Louanna Furbee-Losee. International Journal of American Linguistics–Native American Texts Monograph 5. Chicago: University of Chicago Press.

Mayers, Marvin K.

1958    *Pocomchí Texts, with Grammatical Notes*. A Publication of the Summer Institute of Linguistics. Norman: University of Oklahoma.

1966    *Languages of Guatemala*. The Hague: Mouton.

Maynard, Eileen

1963    The Women of Palin: Comparative Study of Indian and Ladino Women in a Guatemalan Village. PhD diss., Cornell University.

McArthur, Harry

1977    Releasing the Dead: Ritual and Motivation in Aguacatec Dances. *Museum of Anthropology Publications* 4:6–35. Dallas: Summer Institute of Linguistics.

McBryde, Felix

1947    *Cultural and Historical Geography of Southwest Guatemala*. Institute of Social Anthropology, pub. 4. Washington, D.C.: Smithsonian Institution.

McCafferty, Geoffrey, and Sharrise McCafferty

1991    Spinning and Weaving as Female Gender Identity in Post-Classic Mexico. In *Textile Traditions of Mesoamerica and the Andes: An Anthology*, ed. M. B. Schevill, J. C. Berlo, and E. Dwyer. New York: Garland.

McGee, Jon

1989    Flood Myth from a Lacandón Maya Perspective. *Latin American Indian Literatures Journal* 5(1): 68–80.

1990    *Life, Ritual, and Religion among the Lacandon Maya*. Belmont, Calif.: Wadsworth.

Mendelson, E. Michael

1957    Religion and World View in a Guatemalan Village. Microfilm Collection of Manuscripts on Cultural Anthropology, no. 52. Chicago: University of Chicago Library.

1958    A Guatemalan Sacred Bundle. *Man* 58:121–26.

Mendenhall, Celia Douglas, and Julia Supple

1949    Tojolabal Texts and Dictionary. Microfilm Collection of Manuscripts on Cultural Anthropology, no. 26. Chicago: University of Chicago Library.

Merrill, Robert
1945        Maya Sun Calendar Dictum Disproved. *American Antiquity* 10(3): 306–11.

Merrill-Sands, Deborah
1984        The Mixed Subsistence-Commercial Production System in the Peasant Econ-
            omy of Yucatan, Mexico: An Anthropological Study in Commercial Beekeep-
            ing. PhD diss., Cornell University.

Milbrath, Susan
1999        *Star Gods of the Maya*. Austin: University of Texas Press.

Miles, Suzanna
1955        The Sixteenth Century Pokom-Maya: A Documentary Analysis of Social Struc-
            ture and Archaeological Setting. PhD diss., Harvard University.
1957        The Sixteenth Century Pokom-Maya: A Documentary Analysis of Social Struc-
            ture and Archaeological Setting. American Philosophical Society 47(4): 733–81.
1960        Mam Residence and the Maize Myth. In *Culture in History: Essays in Honor of
            Paul Radin*, ed. Stanley Diamond. New York: Columbia University.

Miller, Mary Ellen
1992        The Image of People and Nature in Classic Maya Art and Architecture. In *The
            Ancient Americas: Art from Sacred Landscapes*, ed. Richard F. Townsend. Chicago:
            Art Institute of Chicago.

Miller, Mary Ellen, and Simon Martin
2004        *Courtly Art of the Ancient Maya*. New York: Thames and Hudson.

Millon, René
1955        When Money Grows on Trees: A Study of Cacao in Ancient Mesoamerica.
            PhD diss., Columbia University.

Montejo, Víctor, and Lyle Campbell
1993        The Origin of Corn: A Jacaltec Tale in Comparative Mayan Perspective. *Latin
            American Indian Literatures Journal* 9(2): 99–119.

Morris, Walter F.
1987        *Living Maya*. New York: Harry N. Abrams.
1994        Notes on Lady Feathered Serpent. In *Artes tradicionales maysa de las tierras bajas*.
            Mexico City: Asociación Mexicana de Arte y Cultura Popular.

Nash, June
1970        *In the Eyes of the Ancestors*. New Haven: Yale University Press.

Nations, James
1981        The Rainforest Farmers. *Pacific Discovery* 34(1): 1–9.

Nations, James, and Ronald Nigh
1980        Evolutionary Potential of Lacandon Maya Sustained Yield Tropical Forest Agri-
            culture. *Journal of Anthropological Research* 36(1): 1–30.

Neuenswander, Helen
1981        Vestiges of Early Maya Time Concepts in a Contemporary Maya (Cubulco
            Achi) Community. *Estudios de cultura maya* 13:125–63.

Nicholson, Henry
1971        Religion in Pre-Hispanic Central Mexico. In *Handbook of Middle American Indians*, vol. 10:395–446. Austin: University of Texas Press.

Nuttall, Zelia
1928        *La observación del paso del sol por el zénit por los antiguos habitantes de la América Tropical*. Mexico: Talleres Gráficos de la Nación.

Oakes, Maud
1951        *Two Crosses of Todos Santos*. New York: Pantheon.

O'Brien, Linda
1975        Songs of the Face of the Earth: Ancestor Songs of the Tzutuhil Maya of Santiago Atitlán, Guatemala. PhD diss., University of California at Los Angeles.

Orellana, Sandra
1984        *The Tzutujil Maya*. Norman: University of Oklahoma Press.
1987        *Indian Medicine in Highland Guatemala*. Albuquerque: University of New Mexico Press.

Paul, Lois, and Benjamin Paul
1962        *Ethnographic Materials on San Pedro La Laguna, Sololá, Guatemala*. Microfilm Collection of Manuscripts on Cultural Anthropology, no. 54. Chicago: University of Chicago Library.
1975        The Maya Midwife as Sacred Professional: A Guatemalan Case. *American Ethnologist* 2:707–26.

Peck, Horace
1970        Practices and Training of Guatemalan Mam Shamans. PhD diss., Hartford Seminary Foundation.

Perera, Victor, and Robert Bruce
1982        *Last Lords of Palenque: The Lacandon Mayas of the Mexican Rain Forest*. Berkeley: University of California Press.

Pérez Toro, Augusto
1942        *La Milpa*. Merida, Mexico: Talleres Gráficos del Sudeste.

Pieper, Jim
2002        *Guatemala's Folk Saints*. Los Angeles: Jim Pieper and Associates.

Piña Chan, Román, Chan Kin Nohol, and Alberto Davidoff
1992        *Arenas del tiempo recuperadas*. Campeche: Gobierno del Estado de Campeche.

Pohl, John M. D.
1994        Weaving and Gift Exchange in the Mixtec Codices. In *Cloth and Curing: Continuity and Change in Oaxaca*, ed. Grace Johnson and Douglas Sharon. San Diego: San Diego Museum of Man.
1999        Lintel Paintings of Mitla and the Function of the Mitla Palaces. In *Mesoamerican Architecture as a Cultural Symbol*, ed. Jeff K. Kowalski. Oxford: Oxford University Press.
2003        Royal Marriage and Confederacy Building among the Eastern Nahuas, Mixtecs, and Zapotecs. In *The Postclassic Mesoamerican World*, ed. Michael E. Smith and Frances F. Berdan. Salt Lake City: University of Utah Press.

Pohl, John M. D., and Bruce Byland
1996        The Identification of the Xipe Bundle–Red and White Bundle Place Sign in the Mixtec Codices. *Journal of Latin American Lore* 19(1): 3–29.

Powell, Christopher
1997        A New View on Maya Astronomy. Master's thesis, University of Texas at Austin.

Prechtel, Martin, and Robert Carlsen
1988        Weaving and Cosmos amongst the Tzutujil Maya of Guatemala. *Res: Anthropology and Aesthetics* 15:122–32.

Prescott, William II.
1979        *History of the Conquest of Mexico.* New York: Random House.

Preuss, Mary
1993        The Origin of Corn and Preparation for Planting in K'ekchi' and Yucatec Mayan Accounts. *Latin American Indian Literatures Journal* 9(2): 121–33.

Proskouriakoff, Tatiana
1960        Historical Implications of a Pattern of Dates at Piedras Negras, Guatemala. *American Antiquity* 25:454–75.
1961        Portraits of Women in Maya Art. In *Essays in Pre-Columbian Art and Archaeology*, ed. Samuel K. Lothrop. Cambridge, Mass.: Harvard University Press.

Quenon, Michel, and Geneviève Le Fort
1997        Rebirth and Resurrection in Maize God Iconography. In *The Maya Vase Book*, vol. 5, ed. Justin Kerr, 884–902. New York: Kerr Associates.

Quirín, Herbert
1974        Leyenda de los cerros y el maíz. In *Tradiciones de Guatemala*. Guatemala: Editorial Universitaria.

Rands, Robert
1955        Some Manifestations of Water in Mesoamerican Art. *Bureau of American Ethnology*, bull. 157 (48): 265–393. Washington, D.C.: Smithsonian Institution.

Rands, Robert, Ronald Bishop, and Garman Harbottle
1978        Thematic and Compositional Variation in Palenque Region Incensarios. In *Tercera Mesa Redonda de Palenque*, vol. 4, ed. Merle Greene Robertson and Donnan Call Jeffers, 19–30. Palenque, Mexico: Pre-Columbian Research Center.

Recinos, Adrián
1950        *Popol Vuh*. Norman: University of Oklahoma Press.

Recinos, Adrián, and Delia Goetz, trans.
1953        *The Annals of the Cakchiquels*. Norman: University of Oklahoma Press.

Redfield, Robert
1936        The Coati and the Ceiba. *Maya Research* 3:231–43.
1941        *The Folk Culture of Yucatan*. Chicago: University of Chicago Press.
1945        Notes on San Antonio Palopó. Microfilm Collection of Manuscripts on Cultural Anthropology, no. 4. Chicago: University of Chicago Library.

Redfield, Robert, and Alfonso Villa Rojas
1934        *Chan Kom*. Washington, D.C.: Carnegie Institute.

Reents, Dorie
1985        *The Late Classic Maya Holmul Style Polychrome Pottery*. PhD diss., University of
            Texas at Austin.

Reents-Budet, Dorie
1991        The Holmul Dancer Theme in Maya Art. In *Sixth Palenque Round Table, 1986*,
            ed. Merle Greene Robertson and Virginia Fields. Norman: University of Okla-
            homa Press.
1994        *Painting the Maya Universe*. London: Duke University Press.
2000        Feasting among the Classic Maya: Evidence from the Pictorial Ceramics. In *The
            Maya Vase Book*, vol. 6, ed. Justin Kerr, 1022–1037. New York: Kerr Associates.

Reina, Rubén E.
1966        *The Law of the Saints: A Pokomam Pueblo and Its Community Culture*. Indianapolis:
            Bobbs-Merrill.
1967        Milpas and Milperos: Implications for Prehistoric Times. *American Anthropologist*
            69:1–20.

Reina, Rubén E., and Robert Hill
1980        Lowland Maya Subsistence: Notes from Ethnohistory and Ethnography. *Ameri-
            can Antiquity* 45(1): 74–79.

Reina, Rubén E., and John Monaghan
1981        Ways of the Maya; Salt Production in Sacapulas, Guatemala. *Expedition* 23(3): 13–33.

Remington, Judith
1977        Current Astronomical Practices among the Maya. In *Native American Astronomy*,
            ed. Anthony F. Aveni. Austin: University of Texas Press.

Ringle, William
1988        *Of Mice and Monkeys: The Value and Meaning of T1016, the God C Hieroglyph*.
            Research Reports on Ancient Maya Writing, 18. Washington, D.C.: Center for
            Maya Research.
2004        On the Political Organization of Chichén Itzá. *Ancient Mesoamerica* 15:167–218.

Robicsek, Frances
1978        *The Smoking Gods*. Norman: University of Oklahoma Press.

Robicsek, Frances, and Donald Hales
1981        *The Maya Book of the Dead: The Ceramic Codex*. Charlottesville, Va.: University of
            Virginia Art Museum/University of Oklahoma Press.

Rodas, Flavio, Ovidio Rodas, and Laurence Hawkins
1940        *Chichicastenango: The Kiche Indians, Their History and Culture, Sacred Symbols of
            Their Dress and Textiles*. Guatemala: Union Tipográfica.

Rosenbaum, Brenda
1993        *With Our Heads Bowed: The Dialectics of Gender in a Mayan Village*. Austin: Uni-
            versity of Texas Press.

Roys, Ralph
1931        *The Ethno-Botany of the Maya*. Middle American Research Series, pub. 2. New
            Orleans: Tulane University.

1933      *The Book of Chilam Balam of Chumayel.* Carnegie Institution of Washington, pub. 523, contribution 31. Washington, D.C.: Carnegie Institution.

1965      *Ritual of the Bacabs.* Norman: University of Oklahoma Press.

Ruppert, Karl, J. Eric S. Thompson, and Tatiana Proskouriakoff

1955      *Bonampak, Chiapas, Mexico.* Washington, D.C.: Carnegie Institution of Washington.

Ruz, Mario Humberto

1982      *Los legítimos hombres.* Mexico City: Universidad Nacional Autónoma de México.

Sahagún, Fray Bernardino de

1959–63      *Florentine Codex: General History of the Things of New Spain,* trans. Charles E. Dibble and Arthur J. O. Anderson. Monographs of the School of American Research and the Museum of New Mexico. 13 vols. Salt Lake City: University of Utah and School of American Research.

Saler, Benson

1960      The Road from El Palmar: Change, Continuity and Conservatism in a Quiché Community. PhD diss., University of Pennsylvania.

Sapper, Carl

1897      *Northern Central Mexico, with a Trip to the Highlands of Anahuac: Travels and Studies of the Year 1888–1895.* Brunswick: Friedrich Viewig and Son.

Saturno, William

2006      The Dawn of Maya Gods and Kings. *National Geographic Magazine* (January 2006): 68–77.

Saturno, William, Karl Taube, and David Stuart

2005      *The Murals of San Bartolo, El Petén, Guatemala. Pt. 1: The North Wall.* Barnardsville, N.C.: Center for Ancient American Studies.

Saville, Marshall

1921      Reports on the Maya Indians of Yucatan by Santiago Méndez, Antonio García y Cubas, Pedro Sánchez de Águilar, and Francisco Hernández. *Indian Notes and Monographs* 9:133–226. Museum of the American Indian, Heye Foundation.

Schackt, Jon

1984      A Kekchi Account of an Encounter with the Chol Indians. *Belizean Studies* 9(3): 21–24.

1986      *One God—Two Temples: Schismatic Process in a Kekchi Village.* Occasional Papers, no. 13. Oslo: University of Oslo, Department of Social Anthropology.

Schele, Linda

1990      Ba as "First" in Classic Period Titles. *Texas Notes on Pre-Columbian Art, Writing and Culture* 5. Austin: University of Texas.

1992      *Notebook for the Sixteenth Maya Hieroglyphic Workshop at Texas.* Austin: University of Texas at Austin, Institute of Latin American Studies.

n.d.      The Puleston Hypothesis: The Waterlily Complex in Classic Maya Art and Writing. Unpublished manuscript.

Schele, Linda, Nikolai Grube, and Federico Fahsen
1992      The Lunar Series in Classic Maya Inscriptions: New Observations and Interpreta-
          tions. *Texas Notes on Pre-Columbian Art, Writing and Culture* 29. Austin: University
          of Texas.

Schele, Linda, and Matthew Looper
1996      *Notebook for the Twentieth Maya Hieroglyphic Workshop at Texas: The Inscriptions of
          Quirigua and Copan.* Austin: University of Texas at Austin, Institute of Latin
          American Studies.

Schele, Linda, and Peter Mathews
1998      *The Code of Kings: The Language of Seven Sacred Maya Temples and Tombs.* New
          York: Simon and Schuster.

Schele, Linda, Peter Mathews, and Floyd Lounsbury
1990      Redating the Hauberg Stela. *Texas Notes on Pre-Columbian Art, Writing and Culture*
          1. Austin: University of Texas.

Schele, Linda, and Jeffrey Miller
1983      *The Mirror, the Rabbit, and the Bundle.* Studies in Pre-Columbian Art and Archaeo-
          logy. Washington, D.C.: Dumbarton Oaks.

Schele, Linda, and Mary Miller
1986      *Blood of Kings.* Fort Worth: Kimbell Art Museum.

Schele, Linda, David Stuart, and Nikolai Grube
1989      A Commentary on the Restoration and Reading of the Glyphic Panels from
          Temple 11. *Copan Notes,* no. 64. Austin: Copan Mosaics Project; Instituto Hon-
          dureño de Antropología e Historia.

Schellhas, Paul
1904      *Representation of Deities of the Maya Manuscripts.* Papers of the Peabody Museum
          of American Archaeology and Ethnology, Harvard University. Cambridge, Mass.:
          Peabody Museum.

Schmidt, Peter, Mercedes de la Garza, and Enrique Nalda
1998      *Maya.* New York: Rizzoli.

Scholes, Francis, and Ralph Roys
1948      *The Maya Chontal Indians of Acalan-Tixchel.* Washington, D.C.: Carnegie Institute
          of Washington.

Schultze Jena, Leonard
1944      *Popol Vuh: Das heilige Buch der Quiché-Indianer von Guatemala.* Stuttgart: W.
          Kohlhammer.
1954      *La vida y las creencias de los indígenas quichés de Guatemala.* Biblioteca Cultura Pop-
          ular 49. Guatemala: Ministerio de Educación Pública.

Scotchmer, David
1986      Convergence of the Gods: Comparing Traditional Maya and Christian Maya
          Cosmologies. In *Symbol and Meaning Beyond the Closed Community,* ed. Gary H.
          Gossen, 197–226. Albany: Institute for Mesoamerican Studies, State University
          of New York at Albany.

Seitz, R., G. E. Harlow, V. B. Sisson, and Karl E. Taube

2001      Olmec Blue and the Formative Jade Sources: New Discoveries in Guatemala. *Antiquity* 5:687–88.

Shaw, Mary

1971      *According to Our Ancestors.* Summer Institute of Linguistics, pub. 32. Norman: University of Oklahoma.

Siebers, Hans

1999      *We Are Children of the Mountain: Creolization and Modernization among the Q'eqchi'es.* Amsterdam: CEDLA (Centre for Latin American Research and Documentation).

Siegel, Morris

1941      Religion in Western Guatemala. *American Anthropologist* 43:63–76.

1943      The Creation Myth and Acculturation in Acatán, Guatemala. *Journal of American Folklore* 56:120–26.

Slocum, Marianna

1965      The Origin of Corn, and Other Tzeltal Myths. *Tlalocan* 5: 1–45.

Smith-Stark, Thomas

1978      The Origin of Corn. In *Codex Wauchope: A Tribute Roll*, ed. Marco Giardino, Barbara Edmonson, and Winifred Creamer, 57–60. New Orleans: Human Mosaic.

Smythe, Frank

1966      *Birds of Tikal.* Garden City, N.Y.: Natural History Press, American Museum of Natural History.

Solano, Francisco

1977      *Tierra y sociedad en el reino de Guatemala.* Guatemala: Editorial Universitaria.

Sosa, John

1985      The Maya Sky, the Maya World: A Symbolic Analysis of Yucatec Maya Cosmology. PhD diss., State University of New York at Albany.

1989      Concepts of Astronomical Order. In *Symbol and Meaning Beyond the Closed Community*, ed. Gary Gossen. Albany: State University of New York at Albany.

Spero, Joanne

1987      Lightning Men and Water Serpents: A Comparison of Mayan and Mixe-Zoquean Beliefs. Master's thesis, University of Texas at Austin.

Stadelman, Raymond

1940      Maize Cultivation in Northwestern Guatemala. In *Contributions to American Anthropology and History* 6(33): 83–263. Washington, D.C.: Carnegie Institution of Washington.

Standley, Paul

1923      *The Trees and Shrubs of Mexico.* Washington, D.C.: Government Printing Office.

1930      *Flora of Yucatan.* Chicago: Field Museum of Natural History.

Starr, Frederick

1908      *In Indian Mexico: A Narrative of Travel and Labor.* Chicago: Forbes and Company.

Steggerda, Morris

1941    *Maya Indians of Yucatan.* Washington, D.C.: Carnegie Institution of Washington.

1943    A Description of Thirty Towns in Yucatan, Mexico. Bureau of American Ethnology, Anthropological Papers, no. 30. Washington, D.C.: Smithsonian Institution.

Stephens, John Lloyd

1841    *Incidents of Travel in Central America, Chiapas, and Yucatan.* New York: Harper and Brothers.

Stone, Andrea

1989    Disconnection, Foreign Insignia and Political Expansion: Teotihuacán and the Warrior Stelae of Piedras Negras. In *Mesoamerica After the Decline of Teotihuacán, A.D. 700–900*, ed. Richard A. Diehl and Janet C. Berlo, 153–72. Washington, D.C.: Dumbarton Oaks Research Library and Collection.

1991    Aspects of Impersonation in Classic Maya Art. In *Sixth Palenque Round Table, 1986, ed.* Merle Greene Robertson and Virginia Fields. Norman: University of Oklahoma Press.

2002    Spirals, Ropes, and Feathers: the Iconography of Rubber Balls in Mesoamerican Art. *Ancient Mesoamerica* 13(1): 21–39.

Stone, Doris

1932    Some Spanish Entradas 1524–1695: A Revision of the Data on Spanish Entradas into the Country of the Lacandon and Ahitza, containing a Full Translation of Antonio de León Pinelo's Report, and First Publication of Juan Delgado's Manuscripts. In *Middle American Research Series*, pub. 4: 209–96. New Orleans: Tulane University.

Stuart, David

1987    *Ten Phonetic Syllables.* Research Reports on Ancient Maya Writing, 14. Washington, D.C.: Center for Maya Research.

1988    Blood Symbolism in Maya Iconography. In *Maya Iconography*, ed. Elizabeth Benson and Gillett Griffin. Princeton: Princeton University Press.

1989    The Maya Artist. BA thesis, Princeton University.

1995    A Study of Maya Inscriptions. PhD diss., Vanderbilt University.

1996    Kings of Stone. *Res: Anthropology and Aesthetics* 29/30:148–71.

1998    The Fire Enters His House. In *Function and Meaning in Maya Architecture.* Washington, D.C.: Dumbarton Oaks.

2000a    Arrival of Strangers. In *Mesoamerica's Classic Heritage: from Teotihuacan to the Aztecs*, ed. David Carrasco, Lindsay Jones, and Scott Sessions. Boulder: University Press of Colorado.

2000b    Ritual and History in the Stucco Inscription from Temple 19 at Palenque. *PARI Journal* 1(1): 13–19.

2003a    A Cosmological Throne at Palenque. www.mesoweb.com

2003b    On the Paired Variants of Tz'ak. www.mesoweb.com

2004    New Year Records in Classic Maya Inscriptions. *PARI Journal* 5(2): 1–6. San Francisco: Pre-Columbian Art Research Institute.

2005a    Sourcebook for the 29th Maya Hieroglyphic Forum. Austin: Department of Art and Art History, University of Texas at Austin.

2005b    *The Inscriptions from Temple 19 at Palenque*. San Francisco: Pre-Columbian Art Research Institute.

2006    Sourcebook for the 30th Maya Meetings. University of Texas at Austin.

Stuart, David, and Stephen Houston

1994    *Classic Maya Place Names*. Washington, D.C.: Dumbarton Oaks.

Stuart, David, Stephen Houston, and John Robertson

1999    *Notebook for the 23rd Maya Hieroglyphic Workshop at Texas: Recovering the Past.* Austin: University of Texas at Austin, Institute of Latin American Studies.

Stuart, George, and Gene Stuart

1993    *Lost Kingdoms of the Maya*. Washington, D.C.: National Geographic Soceity.

Sullivan, Thelma

1966    Pregnancy, Childbirth, and the Deification of the Women Who Died in Childbirth. *Estudios de cultura náhuatl* (Mexico City) 6:63–95.

Sutton, George

1951    *Mexican Birds: First Impressions*. Norman: University of Oklahoma Press.

Tarn, Nathaniel, and Martin Prechtel

1981    Metaphors of Relative Elevation. *Estudios de cultura maya* 13:105–23.

1986    Constant Inconstancy: The Feminine Principle in Atiteco Mythology. In *Symbol and Meaning Beyond the Closed Community*, ed. Gary Gossen. Albany: Institute of Mesoamerican Studies, State University of New York at Albany.

Taube, Karl

1983    The Teotihuacan Spider Woman. *Journal of Latin American Lore*, 9(2): 107–89.

1985    The Classic Maya Maize God: A Reappraisal. In *Fifth Palenque Round Table, 1983,* vol. 7, ed. Merle Greene Robertson and Virginia Fields, 171–81. San Francisco: Pre-Columbian Art Research Institute.

1986    The Teotihuacan Cave of Origin. *Res: Anthropology and Aesthetics* 12:51–82.

1987    *A Representation of the Principal Bird Deity in the Paris Codex*. Research Reports on Ancient Maya Writing, 6. Washington, D.C.: Center for Maya Research.

1988a   A Prehispanic Maya Katun Wheel. *Journal of Anthropological Research* 44(2): 183–203.

1988b   *The Ancient Yucatec New Year Festival: The Liminal Period in Maya Ritual and Cosmology*. PhD diss., Yale University.

1989    *Itzam Cab Ain: Caimans, Cosmology and Calendrics in Postclassic Yucatan*. Research Reports on Ancient Maya Writing, 26. Washington, D.C.: Center for Maya Research.

1992a   *The Major Gods of Ancient Yucatan*. Washington, D.C.: Dumbarton Oaks.

1992b   The Iconography of Mirrors at Teotihuacan. In *Art, Ideology, and the City of Teotihuacan*, ed. Janet Berlo. Washington, D.C.: Dumbarton Oaks.

1992c   The Temple of Quetzalcoatl and the Cult of Sacred War at Teotihuacan. *Res: Anthropology and Aesthetics* 21:53–87.

1994    The Birth Vase: Natal Imagery in Ancient Maya Myth and Ritual. In *The Maya Vase Book,* vol. 4, ed. Justin Kerr, 650–85. New York: Kerr Associates.

1996    The Olmec Maize God: The Face of Corn in Formative Mesoamerica. *Res: Anthropology and Aesthetics* 29/30:39–81.

1998    The Jade Hearth: Centrality, Rulership, and the Classic Maya Temple. In *Function and Meaning in Classic Maya Architecture*, ed. Stephen Houston. Washington, D.C.: Dumbarton Oaks.

2000    The Turquoise Hearth: Fire, Self-Sacrifice, and the Central Mexican Cult of War. In *Mesoamerica's Classic Heritage: From Teotihuacan to the Aztecs*, ed. David Carrasco, Lindsay Jones, and Scott Sessions. Boulder: University Press of Colorado.

2001    The Breath of Life: The Symbolism of Wind in Mesoamerica and the American Southwest. In *The Road to Aztlan: Art from a Mythic Homeland*, ed. Virginia Fields and Victor Zamudio-Taylor, 102–23. Los Angeles: Los Angeles County Museum of Art.

2003    Maws of Heaven and Hell: The Symbolism of the Centipede and Serpent in Classic Maya Religion. In *Antropología de la eternidad: La muerte en la cultura maya*, ed. Andrés Ciudad Ruiz, Mario Humberto Ruz Sosa, and María Josefa Iglesias Ponce de León. Madrid: Sociedad Española de Estudios Mayas.

2004    Flower Mountain: Concepts of Life, Beauty, and Paradise among the Classic Maya. *Res: Anthropology and Aesthetics* 45:69–98.

2005    The Symbolism of Jade in Classic Maya Religion. *Ancient Mesoamerica* 16:23–50.

Taylor, Dicey
1992    Painted Ladies: Costume for Women on Tepeu Ceramics. In *The Maya Vase Book*, vol. 3, ed. Justin Kerr, 513–25. New York: Kerr Associates.

Tedlock, Barbara
1982    *Time and the Highland Maya*. Albuquerque: University of New Mexico Press.

1985    Hawks, Meteorology and Astronomy in Quiché-Maya Agriculture. *Archaeoastronomy* 8:80–88.

1992    The Road of Light. In *The Sky in Mayan Literature*, ed. Anthony F. Aveni. New York: Oxford University Press.

Tedlock, Dennis
1985    *Popol Vuh*. New York: Simon and Schuster.

1996    *Popol Vuh*. Rev. ed. New York: Simon and Schuster.

Termer, Franz
1957    *Etnología y etnografía de Guatemala*. Guatemala: Editorial del Ministerio de Educación Pública.

Thompson, Edward H.
1932    People of the Serpent: Life and Adventure among the Mayas. Boston: Houghton Mifflin.

Thompson, J. Eric S.
1930    Ethnology of the Mayas of Southern and Central British Honduras. *Field Museum of Natural History, Anthropological Series* 17(1). Chicago: University of Chicago.

1934    *Sky Bearers, Colors and Directions in Maya and Mexican Religion*. Carnegie Institution of Washington, pub. 436, contribution 10, 209–42. Washington, D.C.: Carnegie Institution.

1939    *The Moon Goddess in Middle America, with Notes on Related Deities*. Carnegie Institution of Washington, pub. 509, contribution 29, 121–73. Washington, D.C.: Carnegie Institution.

1950    *Maya Hieroglyphic Writing: An Introduction.* Carnegie Institution of Washington, pub. 589. Washington, D.C.: Carnegie Institution.

1954    *The Rise and Fall of Maya Civilization.* Norman: University of Oklahoma Press.

1958    *Thomas Gage's Travels in the New World.* Norman: University of Oklahoma Press.

1959    The Role of Caves in Maya Culture. *Mitteilungen aus dem Museum Völkerkunde in Hamburg* 25:122–29.

1964    *A Catalog of Maya Hieroglyphs.* Norman: University of Oklahoma Press.

1970    *Maya History and Religion.* Norman: University of Oklahoma Press.

1972    *A Commentary on the Dresden Codex.* Memoirs of the American Philosophical Society 93. Philadelphia: American Philosophical Society.

1975    Introduction. In *The Hill-Caves of Yucatan,* by Henry C. Mercer, vii–xliv. Norman: University of Oklahoma Press.

Tobriner, Stephen
1972    The Fertile Mountain: An Investigation of Cerro Gordo's Importance to the Town Plan and Iconography of Teotihuacan. In *Teotihuacan: 11th Mesa Redonda.* Mexico: Sociedad Mexicana de Antropología.

Torquemada, Juan de
1975    *Monarquía indiana.* 5th ed. 3 vols. Mexico: Porrúa.

Tozzer, Alfred
1907    *Comparative Study of the Mayas and Lacandones.* Archaeological Institute of America. London: Macmillan.

1912    A Spanish Manuscript Letter on the Lacandones in the Archives of the Indies in Seville. *18th International Congress of Americanists* 1(2): 497–509.

1941    *Landa's Relación de las cosas de Yucatán: A Translation.* Papers of the Peabody Museum of American Archaeology and Ethnology, Harvard University, vol. 18. Cambridge, Mass.: Peabody Museum.

Vail, Gabrielle, and Andrea Stone
2002    Representations of Women in Postclassic and Colonial Maya Literature and Art. In *Ancient Maya Women,* ed. Traci Ardren, 203–28. Walnut Creek, Calif.: Altamira.

Valey, Alberto, and Benedicto Valey
1979    *Tzijobal pa Kach'abal.* Guatemala: Leyendas de Rabinal.

Valladares, León
1957    *El hombre y el maíz: Etnografía y etnopsicología de Colotenango.* Guatemala: Universidad de San Carlos.

Villa Rojas, Alfonso
1945    *The Maya of East Central Quintana Roo.* Carnegie Institute of Washington, pub. 559. Washington, D.C.: Carnegie Institute of Washington.

1969    The Tzeltal. In *Handbook of Middle American Indians,* ed. Evon Vogt. Austin: University of Texas Press.

Vogt, Evon
1969    *Zinacantán.* Cambridge, Mass.: Harvard University Press.

1976    *Tortillas for the Gods: A Symbolic Analysis of Zinacanteco Rituals.* Cambridge, Mass.: Harvard University Press.

1997        Zinacanteco Astronomy. *Mexicon* 19(6): 110–17.

Wagley, Charles
1941        *Economics of a Guatemalan Village.* [Menasha, Wis.]: American Anthropological
            Association, Memoir 58.
1949        *The Social and Religious Life of a Guatemalan Village.* [Menasha, Wis.]: American
            Anthropological Association.

Wald, Robert, and Michael Carrasco
2004        Rabbits, Gods, and Kings: The Interplay of Myth and History on the Regal Rabbit
            Vase. Paper presented at the Maya Meetings, University of Texas at Austin.

Watanabe, John
1992        *Maya Saints and Souls in a Changing World.* Austin: University of Texas Press.

Wauchope, Robert
1938        *Modern Maya Houses: A Study of Their Archaeological Significance.* Washington, D.C.:
            Carnegie Institution of Washington.

Wetmore, Alexander
1965        *The Birds of the Republic of Panama,* pt. 1. Washington, D.C.: Smithsonian Institution.

Whittaker, Arabelle, and Viola Warkentin
1965        *Chol Texts on the Supernatural.* Norman: Summer Institute of Linguistics, Uni-
            versity of Oklahoma.

Wichmann, Soren
2004        The Names of Some Major Classic Maya Gods. In *Continuity and Change: Maya
            Religious Practices in Temporal Perspective,* ed. Daniel Graña Behrens, et al., 77–86.
            Markt Schwaben, Germany: A. Saurwein.

Wilks, Richard
1991        *Household Ecology: Economic Change and Domestic Life among the Kekchí Maya of
            Belize.* Tucson: University of Arizona Press.

Wilson, Michael
1972        A Highland Maya People and Their Habitat: The Natural History, Demography
            and Economy of the Kekchi. PhD diss., University of Oregon.

Wilson, Richard
1990        Mountain Spirits and Maize: Catholic Conversion and Renovation of Traditions
            among the Q'eqchi' of Guatemala. PhD diss., University of London.
1995        *Maya Resurgence in Guatemala.* Norman: University of Oklahoma Press.

Wisdom, Charles
1940        *Chorti Indians of Guatemala.* Chicago: University of Chicago Press.
1950        Materials on the Chortí Language. Microfilm Collection of Manuscripts on Cul-
            tural Anthropology, no. 28. Chicago: University of Chicago Library.

Woods, Clyde
1968        Medicine and Culture Change in San Lucas Tolimán: a Highland Guatemalan
            Community. PhD diss., Stanford University.

Zender, Marc

1999        Diacritical Marks and Underspelling in the Classic Maya Script: Implications for
            Decipherment. Master's thesis, University of Calgary.

2004a       The Glyphs for "Handspan" and "Strike" in Classic Maya Ballgame Texts. *PARI
            Journal* 4, no. 4:1–9.2004b
            A Study of Classic Maya Priesthood. PhD diss., University of Calgary.

2005        The Raccoon Glyph in Classic Maya Writing. *PARI Journal* 5, no. 4:6–16.

Zotz, Gerhard, and Klaus Winter

1994        Photosynthesis of a Tropical Canopy Tree, *Ceiba pentandra*, in a Lowland Forest
            in Panama. *Tree Physiology* 14:1291–1301.

# INDEX